The 𝔅ook

An Actor's Guide to Chicago

Kevin Heckman
Editor

Published by Per*for*m*ink* Books, Ltd.

PerformInk Books, Ltd.
3223 N. Sheffield
Chicago, IL 60657

Copyright © 2001
PerformInk Books, Ltd.
All rights reserved.

No part of this book may be reproduced in any form or by any means without prior, written permission of the publisher, except brief quotes in connection with critical articles or reviews.

Carrie L. Kaufman, Publisher
ISBN: 1-892296-03-9

Design and production by Marty McNulty
Illustrations by Zak Brown
Additional editing by Mechelle Moe

All advertisements are published with the understanding that the advertiser/agency has obtained authorization for use of materials.

PerformInk Books, Ltd. does not take responsibility
for claims made by advertisers.

For advertising information, call Steve Abbott at 773/296-4600

Successor to "Acting, Modeling and Dance," Founding Editors: Allyson Rice-Taylor, Emily Gerson-Saines

Editors' Notes

In 1996, Carrie Kaufman, editor of PERFORMINK, approached me with a publication she had just bought, "The Acting, Modeling and Dance Guide." At the time, it was mostly picked up for free at agencies and was only moderately useful, as much of the information therein was out of date, addresses and phone numbers were wrong, and even PERFORMINK's listing was incorrect. We looked it over and, while the idea had merit, the guide at that time was not useful.

Now, after four editions of what came to be known as "The Book", we have created an institution. Each year, more actors take advantage of this handy, one stop information source to help them move to Chicago, live in Chicago and have careers in the arts in Chicago. This would not have been possible without the many staffers at PERFORMINK that have helped us out along the way; the readers who have come to us with suggestions; the theatre and film professionals who have contributed time and information to help us compile the most complete source for the Chicago actor.

In particular, thanks have to go out to Rob Mello, Steve Abbott and Mechelle Moe at PERFORMINK for their ideas and assistance. Our proofreader Claire Kaplan and layout artist Marty McNulty both deserve kudos for having been in it since the beginning. Their ideas have been invaluable. Thanks to Adam Cook for his help in keeping the listings up to date, no small task! Thanks to Christine Gatto for again doing the research necessary to keep our Neighborhood stats up to date. Also, thanks to contributers Jonathan Abarbanel, Ben Winters, Adrienne Duncan, Julie Franz Peeler, Susan Hubbard, Kyle Hillman, Julie Daly, Dexter Bullard, Jason Chin, Bob LaBate and Karin McKie for their expertise and their prose. Thanks to the theatres and actors that took the time to tell us of their audition nightmares. Finally, thanks to everyone who was interviewed, who provided data and who went out of their way to help us out in compiling this resource.

I have strived from the beginning to create the resource I wish I had when I first moved to Chicago. It seems, from the comments of readers and industry professionals, that we have succeeded. Nothing is perfect, and "The Book" will continue to improve in the future with the help of your suggestions. Thanks for your support and your help.

Break a leg!

Table of Contents

1. Coming to Chicago 1
    State of the Art 2
    Car Complications Checklist 8
    Public Transportation Info 10
    It's a Beautiful Day in the Neighborhood 11
    Finding an Apartment Checklist 25
        Apartment Services 27
        Housing Spots 28
        Utilities 28
        Temp Agencies 29
        Actor-Friendly Jobs 35
    First Steps... 2

2. Training 39
    The Many Methods of Acting 36
    Acting Training Checklist 45
    Classes 47
        Acting 47
        Kid's 52
        Dance 54
        Stage Combat 58
        Modeling 58
        Scriptwriting 58
    Coaches 59
        Acting 59
        Voice-Over 62
        Dialect 64
        Voice/Speech 65
        Accompanists 66
        Singing 66
        Instrument 69
        Movement 70
        Speech Therapy 70
        Universities with MFAs in Theatre 71

3. The Actor's Tools 77
    The Headshot Market 78
    Photographer Checklist 84
        Photographers 87
        Photo Reproductions 97
        Photo Retouching 99
        Makeup Artists 100
    New Technology 102
    A Look at the Bad Side of Resumés 106
    Resumé & Cover Letter Checklists 110
        Resumé Services 113
        Trade Papers 113
        Answering Services 115
        Beepers 116
        Cell Phones 117
        Makeup 117
        Stage Weapons 119

  Sheet Music 119
  Lighting Rental 119
  Dance Supplies 120
  Costume Shops 120
  Thrift Stores 122
  Libraries 123
  Bookstores 123
  Casting Hotlines 123

4. Agencies - Talent and Casting 125
 The Agent Biz 126
 Getting an Agent Checklist 132
  Talent Agencies 136
  Talent Agencies – Milwaukee 140
  Tradeshow Agencies 141
  Casting Directors 142
  Extras Casting 143
  Literary Agents 144

5. Film, TV and Industrials 145
 Cutting a Demo Tape 146
  Demo Tapes 148
 To Reel, or not to… 151
  Reels 153
 Using an Ear Prompter .155
  Ear Prompters 158
 Getting Paid 159
 Acting on Film 164
 Heading West 168

6. Unions and Organizations 177
 Actors Equity Association 178
 AFTRA & SAG 183
  List of Unions 187
 Legal Resources 188
  Similar Organizations .190

7. Theaters 191
 Director's Directing 192
 Audition Nightmares! 201
 Audition Checklist 205
  Equity Theatres 208
  Non-Equity Theatres .222

8. Improv 247
 Improv and the Actor .248
  Improv Training 252
  Improv-Friendly Theatres 253
  Improv Groups 244

9. Running a Small Theatre Company ...255
- Theatres for Rent 256
- Rehearsal Spaces for Rent 260
- A Brief Guide to Forming a Not-For-Profit 263
- Management Training for the Arts 269
  - Grants 274
- Recruiting an Active Board of Directors 276
- Developing a Pitch 285
  - PR Firms 288
- Five Steps for Audience Development 289
- The Joseph Jefferson Awards 292
  - Helpful Organizations 299

10. Living 301
- Legal, Tax and Insurance 302
  - Accountants and Tax Preparers 302
  - Attorneys 303
  - Insurance 304
- Movie Theaters 304
- Health and Fitness 305
  - Health Clubs 305
  - Health Food Stores 306
  - Nutritionists 306
  - Weight Control 307
  - Counselors 307
  - Hypnotists 308
  - Meditation 309
  - Religious Groups 309
  - Chiropractors 310
  - Naprapaths 311
  - Acupuncture 311
  - Massage 312
  - Alexander Technique 313
  - Yoga 314
  - Tai Chi 315
  - Physicians 315
  - AIDS Resources 316
- Grooming and Appearance 316
  - Salons 316
  - Cosmetic Surgery 317
  - Skin Care 318
  - Electrolysis 319
  - Dentists 319
- Public Service Phone Numbers 320

Calendar 321
- Biographies 334
- CTA Map 342
- Advertisers Index 343
- Order Forms 344

Coming to Chicago

Shattered Globe, "The Batting Cage"

State of the Art

There's no news at the court sir, but the old news.

by Jonathan Abarbanel

Ho-hum. Another year gone by, another 700 productions, another 12,000 performances, another three million-plus tickets sold, another 5,000 artists and staff employed. Just a typical year in Chicago theatre. Again. Ho-hum.

People and theatres come and go (and talk of Michaelangelo, of course). We all benefit, if indirectly, from the thrust of bricks-and-mortar which continues to remake our downtown theatre district and spearheaded by a mayor and city government that actually like the arts in general, and theatre in particular. In fact, the downtown door now is open—if just a crack—for off-Loop and even off-off-Loop theatre troupes.

Both coasts and the big/little screens benefit from the steady flow of Chicago artists, many of whom remember us and return from time to time—Harry J. Lennix, Laurie Metcalf, Joe Mantegna to toss off a few. Predatory old dinosaurs like me remember when Skip Sudduth was laboring in the off-Loop vineyards, and that recent Emmy Award win-

State of the Art

ners Sean Hayes and Megan Mullaly started here. Ditto screenwriter John Logan, who remains a member of the Victory Gardens Playwrights Ensemble despite the success of his films "The Gladiator" and "On Any Given Sunday." Others, such as directors Robert Falls, Mary Zimmerman, Jonathan Wilson and Frank Galati, producer Michael Leavitt and actors John Mahoney, Amy Morton and William L. Petersen, continue to make their homes here in Chicago even as their careers take them cross country or around the world.

Ho-hum. Plus ça change, plus ça même.

During the Year 2000, the edifice complex continued to dominate theatre industry news, especially downtown. The Goodman Theatre finally opened the doors of its impressive, $46 million new complex on Dearborn Street in the North Loop, after 10 years of planning, funding and construction. The center boasts theatres of 850 seats and 400 seats, plus a mixed-use complex of shops and restaurants. In the process, the Goodman saw its subscribership jump from 23,000 to 27,000. Drawing up to 1,250 people a night, the Goodman will be the lynchpin of the North Loop Theatre District, despite the fact that the nearby Ford Center/Oriental, Cadillac Palace, Chicago and Shubert theatres have much larger seating capacities. Thing is, those commercial houses typically have been dark for weeks or months on end. And there hasn't been even one week yet when all of them have shows at the same time. The Goodman, however, will be in operation nearly year round, drawing a steady audience six nights a week.

The Noble Fool, the comedy-based company that produces the long-running, audience interactive hit *Flanagan's Wake,* planned to open its complex of three little houses within the School of the Art Institute Building before the end of the year, but had to postpone until after January 1. Still, it's a Year 2000 story, as The Noble Fool became the first off-Loop company to build itself a permanent home in the North Loop Theatre District, and they did it without TIF (public tax) dollars or help from the City of Chicago.

The city, nonetheless, has encouraged Loop incursions by off-Loop troupes through its Gallery 37 Theatre, a beautiful black box of 99 seats on Randolph Street, across from the Cultural Center (which also houses occasional visiting theatre and dance companies). The Gallery 37 Theatre opened last year and invites companies from all over the city to bring their best shows downtown for runs of up to four weeks. This space may be unique: We can think of no similar American examples of theatres owned and operated by a city government.

Nearby, at the northeast corner of State and Lake streets, the Joffrey

State of the Art

Ballet of Chicago announced last October a $24 million plan to convert a nondescript five-story office building into a nine floor administrative and studio center for the troupe, with a TIF contribution of $4 million from the city. So the North Loop is becoming quite the tidy little artsy-fartsy neighborhood. Now, how about some subsidized artist housing down there?

Also last year, ground was broken at long, long last for Chicago Music and Dance Theatre, a 1500-seat house on East Randolph Street (at Lake Shore Drive) that will be home to a dozen medium sized organizations including Hubbard Street Dance Chicago, Chicago Opera Theatre, Performing Arts Chicago and Music of the Baroque. This $35 million project has been more than a decade in the planning. An opening is projected next year.

Outside the Loop, there were edifice connections, too. Lookingglass Theatre Company, the State of Illinois and the City of Chicago announced plans for a $6.5 million home base for the award-winning ensemble in the form of a 250-seat theatre within the Water Tower Pumping Station at Michigan and Chicago avenues. Lookingglass may be able to produce a show there by the end of this year, but don't hold your breath. Also, the Chicago Center for the Performing Arts (CCPA) on Green Street at Chicago Avenue opened the first of its four planned theatres, a 350-seat cabaret, after six years of slow progress.

Of more particular interest to actors, the CCPA in 2001 expects to introduce a school that will offer professional-level classes in everything from musical theatre to auditioning and on-camera technique. The announced faculty roster includes some of the city's senior people. The CCPA also will have studio space available for rental as well as its four theatre spaces, ranging from 150-350 seats and including two cabaret set-ups.

Further out in the neighborhoods, 2000 saw ComedySportz move into the historic theatre space at 2851 N. Halsted, previously occupied by the St. Nicholas, Steppenwolf and Organic/Touchstone theatre companies. Meanwhile, WNEP moved into ComedySportz' previous space, the tiny Turnaround Theatre on Halsted at Belmont. In the wake of a building code and fire code crackdown by city inspectors on off-Loop houses, the year also saw the Footsteps/Factory Theatre space at 5230 N. Clark Street shuttered for good, and ditto the Shattered Globe space at 2856 N. Halsted. Both troupes, however, survive and continue to produce. The Annoyance Theatre at 3747 N. Clark and the Raven Theatre at 6931 N. Clark also shuttered; the former when the building was sold and the latter when the City condemned the building in order

State of the Art

to construct a new school. Both troupes remain vigorous, and are producing elsewhere at this time.

One result of the late 1999 onslaught by City of Chicago building and fire inspectors was an initiative by the League of Chicago Theatres and the Department of Cultural Affairs that has engaged the city's Department of Inspectional Services and Department of Revenue (issuers of the necessary Place of Public Amusement licenses). That initiative resulted last year in rewrites and clarifications to the city's confusing and even conflicting codes, less costly downgrades of emergency lighting provisions for smaller off-Loop theatres, and the appointment of ombudsmen for the theatre industry in the various departments.

Also on Clark Street at Wellington, the partnership that owns and operates the Ivanhoe Theatre sold it to the neighboring liquor store, which will expand into the space. The venue includes three theatres and has been home to a very large chunk of Chicago theatre history since first opening its doors in the late 1960's. The Ivanhoe will continue to operate until next year, but the deal is done.

Even further afield, the Metropolis Centre for the Performing Arts opened in Arlington Heights, with a 350-seat theatre that will provide a second home for the Apple Tree and Second City theatres, plus visiting dance, concert and cabaret performances. The $21 million mixed-use facility is the latest in a string of suburban arts centers.

But enough of cold, hard bricks-and-mortar. Theatre is a profession of human beings: a people thing. So let's talk of cold, hard people—agents. You remember what the great comedian Fred Allen said: "You can take all the sincerity in Hollywood and fit it into a flea's navel, and still have room for two agents' hearts." Just kidding! He also said, "Imitation is the sincerest form of television." Not kidding. We can't speak for LA or The Big Apple, but our agents in Chicago truly are a wonderful and hard-working lot. Actors don't get rich in Chicago (although actors get rich FROM Chicago), and neither do agents.

The Year 2000 was a tough one for the representation biz. Severely challenged by the six month commercials strike, three agencies shut their doors over the summer starting with Harrise Davidson and Associates, perhaps our top theatrical agency. Davidson semi-retired from the business, retaining only a handful of close, longterm clients to work with personally. The well-established Sa-Rah Talent also closed, as did CED.

In other labor matters, Actors Equity Association and the Producers Association of Chicago-area Theatres (PACT) continued to sail

State of the Art

smoothly along as they passed the halfway point in the current four-year CAT contract— the agreement that governs most key off-Loop companies including Steppenwolf, Victory Gardens, Organic, American Theatre Company, Black Ensemble, Apple Tree, Festival Theatre, Raven, Chicago Shakespeare, Illinois Theatre Center, Remy Bumppo, Writers Theatre and many more. That halfway point, however, included modifications to CAT Tier N.

The CAT contract provides six salary tiers linked to the size of the house. Over the last six years, it's also provided a seventh tier, known as Tier N as in "new," devised as an entry-level tier for non-union Off-Loop theatres. It requires only one Equity actor per show (and no union stage manager). Last year, "The Book" listed no fewer than 23 troupes utilizing Tier N, making it by far the most frequently used contract category.

As originally conceived, after a year or two at Tier N, an Off-Loop theatre would move up the CAT ladder to Tier I or Tier II, paying a higher weekly minimum and engaging an Equity stage manager. What has happened, though, is that small Off-Loop houses have remained at Tier N for three, four or even five years— defining themselves as Equity houses, winning Equity Jefferson Awards, but not increasing their use of Equity members. The union and PACT now have agreed that a Tier N house must move up to Tier I in its third CAT year (although exceptions can be made by Equity), paying the going weekly minimum rate. The Tier N modifications impact the acting community in a direct, if not an earthshaking, way.

The year saw the usual number of staff comings-and-goings, the most significant being the retirement of the engaging and well-regarded Kary M. Walker as producer of the Marriott Theatre in Lincolnshire, the giant musical theatre house. Walker was succeeded by his Number Two, Terry James, who promptly announced that artistic director Dyanne Early would step down at the end of the year, to be succeeded by performer-turned-casting director Rick Boynton (who gives up his post at Chicago Shakespeare Theatre to go back to his first love, musical theatre). Also, Alan Salzenstein stepped down as managing director of Apple Tree Theatre to become executive director of the Metropolis Centre (where Apple Tree will produce three shows a year). His successor at Apple Tree is Todd Schmidt, who retains his longtime post as general manager of the summertime Peninsula Players in Fish Creek, WI.

Two Chicago actors and playwrights took top national honors, winning the annual prizes bestowed by the American Theatre Critics Association. Coby Goss, of the Seanachai ensemble, won the Osborn

State of the Art

Prize for an outstanding emerging playwright, while Regina Taylor won the $25,000 Steinberg Prize for "Oo-Blah-Dee," which premiered at the Goodman Theatre.

On the journalistic scene, columnist Lewis Lazare left The READER after writing the weekly Culture Club feature for 11 years. He moved in late November to the Chicago Sun-Times as a marketing and advertising columnist. Always lively, and always controversial, Lazare brought a style and point-of-view to Culture Club that cannot be replaced.

During Year 2000, the theatre community also endured some heavy personal losses with the deaths of actors Ted Bales (brilliant comedian), Nathan Rankin (intense and diverse), George Busse (World War II vet, ordained minister and gay pioneer), and Patti Wilkus (Jeff Award winning singer, actor and voice-over talent). We also lost one of our most distinguished directors and personal miracle man, a shaper of Off-Loop theatre, Michael Maggio, who was only 49 years old. Finally, former Congressman Sidney R. Yates died in October at age 91. Yates represented Chicago's North Side for 24 terms in the House of Representatives. Known as "Mr. Arts," he co-sponsored the legislation that established the National Endowment for the Arts and was its mightiest defender over the last decade until his retirement in 1998.

Of course, there was the usually potpourri of minor bits and pieces of news: The League of Chicago Theatres endured an embezzlement scandal that resulted in a $200,000 loss and a great deal of embarrassment for present and past management; at Victory Gardens Theater, artistic director Dennis Zacek and managing director Marcelle McVay beat back a scheme by their own board of directors that would have undercut their authority (with the theatre community, subscribers and press rallying to their defense); the Illinois Arts Council saw its base funding rise to the highest level in its history, $19.9 million.

Ho-hum. Just another, typical quiet year in Chicago theatre.

Car Considerations Checklist

Owning a car in Chicago can be both helpful and aggravating. There's a lot of things to keep in mind. Check it out.

The Pros

Ever try to carry your groceries on the eL?

Suburban theatres.

The eL's inconsistent scheduling.

Wider choice of neighborhoods to live in.

Less accessible neighborhoods are usually cheaper neighborhoods. In this case, owning a car can actually save you money.

Flexibility.

The Cons

High insurance rates.

Poorly maintained streets.

Confusing highway systems. This merits a checklist all its own. Each Chicagoland highway has its own name that won't appear on most maps, but without knowing them you'll never understand the traffic report. Some main examples:

- The Kennedy refers to I90 north of the Loop including the portion where I90 and I94 merge.
- The Eisenhower is actually I290.
- The Edens means I94 north of the I90/I94 merge.
- The Dan Ryan actually means I94 south of the Loop.
- The Stevenson is I55.
- The Tri-State refers to I294.
- The Skyway is actually I90 south of the Loop after I90 and I94 separate.
- Why is it this way? Who knows. Chicago works in mysterious ways.

Tollways.

High gas prices.

Other Chicago drivers.

Difficult parking.

Street cleaning (watch for the orange signs).

8   The Book: An Actor's Guide to Chicago

The Procedure
If you're still planning on driving in Chicago (and many people, including this author, do), there are some steps you're going to need to take.

Visit the Secretary of State
Within 90 days of your arrival in Chicago, you're supposed to switch over your license and registration. To get an Illinois license, you'll need to have your old license, a social security card, proof of your current address (a piece of mail addressed to you will suffice) and you'll need to take a written test. Additionally, you'll need $10. To transfer your registration, you'll need an Illinois license, $13 to transfer your title and $48 for plates. If you've owned your car "for a while"(vague terms courtesy of the Secretary of State's office), you shouldn't have to pay tax on the updated registration. Call 312/793-1010 for more information.

Visit the City of Chicago Department of Revenue
Every Chicago resident who drives has to pay a "wheel tax" of $60 called a city sticker. The cost is actually going up soon, so be sure to call and confirm the costs. If you don't get it right away, they'll penalize you, and if you don't get one, you can be ticketed. Your city at work. Additionally, some neighborhoods require that you have a residential parking pass, which is a completely different animal from your city sticker. For that you'll need a city sticker, proof of residence and $10. You may be able to take care of both these things at your local currency exchange. Check one out before you bother with the trip downtown. For more information, call 312/744-7409.

Ch. 1 Coming to Chicago

Getting Around

Chicago Transit

In the city, the eL, the bus, and your feet get you where you're going. Mastering the eL is quite fun and adventurous. CTA fares are $1.50 per ride. If taken within two hours, the first transfer is 30 cents, the second is free. Take an eL, then transfer to a bus and get to your destination on $1.80. The CTA doesn't use coins. All riders — bus and eL — use fare cards. Machines are set up in eL stations to purchase cards or add money onto existing ones. To get information about the CTA, check out their website at **www.transitchicago.com** or call **1-888-968-7282**.

What the "eL"?

The eL is a network of frequently-stopping trains that run on *elevated* platforms one-story above street level.

The color-coded eL lines culminate in the heart of the city and "loop" around downtown. Two exceptions, the Red and Blue Lines, descend into subways downtown and tunnel under the Loop.

See page 342 for a detailed map of all Chicago CTA eL stops.

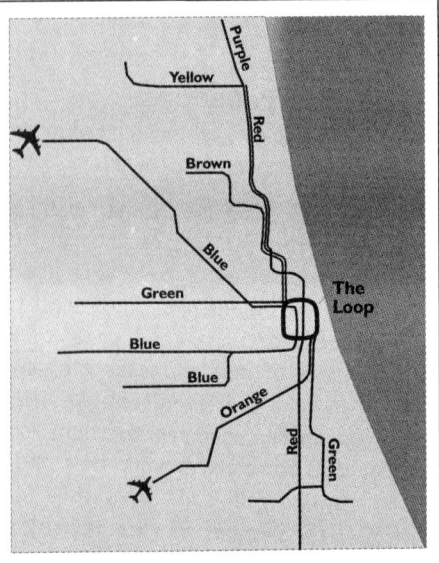

Metra: Training in from the suburbs

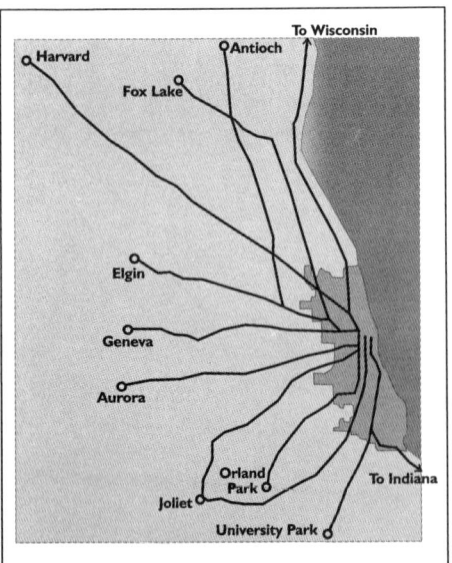

Metra trains can get you into Chicago from all corners of suburbia.

Metra is the train that runs from almost all the Chicago suburbs to the city. Metra riders swear by it and seem to feel sorry for folks dealing with congestion in the city. For under $10, you can travel from the farthest reaches of suburbia, and even parts of Indiana and Wisconsin. The trains are quiet, comfortable and great for reading.

For more about Metra, log on to **www.metrarail.com** or call **312/322-6777**.

Regional Transit Authority has a special hotline that can help you figure out how to get from any point A to any point B. Call the Hotline– **836-7000,** in any area code– and get advice regarding the use of Metra, CTA buses, eL trains, and the PACE suburban bus system.

10 The Book: An Actor's Guide to Chicago

Neighborhoods

It's a Beautiful Day in the Neighborhood

I like this place, and willingly could waste my time in it.

Chicago is a very simple city. It's laid out on a grid, with the exception of a few conveniently placed diagonal streets. All highways lead downtown, as do all train routes. A new arrival to the city will find it surprisingly easy to make one's way, whether driving or on foot.

Chicago is a very confusing city. All of the highways have names in addition to route numbers that everyone uses, but that don't appear on most maps. If you ask a Chicagoan where they live, they won't say Chicago, and they won't give the street. They'll say they live in Bucktown or Logan Square or Rogers Park. Public transportation, though conveniently color-coded, is referred to, instead, by its final stops. It's not the Red Line, it's the Howard-Dan Ryan.

Both of these paragraphs are true. Chicago is a simple city that seems to be full of strange codes to a newcomer. No one really knows where particular neighborhoods begin or end, or why it is that I-94 West actually heads north. It may take a new arrival months to understand all of the names of the interstates and be able to make sense of a traffic report. What's a newcomer to do?

When it comes to neighborhoods, we can help. Neighborhood names are particularly useful when apartment hunting, as most papers and realtors separate listings this way. Below is a breakdown of information

Ch. 1 Coming to Chicago **11**

Neighborhoods

on a selection of Chicago neighborhoods. Included are the boundaries (roughly), average rents for studios, one bedrooms, and two bedrooms, crime ratings and comments from PERFORMINK readers and staffers familiar with the area.

Neighborhood Breakdowns

These description come from the experience of PERFORMINK staffers and subscribers. Please remember these are the compiled thoughts of 2-7 people a neighborhood. The comments are completely unscientific, and should be taken as such. The best way to get a feel for a neighborhood is to go there and walk around.

Rent averages are based on those quoted on the Chicago Reader's Spacefinder at www.chireader.com. Those numbers should be taken with a grain of salt, as apartment prices can range widely depending on what's being offered. Crime ratings are based on stats found on the Chicago Police Website for January-September of 2000. Each neighborhood gets two grades, one for violent crime and one for total crime. Each neighborhood has been measured relative to the others listed. Crime rates are given by letter grades. A, of course, is safest. F is least safe, relative to the neighborhoods listed.

Neighborhood Map Key: M –*Metra Train Stop*   ++++++++ –*Train Tracks*
L – *eL Train Stop*   <u>Street name</u> –*Streets*

These streets do have names .... and numbers!

The streets of Chicago form a grid that is conveniently numbered for your navigational sanity. Mastering this system will greatly assist you in getting to know the neighborhoods and help you get around town.

Madison and State Street are the starting lines for this system. The major streets that form the grid increase in number by hundreds. Streets are numbered and tagged with an N, S, E, or W.

Examples: Fullerton is 2400 N., or 24 blocks north of Madison. Halsted is 800 W., or 8 blocks west of State Street.

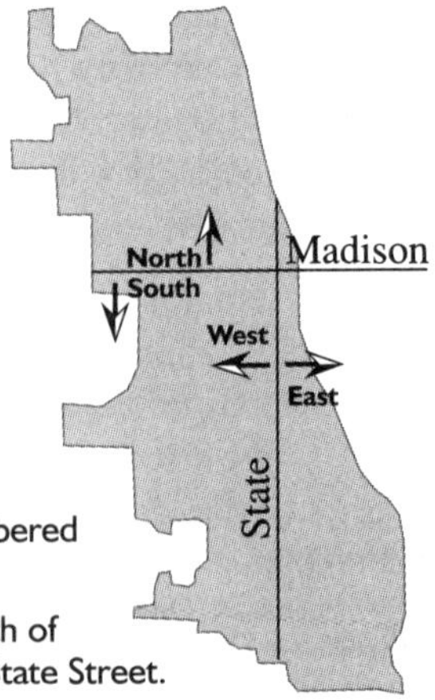

12   The Book: An Actor's Guide to Chicago

Neighborhoods

Andersonville

Comments: Residents cite the easy parking, affordable rents and great international restaurants in recommending Andersonville. It is home to many artists. Theatres in the neighborhood include The Neo-Futurists and Griffin. There are also a number of actor hangouts: Simon's Tavern (where you can pick up a **PERFORMINK**), the Hop Leaf and Kopi, "a traveler's cafe." It also boasts the original Ann Sathers, which is the place for Sunday brunch and cinnamon rolls. The neighborhood is quite multicultural, with Scandinavian, Latino and Asian populations — and eateries. It also has a very big lesbian population. Women and Children First — a well-known feminist bookstore — has many special events with authors from around the country.

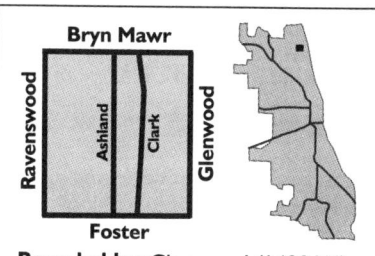

Bounded by: Glenwood (1400 W.), Ravenswood (1800 W.), Foster (5200 N.) and Bryn Mawr (5600 N.)

Rent: Studio: $620 1 Bedroom: $700 2 Bedroom: $1120

Violent Crime: A **Total Crime:** A

Bucktown

Comments: Right off the expressway, this is a less accessible area by public transportation. A lot of small restaurants and bars are scattered throughout this area. It is quickly being gentrified and is often referred to in conjunction with its neighbor to the south, Wicker Park. There are a lot of filmmakers in Bucktown, many of whom can be found at a local tavern called The Charleston. It is both yuppie and artsy and is quickly rising in price. Trap Door Theatre is in Bucktown.

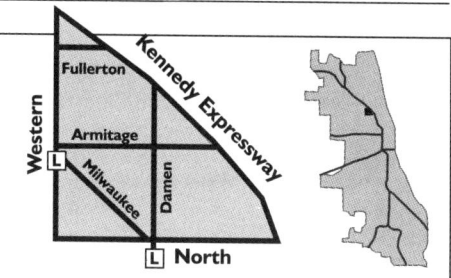

Bounded by: Kennedy Expressway, Western (2400 W.), North (1600 N.) and Fullerton (2400 N.)

Rent: Studio: $600 1 Bedroom: $770 2 Bedroom: $1400

Violent Crime: D **Total Crime:** C

Buena Park

Comments: This quiet neighborhood is "homey for being urban," says one resident. Buena Park is conveniently close to most things — the lake, Lake Shore Drive, Lakeview and public transportation. It is within easy walking distance of an eL, and many major bus routes run through the area, including express buses during the week down to the Loop. Parking is do-able if not always easily found. The neighborhood is praised by the many actors who live here.

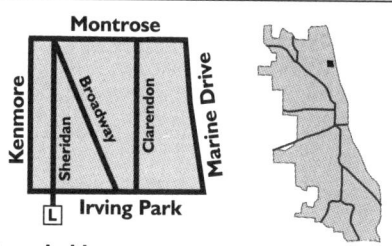

Bounded by: Marine Drive, Kenmore, Irving Park (4000 N.) and Montrose (4400 N.)

Rent: Studio: $580 1 Bedroom: $815 2 Bedroom: $1180

Violent Crime: A **Total Crime:** A

Ch. 1 Coming to Chicago 13

Neighborhoods

Edgewater

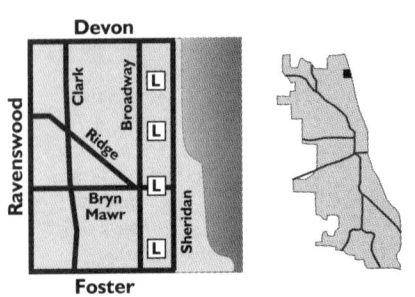

Comments: Originally settled by German, Swedish, and Irish immigrants, this community was originally designed as a posh residential subdivision for some of Chicago's more prosperous families. But, like many Chicago neighborhoods, Edgewater fell the way of urban decay after the Depression. Due to the combined efforts of the Edgewater Community Council and community volunteers, however, areas of Edgewater have been reclaimed and revitalized by identifying and removing absentee slumlords and renovating these historic properties. Cheaper rents have attracted many actors and artist types. The "Artists in Residence" building — a residence which solely houses artists of all persuasions — is located here. Parking accessibility isn't always top notch depending on where you're located.

Bounded by: Lake Michigan, Ravenswood (1800 W.), Foster (5200 N.) and Devon (6400 N.)

Rent: Studio: $545
1 Bedroom: $700   2 Bedroom: $1270

Violent Crime: C   **Total Crime:** B

Gold Coast

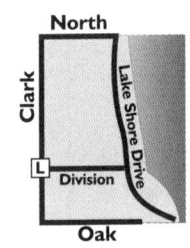
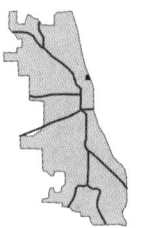

Comments: This is a "great place to live" if you can afford it. Close to the lake with a lot of (very expensive) shops, "There's always a lot going on in the neighborhood." Again, many of the residents here own rather than rent, and the price for ownership runs in the millions, or at least the high six figures. This is the place, incidentally, where you can find Chicago's Magnificent Mile. It also boasts Mr. J's — one of the best hot dog stands in Chicago. It is very accessible to public transportation and within healthy walking distance of most agents' offices.

Bounded by: Lake Michigan, Clark, Oak (1000 N.) and North (1600 N.)

Rent: Studio: $915
1 Bedroom: $1255   2 Bedroom: $2200

Violent Crime: B   **Total Crime:** D

14   The Book: An Actor's Guide to Chicago

Humboldt Park

Comments: *"There's a strong sense of community, lots of artists and lots of gangs,"* says one resident. The park itself (part of the vast boulevard system designed to link all of Chicago's parks from the north to the south side) is quite beautiful. Gentrification has begun here, but long-time residents — most of whom are Latino — are determined that they will not be priced out by development.

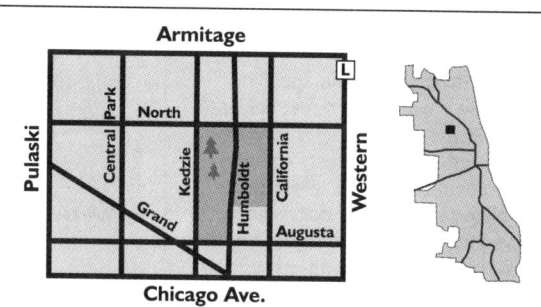

Bounded by: Western (2400 W.), Pulaski (4000 W.) Chicago (800 N.) and Armitage (2000 N.)

Rent: Studio: $515
1 Bedroom: $780 2 Bedroom: $875

Violent Crime: D **Total Crime:** D

Hyde Park

Comments: Centered around the University of Chicago, this is a college neighborhood tucked in the South Side. It's a very diverse area with a lot of bookstores, and it has the highest percentage of Nobel prize winners living in the city. Some great old buildings can be found there. If you're an architecture buff, it's definitely the place to be. The neighborhoods surrounding Hyde Park are not the best, so a car is definitely recommended. The Metra station, for instance, is on the boundary and is not quite as safe as the rest of the neighborhood. Court Theatre is in Hyde Park. The South Shore Cultural Center is also close by.

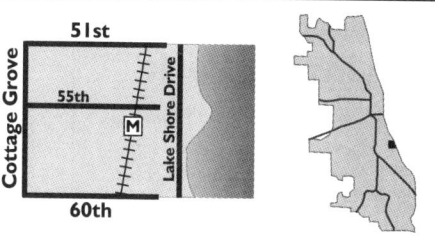

Bounded by: Lake Michigan, Cottage Grove, 60th (6000 S.) and 51st (5100 S.)

Rent: Studio: $445
1 Bedroom: $570 2 Bedroom: $725

Violent Crime: B+ **Total Crime:** A

Neighborhood Map Key:
M – *Metra Train Stop*
L – *eL Train Stop*
┼┼┼┼┼┼┼┼ – *Train Tracks*
Street name – *Streets*

Ch. 1 Coming to Chicago **15**

Neighborhoods

Lakeview

Comments: *Statistically speaking, Lakeview is one of the safest neighborhoods in the city. Parking is very difficult — especially at night. The only other complaint is that, while this is largely regarded as a great neighborhood, yuppification has begun in earnest. Frame houses have been torn down to make room for large brick and stone condos.* PERFORMINK'S *offices are in Lakeview, as are many theatres, including the Theatre Building, Bailiwick Repertory, Ivanhoe, Briar Street, Stage Left, ComedySportz, ImprovOlympic and About Face. Actor hangouts include the L&L Tavern, Melrose Diner, and Bar San Miguel. It's a very young, post-college crowd with not too many families. Part of Lakeview is also known among the gay community as "Boys' Town."*

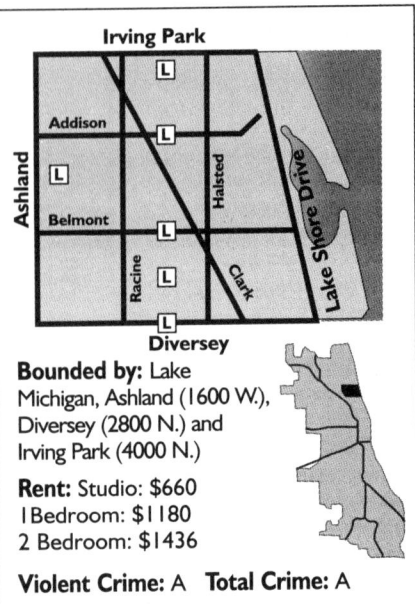

Bounded by: Lake Michigan, Ashland (1600 W.), Diversey (2800 N.) and Irving Park (4000 N.)

Rent: Studio: $660
1 Bedroom: $1180
2 Bedroom: $1436

Violent Crime: A   **Total Crime:** A

Lincoln Park

Comments: *Just south of Lakeview, this is clearly an upper-class neighborhood. Its residents enjoy a great deal of safety and convenience, although parking is, again, very difficult. Lincoln Park was the up and coming neighborhood a decade ago and still boasts a lot of theatres. In fact, the Off-Loop theatre scene pretty much started in Lincoln Park (with a nod to Lakeview just to its north) in the 70's. Victory Gardens is located here in a building that once also housed the famed Body Politic Theatre. Steppenwolf and the Royal George are across the street from each other on Halsted. DePaul University is in Lincoln Park, which makes for an interesting mix of theatre folk, yuppies and frat boys. John Barleycorn is one notable actor hangout, as is Sterch's. The Biograph (where John Herbert Dillinger was shot) is in this neighborhood, along with the Three Penny movie theatre. Most importantly, Act I Bookstore is on Lincoln, next to the Apollo Theatre.*

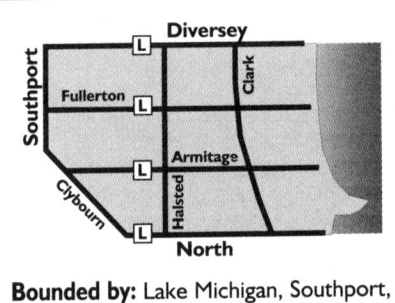

Bounded by: Lake Michigan, Southport, North (1600 N.) and Diversey (2800 N.)

Rent: Studio: $725
1 Bedroom: $1130
2 Bedroom: $1530

Violent Crime: A

Total Crime: A

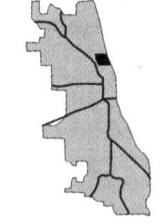

16   The Book: An Actor's Guide to Chicago

Neighborhoods

Lincoln Square

Comments: *This neighborhood gets raves from its residents for the people and the community. It's less congested than the lakeside neighborhoods. A car is advantageous, but the eL does have a stop on Western and Lincoln, and there's a bus depot on Western. The buildings have a very German feel, though the population is more a mix of White, Latino and Asian. Great Thai restaurants can be found in the area. There are also wonderful German bakeries. A number of theatres have opened in this area recently, including TinFish, Cornservatory and Phoenix Ascending.*

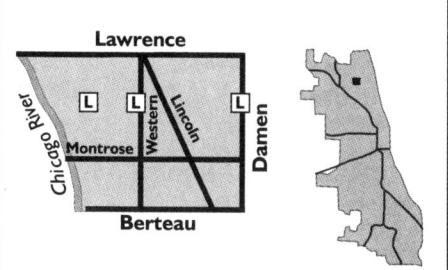

Boundaries: Damen (2000 W.), the Chicago River, Berteau (4200 N.) and Lawrence (4800 N.)

Rent: Studio: $580
1 Bedroom: $765 2 Bedroom: $1050

Violent Crime: A **Total Crime:** B+

Logan/Palmer Square

Comments: *Logan Square is one of the top areas for artists. In fact, artists moving into the neighborhood in the mid-80's helped to start the gentrification that has rapidly spread west and south. It's very community based and multi-everything — race, culture, class. It is marked by large graystones and red brick mostly two and three flats, in a very German/Swedish style of architecture. There are also some mansions that are still single family homes, especially in the Palmer Square area. Logan Square is the beginning of the Boulevard system still in existence. Redmoon Theatre Company is located in the Logan Square area.*

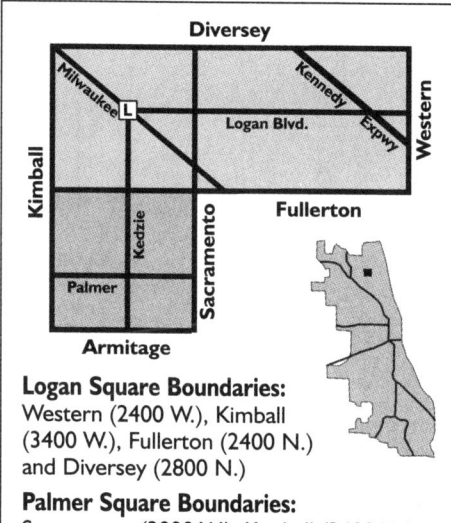

Logan Square Boundaries:
Western (2400 W.), Kimball (3400 W.), Fullerton (2400 N.) and Diversey (2800 N.)

Palmer Square Boundaries:
Sacramento (3000 W.), Kimball (3400 W.), Armitage (2000 N.) and Fullerton (2400 N.)

Rent: Studio: $460
1 Bedroom: $845 2 Bedroom: $1020

Violent Crime: D **Total Crime:** D

Ch. 1 Coming to Chicago **17**

Neighborhoods

Old Town

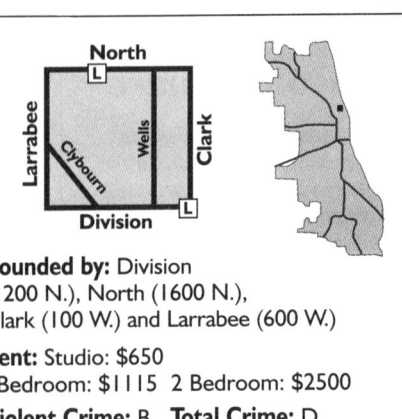

Comments: *"The area's great! It's eclectic, has theatres, bars, restaurants and it's convenient."* This sums up the opinions of the residents we spoke with. Second City is in Old Town and, consequently, there are lots of actors' bars and hangouts. The Last Act is across from Second City on Wells. Old Town Ale House is across from Second City on North. A Red Orchid Theatre is also in Old Town, as is Zanies comedy club. Pipers Alley movie theatre is on the corner of North and Wells in the

Bounded by: Division (1200 N.), North (1600 N.), Clark (100 W.) and Larrabee (600 W.)

Rent: Studio: $650
1 Bedroom: $1115 2 Bedroom: $2500

Violent Crime: B   **Total Crime:** D

same building that houses Second City. Parking is quite horrendous, unless you pay for it. Old Town butts up against the Gold Coast and Lincoln Park, so it can be kind of pricey.

Pilsen

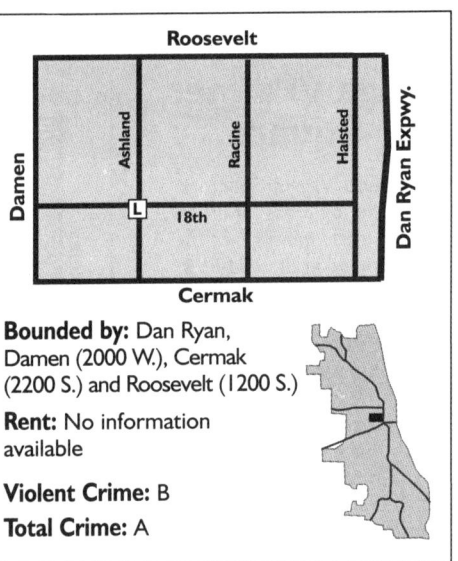

Comments: *Pilsen boasts a very large Mexican population and is home to the Mexican Fine Arts Museum. Decades ago, it was mostly Irish and Polish, and the remnants of those cultures can still be seen. It's currently going through gentrification, which is causing many political problems with longtime, mostly Spanish-speaking residents. There are lots of schools in the area — both Catholic and public. There are also lots of warehouses, which attract both theatre companies and developers. There is a very large artistic population due to the low rents and large spaces. Duncan YMCA Chernin Center for*

Bounded by: Dan Ryan, Damen (2000 W.), Cermak (2200 S.) and Roosevelt (1200 S.)

Rent: No information available

Violent Crime: B

Total Crime: A

the Arts resides in this area and is the home to several small companies. The University of Illinois at Chicago (UIC) anchors the area to the north.

Neighborhood Map Key:
[M] –Metra Train Stop
[L] – eL Train Stop
++++++++++ –Train Tracks
<u>Street name</u> –Streets

---

18   The Book: An Actor's Guide to Chicago

Neighborhoods

Printer's Row/South Loop

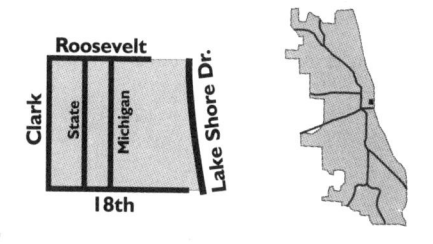

Comments: *This area was a vast wasteland at the beginning of the 90's, but rapid gentrification has made it one of the highest priced neighborhoods in Chicago. New construction overlooks the abandoned freight yards, which only seems to add a quaintness to the area. It helps that Mayor Daley moved from his boyhood neighborhood of Bridgeport (in the shadow of Comiskey Park) to this trendy area a few years ago, leaving traditionalists aghast. Transportation is accessible, with the eL running from the Loop just a mile or so to the north. Buses also are always on time. Parking isn't wonderful — unless you have a garage with your home or apartment, as many do. There are some nice restaurants in Printer's Row, but other than that it's very residential.*

Bounded by: the Lakefront, Clark (100 W.), 18th (1800 S.) and Roosevelt (1200 S.)

Rent: Studio: $750
1 Bedroom: $1250 2 Bedroom: $1960

Violent Crime: A **Total Crime:** C

Ravenswood

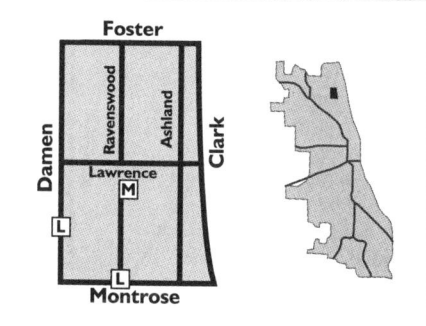

Comments: *"Move here before the rents go up," says one resident. This affordable area is diverse and pretty blue collar, with lots of single family homes. This is a neighborhood in which you will see kids playing in the yard or riding their bikes down the street. It's becoming yuppie, and there is a growing gay population as Andersonville to the northeast becomes too expensive. Pauline's is a great breakfast restaurant that is always crowded. The Zephyr, for ice cream and diner food, is very popular too. Otherwise, there aren't too many hangouts in this residential area. The Ravenswood eL (or the Brown Line) goes through Ravenswood and the Clark bus is always available.*

Bounded by: Clark, Damen (2000 W.), Montrose (4400 N.) and Foster (5200 N.)

Rent: Studio: $580
1 Bedroom: $820 2 Bedroom: $1120

Violent Crime: A **Total Crime:** A

Ch. 1 Coming to Chicago **19**

Neighborhoods

River West

Comments: River West is bounded on the east by its namesake landmark, the Chicago River, which was altered in 1900 by reversing the flow of current, and is also dyed bright green (as opposed to the usual tint of fatigue green) for the annual St. Pat's Day celebrations. Large warehouses and loft spaces make up River West, which made it a prime target for revitalization in the late 80's and early 90's. After a fizzle in the area a few years ago, it is starting to live up to its potential. Chicago Dramatists Workshop is in River West, as is The Chicago Academy for the Arts — Chicago's answer to "Fame." Lots of good restaurants are popping up every day. There are a lot of filmmakers and companies in River West, more so than theatre artists. You definitely need a car in this area. The closest grocery store, for instance, is across the river in the Gold Coast.

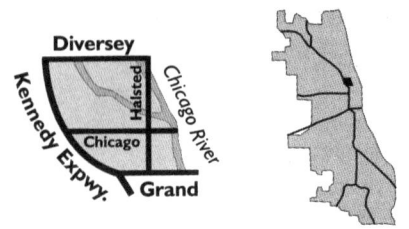

Bounded by: the Chicago River, the Kennedy Expressway, Grand (500 N.) and Division (1200 N.)

Rent: Studio: $775
1 Bedroom: $1225 2 Bedroom: $1675

Violent Crime: D **Total Crime:** C

Rogers Park

Comments: This is a huge neighborhood that forms Chicago's northern border. There's a large diverse community — probably the most diverse of all the neighborhoods in Chicago — including orthodox Jewish, Indian and Middle Eastern populations. Gay men moved up to the condos in West Rogers Park in the early 90's. "It's a melting pot," says one resident. Diverse can describe the income ranges, too. Some areas are quite affluent, while others are very poor. Loyola University is in Rogers Park. Raven, Center, Boxer Rebellion and Lifeline are some of the theaters in this area. Don't take safety for granted. In some areas it's fine. In others — like on Howard street bordering Evanston — it's quite unsafe day or night.

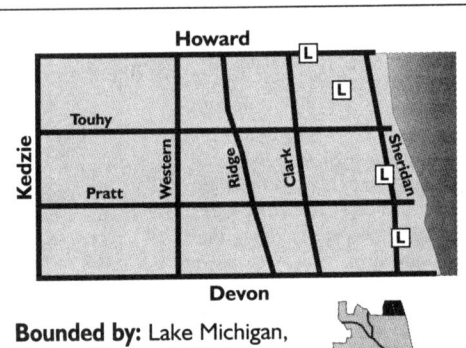

Bounded by: Lake Michigan, Kedzie, Devon (6400 N.) and Howard (7600 N.)

Rent: Studio: $500
1 Bedroom: $670
2 Bedroom: $865

Violent Crime: C **Total Crime:** B

20 The Book: An Actor's Guide to Chicago

Neighborhoods

Roscoe Village

Comments: This is a close neighborhood, but residents will need to go elsewhere for their entertainment. It's definitely a place where "you can know your neighbors." The Village Tap is an actors bar. Of particular note is the Four Moon Tavern, a bar owned and managed by four actors. Many small boutiques and restaurants are just starting to open in this neighborhood. Also, many Chicago filmmakers call this neighborhood home. It borders Lakeview to the east, and rents are rising as people are priced out of Lakeview.

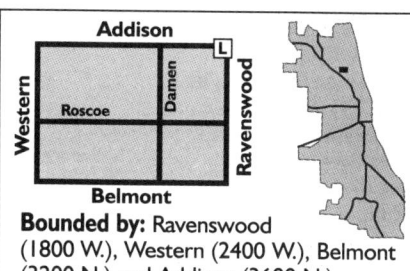

Bounded by: Ravenswood (1800 W.), Western (2400 W.), Belmont (3200 N.) and Addison (3600 N.)

Rent: Studio: $725
1 Bedroom: $1020   2 Bedroom: $1245

Violent Crime: A   **Total Crime:** B+

Saint Ben's

Comments: This is a working class neighborhood that most residents feel is a "great place to live." One resident complained of the noise, but others praised the quiet feel, so it probably depends on where you are. It's between Roscoe Village and Ravenswood and is going through the same kind of gentrification. American Theater Company (formerly American Blues Theater) and Breadline Theatre Group are located in this neighborhood.

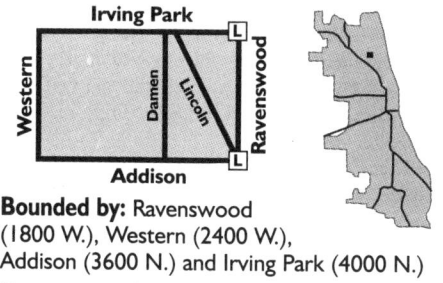

Bounded by: Ravenswood (1800 W.), Western (2400 W.), Addison (3600 N.) and Irving Park (4000 N.)

Rent: Studio: $725   1 Bedroom: $880
2 Bedroom: $1200

Violent Crime: A   **Total Crime:** B

Ukrainian Village

Comments: This neighborhood lives up to its name. Still, while a concentrated number of first and second generation Ukranians live here, it is also home to a number of other ethnicities, including Italians, Hispanics, and African Americans. These populations are augmented by artists who have flocked to housing in this area, which remains affordable. It's a close knit community where people watch out for one another, which can be relief or a nuisance, depending on whether you consider such behavior considerate or nosy. The neighborhood is an even mix of families, elderly, and young artists. The Western Avenue

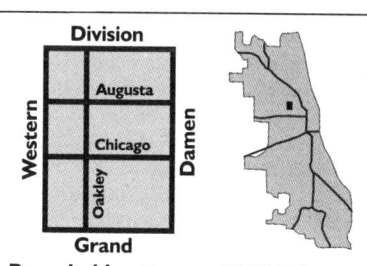

Bounded by: Damen (2000 W.), Western (2400 W.), Grand (500 N.) and Division (1200 N.)

Rent: Studio: $400
1 Bedroom: $750   2 Bedroom: $950

Violent Crime: A   **Total Crime:** A

border can be a bit dicey on the safety side, but the area is generally well-liked by residents. Public trans can be a hassle, since the area is served only by the buses, not the eL.

Ch. 1 Coming to Chicago   **21**

Neighborhoods

Uptown

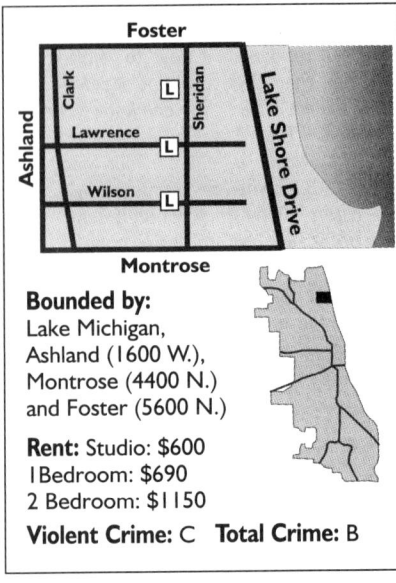

Comments: Uptown is as culturally diverse as its neighbor to the north, Rogers Park. But Uptown holds a unique place in the history and development of entertainers and their industry over the last century. The Aragon Ballroom, The Green Mill, The Equator Club, and the former Essanay Movie Studios (now St. Augustine College), one of the cradles of early American film, are all located in Uptown. Charlie Chaplin had a studio here before heading west. In the years following, Al Capone roamed this area fostering drama to rival any movie plot line. Eventually, the area fell into a slump, attracting seedier types and diversions. Over the last 5-10 years, however, the neighborhood has been on an upswing through rehab projects and community involvement. People deem this area "up and coming," but its arrival has become a slow one. Pegasus Players is in the area, as part of Truman College. The theatre is safe and quite nice, but people often complain about walking from their cars.

Bounded by: Lake Michigan, Ashland (1600 W.), Montrose (4400 N.) and Foster (5600 N.)

Rent: Studio: $600
1 Bedroom: $690
2 Bedroom: $1150

Violent Crime: C   **Total Crime:** B

Wicker Park

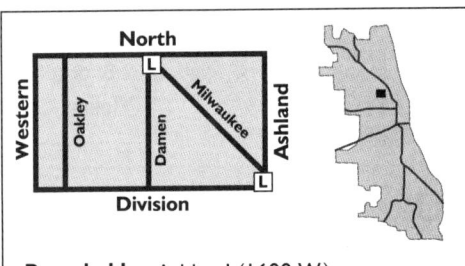

Comments: Wicker Park is the neighborhood for any trendy artist in Chicago. If you want to be "in," you want to be in Wicker Park. Architecturally, it is defined by large Victorian mansions that were once grand and graceful and now have been cut up into apartments. There has also been a lot of rehab in the area over the past few years, resulting, sometimes, in a strange mix of brand new brick and stone next door to an old Victorian. This is the area where Nelson Algren lived and wrote and the neighborhood is as tough and beautiful as an Algren book. Accessibility is somewhat of an issue, but not bad. The eL is the O'Hare line, which runs diagonally across the city to the airport. If you want to get up to Lakeview, where many theatres are, you have to go downtown first, then switch trains and head north. But buses do run regularly down North Avenue, Ashland and Damen.

Bounded by: Ashland (1600 W.), Western (2400 W.), Division (1200 N.) and North (1600 N.)

Rent: Studio: $475
1 Bedroom: $970   2 Bedroom: $1390

Violent Crime: D   **Total Crime:** C

22   The Book: An Actor's Guide to Chicago

Wrigleyville

Comments: The home of the Cubs receives high praise from its residents, though parking can be difficult, particularly during baseball season. "I love it. I would recommend it to first-time Chicagoans. Easy access to bars and theatres," says one resident. Wrigleyville is home to many young families, as well as artists. Wrigleyville is technically in Lakeview, but they are proud of their separate identity.

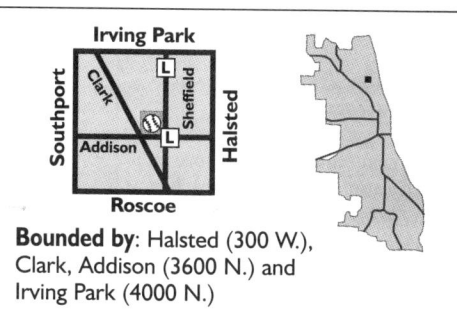

Bounded by: Halsted (300 W.), Clark, Addison (3600 N.) and Irving Park (4000 N.)

Rent: Studio: $660
1 Bedroom: $1025 2 Bedroom: $1420

Violent Crime: A **Total Crime:** A

Suburbs

Evanston

Comments: The first of our selected suburbs. Evanston lies just to the north of the city along the lake. Home to Northwestern University, this is a "down to earth, well rounded community," says one resident. "The neighbors are great because they look out for each other. It's convenient without being crowded," says another. Evanston is mostly made up of houses and mansions. It can be quite exclusive, yet it can also

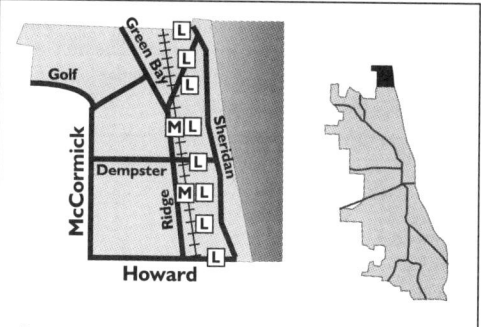

Rent: Studio: $650
1 Bedroom: $800 2 Bedroom: $1300

be affordable around the university or west of the Ridge Street dividing line. Even so, living in Evanston is more expensive than living in Chicago. Taxes alone, if you're in the buying mood, can be more than your mortgage payment. Public transportation in Evanston is pretty much limited to buses, but the Evanston Express eL line runs all the way down the lake to the Loop. One can go door to door from their apartment in Evanston to the Theatre Building in Lakeview in 20-30 minutes. Fleetwood Jourdain is an African American theatre that has been there for years. The famed Piven Theatre Workshop and Next Theatre are also in Evanston. And the city is expanding its commitment to the arts by building a new cultural center.

Ch. 1 Coming to Chicago

Suburbs

Oak Park

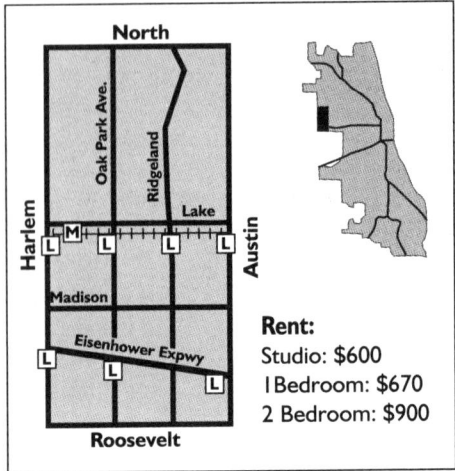

Rent:
Studio: $600
1 Bedroom: $670
2 Bedroom: $900

Comments: *This suburb lies just west of Chicago along the Eisenhower Expressway.* "It's a diverse community, and we have a lot of cultural things. Oak Park has a lot of actors. You'll always run into someone who's in the business," says a resident. *Residents also cite the great schools and the supportive neighborhoods in recommending this suburb. Oak Park is a village and feels like one. You can walk almost anywhere. Some apartments are more affordable than others, but it can be pretty pricey in some areas. Taxes are also a consideration here — the price for those wonderful schools and clean streets. There is also a considerable gay population in Oak Park. In fact, this progressive city is one of the few in the country who give domestic partnership benefits to gay spouses of city employees. Circle Theatre is in Oak Park, as is Oak Park Village Players. And the Oak Park Shakespeare Festival is a staple for actors and theatregoers every summer. You can live in Oak Park without a car. The eL Green and Blue Lines go to Oak Park, but it passes through some very poor neighborhoods on Chicago's west side first. More importantly, Metra runs directly from Oak Park to the city.*

Skokie

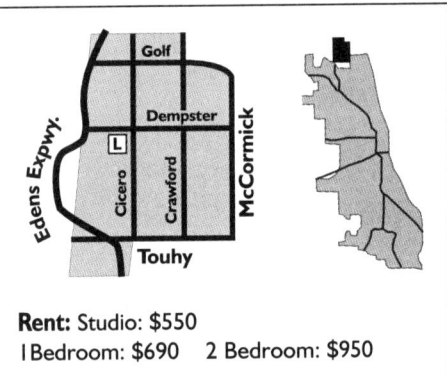

Rent: Studio: $550
1 Bedroom: $690   2 Bedroom: $950

Comments: *Skokie is more diverse and less expensive than its neighborhood to the east, Evanston. While the suburb is largely thought of as the Jewish center of the North Shore, the area has opened up to include many Asians and Latinos. The schools have a solid reputation, and there is an active park district. Convenient bus routes make it easy to reach the Howard eL stop in Evanston and many of the area's shopping and entertainment complexes. You can also take the "Skokie Swift," the one-stop extension of the eL that deposits riders at the Greyhound bus terminal. With the opening of The Northshore Center for the Performing Arts, Skokie became a big-time player on the theatre scene. Northlight Theatre is in the Northshore Center, along with the presenting company Centre East. Many companies also rent space in the North Shore Center.*

Finding an Apartment Checklist

Your living arrangement can make or break your Chicago experience. As you search for the perfect place to live, keep the following items in mind:

Rooms
How many rooms do you need? Where do you spend your time? How's the layout for sound? For privacy?

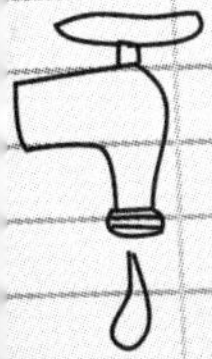

Water Pressure
How's the water pressure in the kitchen and bathroom? Can you get hot water from both sinks simultaneously? Check the shower too.

Parking
If you own a car, how tough is parking going to be? Do you need a sticker? Check the neighborhood during both the day and night.

Storage
Do you need places for stuff? Are there enough of such places?

Laundry
Are there facilities on-site? If not, where's the nearest laundromat?

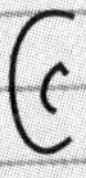

Sound
How much sound is there from the street? Is the eL nearby?

Natural Light
When and from what direction will the apartment get sunlight? Is the light going to wake you in the morning? Will your plants flourish?

Security
How well lit are the entrances to the building? Are there good locks on the doors? If the apartment is on the first floor, are there grills on the windows? Be sure to check the neighborhood at night as well.

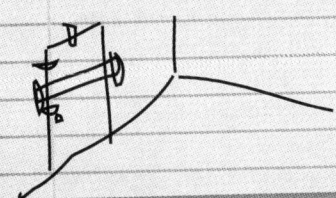

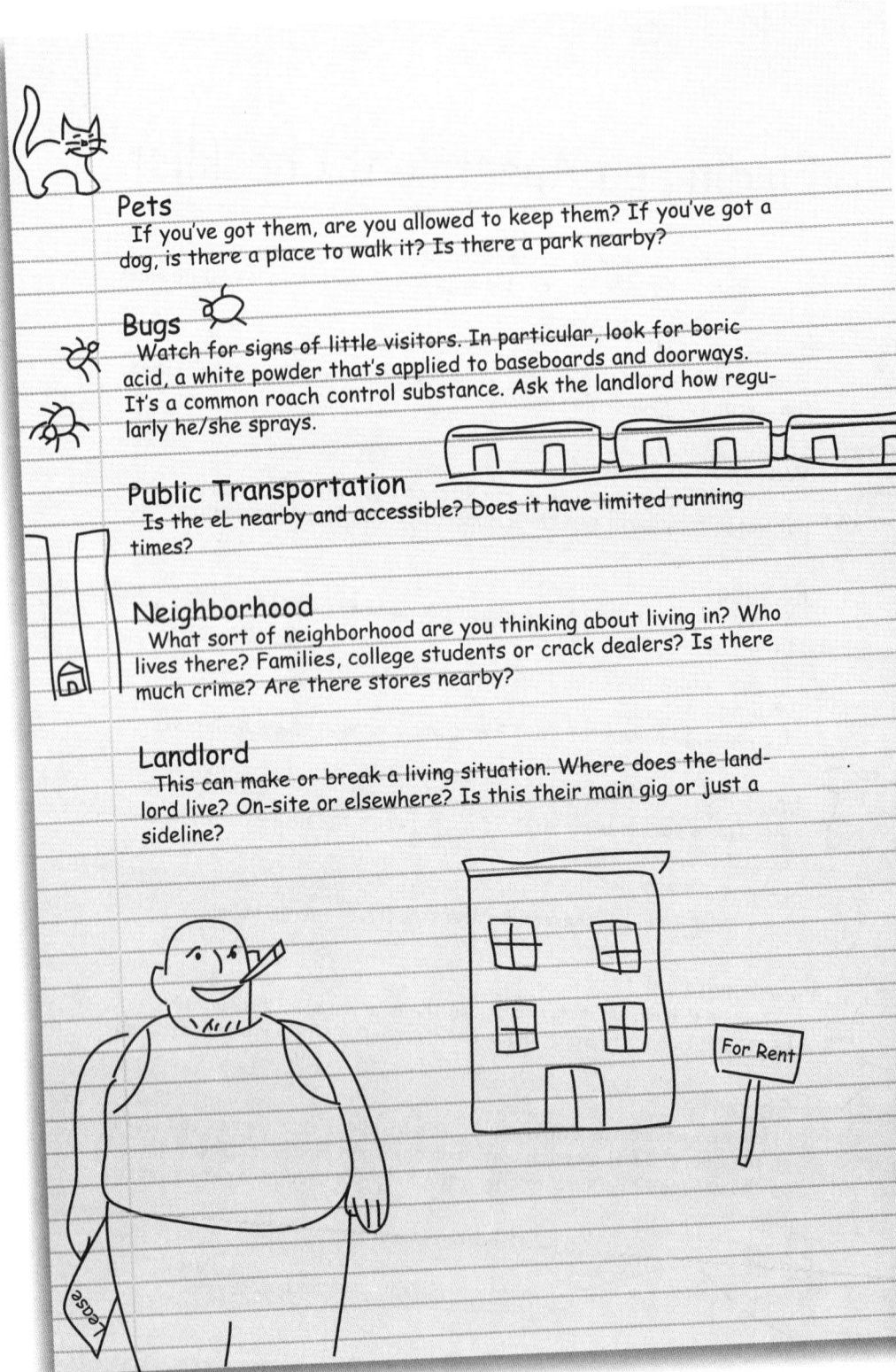

Pets
If you've got them, are you allowed to keep them? If you've got a dog, is there a place to walk it? Is there a park nearby?

Bugs
Watch for signs of little visitors. In particular, look for boric acid, a white powder that's applied to baseboards and doorways. It's a common roach control substance. Ask the landlord how regularly he/she sprays.

Public Transportation
Is the eL nearby and accessible? Does it have limited running times?

Neighborhood
What sort of neighborhood are you thinking about living in? Who lives there? Families, college students or crack dealers? Is there much crime? Are there stores nearby?

Landlord
This can make or break a living situation. Where does the landlord live? On-site or elsewhere? Is this their main gig or just a sideline?

Apartment Services

Apartment Connection
1000 W. Diversey
Chicago, IL 60614
773/525-3888
773/525-0210 - fax

The Apartment People
3121 N. Broadway
Chicago, IL 60657
773/248-8800
773/248-1007 - fax
www.apartmentpeople.com

Apartment Source
2638 N. Halsted
Chicago, IL 60614
773/404-9900
773/404-0669 - fax

Cagan Management
3856 W. Oakton St.
Skokie, IL 60076
847/679-5512 • 847/679-5516 - fax

Century 21 - Amquest
2843 N. Halsted
Chicago, IL 60657
773/404-2100 • 773/404-6034 - fax
www.century21amquest.com

City Living Apartment Rentals
1300 W. Belmont
Chicago, IL 60657
773/525-6161

Oak Park Regional Housing Center
1041 South Blvd.
Oak Park, IL 60302
708/848-7150
members.aol.com/RENTinOP/oprhc.html

Realty & Mortgage
928 W. Diversey
Chicago, IL 60614
773/549-8300
www.aptrentals.com

Relcon Apartment Finders
21 W. Elm - 2nd floor
Chicago, IL 60610
312/255-9920
312/255-9928 - fax
www.relconapartments.com

Urban Equities R.E.C.
6240 N. Clark
Chicago, IL 60660
773/743-4141
773/465-4672 - fax

Near any theatres?
Check out the Theatre Listings on page 208

Housing Spots

Artist in Residence
6165 N. Winthrop
Chicago, IL 60660
800/LIVE-ART
773/743-8900
773/743-8259 - fax
www.artistsinresidence.com

Artist in Residence has been a home to artists since 1979. We rent solely to people active in fine or applied arts. We have facilities available for use by our residents, including rehearsal spaces, painter's and sculptor's workshops and darkroom. For more information and appointment, call 773/743-8900 or 1-800-LIVE-ART.

Eleanor Residence
Women Only
1550 N. Dearborn
Chicago, IL 60610
312/664-8245
312/664-0888 - fax
eleanorresidence.com

Sovereign Apartments
1040 W. Granville
Chicago, IL 60660
773/274-8000
773/274-1321 - fax

Three Arts Club (for women)
(men - June, July, August only)
1300 N. Dearborn
Chicago, IL 60610
312/944-6250
312/944-6284 - fax
www.threearts.org

Utilities

Chicago-based utilities Ameritech, ComEd and People's Gas are vilified by residents frequently and with great imagination. Poor service, uninformed representatives and order errors are all too common. The secret to a good (or tolerable anyway) relationship with these fine institutions is to call. Then call to confirm. You may want to follow up to confirm the confirmation.

Ameritech
800/244-4444

AT&T
800/222-0300

Commonwealth Edison
800/334-7661

MCI
800/950-5555

Peoples Gas Light & Coke Co.
130 Randolph
Chicago, IL 60601
312/240-4000

Sprint
800/877-7746

Temp Agencies

A Personnel Commitment
(See our ad on page 346)
208 S. LaSalle #189
Chicago, IL 60604-1003
312/251-5151
312/251-5154 - fax

Active Temporary Services
(See our ad on page 31)
25 E. Washington #1717
Chicago, IL 60602
312/726-5771
312/726-3273 - fax

Active Temporary Services
3145 N. Lincoln - Main Level
Chicago, IL 60657
773/404-5700
773/404-9635 - fax

Advanced Personnel
(See our ad on this page)
1020 Milwaukee Ave. #105
Deerfield, IL 60015
847/520-9111
847/520-9489 - fax
www.advancedresources.com

Advanced Personnel is a staffing firm supplying office support employees to major financial, healthcare and Fortune 1000 corporations in Chicagoland. Our flexible scheduling helps match actors with temporary and full-time positions. Corporate positions, executive assistants, customer service professionals, production specialist, desktop publishers and administrative assistants. Contact us at 312/422-9333.

Temp Agencies

Appropriate Temporaries
(See our ad on the back cover)
79 W. Monroe #819
Chicago, IL 60603
312/782-7215
312/704-4195 - fax

ASI Staffing Service, Inc.
333 N. Michigan #2106
Chicago, IL 60601
312/782-4690
312/782-4697 - fax

BPS Staffing
200 N. LaSalle #1750
Chicago, IL 60601
312/920-6710
312/920-6744 - fax

The Choice for Staffing
(See our ad on page 31)
100 N. LaSalle #1900
Chicago, IL 60602
312/372-4500
312/853-4068 - fax
www.choicestaff.com

City Staffing
(See our ad on this page)
2 N. LaSalle #630
Chicago, IL 60602
312/346-3400
312/346-5200 - fax

Dunhill Staffing Systems
211 W. Wacker #1150
Chicago, IL 60606
312/346-0933
312/346-0837 - fax
www.dunhillstaff.com

Temp Agencies

Interim Office Professionals
11 S. LaSalle #2155
Chicago, IL 60603
312/781-7220
www.interim.com

Kelly Services
949C N. Plum Grove Rd.
Schaumburg, IL 60173
847/995-9350 • 847/995-9366 - fax
www.kellyservices.com

Larko Group
(See our ad on inside of front cover)
11 S. LaSalle #1720
Chicago, IL 60603
312/857-2300
312/857-2355 - fax
www.@thelarkogroup.com

Loftus & O'Meara
166 E. Superior #410
Chicago, IL 60611
312/944-2102
312/944-7009 - fax

Mack & Associates Personnel, Ltd.
att. Boula Proutsos
100 N. LaSalle #2110
Chicago, IL 60602
312/368-0677 • 312/368-1868 - fax
www.mackltd.com

Manpower Temporary Services
500 W. Madison #2950
Chicago, IL 60661
312/648-4555
312/648-0472 - fax
www.manpowerchicago.com

Paige Temporary, Inc.
5215 Old Orchard Rd.
Skokie, IL 60077
847/966-0111
847/966-8479 - fax
www.paigepersonnel.com

Prestige Employment Service
19624 Governors Highway
Flossmoor, IL 60422
708/798-7666
708/798-9099 - fax
www.prestigeemployment.com

Pro Staff Personnel Services
10 S. Wacker #2250
Chicago, IL 60606
312/575-2120
312/641-0224 - fax
www.prostaff.com

Profile Temporary Service
222 N. LaSalle #450
Chicago, IL 60601
312/541-4141
312/641-1762 - fax

ACTIVE TEMPORARY SERVICES, INC.

Loop
25 E. Washington St.
Suite 1717
Chicago, IL. 60602
312.726.5771

Lakeview
3145 N. Lincoln Ave.
Main Level
Chicago, IL. 60657
773.404.5700

Women Owned Award Winning

Benefits
- Same Week Pay
- Top Pay Rates
- Discount Health & Dental
- Free Software Training

Temp Agencies

PUT YOUR OTHER CAREER IN THE SPOTLIGHT

We Have Great Day Jobs For All You Proven Performers!!

ASK ABOUT OUR SPECIAL SIGN ON BONUS

★ Admin/Exec. Asst. ★
★ Accounting/Bookkeeping ★
★ Project Asst./Coordinators ★
★ Desktop Publishing/Graphics ★
★ Marketing Research ★
★ Reception/General Office ★
★ Brokerage/Financial ★
★ Event Planners ★

★ Advertising ★
★ Public Relations ★
★ Marketing ★ Accounting ★
★ Consulting ★
★ Human Resources ★
★ Health Care ★ Real Estate ★
★ Financial ★
★ Investment Banking ★
★ Banking ★

★ Immediate Jobs ★
★ Premium Pay Rates ★
★ Paid Sick/Personal Days ★
★ Software Training Programs ★
★ Insurance & Bonus Plans ★
★ Medical, Dental, Vision ★
★ Holidays, Vacations ★

PROVEN PERFORMERS
Downtown Chicago
PH. 312-917-1111   FAX 312-917-0474
www.greatchicagojobs.com

Temp Agencies

Proven Performers
(See our ad on page 32)
70 W. Madison #530
Chicago, IL 60602
312/917-1111
312/917-0474 - fax
www.greatchicagojobs.com

Randstad, Inc.
542A W. Dundee Rd.
Wheeling, IL 60090
847/541-6220
847/541-6235 - fax
www.accustaff.com

Right Employment Center
53 W Jackson
Chicago, IL 60604
312/427-3136
www.rightservices.com

Select Staffing
208 S. LaSalle #1244
Chicago, IL 60604
312/849-2229
312/849-2234 - fax

Seville Staffing
180 N. Michigan #1510
Chicago, IL 60601
312/368-1272
312/368-0207 - fax
www.sevillestaffing.com

Seville Staffing has been providing Chicago-area talent with temporary Office Support jobs such as: Administrative Assistant, Word Processor, Reception, Data Entry and Customer Service Clerk positions since 1979. We also offer weekly pay, vacation pay, health insurance, and respect for the work you do. Call 312/368-1272 for an appointment.

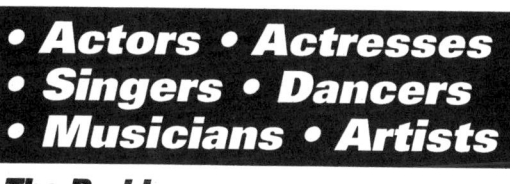

- *Actors* • *Actresses*
- *Singers* • *Dancers*
- *Musicians* • *Artists*

The Problem: The Performance is Over.
And you need extra money to pay your bills.

The Solution: The Choice for Staffing

A leader in the placement of quality temporary administrative and clerical personnel, The Choice for Staffing has several immediate openings with Fortune 500 companies throughout Chicago and the suburbs for individuals with a professional demeanor and good computer skills.

- **Administrative Assistants** • **Executive Admin Assts**
- **Receptionists** • **General Office** • **Data Entry**

Full-Time & Part-Time • Temp/Temp-to-Hire/Direct Hire
Great Pay & Benefits including 401(k)!
Don't wait! Call Today.

THE CHOICE For Staffing INC

CHICAGO
312-372-4500
Fax:
312-853-4068

DEERFIELD
847-267-1353
Fax:
847-267-9077

equal opportunity/ada employer

Temp Agencies

Smart Staffing
(See our ad on page 131)
29 S. LaSalle #635
Chicago, IL 60603
312/696-5306
312/696-0317 - fax
www.smartstaffing.com

Today's Office Staffing
1701 E. Woodfield Rd. #903
Schaumburg, IL 60173
847/240-5300
847/240-5310 - fax

Temporary Opportunities
(See our ad on the inside back cover)
53 W. Jackson #215
Chicago, IL 60604
312/922-5400
312/347-1206 - fax
www.opgroup.com

Temporary Professionals
Personnel Staffing Services
625 N. Michigan #600
Chicago, IL 60611
773/622-1202
773/622-1303 - fax

Soon to be moving to a new location! Call for mailing address. Personnel staffing services for trade shows and promotions.
Models - Talent - Costume Characters - Samplers - Temporaries - Bi Lingual Personnel.
Member of the Chicago Convention & Tourism Bureau
Mail Headshot and resumes. Agency will contact. No drop-ins.
Put your personality to work!

Unique Office Services
203 N. Wabash #608
Chicago, IL 60601
312/332-4183 • 312/332-2688 - fax

Watson Dwyer Staffing
25 E. Washington
Chicago, IL 60602
312/899-8030 • 312/899-8036 - fax
www.watsondwyer.com

Wordspeed
200 N. Dearborn #4006
Chicago, IL 60601
312/201-1171 • 312/201-1279 - fax

Want some crack?
Check out the Chiropractors on page 310

Actor-Friendly Jobs

A supportive job that allows you to pursue your career while still paying the bills is a rare and precious thing. These employers offer work that is particularly suited for the actor's schedule.

Bridgeman Institute
847/358-2010

Chicago Children's Museum
Tim Rey
312/464-7711

Chicago Housesitting & Pet Care
1341 W. Fullerton #177
Chicago, IL 60614
773/477-0136
773/477-0896 - fax
www.chicagopetcare.com

Chicago Trolley Co.
1709 S. Prairie
Chicago, IL 60616
312/663-0260

Museum of Science & Industry
57th and Lake Shore
Chicago, IL
773/684-9844
773/684-0019 - fax
www.msichicago.org

The Princeton Review
attn. Robb Rabito
2847 N. Sheffield
Chicago, IL 60657
773/868-4400
800/2REVIEW
www.review.com

Spirit of Chicago
Ed Carrella
312/836-7888

SST Communications
(Associated with SST)
1840 S. Halsted
Chicago, IL 60608
312/563-1644
www.sstcommunications.com

Steppenwolf Theatre Telemarketing
Chuck Winans
312/932-2462

A Taste of California
2211 N. Elston
Chicago, IL 60614
773/235-9463
773/235-2633 - fax

Those Funny Little People Enterprises
8128 S Madison
Burr Ridge, IL 60521
630/325-3320
630/325-8489 - fax
www.thosefunnylittlepeople.com

Ugly Duck
Karen Healy
312/396-2205

First Steps

First Steps...

Speak you so gently?
Pardon me I pray you,
I thought that all things
had been savage here,
And therefore put I on
a countenance Of stern
commandment.

By Kevin Heckman

Welcome to Chicago!

At this point, you've arrived. You've found an apartment, found a survival job, gotten a cat, done all the things required to settle in and now it's time to get to the point. It's time to work.

Fortunately, Chicago is one of the easiest places to get started acting, whether you're a beginner or an experienced professional. Just get to it. But if you'd like a more specific set of directions, keep reading.

I. Get Ready...

First, make sure all your tools are in order. How recent are your headshots? Monologues ready to go? Resume clean?

Chicago headshots don't glorify their subjects. Glamour is out; reality is in. The headshot is your calling card, and if you're not happy with yours, you might consider getting new ones done locally. Check out the Actors Tools chapter for information on finding a headshot photographer. If you're not sure whether you even need them, go online and poke around. National Photo (www.nationaltalent.com) posts actor photos on its website as do many photographers. Compare the quality of yours with what you see there.

Your resume should mainly be clean and easy to read. Check Actors Tools again for the resume checklist to be sure you're not falling into any common traps. Most importantly (it's there in Actors Tools, but it's important enough to repeat), be sure your contact information is on your resume! No way to contact you equals no way to hire you. 'Nuff said.

Finally, your monologues. Most Chicago auditions will involve a monologue somewhere along the line, so if you're auditioning for theatre, you need to have a few. You'll usually be asked for either one minute or two minute, either comedic or dramatic and either classical or contemporary monologues. That means you should have selections available in each possible flavor. Furthermore, as you keep auditioning, you may want to have multiple selections in each category to prevent having to repeat the same piece in front of a director.

Needless to say, this means a lot of monologues, and the search for them should be ongoing. Keep adding to your repertoire so that when the time comes you have something prepared that fits what they seek.

II. Get Set...

Your support materials are ready to go, now what? Now you get informed about the Chicago scene. In your hands you have one great resource about all things Chicago. PERFORMINK newspaper is another, available both as a subscription or online (www.performink.com). Another good publication is *Acting In Chicago* by Belinda Bremner. The style rambles a little, but there's tons of good information, particularly about the agent scene here. Act I Bookstore is Chicago's only theatre bookstore and a good location for getting information, finding plays and generally learning what's going on (check the Bookstores listing for location and contact info). Act I also carries the Act One Reports which contain a lot of the agent information you can find here in *The Book*, but they update three times a year, so it can be a good addition.

One of the best ways to get informed is to go see shows. Many small to mid-sized theatres have industry nights when professionals get in for a reduced price. Take advantage of those to see what everyone else is doing. Industry nights are advertised in PERFORMINK in the Hotlines section after the audition notices.

Finally, once you're informed, get everyone else informed about you. Time to do a mailing. Some opt for the uber mailing to every casting director, agent or theatre they can find. Others narrow their focus to agents or non-Equity theatres. If you want to focus on theatre, mail to the theatres. If you're looking to get into industrials, commercials, film

First Steps

or TV, then mail to the agents. It's hard to figure exactly how much work comes from those sorts of mailings, but if they don't know you're out there, they're certainly not going to cast you, right?

Some agents have drop-in hours. Take advantage of them if you can. Never drop by outside of those hours though. Agents are rarely pleased to see someone appear out of the blue. Be sure of the times they're willing to see you before you swing by.

III. GO!!

Time to get out there and make contacts. Like any scene, it's all in who you know. How do you build that list of faces who'll light up when they see you? Well, you have some choices.

Audition. Many Chicago theatres have open auditions, so if they're casting call up and reserve your slot. Every show you do is another group of people who know you and (hopefully) know what a wonderful, talented, hard-working person you are. Even if an audition doesn't yield a part, that director may have you in mind for her next project or for next season.

Take a class. There's tons of good training centers here (check the Training chapter) and, odds are, there's one that would fit you. Taking a class gets you in with a group of peers who can help you out down the road. While you should never take a class just to meet the teacher, that person is presumably an experienced professional who's also in a position to give you advice when you need it.

Hang out. If you're the social type, use those skills to make friends and influence people. When you have the opportunity to hobnob with industry people, whether at a party, a bar or at an opening event take it. Don't be annoying, but take advantage of those opportunities. If you're not social, don't force it. The most important thing is to work hard and work well.

Work at PERFORMINK. Well, it worked for me, but isn't open to everyone.

Over the long term, work begets work. Once you get started, you'll find it easier and easier to keep going so…get to it!

Training

Centre East, "Les Ballet Trockadereo de Monte Carlo"

The short one may need more work...

Training

The many methods of acting

> You have train'd me like a peasant, obscuring and hiding from me all gentleman-like qualities. The spirit of my father grows strong in me, and I will no longer endure it.

By Dexter Bullard

If you want to be a successful actor, you must be willing to grow. Technique, presence, creativity, and experience are what get an actor noticed, hired, and launched on a career. These attributes can only be built and enhanced through training. Every actor at any point of his/her career should continue study in acting. Even if you've been working for years, acting is an art that requires re–dedication. Being in shows and getting work are vital learning experiences in themselves, but classes and workshops provide the foundation and continuation of successful stage, screen, and commercial work. A headshot and a dream alone cannot do the acting for you. Acting is life–work. Get to it.

There are many "methods" and schools of acting training. "Methods" of acting training don't really exist. Most of these are based on the work of an important teacher who has influenced a generation of actors. The real method of an acting class is the character of the teacher and the studio's program. Every teacher approaches her/his work from the traditions and "Methods" that she/he has studied. Just like actors, each is unique in expressing what he or she knows and believes.

Finding a good acting class is finding a good teacher. That is someone with whom you connect, someone you respect, and someone who challenges you. We are lucky that the many studios and programs throughout the city have some of the best teachers in America.

What follows is a breakdown or glossary of sorts to help you pinpoint a good class for you. There are many more than this. I have divided them into three areas, Technique, Presence, and Physicality. I recommend taking from each category. It is important to stick to something you like. One class is not going to make much impact. Changes in acting technique and presence take months and years to manifest. Give your program the time to sink in.

Technique

Constantin Stanislavski Stanislavski was a Russian actor, teacher, and founder of The Moscow Art Theatre. He created a revolution in American acting training when his work was brought to New York in the 1930's and was termed "Method Acting." Many of the great American acting teachers were inspired by his observations about truth–in–action, objectives, and emotional memory. He created much of the terminology we use to talk about acting including, "beats," "inner–life," and "through-line."

Lee Strasberg Strasberg was one of the Method teachers who incorporated Stanislavski and Boleslavski's work. He co-founded the Group Theatre and The Actors' Studio in New York. His work focused on the actor's use of specific details from his/her life to generate emotion and connection to the theatrical moment. His work is controversial in that he demanded great depth of inner pain and exposure from his students. He taught Marlon Brando, Anne Bancroft, and Robert DeNiro.

Sanford Meisner Meisner belongs in the Method pack and was a Group Theatre member, but is unique in his attention to communication rather than emotional life. Meisner exercises including "repetition" and "preparation" emphasize an actor's concentration on and response to the actual moment with a scene partner. Truth and action are found in observation and immediate response to the scene partner. Preparations use the actor's own sense of purpose and need to "load" the actor for effectively driving a scene. The Actors' Center is an excellent Meisner–based program.

Training

Uta Hagen Hagen is a famous actor and acting teacher. Her work emphasizes the use of "inner objects," "active listening," and "endowment." Inner objects are personal images that fuel an actor's imagination and belief. Active listening is an actor listening through his or her character's point of view and responding in a constant and active state. Endowment is giving moments and objects on stage a heightened value to intensify response.

Michael Shurtleff Shurtleff is a Broadway and Hollywood casting director and acting teacher who came up with a very practical way of looking at audition material. His "Guideposts" were designed to help actors make immediate strong choices on cold reading material. The Guideposts have since developed into a powerful analytic tool for actors to bring action to texts. The Guideposts focus on relationship, active moments, discoveries, and the specific mix of love and fight between characters. The Audition Studio is an excellent Shurtleff–based program.

Presence

Viola Spolin Spolin is a Chicago original. She adapted games from Neva Boyd into exercises designed to teach young actors and bring spontaneity into rehearsals. Her work emphasizes a "poor" stage (no real objects or things) to challenge the imagination and inspire detail–orientation. Her work is taught in "game" forms that build ensemble and listening skills. The Piven Workshop in Evanston is in many ways a Spolin–based studio.

Improvisation Improvisation is a Chicago tradition with roots back to the 1950's. Originally The Compass and then The Second City adapted Spolin's games, political and social satire, and vaudeville revue into a form of theatrical expression that is famous around the world. Improvisation is the study of instant scene creation. Also emphasizing a "poor" stage, improvisation classes build imagination, play, listening, courage, and ensemble in an extremely effective way. The Second City Training Center is an excellent, world–reknown program that focuses on sketch comedy and social satire. ImprovOlympic covers longer form improvisation and Player's Workshop is closer to the early work of Chicago improvisation.

Jerzy Grotowski Though not common in Chicago, Grotowski's work has influenced many teachers. Grotowski was the founder of The

Polish Lab Theatre, who astonished the theatre world in the 60's with highly physical, visceral and ritualistic theater work. His training is very physical, self–penetrating, and looks to create a "holy" actor. His study of acting in various cultures led him to focus exclusively on the particular energy that exists between the actor and the spectator.

The Viewpoints The Viewpoints are one of the hottest training "methods" of the 1990's. Popularized by director Anne Bogart, the Viewpoints are a series of focal points (tempo, repetition, shape, architecture,...) that can be used to create improvisational play or analyze scenic material. The Viewpoints were created by modern dance teacher Mary Overlie to teach and inspire choreographic ideas for dancers. The Viewpoints release actors from "psychological" analysis of acting and build creativity and theatricality.

Tadashi Suzuki Suzuki is a Japanese theatre director and acting teacher. His company amazed the world on the 80's with its stylization and awesome acting power. He created training that emphasizes physical control, balance, and body–centered vocalization. Suzuki work is very strenuous and builds actors with strong centers and powerful communication skills. Suzuki training has been coupled with Viewpoints work at the Saratoga Institute and grows in popularity.

Physicality

Physical Theater Physical theater is a very broad area but includes clowning, commedia, circus, drumming and puppetry. These forms of ancient theatrical practice are fun to learn, watch, and play. All these forms build an actor's flexibility and playing range. They also require physical skills and courage. Many Chicago theatre companies look for actors with these skills, including Redmoon Lookingglass, Defiant, and Plasticene. The Actor's Gymnasium and these companies offer excellent classes.

Mime Mime is misunderstood. It is thought of as an annoying white-faced loser trying to fight a non-existent stiff breeze or escape an invisible box. Mime is actually the study of theatrical gesture. It is very hard to master and builds awesome powers of articulation and theatrical expression.

Combat Combat is essential training for those looking for classical work or rip-roaring nitty-gritty Chicago theatre. Combat is a fun and complementary skill that gets actors hired. Combat trains the body and

Training

introduces safe ways of creating the illusion of violence via fist, sword, knife, stick, and anything else nearby.

Dance Dance is not just for musical theatre actors. If you can walk, you can dance. Dance is the quickest way to physical conditioning and control. Many plays and theatres incorporate dance. Classes in jazz, ballet, modern dance, contact improvisation, and ethnic, historical, or cultural dance are great ways to tone up and wake up your body. Check out Link's Hall, Hedwig Dances, Joel Hall, Lou Conte, Chicago Moving Company and many others.

Martial Arts and Yoga There is no better practice for actors than these. Mental, physical control and agility are excellent for actors. This is a big secret of many famous actors. Martial arts instill courage, discipline and power. There are many great programs in Yoga, Tai Chi, Tae Kwon Do, Aikido, and Karate in Chicago.

Voice Voice is extremely important and the most neglected area of actor training. How you sound is how you seem. Many actors are stuck here and will be until they get coaching or into a class. Voice is not just singing — although that is excellent training. Voice classes and training remove bad habits and obstructions while building greater power, control, and flexibility. Many actors don't have the oratorical ability or power to handle the classical and benchmark roles that make a career.

Finally, anything you do contributes to your acting. Your mind, body, and soul are your resources and tools. So choose what you do carefully — what you watch, what you read, where you go, what you feel. Read, experience and discuss things beyond the mundane and the commercial mainstream. Expanding your point of view and your passion expands who you are and, as the night follows the day, the kind of actor you are. Travel. Write a journal. Go to therapy. Join AA. Eat healthy. Stop picking on yourself. Actually listen to someone. Be with family. Acting is life–work. By working on yourself, you are working on acting.

Recommended reading:

An Actor Prepares, Constantin Stanislavki

Respect For Acting, Uta Hagen

Sanford Meisner on Acting, Sanford Meisner

Audition, Michael Shurtleff

Towards A Poor Theater, Grotowski

Improvisation for the Theater, Viola Spolin

Anne Bogart: Viewpoints, Michael Dixon, Joel A. Smith

Acting Training Checklist!

Training should be an ongoing process in an actor's life. There are skills to be acquired and maintained. However, you're most likely to get the most for your money if you ask yourself a few questions first.

What Are Your Skills?
This is the first question you have to ask yourself. What are you already good at? What have you done? What do you list under special skills?

What Are Your Weaknesses?
What are you bad at? What skills do you need to acquire to make yourself more marketable?

What Are Your Goals?
Anyone can take a class, but if you've got a plan you're more likely to get the best out of the money you spend on training. Most training goals fall into one of two categories:

1. Maintenance
What skills have you acquired but haven't used recently? These are the skills you may need to maintain through a class.

2. Acquisition
What skills would you like to acquire? What skills do you need in order to get work?

Choosing a Class
There are a lot of aspects to a positive class experience. Some you can control, some you can't. Instructors are the most important aspect of the class. If possible, sit in on a class they teach. They may have a fabulous reputation, but does their style mesh with yours?

Coaches
Getting a coach is quite different from taking a class. They're especially useful for prepping audition pieces or getting help with a particularly difficult role. As with a class, carefully interview a potential coach. They're expensive, so be picky.

Summer Programs
A summer program can provide a period of intensive training. Unfortunately, they're also expensive and time-consuming. This is a major investment, and one you should research before enrolling.

Graduate Programs
The ultimate amount of training, of course, is going back to school for your MFA or MA. An MFA is considered, by many institutions, to be a terminal degree, which means that once you've acquired the degree you can teach. Such a program can also hook you up with a peer group of serious artists that can lead to opportunities later.

Classes—Acting

If You're Serious About Acting

act one STUDIOS

TV & Film I & II   Commercial Technique I
Fundamentals Of Acting
Industrial Film & Ear Prompter
Movement Scene Study
Meisner Technique I & II
Acting Instinctively   Audition Techniques I & II
Monologue Workshp   Masters Scene Class

Check out our
Conservatory Program

We have over thirty different classes for you to choose from. All taught by working professionals who really know the business. Classes for beginners to working actors.

Call for a free consultation.
312-787-9384

http//www.actone.com

640 N. LaSalle, Suite 535   Chicago, IL 60610

The Book: An Actor's Guide to Chicago

Classes—Acting

Acting Classes

Act One Studios, Inc.
(See our ad on page 46)
640 N. LaSalle #535
Chicago, IL 60610
312/787-9384
312/787-3234 - fax
www.actone.com
Commercial Technique I - Get "camera-ready" for all types of commercial auditions.
Industrial Film & Ear Prompter - Learn to analyze and perform technical scripts and use an ear prompter.
TV & Film I, II & Workshop - Learn the "ins and outs" of the film and television world.
Fundamentals I, II & Scene & Monologue Workshop - Learn to make efffective choices from the script.

Acting Instinctively - Flexibility, creativity, and imaginative freedom are explored.
Meisner Technique I, II & Workshop - Leads to a very truthful moment-to-moment style of acting.
Monologue Workshop - Prepare two to four monologues for auditions.
Audition Technique I & II - Learn the art of cold reading theatre auditions.
Shakespeare Beg. & Adv. - Approaches based on the work of Shakespeare & Co.
Masters Class - An on-going scene study class taught by Steve Scott
Voice-Over I & II - Learn what it takes to be successful in the voice-over market.
Movement Scene Study - Learn to bring a physical life to your character.

Actors' Center
Kay Martinovich
3047 N. Lincoln #390
Chicago, IL 60657
773/549-3303
773/549-0749 - fax
Technique (based on Meisner)
Monologues

Scene Study
Physical Character Work
Technique on Camera
TV/Film on Camera
Beginning Scene Study
Auditioning Technique
Acting in Chicago: Where Do I Start?
Master Meisner Technique

The Actors Gymnasium & Performing Arts School
Noyes Cultural Arts Center
927 Noyes St.
Evanston, IL 60201
847/328-2795
847/328-3495 - fax
www.actorsgymnasium.com
Acro-Dance
Adaptation for the Stage
Dance 101
Drum Performance
Gymnastics

Movement for Actors
Physical Comedy
Scene Study
Viewpoints
Circus Arts
Your body is an instrument--we'll teach you to play it. A variety of physical performance skills, from trapeze to slapstick, juggling to mime. Professional-level classes, run jointly with the Lookingglass Theatre Company. Convenient Chicago and Evanston locations. SAFD stage combat certification workshops. Master classes with renowned performers.

Ch. 2 Training 47

Classes—Acting

Actors Workshop
(See our ad on page 52)
Michael Colucci
1350 N. Wells #F521
Chicago, IL 60610
312/337-6602 • **888/COLUCCI**
312/337-6604 - fax
www.actorsworkshop.org
Beginning Acting-On Camera

Advanced Acting-On Camera
Private Coaching: Ear Prompter, Monologue, Cold Reading, Commercial
Actors Workshop offers weekly ongoing classes for all levels. Each class starts with vocal warm-up, then commercials & scenes on-camera, which you can add to your demo reel. Call 1-888-COLUCCI to arrange a free visit and consultation with director Michael Colucci, author of Vocal Workout Booklet.

The Audition Studio
(See our ad on page 49)
20 W. Hubbard #2E
Chicago, IL 60610
312/527-4566 • 312/527-9085 - fax
Beginning Acting - Part 1 & 2: Weekly scene work, improvisation and script analysis help you build a strong foundation.
Cold Reading - The twelve guideposts are taught through weekly cold reading situations.
On Camera - Strengthen your on-camera auditions. These courses cover all aspects of the commercial industrial and film audition.
Scene Study (Beginning and Advanced) - In depth scene work, this class focuses on performance and the rehearsal process.
Monologue - Prepare audition pieces for theatres and agents. Actors will be assigned three pieces from classical to contemporary.
Voice Technique - Based on Kristin Linklater's vocal progression.
Voiceover (Beginning and Advanced) - Get an inside look into the world of voiceover. Explore various techniques for breaking down copy. Includes three sessions in a professional recording studio.
Shakespeare Workshop
On Going Workshop Series - Voiceover, Directing, Getting Started in the Business, Commercial On Camera
List of Instructors: Kurt Naebig, Rachael Patterson, Jack Bronis, Linda Gillum, Chris Stolte, Jim Johnson, Pat Van Oss, Lawrence Grimm, Barb Wruck Thometz, Brighid O'Shaughnessy, Greg Vinkler, Molly Glynn Hammond, Jeff Lupetin, Deb Doetzer

Center Theater's Training Program for Actors, Directors, Playwrights, and Singers
1346 W. Devon
Chicago, IL 60660
773/508-0200 • 773/508-9584 - fax

Professional Classes for beginning to advanced levels:
Technique - Scene Study - Monologues
Camera Technique - Playwriting
Directing - Advanced Characterization
Audition Intensive - Shakespeare - Singing

The New Actors Workshop
study with **George Morrison, Mike Nichols, Paul Sills**
and an outstanding faculty
two-year professional training program starts October 9, 2001
scholarships and financial aid available
three-week summer sessions • July & August
259 West 30th St., 2nd flr, New York, NY 10001 • 212-947-1310 • 1-800-947-1318
www.newactorsworkshop.com

Classes—Acting

Chicago Actors Studio
1567 N. Milwaukee
Chicago, IL 60622
773/645-0222
773/645-0040 - fax
www.actors-studio.net

Scene Study - Film Tech
Commercials - Industrials
Characterization - Voice & Diction
Shakespeare - Auditioning & Marketing
The Ear Prompter - Trade Shows

Chicago Center for the Performing Arts Training Center
(See our ad on page 142)
777 N. Green
Chicago, IL 60622
312/327-2040
312/327-2046 - fax
www.theaterland.com
Acting: Relationship with Energies
Acting: Understanding Action Within Conflict

Script Analysis
Improv to Scene Study Class
Improvisation
Scene Study: A Diagnostic Tool
Auditioning Strategies for the Stage
Monologues
Auditioning for Film and Television
Acting the Song

■ MYSTERY & SECRET ■ RELATIONSHIP ■ DISCOVERIES ■

You're Brilliant.
Are your auditions?
Get the training that helps you get the job.

THE
Audition
S T U D I O

312.527.4566
Observe a class for free. **Then decide.**

■ MYSTERY & SECRET ■ RELATIONSHIP ■ DISCOVERIES ■

Ch. 2 Training 49

Classes—Acting

Join our community of performers & have a venue where agents can see you perform. All of Chicago's best improvisers trained at the I.O., including Mike Meyers, Chris Farley, Tina Fey, Rachael Dratch & more.

"This is the most important group work since they built the pyramids." - Bill Murray
Call 773-880-0199 for show & class info.

Duncan YMCA Chernin Center for the Arts
1001 W. Roosevelt
Chicago, IL 60608
312/738-7980
312/738-1420 - fax

Eileen Boevers Performing Arts Workshop
595 Elm Pl. #210
Highland Park, IL 60035
847/432-8223
847/432-5214 - fax
www.appletreetheatre.com

ETA Creative Arts
7558 S. South Chicago
Chicago, IL 60619
773/752-3955
773/752-8727 - fax
Adult Acting - Beginning and Advanced
Sound
Lighting
Stage Management
How to Audition for Commercials

GATE
Gregory Abels Training Ensemble
28 W. 27th St.
New York, NY 10001
212/689-9371
888/277-GATE
www.GATEacting.com

Illinois Theatre Center
P.O. Box 397
Park Forest, IL 60466
708/481-3510
708/481-3693 - fax
Acting Workshop (by invitation only)
Advanced Acting Ensemble (permission of instructor only)
Beginning Acting for Adults

John Robert Powers Entertainment Company
27 E. Monroe #200
Chicago, IL 60603
312/726-1404
312/726-8019 - fax
www.johnrobertpowers.com
TV 1   TV 2   TV 3
Image Development
Commercial Print
Runway

Moving Dock Theatre Company
Dawn Arnold
2970 N. Sheridan #1021
Chicago, IL 60657
773/327-1572

The Neo-Futurists
5153 N. Ashland
Chicago, IL 60640
773/275-5255
www.neofuturists.org
Neo-Futurist Performance Workshop
Advanced Neo-Futurist Performance Workshop - both classes are studies in writing, directing and performing your own work.

50   The Book: An Actor's Guide to Chicago

Classes—Acting

Piven Theatre Workshop
927 Noyes
Evanston, IL 60201
847/866-6597
847/866-6614 - fax
www.piventheatreworkshop.com
This renowned training center offers beginning, intermediate and professional level classes in improvisation, theatre games, story theatre, and scene study. Submit H/R for intermediate and advanced scene study. Call for current class information.

Plasticene
2122 N. Winchester #1F
Chicago, IL 60614
312/409-0400
www.plasticene.com
Summer Physical Theatre Intensive
Ongoing Workshops

Roadworks
1144 Fulton Market #105
Chicago, IL 60607
312/492-7150
312/492-7155 - fax
www.roadworks.org

Sarantos Studios
2857 N. Halsted
Chicago, IL 60657
773/528-7114 • 773/528-7153 - fax
Feature Film Acting
Scene Study
Monologue Preparation
On Camera Auditioning
Basic Acting Technique

Scrap Mettle Soul
773/275-3999 • 773/561-3852 - fax
Story Gathering for Performance
Verbal and Physical Storytelling

T. Daniel and Laurie Willets
c/o T. Daniel Productions
1047 Gage St.
Winnetka, IL 60093
847/446-0183
847/446-0183 - fax
www.tdanielcreations.com
Basic Mime Techniques & Concepts
Intermediate Mime Techniques & Concepts
Mime Concepts & Techniques for the Disciplined Performing Artists
Mime as a Tool for the Verbal Storyteller
Mime Concepts Applied to the Fine Arts Students/Professional Artists
Understanding the Effectiveness of Corporeal Movement In Speech Presentations: For Business/Corporate People Only
An ACTOR must gain the physical skills, imagination and confidence necessary to be as articulate with his Body as he is with Words. T. Daniel and Laurie Willets, internationally-acclaimed Mime and Theatre Movement performers perform, consult, choreograph and teach for Stage, Film, Animation, Opera and Music. Contact 847/446-0183.

Victory Gardens Theatre
2257 N. Lincoln
Chicago, IL 60614
773/549-5788
773/549-2779 - fax
www.victorygardens.org
Basic Acting
Introduction to Scenes & Monologues
Musical Theater
Speech & Movement
Dialects
Building a Character
Monologues
Scene Study
Improvisational Scene Study
Comedy Styles

Classes—Kid's

California Dreamin?

Let the Actors Workshop be your connection to the most respected showcase in the Los Angeles market. *The Actors Workshop* and *Reel Pros* announce a joint venture offering regular showcases in L.A. for Chicago actors.

www.actorsworkshop.org

Get ready in Chicago!
Let us enchance your cold reading skills to audition effectively for the top casting directors in Film & TV
Ongoing weekly workshops, month by month, year round

888-colucci   colucci@actorsworkshop.org

CELEBRATING 10 YEARS OF TRAINING CHICAGO ACTORS!

Kid's Classes

ALYO Children's Dance Theatre
P.O. Box 198672
Chicago, IL 60619
773/723-2596
773/723-7995 - fax

Beverly Art Center
2153 W. 111th
Chicago, IL 60643
773/445-3838
773/445-0386 - fax

Boitsov Classical Ballet
410 S. Michigan #300
Chicago, IL 60605
312/663-0844
312/939-2094 - fax

Chicago Academy for the Arts
1010 W. Chicago
Chicago, IL 60622
312/421-0202
312/421-3816 - fax
www.chicagoacademyforthearts.org

Chicago Ballet Arts
Claire Carmichael - Director
7416 N. Ridge
Chicago, IL 60645
773/381-0000
847/657-8121 - fax

Chicago Moving Company
3035 N. Hoyne
Chicago, IL 60618
773/880-5402

Classes—Kid's

Chicago Theatre Company
500 E. 67th
Chicago, IL 60637
773/493-0901
773/493-0360 - fax

Dancecenter North
540 N. Milwaukee
Libertyville, IL 60048
847/367-7970
847/367-7905 - fax
www.dancecenterNorth.com

DancEd
3131 Dundee Rd.
Northbrook, IL 60062
847/564-9120

**Eileen Boevers
Performing Arts Workshop**
595 Elm Pl. #210
Highland Park, IL 60035
847/432-8223
847/432-5214 - fax
www.appletreetheatre.com

**Fieldcrest School
of Performing Arts**
11639 S. Ashland
Chicago, IL 60643
773/568-6706

Free Street Programs
1419 W. Blackhawk
Chicago, IL 60622
773/772-7248
www.freestreet.org

Golden's School of Dance
1548 Burgundy Pkwy.
Streamwood, IL 60103
630/540-0996
630/540-9650 - fax

Illinois Theatre Center
P.O. Box 397
Park Forest, IL 60466
708/481-3510 • 708/481-3693 - fax
*Acting Workshop (by invitation only)
Advanced Acting Ensemble (permission of instructor only)
Beginning Acting for Adults*

Midwest Academy of Gymnastics
Body Xpressions Ltd.
30W315 Calumet Ave.
Warrenville, IL 60555
630/393-6225 • 630/393-6693 - fax
www.mwaogymnastics.org

Northlight Theatre
9501 N. Skokie Blvd.
Skokie, IL 60076
847/679-9501
www.northlight.org

Old Town School of Folk Music
4544 N. Lincoln
Chicago, IL 60625
773/728-6000 • 773/728-6999 - fax
www.oldtownschol.org

Piven Theatre Workshop
927 Noyes
Evanston, IL 60201
847/866-6597 • 847/866-6614 - fax
www.piventheatreworkshop.com
Come learn to play again at the theatre school that launched John & Joan Cusack, Aidan Quinn, Lili Taylor, Jeremy Piven and many more! Classes for young people from 4th grade through high school. Call for current class information.

Shakespeare on the Green
Barat College - 700 E. Westleigh Rd.
Lake Forest, IL 60045
847/604-6344 • 847/604-6342 - fax
www.sotg.pac.barat.edu

Classes—Dance

Dance Classes

Academy of Movement and Music
605 Lake St.
Oak Park, IL 60302
708/848-2329
708/848-2391 - fax
Ballet, Jazz, Modern, Creative Movement,

American Dance Center Ballet Co.
10464 W. 163rd Pl.
Orland Park, IL 60462
708/747-4969
708/747-0424 - fax
Ballet, Point, Jazz, Hip-Hop, Modern, Tap, Swing

The Academy of Dance Arts
1524 Centre Cr.
Downers Grove, IL 60515
630/495-4940
Ballet (ages 3 to Adult), Point, Jazz (ages 3 to adult), Hip-Hop, Tap (ages 3 to adult), Acrobat, Lyrical, Proffesional Ballet Program

Authentic Mid East Belly Dance
Jasmin Jahal
P.O. Box 56037
Chicago, IL 60656-0037
773/693-6300
773/693.6302 - fax
www.jasminjahal.com
Traditional Middle Eastern & Classical Egyptian Dance

Ballet Chicago
185 N. Wabash #2305
Chicago, IL 60601
312/251-8833
312/251-8840 - fax
www.balletchicago.org
Ballet, Pre Ballet/Creative Movement to Pre Professional Positions, Beginner Adult Ballet

Belle Plaine Studio
2014 W. Belle Plaine
Chicago, IL 60618
773/935-1890
773/935-1909 - fax
Ballet, Jazz, Modern, Tap, Belly Dance, Flamenco, NIA, Swing

Beverly Art Center
2153 W. 111th
Chicago, IL 60643
773/445-3838
773/445-0386 - fax
Ballet, Jazz, Modern, Tap, Stretch and Strength, African

Boitsov Classical Ballet
410 S. Michigan #300
Chicago, IL 60605
312/663-0844
312/939-2094 - fax
Ballet - Vaganova Technique (Moscow Bolshoi Theatre system of training)

Chicago Moving Company
3035 N. Hoyne
Chicago, IL 60618
773/880-5402
Modern, Aerobic Jazz, Creative Movement, Special Populations, Special Summer and Spring Break Camps

Chicago Multicultural Dance Center
806 S. Plymouth
Chicago, IL 60605
312/461-0030
312/461-1184 - fax
Ballet, Jazz, Tap, Latin, West African

Classes—Dance

Chicago National Association of Dance Masters
5411 E. State St. #202
Rockford, IL 61108
815/397-6052
815/397-6799 - fax
www.cnadm.com
Workshops only; no ongoing classes.

Teresa Cullen
729 Lake Ave.
Wilmette, IL 60091
847/256-6614
847/256-5318 - fax
Ballet, Flamenco

Dance Center Evanston
610 Davis St.
Evanston, IL 60201
847/328-6683 • 847/328-6656 - fax
Ballet, Jazz, Modern, Tap, Ballroom, Character, Just For Boys, Pilates

Dance Center of Columbia College
1306 S. Michigan
Chicago, IL 60605
312/344-8300
312/344-8036 - fax
www.colum.edu
Ballet, Modern, Jazz, Tap, African

Dance Dimensions
595B N. Pinecrest Rd.
Bolingbrook, IL 60440
630/739-1195
Ballet, Jazz, Tap, Ballroom, Swing, Tumbling, Salsa

Dance Therapy Center
Fine Arts Building
410 S. Michigan
Chicago, IL 60605
312/461-9826 • 312/461-9843 - fax
Ballet, Modern, Ballroom

Dancecenter North
540 N. Milwaukee
Libertyville, IL 60048
847/367-7970
847/367-7905 - fax
www.dancecenterNorth.com
Classical Ballet, Point, Jazz, Tap, Irish Step Dance, Social Dance, Jazz and Funk

Domenick Danza
5116 N. Glenwood
Chicago, IL 60640
773/728-7305
Musical Theatre Dance

Diana's Dance and Fitness Dynamics, Ltd.
Diana Duda
429 Park Dr.
Glenwood, IL 60425
708/755-8292
708/799-7613 - fax
Ballet, Jazz, Tap, Ballroom

Discovery Center
2940 N. Lincoln
Chicago, IL 60657
773/348-8120
773/880-6164 - fax
www.discoverycenter.cc
Ballet, Jazz, Modern, Tap, Bachta, Ballroom, Belly Dance, Contemporary Latin, Hip-Hop, Salsa, Social Dance, Swing, Tango, Kardio Kickboxing

Barbara Dubosq
1068 Hillcrest
Highland Park, IL 60035
847/831-3383
Ballet, Tap, Creative

Classes—Dance

Emergence Dance Theatre
804 1/2 Market
P.O. Box 186
DeKalb, IL 60115
815/758-6613
Ballet, Jazz, Modern, Tap

Evanston School of Ballet Foundation
1933 Central St.
Evanston, IL 60201
847/475-9225
Ballet

Golden's School of Dance
1548 Burgundy Pkwy.
Streamwood, IL 60103
630/540-0996 • 630/540-9650 - fax
Ballet, Jazz, Tap, Ballroom, Clogging, Lyrical

Gus Giordano Dance Center
614 Davis
Evanston, IL 60201
847/866-9442
847/866-9228 - fax
Ballet, Jazz, Modern, Tap, Hip-Hop, Ballroom, Children's programs

Hedwig Dances
Administrative Offices
2936 N. Southport #210
Chicago, IL 60657
773/871-0872
773/296-0968 - fax
www.enteract.com\~hedwig
Ballet, Modern, African, Butoh (Japanese Theatrical Dance form), Contemporary and World Dance, Yoga, Spanish Flamenco, Company Class, Visiting Artist Series

Jo's Footwork Studio
1500 Walker
Western Springs, IL 60558
708/246-6878
Ballet, Jazz, Modern, Tap, Hip-Hop,

Joel Hall Dance Center
1511 W. Berwyn
Chicago, IL 60640
773/293-0900
773/293-1130 - fax
www.joelhall.com
Ballet, Jazz, Modern, Tap, Hip-Hop, African, Egyptian, Jamaican Folk.

Lou Conte Dance Studio
1147 W. Jackson
Chicago, IL 60607
312/850-9766
312/455-8240 - fax
Ballet, Jazz, Modern, Tap, Dance Fitness, Hip-Hop

Mayfair Academy of Fine Art
1025 E. 79th
Chicago, IL 60619
773/846-8180
Ballet, Jazz, Modern, Tap, Tumbling

Muntu Dance Theatre of Chicago
6800 S. Wentworth #3E96
Chicago, IL 60621
773/602-1135
773/602-1134 - fax
African, African American

Najwa Dance Corps
1900 W. Van Buren #0505
Chicago, IL 60612
312/850-7224
312/850-7141 - fax
Modern, Jazz, Tap, African, Caribbean

North Shore School of Dance
107 Highwood
Highwood, IL 60040
847/432-2060 • 847/432-4037 - fax
www.northshoredance.com
Ballet, Jazz, Modern, Tap, Hip Hop, Irish, Yoga

Classes—Dance

Old Town School of Folk Music
4544 N. Lincoln
Chicago, IL 60625
773/728-6000
773/728-6999 - fax
www.oldtownschool.org
Ballet, Jazz, Tap, African, Aztec, Belly, Breakdance, Flamenco, Flat-Foot, Hip-Hop, Hula, Indian, Irish, Latin, Mexican, Swing, Tango

Patterson School of Ballroom Dance
1240 Sunset Rd.
Winnetka, IL 60093
847/501-2523
Ballroom Dance

PerformInk
3223 N. Sheffield - 3rd floor
Chicago, IL 60657
773/296-4600
773/296-4621 - fax
www.performink.com
Swing Dancing, Barn Dancing

Rockford Dance Company
711 N. Main
Rockford, IL 61103
815/963-3341
815/963-3541 -fax
www.rockforddancecompany.com
Ballet, Jazz, Modern, Tap, Ballroom, Tango Argentino, Irish, Folk

Ruth Page Foundation
School of Dance
1016 N. Dearborn
Chicago, IL 60610
312/337-6543
312/337-6542 - fax
www.ruthpage.com
Ballet, Jazz, Tap, Pilates

School of Performing Arts
200 E. 5th Ave. #132
Naperville, IL 60563
630/717-6622
630/717-5131 - fax
www.performing-arts.org
Ballet, Jazz, Modern, Tap, Hip-Hop, Fine Arts Adventures (Preschool)

Shelley's School of Dance and Modeling, Ltd.
450 Peterson Rd.
Libertyville, IL 60048
847/816-1711
Ballet, Jazz, Modern, Tap, Hip Hop, Lyrical, Pilates, Point, Ensemble Classes

Teresa y los Preferidos
729 Lake Ave.
Wilmette, IL 60091
847/256-6614
Ballet, Flamenco

Tina Mangos Dance
773/282-5108
www.tinamangosdance.com
Ballroom, Latin, Movement for Performers, Swing

Von Heidecke School of Ballet
1239 S. Naper Blvd.
Naperville, IL 60540
630/527-1052
630/527-8427 - fax
www.chicagofestivalballet.org
Ballet

Stage Combat Classes

The Actors Gymnasium & Performing Arts School
Noyes Cultural Arts Center
927 Noyes St.
Evanston, IL 60201
847/328-2795
847/328-3495 - fax
www.actorsgymnasium.com
Your body is an instrument--we'll teach you to play it. A variety of physical performance skills, from trapeze to slapstick, juggling to mime. Professional-level classes, run jointly with the Lookingglass Theatre Company. Convenient Chicago and Evanston locations. SAFD stage combat certification workshops. Master classes with renowned performers.

Fencing 2000
328 S. Jefferson
Chicago, IL 60606
312/879-0430

Raoul Johnson
Loyola University
6525 N. Sheridan
Chicago, IL 60626
773/508-3841

R & D Choreography
7443 N. Hoyne #1N
Chicago, IL 60645
847/333-1494
www.theatrechicago.com/randd

Stunts & Swords
262/215-3983
www.stuntsandswords.com
Stunts & Swords provides professional stunt coordinating and dynamic fight choreography for film, television, and theatre. We have an extensive talent network and can provide any necessary equipment.

Modeling Classes

Model Image Center
1218 W. Belmont
Chicago, IL 60657
773/348-9349 - fax
773/348-9366
www.modelimagecenter.com

Shelley's School of Dance and Modeling, Ltd.
450 Peterson Rd.
Libertyville, IL 60048
847/816-1711

Scriptwriting Classes

Center Theater's Training Program for Actors, Directors, Playwrights, and Singers
1346 W. Devon
Chicago, IL 60660
773/508-0200
773/508-9584 - fax

Chicago Alliance for Playwrights
1225 W. Belmont
Chicago, IL 60657
773/929-7367
773/327-1404 - fax

Coaches—Acting

Chicago Dramatists
1105 W. Chicago
Chicago, IL 60622
312/633-0630
312/633-0610 - fax

ETA Creative Arts
7558 S. South Chicago
Chicago, IL 60619
773/752-3955
773/752-8727 – fax

New Tuners Theatre
(See our ad on page 218)
1225 W. Belmont
Chicago, IL 60657
773/929-7367

Victory Gardens Theatre
2257 N. Lincoln
Chicago, IL 60614
773/549-5788
773/549-2779 - fax
www.victorygardens.org

Coaches
Acting Coaches

Dawn Arnold
773/327-1572

Bud Beyer
1979 S. Campus Dr.
Evanston, IL 60208
847/491-3372

Belinda Bremner
773/871-3710
An audition is a job interview using someone else's words. The key to a successful audition is finding an author who tells your story in your words. Your choice of audition material speaks volumes. Decide what that message is and then craft your audition. Ideally suited for the well-trained actor looking for an edge.

The Second City training center

"The entire recent tradition of American satire can be summed up in three words: THE SECOND CITY."
— Clive Barnes, The New York Times

- Conservatory Program
- Improv for Actors
- Beginning Program
- Comedy Writing Program
- Acting Program
- High School Program
- Special Workshops

CALL: 312.664.3959 or log on to:
www.secondcity.com

Ch. 2 Training 59

Coaches—Acting

Dexter Bullard
2122 N. Winchester
Chicago, IL 60614
773/227-6487
Dexter Bullard is a Jefferson Cited Chicago director, Artistic Director of Plasticene Physical Theater, and a director for The Second City. Dexter has taught acting, improvisation, and audition technique for over six years at University of Illinois, Columbia College, The Actors' Center, The Audition Studio, and at The Second City Training Center. Gain immediate results for auditions or breakthroughs in acting over a few sessions. Very affordable sliding scale.

Dale Calandra
773/508-0397

Michael Colucci
Actor's Workshop
1350 N. Wells #F521
Chicago, IL 60610
312/337-6602 • 888/COLUCCI
312/337-6604 - fax
www.actorsworkshop.org

T. Daniel and Laurie Willets
c/o T. Daniel Productions
1047 Gage St.
Winnetka, IL 60093
847/446-0183 • 847/446-0183 - fax
www.tdanielcreations.com

Ann Filmer
1539 N. Bell
Chicago, IL 60622
773/489-0843

Linda Gillum
773/878-3077
Linda Gillum is an acting instructor at the Audition Studio and freelance director. She has a B.F.A. in theatre form the University of Illinois at Urbana-Champaign. Linda is a member of Defiant Theatre in Chicago and SAG/AFTRA.

Kevin Heckman
7466 N. Ashland #2N
Chicago, IL 60626
312/562-3748

Illinois Theatre Center
P.O. Box 397
Park Forest, IL 60466
708/481-3510 • 708/481-3693 – fax

**Jeremy Sklar's
Monologue Workout**
(See our ad on this page)
1710 W. School #3F
Chicago, IL 60657
773/248-1543 x1

Lori Klinka
916 Rainbow Dr.
Glenwood, IL 60425
708/709-0880
708/709-0881 - fax

Bob Kulhan
3638 N. Pine Grove #1
Chicago, IL 60613
773/296-4887

One hour! $20! - It's the **Monologue Workout**
SAG/AFTRA actor and director
Jeremy Sklar
will work your audition pieces into shape. Classical and contemporary monologues to last minute auditions.

Call Jeremy for free consultation at
773/430-2827
The Monologue Workout. Work hard. Get cast.

Coaches—Acting

Ruth Landis
B.S., M.A.,
773/991-777
Private Coaching- $65.00 hourly

Ruth Landis, Inc.
773/991-7777
773/463-3683 - fax
A mind/body/spirit holistic approach to acting for theatre (monologues, scenes, cold-reading), on-camera, and voice-over, striving to make auditioning and artistry a joyous experience, focusing on personal on personal empowerment and relief of performance anxiety. Ruth has taught at Northwestern, Columbia, Roosevelt University, Victory Gardens and privately.

Jaclyn Loewenstein
(formerly Greenberg)
2151 Ridge Ave. #2D
Evanston, IL 60201
847/866-8651

Richard Marlatt
773/338-8755
For actors at all levels of experience. Work with contemporary to classical material, or cold readings. Diction and Dialect training available. A working professional Regional and Chicago actor/director, Richard has experience as a private coach and workshop instructor since 1981. $25-$45/hour.

Michael Menendian
Raven Theatre
2549 W. Fargo
Chicago, IL 60645
773/338-2177
773/508-9794 - fax
www.raventheatre.com

Janet B. Milstein
773/465-5804
Award-winning Acting Instructor, Janet has trained hundreds of actors, beginners to professionals. Her students continually get cast in Chicago theatre and have been signed by agents in Chicago, NY, and LA. Janet offers affordable private coaching in monologues and cold reading that will teach you the skills to audition powerfully and with confidence. Author of "111 One-Minute Monologues," with a children's monologue book to be released this summer by Smith and Kraus.

Kurt Naebig
20 W. Hubbard
Chicago, IL 60610
630/495-7188
312/527-4566

Kathryn Nash
312/943-0167
312/943-0229 - fax
Acting- Voice- Speech Coach
Member- AEA, AFTRA, VASTA (Voice and Speech Trainers Association)
Private instruction specializing in:
　-vocal techniques for stage and voiceovers
　-Standard American diction
　-dialect acquisition and reduction
　-monologue coaching to integrate "kinesthetic, vocal, and emotional modes" within the acting process.

Cecilie O'Reilly
2023 N. Damen
Chicago, IL 60647
773/486-3649

Rick Plastina
1117 N. Taylor
Oak Park, IL 60302
708/386-8270

Nancy Sheeber
847/266-8425

Coaches—Acting

Fredric Stone
5040 N. Marine #3A
Chicago, IL 60640
773/334-4196
A working professional actor/director with over 25 years experience (New York and Chicago), coaches actors in monologue and scene preparation for auditions - both contemporary and classical. He created and taught The Audition Workshop at Organic Theatre and currently teaches an 8 week Performing Shakespeare class at Victory Gardens Theatre.

Karen Vaccaro
1243 N. Damen
Chicago, IL 60622
773/201-0951
"The moment you lose yourself on stage marks the departure from truly living your part and the beginning of exaggerated false acting" —Stanislavski
I can't say it any better than this. Together we create a space that is both disciplined yet nurturing. From the beginner to the working actor, you'll get the tools and the coaching needed to move your work and your career forward with grace and ease. Coaching for monologues - modern/classical/Shakespeare, career counseling and commercial copy. Credits include: Broadway, Off-Broadway, Steppenwolf, Goodman, Shakespeare Rep., Commercials, Television, Film.

Voice-Over Coaches

Audio One, Inc.
(See our ad on page 64)
325 W. Huron #512
Chicago, IL 60610
312/337-5111 • 312/337-5125 - fax

Bosco Productions
(See our ad on page 149)
160 E. Grand - 6th floor
Chicago, IL 60611
312/644-8300

Helen Cutting
445 E. Ohio #1914
Chicago, IL 60611
312/527-1809
Helen Cutting is a seasoned professional voiceover talent and coach, with 25 years' experience in the business. She is an expert at teaching basic to advanced level voice technique.
Helen provides in-depth coaching for Television /Radio commercials, Promotions, Animation, Narration and demo tape production. Call for private consultation.

Sound Advice
(See our ad on page 63)
Kate McClanaghan, Gina Mazza, Tyrone Dockery
2028 W. Potomac #2 & 3
Chicago, IL 60622
773/772-9539
www.voiceoverdemos.com
Sound Advice is the most complete, start-to-finish voiceover demo production service. We maintain no one does what you do. The copy is written/selected specifically fo you by Professional Producers. Our mailing list and marketing plan is unparalleled. We coach, direct and produce you to get you completely poised to work. Get trained and produced by two of Chicago's top former Talent Agents, Gina Mazza (CED) and Tyrone Dockery (Stewart) and Kate McClanaghan, Producer at top Ad Agency (DDB Worldwide).

Coaches—Acting

VoiceOver 101
Ray Van Steen
325 W. Huron #512
Chicago, IL 60610
312/587-1010
312/337-5125 - fax

Private individual coaching sessions in voicing TV/Radio commercials, narrations. Employs record/playback method in recording studio environment. Basics through production of voice-over demo. Van Steen is a published writer on the subject, and has voiced thousands of commercials.
Phone for free, no-obligation brochure.

Voice Over U
Sherri Berger
773/774-9559
773/774-9555 - fax
sherriberger.voicedemo.com

Voices On
Thomas Test
773/528-7041

Your demo needs cutting-edge scripts and production values to stand out from the crowd. EVERY demo I've produced has resulted in agent representation for my students. Call Telly award-winning v/o talent Tom Test of "Voices On" at 773/528-7041, for private coaching, in-studio audition workshops, and demo production.

Training

sound advice
the most complete voice-over demo service

featuring
- THOROUGH ORIENTATION OF CURRENT TALENT INDUSTRY
  (focusing on how to make yourself known and accessible)
- ONE-ON-ONE VOCAL COACHING
- INTIMATE IN-STUDIO WORKSHOPS
- FULL VOICE-OVER DEMO PRODUCTION
- FLAT RATE AVAILABLE
- STATE-OF-THE-ART FACILITIES DEDICATED SOLELY TO VOICE-OVER RELATED PRODUCTION

Get trained and produced by former Chicago voice-over agents Gina Mazza & Tyrone Dockery.
We endorse Certified Speech Pathologist Lynette Venturella of Professionally Speaking.

www.voiceoverdemos.com
call (773) 772-9539

Coaches—Voice

Dialect Coaches

Martin Aistrope
1243 N. Damen #2
Chicago, IL 60622
773/276-4665
Native Brit. Standard, Regional (Cockney, Scots, Irish, Yorks, Scouse, Geordie, etc.), Colonial (Aussie, NZ, SA, etc.). All technique and no music? Aaargh! Taped personal coaching, customized drill, facial exercises, tapes. You have a better ear than you think: Find out which one it is!

Eric Armstrong
773/588-8977
312/341-4329
faculty.roosevelt.edu/armstrong/
One on one: A complete approach to sharpen skills in the vocal area: voice work, dialect preparation, accent reduction or preparing a complex text. Individual attention in a supportive atmosphere helps you reach your goals.
Company coaching: productions with dialect/accent, voice or text needs. Reasonable rates.

Belinda Bremner
773/871-3710
An audition is a job interview using someone else's words. The key to a successful audition is finding an author who tells your story in your words. Your choice of audition material speaks volumes. Decide what that message is and then craft your audition. Ideally suited for the well-trained actor looking for an edge.

Kate DeVore
4451 N. Hamilton
Chicago, IL 60625
773/334-7203
Character-based dialect acquisition and coaching. The way we speak is an integral part of who we are; this principle informs technical coaching for sound changes, voice placement (resonance), and musicality of a dialect. Non role-specific dialect training also available, as is coaching in Standard American (accent reduction). Materials and personalized coaching tapes provided.

Cecilie O'Reilly
2023 N. Damen
Chicago, IL 60647
773/486-3649

64 The Book: An Actor's Guide to Chicago

Voice/Speech Coaches

Eric Armstrong
773/588-8977
312/341-4329
faculty.roosevelt.edu/armstrong/
One on one: A complete approach to sharpen skills in the vocal area: voice work, dialect preparation, accent reduction or preparing a complex text. Individual attention in a supportive atmosphere helps you reach your goals. Company coaching: productions with dialect/accent, voice or text needs. Reasonable rates.

Randy Buescher
Chicago/Naperville, IL
312/671-3181
708/352-0510

Lia Corinth
847/328-4202

Kate DeVore, M.A.
4451 N. Hamilton
Chicago, IL 60625
773/334-7203
www.KateDeVore.com
Ten years experience as voice, speech and dialect coach; certified voice/speech pathologist specialized in performers' voice. Voice enhancement, exploration and development. Training in vocal projection, resonance, power, flexibility, ease and range. Vocal extremes (shouting and screaming) without injury. Vocal health and maintenance. Holistic approach to voice enhancement also available, incorporating energetic and complementary healing techniques to free and strengthen the voice.

Marina Gilman
5701 S. Dorchester
Chicago, IL 60637
773/955-0016

Deb Kowalczyk
773/562-5452
M.A. in Speech/Language Pathology - 22 years experience. Member ASHA (American Speech/Language/Hearing Association and VASTA (Voice and Speech Trainers Association). Studied with Patsy Rodenburg "The Actor Speaks: Voice and the Performer. Specializing in:
-Standard American English pronunciation
-voice and projection difficulties
-dialect modification
Trained theater professional

Richard Marriott
410 S. Michigan #920
Chicago, IL 60605
312/360-1728

Kathryn Nash
312/943-0167
312/943-0229 - fax
Acting- Voice- Speech Coach
Member- AEA, AFTRA, VASTA (Voice and Speech Trainers Association)
Private instruction specializing in:
-vocal techniques for stage and voiceovers
-Standard American diction
-dialect acquisition and reduction
-monologue coaching to integrate "kinesthetic, vocal, and emotional modes" within the acting process.

Cecilie O'Reilly
2023 N. Damen
Chicago, IL 60647
773/486-3649

Professionally Speaking
2028 W. Potomac - 3rd floor
Chicago, IL 60622
773/218-9183

Coaches—Singing

Ann Wakefield
1500 N. LaSalle #3C
Chicago, IL 60610
312/751-9348

William Rush Voice Consultants
410 S. Michigan #920
Chicago, IL 60604
312/360-1039
630/620-1270 • 630/620-1271 - fax

Accompanists

Bobby Schiff Music Productions
363 Longcommon Rd.
Riverside, IL 60546
708/442-3168
708/447-3719 - fax

Matthew Krause
773/334-6425
Do you need music transposed for an audition or performance? Music transcribed and printed out from a recording? An accompaniment tape made for an audition or rehearsal? Vocal coaching? Call for professional, reasonably priced music or tapes. A musician and actor, Matt will get exactly what you need, fast!

Singing Coaches

Tamara Anderson
1023 Barberry Ln.
Round Lake Beach, IL 60073
847/546-5548
847/546-5717 - fax

Randy Buescher
Chicago/Naperville, IL
312/671-3181
708/352-0510

Mark Burnell
2008C W. Potomac
Chicago, IL 60622
773/862-2665
773/862-2655 - fax
members.aol.com\brunell88\
Mark Burnell (773)862-COOL Cabaret, jazz, Broadway, pop, R & B. Get your show together: repertoire, arrangements, demo recording. Prepare your audition: style, phrasing, transposition, rehearsal tapes. Work your chops: technique, flexibility, improvisation, ornamentation. MFA and 10 years with Carnegie Mellon Music Theatre Department. burnell88@aol.com

The Center For Voice
410 S. Michigan #635
Chicago, IL 60605
312/360-1111
Private voice lessons in all styles located in the fine arts building.

Center Theater's Training Program for Actors, Directors, Playwrights, and Singers
1346 W. Devon
Chicago, IL 60660
773/508-0200
773/508-9584 - fax

Coaches–Singing

Dr. Ronald Combs
917 W. Castlewood
Chicago, IL 60640
773/271-8425
773/271-0364 - fax

Lia Corinth
847/328-4202

Dancecenter North
540 N. Milwaukee
Libertyville, IL 60048
847/367-7970
847/367-7905 - fax
www.dancecenterNorth.com

DEPAUL COMMUNITY MUSIC

MUSICAL THEATER WORKSHOP
Grades 7-12
Acting • Movement • Vocal Techniques

For information, call (773) 325-7262

DePaul University – Community Music Division
(See our ad above)
804 W. Belden
Chicago, IL 60614-3296
773/325-7262
773/325-7264 - fax
music.depaul.edu

The workshop is an intensive, performance-oriented program in musical theatre. Class sessions include vocal and physical warm-ups, theatre games, song preparation, interpretation of text, character analysis, and stage movement. Each student performs in group numbers and at least one solo or scene. Participants take an active role in the developmental process, working as an ensemble toward the final end-of-session performance.

David H. Edelfelt
1243 W. Foster
Chicago, IL 60640
773/878-SING

Jilann Gabriel
410 S. Michigan #630
Chicago, IL 60605
800/831-3139
312/692-1703
773/237-0299 - fax
www.poporchshows.com

Marina Gilman
5701 S. Dorchester
Chicago, IL 60637
773/955-0016

Matthew Krause
773/334-6425

Do you need music transposed for an audition or performance? Music transcribed and printed out from a recording? An accompaniment tape made for an audition or rehearsal? Vocal coaching? Call for professional, reasonably priced music or tapes. A musician and actor, Matt will get exactly what you need, fast!

Richard Marriott
410 S. Michigan #920
Chicago, IL 60605
312/360-1728

Music Workshop
Bob Kalal
4900 W. 28th Pl.
Cicero, IL 60804
708/652-4040
members.xoom.com\musicwkshop

Ch. 2 Training 67

Coaches—Singing

**Northwestern University
School of Music**
(ask for referrals)
711 Elgin Rd.
Evanston, IL 60208
847/491-7485
847/491-5260 - fax

Old Town School of Folk Music
4544 N. Lincoln
Chicago, IL 60625
773/728-6000
773/728-6999 - fax
www.oldtownschool.org

School of Performing Arts
200 E. 5th Ave. #132
Naperville, IL 60563
630/717-6622 • 630/717-5131 - fax
www.performing-arts.org

**Sherwood Conservatory
of Music**
1312 S. Michigan
Chicago, IL 60605
312/427-6267
312/427-6677 - fax

Rak Vocal & Healing Clinic
6056 W. Irving Park
Chicago, IL 60634
773/283-8349

Peggy Smith-Skarry
(See our ad on this page)
1347 W. Winona
Chicago, IL 60640
773/728-5240
There is nothing more exciting than a powerful voice with a great technique. But besides tone quality, what makes the singer unique as a performer? I give my students crucial developmental techniques which provide freedom and confidance - then train them to trust and express their originality through their voices.

The Voice Works
Ruth Allyn
Near North
Chicago, IL 60610
312/944-3867

**What a Voice Productions
(The Vocal Studio)**
Karyn Sarring
P.O. Box 558188
Chicago, IL 60655
708/388-5585
www.whatavoice.com

Established Singer/Pianist/Teacher/Coach/Performer

Peggy! Smith-Skarry

for vocal instruction

"Peggy Smith-Skarry is one of the top singers & voice teachers in the Chicago area. I have great respect for her work." --**George Estevez, Founder/Music Director Choral Ensemble of Chicago**
Member National Association of Teachers of Singing (NATS) and The Musicians Club of Women

Call 773/728-5240 - Detailed brochure upon request

---

68 The Book: An Actor's Guide to Chicago

Coaches—Instruments

William Rush Voice Consultants
410 S. Michigan #920
Chicago, IL 60604
312/360-1039
630/620-1270
630/620-1271 - fax

Wilmette Voice & Piano Studio
847/251-7449

Frank Winkler
1765 George Ct.
Glenview, IL 60025
847/729-1893

Instrument Coaches

Academy of Movement and Music
605 Lake St.
Oak Park, IL 60302
708/848-2329
708/848-2391 - fax

DePaul University – Community Music Division
(See our ad on page 67)
804 W. Belden
Chicago, IL 60614-3296
773/325-7262
773/325-7264 - fax
music.depaul.edu
The workshop is an intensive, performance-oriented program in musical theatre. Class sessions include vocal and physical warm-ups, theatre games, song preparation, interpretation of text, character analysis, and stage movement. Each student performs in group numbers and at least one solo or scene. Participants take an active role in the developmental process, working as an ensemble toward the final end-of-session performance.

Northwestern University School of Music
(ask for referrals)
711 Elgin Rd.
Evanston, IL 60208
847/491-7485
847/491-5260 - fax

Old Town School of Folk Music
4544 N. Lincoln
Chicago, IL 60625
773/728-6000
773/728-6999 - fax
www.oldtownschool.org

School of Performing Arts
200 E. 5th Ave. #132
Naperville, IL 60563
630/717-6622
630/717-5131 - fax
www.performing-arts.org

Sherwood Conservatory of Music
1312 S. Michigan
Chicago, IL 60605
312/427-6267
312/427-6677 – fax

Wilmette Voice & Piano Studio
847/251-7449

Ch. 2 Training

Speech Therapy

Movement Coaches

Chicago Center for the Alexander Technique
Ed Bouchard
5415 N. Sheridan #1005
Chicago, IL 60640
773/728-3235

T. Daniel and Laurie Willets
c/o T. Daniel Productions
1047 Gage St.
Winnetka, IL 60093
847/446-0183
847/446-0183 - fax
www.tdanielcreations.com

An actor must gain the physical skills, imagination and confidence necessary to be as articulate with his Body as he is with Words. T. Daniel and Laurie Willets, internationally-acclaimed Mime and Theatre Movement performers perform, consult, choreograph and teach for Stage, Film, Animation, Opera and Music.

Robin Lakes
1979 S. Campus Dr.
Evanston, IL 60208
773/973-3929

Nana Shineflug
847/724-1931

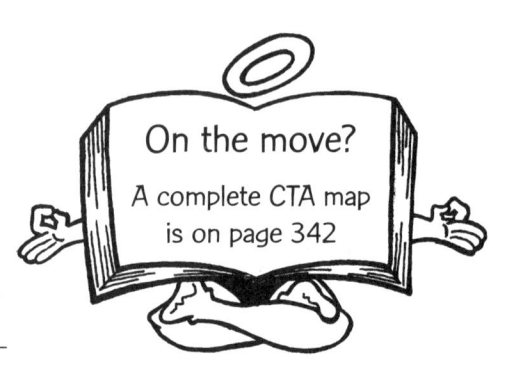

On the move?
A complete CTA map is on page 342

Speech Therapy

Kate DeVore, M.A., CCC-SLP
4451 N. Hamilton
Chicago, IL 60625
773/334-7203

As a voice, speech and dialect trainer as well as a speech pathologist specialized in professional voice, Kate has created a unique combination of artistic and scientifically based techniques for vocal rehabilitation and speech training. She is also specialized in working with people who stutter, using similar prinicples to facilitate a feeling of ease and control in speech.

Center for Stuttering Therapy
9933 Lawler Ave.
Skokie, IL 60077
847/677-7473 • 847/677-7493 –fax
www.cfst.com

Krause Speech & Language Services
Sue Ellen Krause, Ph.D., CCC-SLP
233 E. Erie #815
Chicago, IL 60611
312/943-1927
312/943-2692 - fax

Kathleen E. Long
11142 S. Campbell
Chicago, IL 60655
773/239-8089

Professionally Speaking
2028 W. Potomac - 3rd floor
Chicago, IL 60622
773/218-9183

Universities

Rak Vocal & Healing Clinic
6056 W. Irving Park
Chicago, IL 60634
773/283-8349

Bonnie Smith, Ph.D., CCC-SLP
Division of Speech Pathology
UIC Medical Center
1855 W. Taylor
Chicago, IL 60612
312/996-6520 • 312/996-1527 - fax
www.otol.uic.edu\divisions\speech.htm

Universities (with MFA's in Theatre)

American Conservatory Theater
30 Grant Ave. – 6th floor
San Francisco, CA 94108
415-439-3250
415/834-3326 - fax
MFA's offered in Acting.

Arizona State University
Department of Theatre
P.O. Box 872002
Tempe, AZ 85287-1003
480/965-5359
480/965-5158 - fax
www.asu.edu/graduate
MFA's offered in Acting, Theatre for Youth and Scenography.

Boston University
School for the Arts
855 Commonwealth Ave. #470
Boston, MA 02215
617/353-3390
617/353-4490 - fax
http://web.bu.edu/SFA/
MFA's offered in Directing, Education, Theatre and Design.

Brandeis University
Department of Theatre Arts
Waltham, MA 02254-9110
617/746-3340
617/736-3408 - fax
www.brandeis.edu
MFA's offered Acting, Dramaturgy, Playwriting and Design.

California Institute of the Arts – Theatre School
24700 N. McBean Parkway
Valencia, CA 91355
661/253-7853
661/255-0690 - fax
MFA's offered in Acting, Directing, Directing for Theatre, Video & Cinema, Design, Playwriting, Management and Technical Direction.

Columbia University
Hammerstein Center/Theatre
School of the Arts, Columbia University
New York, NY 10027
212/854-3408
212/854-3344 - fax
www.columbia.edu/cu/arts
MFA's in Acting, Directing, Dramaturgy, Playwriting and Management

Ch. 2 Training 71

Universities

DePaul University
The Theatre School at DePaul University
2135 N. Kenmore
Chicago, IL 60614
773/325-7999
800/4DEPAUL
ttsweb.tht.depaul.edu
MFA's offered in Acting, Directing, Costume Design, Lighting Design and Set Design.

Eastern Michigan State University
Department of Comm. & Theatre Arts
124 Quirk
Ypsilanti, MI 48197
313/487-1153
313/487-1484 - fax
www.emich.edupublic/cta/theatre_Home_page.html
MFA's offered in Theatre for the Young.

Illinois State University
Department of Theatre
Campus Box 5700
Normal, IL 61761
309/438-8783
309/438-7214 - fax
www.orat.ilstu.edu/theatre
MFA's offered in Acting, Directing and Design.

Indiana University
Dept. of Theatre & Drama
Theatre 200
Bloomington, IN 47405
812/855-4503
812/855-4704 - fax
www.fa.indiana.edu/~thtr
MFA's offered in Acting, Directing, Playwriting, Costume Design, Lighting Design, Set Design and Theatre Tech.

Mankato State University
Dept. of Theatre Arts
261 Performing Arts Cevter
Mankato, MN 56001
507/389-2118
507/389-2922 - fax
www.mankato.msus.edu
MFA's offered in Acting, Directing and Design/Tech.

Michigan State University
Department of Theatre
149 Auditorium Building
East Lansing, MI 48824
517/355-6690
517/355-1698 - fax
pilot.msu/theatre/unit
MFA's offered in Acting and Production Design.

National Theatre Conservatory
1050 13th St.
Denver, CO 80204
303/893-4000
www.denvercenter.org/edu
MFA's offered in Acting.

Northern Illinois University
School of Theatre Arts
DeKalb, IL 60115
815/753-1335
815/753-8415 - fax
MFA's offered in Acting and Design/Tech.

Northwestern University
Theatre Department
1979 S. Campus Dr.
Evanston, IL 60208
847/491-3170
847/467-2019 - fax
www.nuinfo.nwu.edu/speech/departments/theatre.html
MFA's offered in Directing and Stage Design.

Universities

Ohio State University
Department of Theatre
1849 Cannon Dr.
Columbus, OH 43210
614/292-5821
614/292-4818 - fax
MFA's offered in Acting, Directing and Design/Tech.

Ohio University
School of Theatre
307 Kantner Hall
Athens, OH 45701
740/593-4818
740/593-4817 - fax
MFA's offered in Acting, Directing, Playwriting, Design, General, Production and Tech.

Pennsylvania State University
School of Theatre Arts
103 Arts Building
University Park, PA 16802-2900
814/865-7586
MFA's offered in Acting, Directing, Design and Tech.

State University of New York/Purchase
Conservatory of
Theatre Arts & Film
735 Anderson Hill Rd.
Purchase, NY 10577
914/251-6830
914/251-6300 - fax
MFA's offered in Directing/Stage Management and Design Technology.

Purdue University
Department of Visual and Performing Arts
1376 Stewart Center
West Lafayette, IN 47907
765/494-3074
765/496-1766 - fax
www.sla.purdue.edu/theatre/acting.html
*MFA's offered in Acting, Directing, Scenography and Technology.
Just 2 hours south of Chicago. Graduate MFA. programs in Acting, Production Design & Technology (Costume, Scenery, Lights, Sound, Theatre Engineering, Theatre Technology); MA program in Stage Management. Assistantships with tuition waiver plus salary in excess of $10,000/year. Member: U/RTA, NAST, ACTF. Info: www.purdue.edu/theatre; e-mail: theatre@purdue.edu. EA/EOU.*

Roosevelt University
The Theatre Conservatory-Chicago
College of Performing Arts
430 S. Michigan
Chicago, IL 60605-1394
312/341-3719
312/341-3814 - fax
www.roosevelt.edu
MFA's in Directing/Dramaturgy, Musical Theatre and Performance.

Southern Illinois University
Department of Theatre
Carbondale, IL 62901-6608
618/453-5741
618/453-7582 - fax
www.siu.edu/~mccleod/
MFA's offered in Directing and Playwriting.

Got Books?
Check out the Bookstore
Listings on page 123

Ch. 2 Training

Universities

Southern Methodist University
Theatre Division
1164 Owens Art Center
Dallas, TX 75275
214/768-2558
www.smu.edu/~meadows/
MFA's offered in Acting and Directing.

University of Alabama
Dept. of Theatre & Dance
Box 870239
Tuscaloosa, AL 35487-0239
205/348-5283
www.asf.net
MFA's offered in Acting, Directing, Playwriting/Dramaturgy, Costume Design, Costume Design/Production, Set Design/Technical Production and Management/Arts Administration.

UCLA
Department of Theatre
Los Angeles, CA
90024-1622
310/825-7008
310/825-3383 - fax
www.tft.ucla.edu
MFA's offered in Acting, Directing, Playwriting and Design & Production.

University of Cincinnati
College-Conservatory of Music
P.O. Box 210096
Cincinnati, OH 45221-0096
513/556-5803
513/556-3399 - fax
www.UC.edu/www/ccm
MFA's offered in Acting, Directing, Musical Theatre, Costume Design, Lighting Design; Make-up & Wig Design, Scenic Design, Sound Design and Stage Management.

University of Delaware
Professional Theatre Training Program
Mitchell Hall, RM 109
Newark, DE 19716
302/831-2201
www.udel.edu/theatre
MFA's offered in Acting, Stage Management and Technical Production.

Linenwood College
Department of Performing Arts
209 S. Kingshighway
St. Charles, MO 63301
314/949-4949 • 314/949-4910 - fax
MFA's offered in Acting, Directing and Design/Technical Theatre.

University of Houston
School of Theatre
Houston, TX 77204-5071
713/743-3003
713/749-1420 - fax
MFA's offered in Acting, Directing, Costume Design and Scenic Design.

University of Illinois, Urbana-Champaign
Dept. of Theatre
4-122 Krannert Center
500 S. Goodwin Ave.
Urbana, IL 61801
217/333-2371
217/244-1861 - fax
www.uiuc.edu/providers/kcpathaater/theat.html
MFA's offered in Acting and Design/Management/Tech.

University of Iowa
Dept. of Theatre Arts 107 TB
Iowa City, IA 52242-1705
319/335-2700
www.uiowa.edu
MFA's offered in Playwriting, Design and Stage Management.

Universities

University of Massachusetts
Department of Theater
Room 112 - Fine Arts Center
Amherst, MA 01003
413/545-3490
413/545-4312 - fax
MFA's offered in Directing, Dramaturgy, Costume Design, Lighting Design and Scenic Design.

University of Michigan
Dept. of Theatre & Drama
2550 Frieze Build.
Ann Arbor, MI 48109-1285
734/764-5350
734/763-5097 - fax
www.theatre.music.umich.edu
MFA's offered in Directing, Playwriting and Design.

University of Missouri-Kansas City
5100 Rockhill Rd.
Kansas City, MO 64110
816/235-2784
816/235-5367 - fax
MFA's offered in Acting and Design/Technology.

University of Nebraska-Lincoln
Dept. of Theatre Arts & Dance
215 Temple Building 12th & R Sts.
Box 880201
Lincoln, NE 68588-0201
402/472-2072
MFA's offered in Acting and Design/Tech

University of North Carolina
Department of Dramatic Art
CB#3230, Graham Mem. 052A
Chapel Hill, NC 27599-3230
919/962-1132
919/966-2611 - fax
MFA's offered in Professional Actor Training Program, Costume Technology and Technical Production.

University of Southern California
School of Theatre
Los Angeles, CA 90089-0791
213-740-1289
213/740-8888 - fax
www.usc,edu/dept.theatre/DramaNet
MFA's offered in Playwriting and Design.

University of Texas at Austin
Department of Theatre & Dance
College of Fine Arts
Austin, TX 78712
512/471-5793
MFA's offered in Acting, Creative Drama/Theatre for Children & Youth, Directing, Playwriting, Design and Theatre Tech.

University of Washington
School of Drama
Box 353950
Seattle, WA 98195-3950
206/543-5140
206/543-8512 - fax
http://artsci.washington.edu/drama/schdram1.html
MFA's offered in Acting, Directing and Design/Tech.

University of Wisconsin-Madison
Theatre and Drama Department
6173 Vilas Hall
821 University Ave.
Madison, WI 53706-1497
608/263-2329
608/263-2463 - fax
http://polyglot.lss.wisc.edu/tnd/theatre.html
MFA's offered in Acting, Directing, Costuming, Design and Technology.

Ch. 2 Training 75

Universities

University of Wisconsin/Milwaukee
Professional Theatre Training Prog.
P.O. Box 413
Milwaukee, WI 53201
414/229-4947
414/229-2728 - fax
www.uwm.edu
MFA's offered in Acting, Costume Production, Stage Management and Technical Production.

University/Resident Theatre Association (U/RTA)
1560 Broadway #414
New York, NY 10036
212/221-1130
212/869-2752 - fax
www.urta.com

Wayne State University
Theatre Department
3225 Old Main
Detroit, MI 48202
313/577-3508
www.comm.wayne.edu/theatre
MFA's offered in Acting, Costuming, Lighting Design, Scenic Design, Stage Management and Theatre Management.

Western Illinois University
Theatre Department
101 Browne
Macomb, IL, 61455
309/298-1543
www.wiu.edu
MFA's offered in Acting, Directing and Design.

Yale University
P.O. Box 208325
New Haven, CT 06520
203/432-1507
203/432-9668 - fax
www.yale.edu./drama
MFA's offered in Acting, Directing, Playwriting/Dramaturgy/Dramatic Criticism, Design, Technical Design/Production and Theatre Management.

Performink

Chicago's Entertainment Trade Paper, The art, the business, the industry.

www.performink.com

Your source for vital industry news

To order PERFORMINK call 773/296-4600.

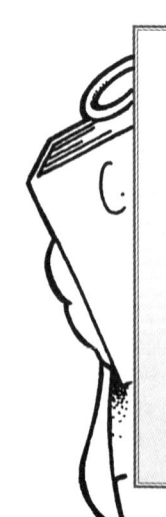

The Actor's Tools

I still might be missing a few things before my audition!

WNEP Theatre Foundation, "The Lindner Briefs"

The Headshot Market

'Tis not her glass, but you that flatters her;
And out of you she sees herself more proper
Than any of her lineaments can show her

By Bob Peterson

"The days of one headshot are over," said Los Angeles photographer Jeffrey Nicholson. Surprised?

"People are bored with the same old generic shot," said Laura Burke, a Los Angeles photographer and former New York agent.

We cornered the experts—including a bevy of agents, photographers and casting directors from around the country—for the skinny on how headshot styles differ in Chicago, New York and Los Angeles as well as how many and what kind of headshots you need in each city.

Auditioning for a commercial? There's one headshot you need. Got a cold reading for an industrial film next week? Yep, you need a different headshot for that, too.

And not only do you need a variety of headshots for different types of auditions, but if you move from Chicago to New York or Los Angeles, you'll need even more headshots.

Here's the breakdown. Actors audition for film, television, theatre, commercials and industrials. Industry experts say that headshots for commercials and industrials, while different from each other, are stylistically similar in all three cities.

But theatre, film and television headshots are city-specific. You can use the same headshot to audition for a production of *Hamlet*, that new pilot and the latest David Fincher movie, but it should look different depending on where you are.

We'll talk about commercial and industrial headshots, hit each of the three cities, their different headshot styles and acting scenes, then discuss the future of headshots.

The Industrial Headshot

Companies are crazy about sharp-dressed men and women when they cast their in-house films. "Industrial headshots are definitely more on the corporate end—in a suit with a cell phone," says Bob Schroeder, director of the on-camera division at Suzanne's A-Plus talent agency. "It's not very interesting, just corporate."

Geddes agency co-owner Elizabeth Geddes and local photographer Brian McConkey agreed that a corporate look is best for an industrial headshot.

President of the now closed Cunningham, Escott, Dipene agency Diane Herro Sanford stressed that a good headshot is key to getting industrial work. "The headshot is more important because the companies usually don't have casting directors," she said. "They just call an agent for a headshot."

The Commercial Headshot

You're a great actor? Commercial casting directors don't care.

"You can have bad teeth and be a good theatre actor," said Chicago photographer Larry Lapidus, who worked in New York for 17 years. "But you can have one chipped tooth and never do a commercial."

Others agreed that you need a radiant headshot—and good teeth—to get commercial work.

"It should show a lot of energy and life," Sanford said. "And you need to show some teeth, especially for food products."

"The commercial shot should be more upbeat and friendly, usually with a smile to it that shows off a person's teeth," says McConkey.

Did we mention you need good teeth?

Also, while most headshots only show actors from the chest up, Sanford said that actors should have a three-quarter or full-body headshot for commercials. "Have a body shot to show your size and how you're built," she said. "Casting directors need to see that."

The Theatre/Film/Television Headshot

This is the meat 'n' potatoes headshot. It's the one you'll use at most auditions because it's not about you selling a product, it's about you selling *you*.

"I'm looking for a headshot that represents who the actor is, not a character they can play," Geddes said. "It should show me the soul of the actor."

Overall, experts said that the theatre/film/TV headshot is more dramatic than the other headshots, with an emphasis on the actor's personality, not their look.

But where's the personality?

"The eyes," Sanford said. "They have to say something."

Schroeder agreed, saying, "I only look at the eyes. If you draw my interest, that's the headshot I pick."

But here's the rub: Your Chicago theatre/film/TV headshot may not turn that casting director's head in New York or Los Angeles.

"Each city has its own style," Schroeder said.

Los Angeles

You can always count on Los Angeles to have the weirdest everything, including headshots. Because of the huge commercial market and surplus of actors, Los Angeles photographers opt—not always by choice—for more outdoor, naturally lit shots.

"In LA, a huge percentage of money is spent on commercials—not theatre, TV or film," said former New York photographer Michael Helms, now working in Los Angeles. "About 65 to 70 percent of the money. Theatre in LA pales in comparison to New York and Chicago."

Los Angeles photographer Jeffrey Nicholson agreed.

"The commercial market is still stronger in LA than in New York," he said, adding that almost no industrials are shot in Los Angeles.

And the style of shot? Well, it's just that—stylish.

"LA is very hip and very cool," said David O'Connor, president of O'Connor Casting in Chicago. "A lot of times they make people look too good."

The fallout from the emphasis on commercials is that actors need more headshots in Los Angeles than any other city. This carries over to the large film and television market. Again, because of the surplus of talent, actors not only need to have something different exhibited in their headshots, but also need to be laser-specific about what type they can play.

"It used to be that the casting director could use their imagination," Nicholson said. "But in LA there are so many applicants that if you don't make a specific choice—even to the extent of wearing a cop uniform—you won't get picked. If that ER casting director is going through a stack of headshots and you're wearing medical scrubs in yours, he'll pick you. It may not be right, but that's what happens."

So how many headshots do you need in Los Angeles? It's up to you, experts say.

"You need several photos in LA," Helms said. "A woman should have an 'I'm a mommy' shot, a business woman and a sexy shot, ideally, if she can pull all those off. It helps to have more than two because casting directors don't have the time."

New York

New York's overwhelmingly strong theatre scene influences their headshots.

"The New York shots are more serious—with depth and soul," Lapidus said. "They're more theatrical with a lot of sex appeal. It's more relaxed. It's a photo about character and not vitality."

As opposed to Los Angeles, most New York headshots are done in a studio to give photographers better light control. But experts agreed that although the New York headshot is darker and deeper, it's not as important as the actor.

"In LA, a casting director might not even look at the resumé, but they will in New York," Helms said. "You find more trained professionals in New York and Chicago than in LA." Helms added that a New York actor usually only has one or two headshots.

"It's more about the craft of acting," he said.

So if you're moving to New York, you better want to act on the stage, sources said. While the sitcom *Spin City* is shot in New York, all others are shot in Los Angeles. But Ron Rinaldi, a longtime New York photographer who recently moved to Los Angeles, added that actors also find work in the "three or four" soap operas filmed in New York, along with a respectable commercial scene.

"TV is not a small business in New York," he said.

Lapidus said that few industrials are shot in New York, unless it's a high-profile company. "Most who come to New York are there for the stage," he said. "Their goal usually is to be seen onstage and sent out to Los Angeles."

A New York actor should have two headshots at the most, a majority of experts said. One dark and mysterious headshot for theatre and maybe one flashier shot for commercials. The main exception, Rinaldi said, is for character actors, who should have a variety of shots that reflect how many roles they can play.

Rinaldi differed with the others, saying actors should have an industrial and commercial headshot in New York, along with a "more glamorous" shot for soap opera auditions.

Chicago

Chicago falls between New York and Los Angeles on the headshot spectrum.

"Chicago has a more conservative feel," said Brooke Tonneman, owner of Big Mouth Talent in Chicago.

Lapidus said Chicago's headshots are more relaxed than New York's. "Chicago headshots are more commercial and smiley," he said.

But while actors can smile in a Chicago headshot, theatre still dominates the acting scene, and your headshot should reflect that.

"Most clients want a good theatre shot with a good dramatic edge," McConkey said. "It shouldn't be so smiley and vivacious like, 'I'm doing an Empire carpet ad.'"

Although theatre dominates the scene here, McConkey said actors don't usually pay the bills by doing plays. "A commercial shot is good to have because Chicago is such a good commercial and industrial town," he said.

Almost all the experts agreed that a Chicago actor should have three headshots: a darker one for theatre and film, a brighter one for commercials and a corporate one for industrials.

Future Trends of the Headshot

While headshot styles in the three cities differ now, experts say that they are growing more similar. The more natural light shots are taking focus in Chicago, as casting directors force photographers to catch up with the coasts.

"Chicago is getting more artistic," Tonneman said. "The typical headshot has fallen by the wayside. The 'just head' headshot is done."

Rick Frederick, casting director of European Repertory, agreed. "For a while only LA was doing the three-quarter and full-body shots, then Chicago got more three-quarter and full-body shots," he said. "I like to see something interesting in the theatre shot—something artistic."

According to Burke, industrial and commercial headshots are getting harder to tell apart, too.

"Even industrials have changed their style. It's not always the stiff, spokesman shot anymore. I've even seen some serious commercial shots." Burke said. "One girl I knew for an industrial wore a leopard print outfit and did a Jewish yenta, saying, 'Like, oh my gawd.' You can't have a boring industrial."

But according to Nicolson, the biggest change coming for headshots is the digital revolution.

"I firmly believe that's where the headshot world is going," he said.

Rinaldi is already there, having converted his studio to digital. Sacrilege? He says no, and that digital will replace old-fashioned film photography.

"We're on the Enterprise and Spock's taking a picture," he ventured. "Is he using film or digital? Film is still beautiful, but the technology should surpass it."

What are the benefits? Actors usually have to wait a week for a final print of their headshot, but a digital camera can get them the final print in as little as 48 hours.

"After a session with a film photographer, actors usually get a sheet with stamp-sized pictures of all their shots to choose from. If they want to blow up one or more to look at, he or she has to pay more money. But digital technology abolishes that inconvenience," said Rinaldi.

"The pictures come out magazine quality on-screen one hour after a session and an actor can walk out the door with 40 to 60 usable prints to choose from on 8"x10" laser paper," he said, adding that actors save "a couple of hundred dollars" by going to him.

But how is the quality?

"I hate to say the photos are better, but they are," he said. "People say they look 3-D." Rinaldi also said he can retouch any image on the computer.

"Re-shoots are obsolete," he said, adding, "Now wrinkles, zits and blemishes can be totally washed out. It's totally undetectable, except to a really well-trained eye."

Photographer Checklist

A good headshot is one of the most important investments an actor can make. It's your calling card, introduction and logo all rolled into one. As a result, it's important to be careful when choosing a photographer to ensure that the money you spend gets you the best shots possible.

1. Research

This is a big investment, so you want to do your research carefully. Though it may be tempting, DON'T SKIMP!! Your headshot is your introduction to many casting people. You want it to look professional. A great deal is one that gets you great shots. Look for photographers whose style you like or who sound appealing to you. Some places to check:

PERFORMINK
This Book
Act One Studios–Act One has a portfolio of many photographers' work.

References

If a friend has had a good experience with a photographer, or if an agent recommends someone, check him or her out. Don't take this reference as gospel, though. What works for your friend may not work for you.

2. Consultation

Any legitimate photographer should offer a free consultation. Look for the following things:

Space

Are you comfortable with the space the photographer shoots in?

Personality

Do you get along with the photographer? Do they listen to you and what you want to do? Are you able to be yourself?

Portfolio

Look at the photographer more closely. Have they shot anyone who's similar to you in appearance? How are those shots? Do all the shots look the same, or does the photographer seem to change his/her style with each subject?

3. Makeup Artist

You may want to hire a makeup artist as well. The photographer may have someone available that they like to work with. Do research. Any makeup you use should enhance your look without changing it. In the end you want to look like you.

4. The Shoot
The day finally arrives. What can I do to be sure of having the best session possible?

Sleep
It's important to be well rested. Schedule your shoot at the time of day when you are at your best.

Clothes
Bring a lot of choices. In particular, bring clothes that show your shape without being too tight or revealing. One photographer recommends bringing clothing that is darker than your skin tone. Above all, bring clothes that you're comfortable in.

Music
Bring music that you love. It'll help you maintain positive energy and a positive mood.

5. Choosing Your Shot
I've got my proof sheets back, but how do I choose between all these tiny shots?

Get a Loupe
Though it may sound like a wolf of some sort, a loupe is actually a small eye piece that will help you get a better idea of what a shot will look like blown up.

Get Advice
See what shots your agent likes. If you have an experienced actor friend, see what they like.

Get a Concept
Know what sort of image you're looking to project and choose shots that reflect that. What are you trying to sell, and how are you going to project that?

Get Some Shots
If necessary, spend the extra money to get extra shots blown up. You'll never know exactly how a shot will look until it's 8" by 10".

Over

6. Retouching

If your shot's almost perfect—if one hair's out of place or if a wrinkle in your sweater is marring an otherwise perfect shot—get it retouched. This is a process, done either by hand or computer, that will remove those imperfections. Retouching should leave you looking like you, however. In the end, the shot has to represent how you look.

7. Reproduction

Now that you've chosen your shots, you have to get them reproduced.

Style

Matte finishes with a border are currently in style in Chicago. Ask your photographer and/or agent for their recommendations.

Font

Even the font your name is in can help express yourself. Print your name out in a bunch of different ones to find one that you like.

Lithographs

Lithographs are made by breaking a picture into dots, like printing a photograph in a newspaper. On the positive side, it's cheaper. On the negative, the quality is not as high. Lithographs might be useful for certain types of mass mailings, but most agents prefer the traditional photographic process.

8. Postcard

Finally, in addition to standard headshots, you may want to make a postcard. Postcards are used for invitations to agents and directors, thank you notes and other "Remember me?" sort of purposes. Postcard photos can be much more wacky than traditional headshots and can even use more than one photograph. Anything that will help them remember you is suitable.

Photographers

Aaron Gang Photography
773/782-4363
www.aarongang.com

Superior Headshots at Reasonable Rates. Polaroids included so you see what you're getting. Comfortable, fun atmosphere. Agent recommended. Excellent makeup/hair stylist available.

Joseph Amenta Photography
555 W. Madison #3802
Chicago, IL 60661
773/248-2488

Art Ketchum Studios
2215 S. Michigan
Chicago, IL 60616
312/842-1406
312/842-6546 - fax

Linda Balhorn
55 E. Washington #113
Chicago, IL 60602
312/263-3513

Basil Fairbanks Studio
Noel Grigalunus
370 S. Hancock
Miller, IN 46403
312/218-6687
773/907-0050 - fax

10 years Professional Working Experience in Chicago. Specializing in Music, Editorial, Fashion, Head Shots, Environmental Portraits. Individual or Corporate Clients. In the Studio or Location. A full service photography/production company.

JOHN ■ KARL ■ BREUN
PHOTOGRAPHER

jkb@classicphoto.com

www.classicphoto.com

847 ■ 259 ■ 8373

Photographers

Brad Baskin
850 N. Milwaukee
Chicago, IL 60622
312/733-2192
www.bradbaskin.com

Sandra Bever
1521 Dearborn St.
Joliet, IL 60435
815/723-3051
815/727-1687 - fax
www.sandrabever.com

Peter Bosy
6435 Indian Head Trail
Indian Head Park, IL 60525
708/246-3778
708.246.1080 - fax
www.peterbosy.com

Guy J. Cardarelli
119 W. Hubbard - 3rd floor
Chicago, IL 60610
312/321-0694 • 708/452-8844

Christopher Jacobs Studio
1443 W. Grand
Chicago, IL 60622
312/563-0987
312/563-0588 - fax
www.jacobs-photography.com

Martin Christopher
801 S. Plymouth #311
Chicago, IL 60605
312/987-9067

VISIT US ON THE WEB: WWW.ANDREWCOLLINGS.COM

Complete conventional & digital services

Quick results

ANDREW COLLINGS
Photography Video Internet
media group

www.andrewcollings.com
1550 N. Damen Chicago, IL 60622
773.384.2200

Photographers

Classic Photography, Inc.
(See our ad on page 87)
John Karl Breun
38 South Main St. #2A
Mount Prospect, IL 60056
847/259-8373 • **847/259-8474** - fax
www.classicphoto.com

Keith Claunch
1417 W. Farragut
Chicago, IL 60640
773/612-3983

Andrew Collings
(See our ad on page 93)
1550 N Damen
Chicago, IL 60622
773/384-2200
www.andrewcollings.com

Costume Images
3634 W. Fullerton
Chicago, IL 60647
773/276-8971 • **773/276-0717** - fax
www.costume-images.com

Daniel Byrnes Photography
113 W. North
Chicago, IL 60610
312/337-1174

Actors, Models, Dancers, Musicians: Whether your needs are for headshots, portfolios, or promotional photos, we have the experience to give you individualized images to be remembered. 20 years experience in Chicago and Los Angeles. Ask about our Scene Stealers Portfolios. VISA and Mastercard accepted.

David Puffer Studio
773/267-6500

Dan DuVerney
1937 W. Division - 1st floor
Chicago, IL 60622
773/252-6639

Edda Taylor Photographie
Courthouse Square #304
Crown Point , IN 46307
219/662-9500

Linn Ehrlich
312/209-2107

Elan Photography
5120 Belmont #A
Downers Grove, IL 60515
630/960-1400
630/969-1972 - fax
www.elanphotography.com

Dale Fahey
773/973-5757

Gerald Peskin Photography
681 Academy Dr.
Northbrook, IL 60062
847/498-0291

Jennifer Girard
1455 W. Roscoe
Chicago, IL 60657
773/929-3730
773/871-7762
773/871-2308 - fax

Steve Greiner
1437 W. Thomas
Chicago, IL 60622
773/227-4375
773/227-4379 - fax

Ch. 3 The Actor's Tools

Photographers

IronHorse Productions
3310 S. Aberdeen #1-A
Chicago, IL 60608
773/890-4355
773/890-4345 - fax

Whether you are looking for images that are straightforward, or cutting edge, we will work with you in a comfortable and relaxed atmosphere to capture the look you desire. Appointments are available to suit your schedule, including evenings/weekends. Ask for Michelle or Kevin. IronHorse Productions is conveniently located 10 minutes south of the Loop.

Deon Jahnke
228 S. 1st St.
Milwaukee, WI 53204
414/224-8360
414/224-8356 - fax
www.execpc.com\~deon

JLB Photography
350 N. Ogden   Chicago, IL
18031 Dixie Hgwy.
Homewood, IL 60430
312/339-3909 • 708/799-0719

Gary Jochim
1470 W. Huron #2F
Chicago, IL 60622
312/738-3204 • 312/738-3204 - fax

Joel DeGrand Photography
2715 S. Archer #2
Chicago, IL 60608
312/543-5999
www.degrand.com

The shortest distance between...
Actor and **Audition**

Brian McConkey Photography
312-563-1357
www.gratefulheads.net

Photographers

Larry Lapidus
2650 W. Belden #304
Chicago, IL 60647
773/235-3333

I am considered by many to be the most reputable "headshot" photographer in Chicago. My directorial technique sets me apart from other photographers. The rapport we develop is the most essential tool in capturing your true individuality. We will express your character in a fashion that is perfect for commercial purposes in theatre, television, or film. Recommended by top talent agents, casting directors, and acting teachers. Satisfaction guaranteed. Photographic fees: $400 includes 45 minute consultation, three rolls, and two 8x10 custom prints. Credit cards accepted.

Laurie Locke
4018 S. Oak Park Ave.
Stickney, IL 60402
708/749-2444

Max Photography
P.O. Box 14620
Chicago, IL 60614
773/477-6548

Brian McConkey
(See our ad on page 90)
312 N. May #6J
Chicago, IL 60607
312/563-1357
312/563-1615 - fax
www.gratefulheads.net

Michael Brosilow Photography
(See our ad on this page)
1370 N. Milwaukee
Chicago, IL 60622
773/235-4696
773/235-4698 - fax

PHOTOGRAPHY BY
MICHAEL BROSILOW

Photography for the Performing Artist and the Performance

Angels in America The Journeyman

John Mahoney

773 235.4696
1370 MILWAUKEE
CHICAGO, IL 60622
HEADSHOTS@BROSILOW.COM

Brosilow PHOTOGRAPHY

VISA/MASTERCARD

Photographers

1001 Working Actors Agree
Don't Panic Get Shot Right Get Potter Shot

Aaron Freeman, Frances Callier, James Belushi, John Malkovich, Chris Farley, Tim Meadows, ...abella... ...ly Wortell, Harry Mu... ...rda, Jef... ...cKay, Tom Gianis, Na... ...Avery S... ...Odenkirk, Michael C... ...yce Sloa... ...stellaneta, Jim Fay, M... ...Fred K... ...en, Mindy Bell, Care... ...lins, A... ...rkel, Amy Morlin, Mi... ...sher, Jim... ...Bernstein, Don DePo... ...ns, Meg... ...river, Lois Kazz, Rosi... ...olson, ...ne Morris, Jeff Micha... ...ey Ande... ...Budd, August Wilso... ...Parede... ...tton, Jaco Pastoria, ...e Army, ..., the Rick Thomas Sh... ...usical), ...One to Eat Cheese W... ...n Stage ... ...Twins, the Seed Show, Richard Simmons, Man & Superman, Mad Long, Katlin Kilpatrick, John Michalski, Mica Michalski, Dan Gillogly, Tracy Frenkel, Mick Napier, Benny the ... ..., Martt... ...A. Slip... ...ndy Du... ...rian Lu... ...son, Da... ...Edgar, ...y Heisl... ...d Sally, ...er, Jean... Hart Littlejohn, Janet Thanken, Marcel Saba, Brett Williams, Angela Daniels, Ellen Craybill, Kristina Mosbo, John Gardner, Alyx Morgan, Robert Sorensen, John Gardner, Doug Glad... ...s Mocka... ...W. Kelch, Justin Bay... ...d Voga... ...n, Christy Ogilvie, M... ...ve Ei... ...ike Avery, Bob Lizd, ...ens, Elis... ...e Chanie, Joan Alma... ...nifer S... ...e Moskal, Monique, ...Lewis, Mike Odeh, Kate Fifrig, Elisa Scott, Tamara Le... ...stin Re... ...Luedtke, Fran Adam... ...Evans, C... ...n, Andrea Bennett, ...Nagel, ...Evanston Dance Cer... ...ple, Esq... ...en's Quarterly, Elle, ...o, The Carzs of Fun, Pig Boy show, Live Bait Production... ...egasus ... ...The Body Politic, Eq... ...ee Shake... ...he Improv Institute, ...e, Para... ...cond City, Walt Disney Productions, Warner Brothers, and The Black Comedy Underground.

(312) 226-2060 chicago-photographer.net
REP3@chicago-photographer.net

92 The Book: An Actor's Guide to Chicago

Photographers

Michael J. Kardas Studio
2635 N. Albany
Chicago, IL 60647
773/227-7925

Michael McCafrey Photography
109 W. Hubbard
Chicago, IL 60610
312/222-9776

Mike Canale Photography
614 Davis St.
Evanston, IL 60201
847/864-0146

$169.00 Headshots. Satisfaction guaranteed. Located in the Giordano Dance Center, one block from CTA & Metra stops. Established 1980.

Rick Mitchell, Inc.
(See our ad below)
652 W. Grand
Chicago, IL 60610
312/829-1700

Moore Photographic
773/276-0249

Joseph A. Nicita
1500 W. Ohio
Chicago, IL 60622
312/666-2443 • 773/283-1674

Papadakis Photography
17 Lexington Rd.
South Barrington, IL 60010
847/428-4400
847/428-4403 - fax
www.papadakisphotography.com

Paul Sherman Photography
955 W. Fulton
Chicago, IL 60607
312/633-0848 • 312/666-1498 - fax
www.paulshermanphotos.com

Payton Studios
Reginald Payton
2701 W. Fulton
Chicago, IL 60612
312/661-0049
www.paytonstudios.com

Pete Stenberg Photography
(See our ad on page 94)
1048 W. Fulton Market
Chicago, IL 60607
312/421-8850
www.petestenberg.qpg.com

Photographic Creations
Robert D. Wright
15 Stratford Ct.
Indian Head Park, IL 60525
708/246-8043

RICK MITCHELL

PHOTOGRAPHY
652 WEST GRAND AVENUE CHI ILL 60610
312-829-1700
WWW.RICKMITCHELLPHOTO.COM

Photographers

Pete stenberg
PHOTOGRAPHY

1048 West Fulton Market Street
Chicago, IL 60607
tel: (312)421-8850   fax: (312)421-8830
email: pdsphoto@aol.com

elizabeth howard
rita reed 
sean paul bryan 
chase kusero
johnny starks  
eigi chiang
perry hampton
leland burbank 
ann whitney 
krissy bailey 

Free Consultation
Makeup Artist On Staff
Over 20 Years of Experience
Agency & Client Recommended

American Express . VISA
Discover . Mastercard
312.421.8850

94   The Book: An Actor's Guide to Chicago

Photographers

Suzanne Plunkett
3047 N. Lincoln #300
Chicago, IL 60657
773/477-3775
773/477-4640 - fax

Robert Erving Potter III
(See our ad on page 92)
Chicago Photographer
2056 W. Superior
Chicago, IL 60612-1314
312/226-2060
www.chicago-photographer.net

"Rob is endlessly patient with Actors who need headshots, and is tremendously generous with his time. His input and suggestions result in not only excellent professional marketing tools for the Actor, but a more confident Actor as well."

Joyce Sloane, producer emeritus, The Second City.

Pret a Poser Photography
231 George St.
Barrington, IL 60010
847/382-2211
847/842-0494 - fax

Isabel Raci
773/486-1980
773/862-4608

Rubinic Photography
319 N. Western
Chicago, IL 60612
312/733-8901
312/733-8902 - fax
www.rubinic.com

Gerber/Scarpelli Photography
1144 W. Fulton Market
Chicago, IL 60607
312/455-1144
312/455-1544 - fax

Sima Imaging
Sid Afzali
1821 W. Hubbard #301
Chicago, IL 60622
312/733-1788
312/733-6890 - fax

Tom Krantz Photography
180 Marsh Ave.
Montgomery, IL 60538
800/898-6282

Gary Trantafil
312 N. May #100
Chicago, IL 60607
312/666-1029
312/666-1259 - fax

Triangle Studio
3445 N. Broadway
Chicago, IL 60657
773/472-1015
773/472-2201 - fax

Tyrone Taylor Photography
1143 E. 81st
Chicago, IL 60619
773/978-1505

Vic Bider Photography
1142 W. Taylor
Chicago, IL 60607
312/829-5540

Michael Vollan
800 W. Huron - 3rd floor
Chicago, IL 60622
312/997-2347

G. Thomas Ward
1949 W. Leland
Chicago, IL 60640
773/271-6813
www.thepeoplephotographer.com

The Actor's Tools

Ch. 3 The Actor's Tools 95

Photo Reproductions

Are you getting the right exposure?

National Photo Service INCORPORATED

114 West Illinois
Chicago, IL 60610
p (312) 644-5211
f (312) 644-6285
email nps@nationalphoto.com
www.nationaltalent.com

Get all the exposure you need!

Make National Photo your source for
8x10 Head Shots,
Model Comp Cards,
Photo Postcards,
Photo Business Cards,
Digital Retouching,
Slide Duplication
and our Free On-line Talent Database!
We can even store your negatives for easy re-ordering.
With over forty-five years serving the acting and modeling community
National Photo has... everything you need to get exposed!

Photo Reproductions

Wayne Cable Photography
312 N. Carpenter
Chicago, IL 60607
312/226-0303
312/226-6995 - fax

Jean Whiteside
6410 N. Glenwood #1S
Chicago, IL 60626
773/274-5545

Winkelman Photography
P.O. Box 531
Oak Park, IL 60303-0531
312/953-2141

Yamashiro Studio
2643 N. Clybourn
Chicago, IL 60614
312/280-4970
773/883-0453 - fax
www.yamashirostudio.com

Photo Reproductions

A&B Photography
(See our ad on page 98)
650 W. Lake - 2nd floor
Chicago, IL 60661
312/454-4554 • 312/454-1634 - fax

ABC Pictures
(See our ad on page 98)
1867 E. Florida
Springfield, MO 65803
417/869-3456 • 417/869-9185 - fax
www.abcpictures.com

Acme Copy Corp.
218 S. Wabash - 4th floor
Chicago, IL 60604
312/922-6975
312/922-6976 - fax

Artisan Printing & Lithography
445 W. Erie
Chicago, IL 60610
312/337-8400 • 312/337-5631 - fax

Bodhis Photo Service
112 W. Grand
Chicago, IL 60610
312/321-1141
312/321-3610 - fax

Composites International
12335 S. Keeler Ave.
Alsip, IL 60803
708/597-3449
708/597-3421 - fax

Ideal Photos of NYC
155 W. 46th St. - 2nd floor
New York, NY 10036
800/929-5688
212/386-2106 - fax
www.idealphotosofnyc.com

Movie Facts, Inc.
1870 Busse Highway #200
Des Plaines, IL 60016
847/299-9700
847/299-2321 - fax

National Photo Service
(See our ad on page 96)
114 W. Illinois
Chicago, IL 60610
312/644-5211
312/644-6285 - fax
www.nationalphoto.com

Ch. 3 The Actor's Tools

Photo Reproductions

ABC PICTURES

HEADSHOTS COMPOSITES

POSTCARDS • BUSINESS CARDS • POSTERS

1867 E. Florida St.
Dept. P
Springfield, MO
65803

(417) 869-3456
Fax
(417) 869-9185

www.abcpictures.com

B&W
8x10's
500 - $80
1000 - $108

COLOR
8x10's
1000 - $396

other sizes available
Prices Include Typesetting &
Freight in Continental U.S.

Request
FREE
Catalog & Samples

Lucy Hatcher

35 years producing high quality lithographs

Custom Quality Headshots

Our Specialty:
the finest in
photo reprints.

A&B
PHOTOGRAPHY, INC.
650 W. LAKE STREET ◆ CHICAGO 60661

312-454-4554
www.a-bphoto.com

P.S. Mention this ad and receive a 10% discount.

Photo Retouching

Photoscan
646 Bryn Mawr St.
Orlando, FL 32804
800/352-6367
407/839-5029
www.ggphotoscan.com

Quantity Photo
(See our ad on this page)
Rich Pace
119 W. Hubbard - 2nd floor
Chicago, IL 60610
312/644-8290 • 312/644-8299 - fax
www.quantityphoto.com

QUANTITY PHOTO
119 W. HUBBARD ST CHICAGO IL 60610
Actors • Models • Musicians
B&W and Color Promo Photos
Photo Postcards, Photo Business Cards
Retouching and Digital Services
312-644-8288
Photographer and Agency Recommended

The Actor's Tools

A-PAKS Portfolio Bags
www.actorpaks.com
The ActorPak and BactorPak - Specially designed to carry and protect "tools" actors need: headshots, resumes, scripts, cellular and pager. Perfect for auditions, rehearsals or class.

1400 W. Devon Ave.   **773-450-2977**
Chicago, IL 60660-1312   777-907-3092 fax

Photo Retouching

John Bresnahan
3320 N. Clifton
Chicago, IL 60657
773/248-7211

G. Mycio Digital Imaging
333 N. Michigan #715
Chicago, IL 60601
312/782-1472 • 312/782-9874 - fax

Bob Faetz Retouching
203 N. Wabash #1320
Chicago, IL 60601
312/759-0933
312/759-0944 - fax

Irene Levy Retouching Studios
300 N. State #3431
Marina Towers
Chicago, IL 60610
312/464-0504 • 312/464-1665 - fax

Ch. 3 The Actor's Tools **99**

Makeup Artists

Sharleen Acciari
1007 W. Webster
Chicago, IL 60614
773/248-1273

Bianco Scotti Productions
2458 W. 38th
Chicago, IL 60632
312/301-9373

**Cat'Ania's Hollywood
Make-up & Hair**
170th Torrence Ave.
2 River Place #L
Lansing, IL 60438
708/889-9800
708/889-9802 - fax

Makeup, Hair, Cases, Set Bags & Chairs. 24 hour delivery service to your set location & More...

Cheryl Channings
54 E. Oak - 2nd floor
Chicago, IL 60611
312/280-1994
312/280-1929 - fax
www.channings.com

Che Sguardo Makeup Studio
500 N. Wells
Chicago, IL 60610
312/527-0821
888/858-9012

Cathy Durkin
1749 N. Wells #1106
Chicago, IL 60614
312/787-0848

Jeanean-Lorrece Eldridge
P.O. Box 21397
Chicago, IL 60621
773/651-5690

Marcus Geeter
655 W. Irving Park #207
Chicago, IL 60613
773/975-8242
773/296-2905 - fax

Robyn Goldman
312/751-8994

Anna Intravatolo
11350 Behrns
Melrose Park, IL 60164
847/455-2596
847/455-5772 - fax

Blair Laden
1864 Sherman Ave.
Evanston, IL 60201
847/328-1177

Dawn Laurrie
312/837-6404

Marianne Strokirk Salon
361 W. Chestnut
Chicago, IL 60610
312/944-4428
312/944-4429 - fax
www.mariannestrokirk.com

Marilyn Miglin Institute
112 E. Oak
Chicago, IL 60611
800/662-1120
312/943-1184 - fax
www.marilyn-miglin.com

Makeup Artists

Tammy McEwen
630/226-9092
630/710-1288 - cell

Darcy McGrath
312/337-1353

Media Hair & Makeup Group
Maureen Kalagian
708/848-8400

Model Image Center
1218 W. Belmont
Chicago, IL 60657
773/348-9349
773/348-9366 - fax
www.modelimagecenter.com

Sandy Morris
773/549-4951

Andrea Nichols
312/851-6754

Nouvelle Femme
1157 Wilmette Ave.
Wilmette, IL 60091
847/251-6698

Suzi Ostos
773/868-1738
312/688-4540

Shelly Rolf
630/262-1142
630/262-0461 - fax

Nancy P. Stanley
773/871-1396

Transformations by Rori
146 N. Oak Park Ave.
Oak Park, IL 60301
708/383-8338 • 708/383-6796 - fax

Transformations by Rori
110 S. Arlington Heights Rd.
Arlington Heights, IL 60005
847/454-0600

Performink

Chicago's Entertainment Trade Paper, The art, the business, the industry.

www.performink.com
Your source for vital industry news

PerformInk Newspaper is a publication with news and information on the theatre industry in Chicago and the Midwest, including job listings and audition notices. PerformInk's mission is to be a catalyst in the healthy growth of the theatre industry.

To order call 773/296-4600.

New Technology

I pray you mar no more trees with
carving love songs in their barks.

By Kyle Hillman

What was once considered the far future is now reality. We go online for books, banking, and e-business spending hours searching for that elusive collectable on eBay. It was only a matter of time until someone found a way to manipulate the information super highway for actors. Back in December of 1998, PERFORMINK awoke Chicago actors to the promise of online portfolios that would soon change the way actors, agents and casting directors would do business. Unfortunately, two years later, this promise has not yet been realized. The resources and technology are there for this segment of the arts to be cyberized, but the lack of uniformity, education, and the willingness of those in the business to change, often make online portfolios a waste of money.

National corporations like Iam.com are created for the sole purpose to create a Web site that will appeal to artists so that the company can be profitable off of subscription purchases. These businesses attempt to create a central location for artists to gather, share ideas and more importantly promote themselves to industry professionals. They carry much more support from casting directors and agents in the business, and, because of their size, they have more resources to market the actors who have signed up. The downside is that most of the information is not relevant to markets like Chicago and the local agents/casting directors do not wish to be required to search through nonlocal resumés for regional casting calls.

Smaller corporations like Chicagoactors.com and NationalTalent.com are regional equivalents to their national competitors. Their local appeal and relevance often make them a preferred destination for Chicago actors. They also have arrangements with photo duplication companies to host online portfolios free of charge. However, these companies are poorly funded and their Web sites are not updated often enough to make them a staple of every actor's routine. They also lack very important safety features that limit access to your information to industry professionals only. It also appears that neither regional company is supported nor used by the local agents/casting directors.

IAM.COM

Created in Spring 2000, Iam.com is a relative new guy on the block of online portfolios. However, with the recent bankruptcy of Castnet.com, they are now the country's only such national corporation. They aim to promote not just actors, but dancers, models and musicians on their site. While Iam.com lacks support from agents/casting directors, their layout is cleaner and easier to navigate then Castnet. They currently have one free basic membership and two types of online portfolio packages, Premiere and Pro that cost only $29.95 and $149.95, respectively. The free basic membership does not allow you an online portfolio but gives you access to the online artist community. The Premiere package contains two photos, one audio sample, a resumé, and basic membership rights; while the Pro package allows you to have 10 photos, three audio samples, one video sample, a resumé and basic membership rights. Iam.com also has a secured network for safety and boasts the support of Hollywood directors like Spike Lee.

New Technology

CHICAGOACTORS.COM

Created in September of 1999, Chicagoactors.com is the leader of regional online portfolios. They have a collection of Chicago-only actors who are searchable by every physical category possible. They also have an extensive list of online resources that point the viewer to the Chicago theatre scene. However, their review section seems out of date and while the online audition list appears current, it will not be a usable resource until other theatre companies and agencies use the posting service more frequently. While Chicagoactors.com costs $35.00 per year (+ $25.00 one time setup fee), the service is free to the clients of Quantity Photo Co. This site with extra funding, spiced up layout, an active Webmaster, and support from the Chicago industry could become a very valuable resource for Chicago actors. However, its current state leaves much to be desired.

NATIONALTALENT.COM

Chicago's other regional online portfolio host, NationalTalent.com, is a branch off service from National Photo's photo duplication business. NationalTalent.com offers online portfolios and a searchable database, but like their competitor, they do not have safety features limiting access to your portfolios. The service costs a hefty $40.00 every 6 months, but they allow free postings to actors who use their service of duplication. The site lacks extra features and their audition line doesn't have the support from industry professionals to make it worth your time.

WHAT SHOULD YOU DO?

If you're getting your headshots duplicated by either service, take advantage of their free offers and get your online portfolio. The process usually takes a couple of weeks, but any type of promotion for artists is a positive one. Due to their lack of security features, make sure you list only your agents number or at minimum, a voicemail account. Besides, it is always beneficial to send your work through your agent; shady companies will steer clear of reputable agencies.

If you have money to burn or are heading to L.A., purchase an account with one of the national companies. The L.A. market seems more open to these technologies than Chicago and having an online portfolio to promote yourself cannot hurt.

If you cannot afford either option and yet you feel you need to have an online presence, go to **www.homestead.com** and sign up for a free Web site. They have a very easy program that will have you up and running in minutes. You can also take your headshot into a local Kinko's to get a digital copy.

Once you're up, forget about it! Despite the possibilities, online portfolios are still not going to land you the job, an agent, or notoriety. Down the road, those things may become possible, but in the meantime, you still need to send in headshots, attend open calls, sign up for classes, and, most importantly, work on your craft.

- E-mail Notifications of New Auditions!
- Featured Actor of the Month
- E-Register for FREE!
- Internet Casting - Get ready for the future

ChicagoActors.com

Resumés

A Look at the bad side of Resumés

O, sir, we quarrel in print, by the book, as you have books for good manners.

By Kevin Heckman

The resumé that is glued, stapled or otherwise affixed (hopefully) to the back of your headshot is a key piece of your presentation. No one gets hired in this business based on their resumé, but a good one garners more respect and a bad one can lose you a job.

For information on what should go into a resumé, check out (appropriately) our checklist. If you'd like to know some of the things that shouldn't, read on.

Actually, these particular points I mention aren't all big no-no's, though some are. I also include things I or other directors have simply found strange. Each of these oddities has appeared in some form on actual resumés.

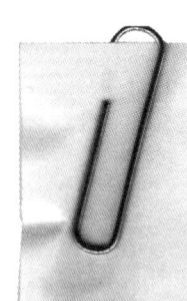

Nadia E. Phektev
EMC

Height: 5'7"
Hair: Ochre
Eyes: Hazel
Voice: High Tenor

The EMC thang

I've never understood why actors list their EMC (Equity Membership Candidate) status under their name. I assume it's a spin-off of listing your union memberships there, but union membership affects casting and EMC doesn't. EMC's gather weeks by working as a non-Equity actor in certain Equity houses. Once they accumulate 50 weeks, they have to join the union with their next Equity job or drop their EMC status. The only situation in which EMC could influence casting is if Nadia has close to 50 weeks. Otherwise, she's just emphasizing something that doesn't matter.

Nadia E. Phektev
EMC

Height: 5'7"
Hair: Ochre
Eyes: Hazel
Voice: High Tenor

Call that actor...

Wow, Nadia gave a great audition. I should definitely give her a call. Many directors separate your headshot and resumé from the cover letter that accompanied it. If your resumé doesn't have contact info, no one will contact you. Of course, many actors don't list an address or their home phone numbers as a security precaution, but you've got to give casting people some way to reach you.

Nadia E. Phektev
EMC

Height: 5'7"
Hair: Ochre
Eyes: Hazel
Voice: High Tenor

Resumés

What does she look like?

If a casting director gets 200 headshots and resumés over a three-day span, and if two percent of the headshots are attached to their accompanying resumés with only a paper clip, what are the odds that that paper clip will successfully keep those resumés with their headshots? If you chose E. Not Good, you're correct!! Those resumés will probably get tossed. Staple, glue, whatever. Just make sure your resumé stays attached to your picture.

Production	Role	Theatre
Ten Little Indians	Tonto	Misaligned Theatre
You're a Good Man Charlie Brown	Calvin	Griffin Ascending
I'm 25 and Who the Fuck Cares	Bette	Stage Left
Dark at the Top of the Stairs	The Electrician	Goomdan Theater
Red Noses	The Pediatrician	Off-Stage Right

Who produced this show?

What's wrong with this picture? Only that Stage Left didn't produce *I'm 25 and Who the Fuck Cares*. It went up at Stage Left, but was produced by Irrelevant Players. Needless to say, if this resumé shows up at Stage Left, this actor's probably not going to get called in. Furthermore, any director who's familiar with Stage Left is probably going to think that this actor's lying about their work. Not the image she wanted to project.

Production	Role	Theatre
Ten Little Indians	Tonto	Misaligned Theatre
You're a Good Man Charlie Brown	Calvin	Griffin Ascending
I'm 25 and Who the Fuck Cares	Bette	Stage Left
Dark at the Top of the Stairs	The Electrician	Goomdan Theater
Red Noses	The Pediatrician	Audience Right Theatre
Tight-Ass Androgynous	The Queen	Theatre Pyu
Glass Meringue	Chef Tom	The Hyperactives
Six Degrees of Being Apart	Sydney Poitier	Eating Crow Theater
Billy Joe and the Remarkably Hued Overcoat	Billy Joe	Downtown Hilton Theater
Goddamn Car	Driver	Well-Known Window Productions
Always Cross-Hatched	Binky	Regal Porgie Playhouse
A Collection of Blue Hominids	The Blue One	Nettles Road Theatre

Get me my magnifying glass, Watson

The fact is, many directors look more closely at your training and skills than they do your credits. There's no reason to cram every show you've ever done on your resumé. Choose those credits that put you in the best light. Include name theatres, well-known shows or anything that got good press. You may even want to have different resumés for different genres: classical work, musicals, children's theatre, etc. Then you can emphasize work that particularly suits you for that genre.

Education & Training
B.A.-Theatre/Astrology-Mulligan University
Physical Theatre-Plastic Bean Performance Group
Vocal Performance-Camilla Rosen

Special Skills
Driver-Moped, Stage Combat, Basic Tumbling, Dialects (New York, Texas, Deep South, Western Pennsylvania), Puppetry, Winking at Boys

Well isn't that special

Actors go to all sorts of lengths to be sure their resumé will be noticed. In this case, the actor has printed her resumé on cloud paper. Unfortunately, clouds or flowers or pink neon paper are more likely to upstage your resumé than call attention to it. They'll remember the paper but not the person. Present yourself as a professional. If your resumé feels sparse, do a student film, take a class, or work for one of Chicago's dozens of small theatres who might see your potential to build your resumé. A cheap attention grabber can annoy casting people and that will hurt instead of help.

Additionally, beware of the cute special skill. First of all, be sure it's a skill. "Winking at boys" isn't really that difficult, and listing it won't necessarily impress anyone. Also, be sure you can do whatever it is the moment they ask. If you list "Belch the Pledge of Allegiance" as a skill, you'd better be able to do it right there. Special Skills can help you get the job, but it's also part of your presentation. If you get too cutesy, casting people are less likely to treat you as a professional.

Chances are, most of these errors or oddities aren't going to make or break your chances at getting the part, but your resumé introduces you and it should introduce you as a professional actor. If you've done that, you're one step closer to convincing a director you should be seriously considered for the part.

Resumé Checklist

Your resumé is often the most important piece of material a casting director or agent will receive from you. Present yourself in the best light possible. Highlight your strengths. Be sure that it's easy to read. And don't forget to include:

1. **Your name**
   This should be at the top and in the largest font.

2. **Your stats**
   Height, weight, hair and eye color are all standard. Don't include your age or age range. They'll figure that out themselves.

3. **Your beeper or contact number**
   Obviously you want to be reachable. Don't include your address unless they specifically ask for it. You never know who'll get their hands on your resumé. Some agencies won't want your number on the resumé. They want all bookings to go through them. If you do have your number on a resumé and you get a call that should go through your agent, refer it to your agent. Work leads to work.

   beep!

4. **Room for an agency stamp or sticker**
   Once you get representation, you don't want to have to completely redesign your resumé!

5. **For theatre, film, etc.**
   a. List production name to the left,
   b. Your role in the middle,
   c. Theatre, studio or production company to the right.

6. **For film, also indicate type of work (i.e. "Day Player" or "Principal")**
   You may have been brilliant in that independent film, but the agent/director may never have seen it. Listing "Queen Anne" on your resumé doesn't tell them anything, but indicating it was a principal does.

7. Training
   Either list
   Areas of training
   Corresponding teachers

   Or
   Schools or studios
   Classes taken

   Use whichever method shows you off best. If you've had impressive teachers, be sure to mention their names. If you've trained at schools that are recognizable, mention them.

8. University degrees
9. Special skills
10. Dialects
11. Sports (Indicate level of skill)
12. Languages spoken (Indicate fluency)
13. Odd skills or talents (Be sure you can do it!!)
    Anything that doesn't fit into the above categories can go here. A lot of actors get cute in this section. That's fine, but if you list "Choking dog impressions" you'd better be able to impersonate a choking dog on a moment's notice.
14. Commercials
    Write "Commercial list available upon request"
    This keeps you from getting into the sensitive and confusing issue of product conflict until you have to.

Ch. 3 The Actor's Tools 111

Cover Letter Checklist

This is often your first introduction to an agent or director. Remember your audience; they see dozens of these letters each day, so you want to be sure that yours is to the point and presents you in a good light. There are a few things you can do to ensure this.

1. ## Confirm the Names
   How would you feel getting a letter that's intended for you, but misspells your name?

2. ## Keep it Short
   Remember, they see dozens of these letters and aren't interested in reading your life story.

3. ## Contents

   ### Name, Number and Address
   You must include your basic stats: name, address and contact numbers on your cover letter. Don't assume that they'll refer to the information on your headshot; make it as easy for them as possible.

   ### It's OK to Name-Drop
   If you know someone who's represented by the agent, mention that (s)he speaks well of that agent. Keep it appropriate. Mentioning that you met John Lennon's cousin once is probably not going to help you.

   ### Give Referrals
   If there's a director or teacher that will speak well of you, mention them. Be sure to OK this with the individual in question first.

   ### Talk About Your Present Work
   Are you doing a good show? Taking an exciting class? Auditioning for anything interesting? Mention it. Anything that indicates that you're pursuing your craft will make you look better.

   ### What Are Your Goals?
   How can this particular agency help you get where you want to go? Keep this brief and fairly specific.

Trade Papers

Resumé Services

Act I Bookstore
2540 N. Lincoln
Chicago, IL 60614
773/348-6757
800/55PLAYS
773/348-5561 - fax
www.act1books.com

Act I Bookstore serves everyone from Chicago to Sao Paolo to Istanbul for its theatre and film book needs. You can find thousands of plays, acting books, screenplays, agent listings, monologues, musicals, audition notices, reading copies of shows currently auditioning, a professional resumé service, theatre games, and many other books for actors, directors, writers, producers, designers, teachers and filmmakers. Open Mon-Wed 10-8 and Thur-Sun 10-6. The best online bookstore for theatre and film is www.act1books.com.

Bob Behr
Resumés by Mac
4738 N. LaPorte
Chicago, IL 60630
773/685-7721
773/283-9839 - fax

CastNet
5757 Wilshire Blvd #124
Los Angeles, CA 90036
888/873-7373
323/964-1050 - fax
www.castnet.com

Ink Well
112 W. Illinois
Chicago, IL 60610
312/644-4700
312/644-4703 – fax

Trade Papers

Act One Reports
640 N. LaSalle #535
Chicago, IL 60610
312/787-9384
312/787-3234 - fax
www.actone.com

Updated listings of Chicago-area agencies, casting directors, photographers, and industry related information.

American Theatre
355 Lexington Ave.
New York, NY 10017
212/697-5230
212/557-5817 - fax
www.tcg.org

National theatre periodical containing news, features, and articles.

Audition News
P.O. Box 250
Bloomingdale, IL 60108
630/894-2278
630/894-8364 - fax

Audition notices for the greater Midwest.

Backstage
1515 Broadway - 14th floor
New York, NY 10036-8986
212/536-5368
800/437-3183 - subscriptions
www.backstage.com

The theatrical trade paper for the east coast.

Trade Papers

Backstage West
5055 Wilshire Blvd. - 5th floor
Los Angeles, CA 90036
323/525-2356
323/525-2354 - fax
www.backstagewest.com

The theatrical trade paper for the west coast.

Breakdown Services, Ltd.
1120 S. Robertson Blvd. - 3rd floor
Los Angeles, CA 90035
310/276-9166
310/276-8829 - fax
www.breakdownservices.com

Creates cast breakdowns for film, TV, theatre and commercials.

Callboard
870 Market St. #375
San Francisco, CA 94102
415/430-1140
415/430-1145 - fax
www.theatrebayarea.org

The theatrical trade paper for the San Francisco area.

Casting News
P.O. Box 201
Boston, MA 02134
617/787-2991

The theatre and film trade for Boston and Eastern Massachusettes.

CastNet
5757 Wilshire Blvd #124
Los Angeles, CA 90036
888/873-7373
323/964-1050 - fax
www.castnet.com

The Chicago Creative Directory
333 N. Michigan #810
Chicago, IL 60601
312/236-7337
312/236-6078 - fax
www.creativedir.com

Equity News
Actor's Equity Association
165 W. 46th
New York, NY 10036
212/719-9570
212/921-8454 - fax

Union news and updates for members.

Hollywood Reporter
5055 Wilshire Blvd.
Los Angeles, CA 90036
323/525-2150
323/525-1583 - fax
www.hollywoodreporter.com

The National Casting Guide
888/332-6700
www.pgdirect.com

Resource directory for the acting industry on a national basis.

PerformInk
3223 N. Sheffield - 3rd floor
Chicago, IL 60657
773/296-4600
773/296-4621 - fax
www.performink.com

Chicago's Entertainment Trade Paper. The art, the business, the industry.

Answering Services

Ross Reports Television and Film
1515 Broadway - 14th floor
New York, NY 10036
800/817-3273
212/536-5178
212/536-5294 - fax
www.backstage.com/rossreports

Updates on production and casting in feature film and television.

Screen Magazine
16 W. Erie - 2nd floor
Chicago, IL 60610
312/664-5236
312/664-8425 - fax
www.screenmag.com

Chicago's film trade paper.

Show Music Magazine
Goodspeed Opera House
Box 466 - Goodspeed Landing
East Haddam, CT 06423-0466
860/873-8664
860/873-2329 - fax
www.goodspeed.org

Side Splitters
P.O. Box 5353
Wheaton, IL 60189
630/942-9710

Theatre Directories
(See our ad on page 118)
P.O. Box 510
Dorset, VT 05251
802/867-2223
800/390-2223
802/867-0144 - fax
www.theatredirectories.com

Publishes Summer Theatre Directory, Regional Theatre Directory and more.

Variety
P.O. Box 16507
North Hollywood, CA 91615-6507
800/323-4345 - weekly
800/552-3632 - daily
www.variety.com

Answering Services

Burke Communications
P.O. Box 4152
Oak Park, IL 60303-4152
708/383-8580
708/386-1336 - fax
www.magicallone.com

Not answering the phone?

Check out the Meditation listings on page 309

Ch. 3 The Actor's Tools **115**

Cell Phones

Beepers

Comm One Wireless
1437 W. Taylor
Chicago, IL 60607
312/850-9400
312/850-9442 - fax

Electronic Beepers Inc.
61 E. Washington
Chicago, IL 60602
312/332-6024

MCI Worldcom
800/571-6682
312/781-6030

PortaCom
531 S. Dearborn
Chicago, IL 60605
312/939-PAGE
312/939-7759 - fax

Skytel
800/456-3333

SmartBeep
800/BEEP-199

The Sound Advantage
2911 N. Clark
Chicago, IL 60657
773/404-1288
773/404-1291 - fax

Verizon Wireless
800/MOBILE-1

Weblink Wireless
800/864-4357
888/304-9899 - fax
www.pagemart.com

FANTASY HEADQUARTERS
OVER 1 MILLION ITEMS IN STOCK • 1 CITY BLOCK LONG

1,000'S OF COSTUMES
RENTALS & SALES FOR ANY OCCASION

- SANTA CLAUS
- EASTER BUNNY
- MASCOT
- MARDI GRAS
- PURIM • HAWAII
- THEATRICAL COSTUMES & WIGS
- EXTENSIVE MAKE UP
- NOVELTIES & GAGS
- ALL SEASONS & HOLIDAYS
- 1000'S OF MASKS
- MAGIC
- PARTY GOODS
- ADULT GIFTS
- ACCESSORIES

OPEN 7 DAYS

BUSINESS • CORPORATE • SCHOOLS
A Huge Selection Of Kids & Adults
Costumes & Accessories All Year Round

(773) 777-0222
4065 N. Milwaukee Ave. • Chicago, IL 60641

---

116 The Book: An Actor's Guide to Chicago

Makeup Supplies

Cell Phones

Verizon Wireless
800/MOBILE-1

AT&T
888/344-3332

Cellular One
800/CELLONE

Comm One Wireless
1437 W. Taylor
Chicago, IL 60607
312/850-9400
312/850-9442 - fax

MCI Worldcom
800/571-6682
312/781-6030

Prime Co.
800/774-6326

The Sound Advantage
2911 N. Clark
Chicago, IL 60657
773/404-1288
773/404-1291 - fax

Makeup Supplies

All Dressed Up Costumes
150 S. Water
Batavia, IL 60510
630/879-5130 • 630/879-3374 - fax
www.alldressedupcostumes.com

Broadway Costumes, Inc.
1100 W. Cermak
Chicago, IL 60608
312/829-6400 • 312/829-8621 - fax
www.broadwaycostumes.com

Cat'Ania's Hollywood Make-up & Hair
170th Torrence Ave.
2 River Place #L
Lansing, IL 60438
708/889-9800 • 708/889-9802 - fax

Offers a Complete Line of Professional Cosmetics, Beauty Products & Accessories for the Television, Theatre & Motion Picture Industry. IMAN, RCMA, Pattie LaBelle, Toni & Tina Aromatherapy, Kryolan, Ben Nye, La Femme, Paul Mitchell, American Crew, Wigs, Hair Pieces, Tools & Accessories, Cases, Professional Seminars & Workshops for TV, Motion Picture & Stage, Costumes, Beauty Salon, Delivery, 24 Hour Service & More.

Center Stage
497 Rt. 59
Aurora, IL 60504
630/851-9191

Che Sguardo Makeup Studio
500 N. Wells
Chicago, IL 60610
312/527-0821
888/858-9012

Chicago Hair Group
734 N. LaSalle
Chicago, IL 60610
312/337-4247
Focusing primarily on wigs.

Fantasy Costumes Headquarters
(See our ad on page 117)
4065 N. Milwaukee
Chicago, IL 60641
773/777-0222
800/USA-WIGS
773/777-4228 - fax
www.fantasycostumes.com

Ch. 3 The Actor's Tools 117

Makeup Supplies

Grand Stage Lighting Company
630 W. Lake
Chicago, IL 60661
312/332-5611
312/258-0056 - fax

Josie O'Kain Costume & Theatre Shop
2419B W. Jefferson St.
Joliet, IL 60435
815/741-9303
815/741-9316 - fax
www.josieokain.com

A Magical Mystery Tour
6010 W. Dempster
Morton Grove, IL 60053
847/966-5090
847/966-7280 - fax

Razzle Dazzle Costumes
1038 Lake St.
Oak Park, IL 60301
708/383-5962
708/383-0069 - fax

Riley's Trick & Novelty Shop
6442 W. 111th
Worth, IL 60482
708/448-0075
708/448-0999 - fax
www.rileystrickshop.com

The Actor's Picture/Resume Book

2nd Revised Edition
by Jill Charles, with photographer Tom Bloom

Finding a Photographer
Styles of P/R's ✳ Clothing & make-up
56 Photographs ✳ Sample Resumes
Worksheets to Help You Get Organized

Available at Act 1 Bookstore, or call

(802) 867-2223

Internet Orders Welcome:
✳ **www.theatredirectories.com** ✳

$16.95 plus $3 s/h ($4.25 priority)

---

118 The Book: An Actor's Guide to Chicago

Lighting Rental

Stage Weapons

The Armoury American Fencers Supply
1180 Folsom St.
San Francisco, CA 94103
415/863-7911
415/431-4931 - fax
www.amfence.com

Arms and Armor
1101 Stinson Blvd. NE
Minneapolis, MN 55413
612/331-6473
www.armor.com

Center Firearms Co.
10 W. 37th St.
New York, NY 10018
212/244-4040 • 212/947-1233 - fax

Sheet Music

Act I Bookstore
2540 N. Lincoln
Chicago, IL 60614
773/348-6757 • **800/55PLAYS**
773/348-5561 - fax
www.act1books.com

Act I Bookstore serves everyone from Chicago to Sao Paolo to Istanbul for its theatre and film book needs. You can find thousands of plays, acting books, screenplays, agent listings, monologues, musicals, audition notices, reading copies of shows currently auditioning, a professional resumé service, theatre games, and many other books for actors, directors, writers, producers, designers, teachers and filmmakers. Open Mon-Wed 10-8 and Thur-Sun 10-6. The best online bookstore for theatre and film is www.act1books.com.

Carl Fisher Music
333 S. State
Chicago, IL 60604
312/427-6652 • 312/427-6653 - fax

Lighting Rental

Chicago Spotlight, Inc.
1658 W. Carroll
Chicago, IL 60612
312/455-1171
312/455-1744 - fax
www.chicagospotlight.com

Designlab
806 N. Peoria - 2nd floor
Chicago, IL 60622
312/738-3305 • 312/738-2402 - fax
www.designlab-chicago.com

Grand Stage Lighting Company
630 W. Lake
Chicago, IL 60661
312/332-5611 • 312/258-0056 - fax

Dance Supplies

American Dance Center Ballet Co.
10464 W. 163rd Pl.
Orland Park, IL 60462
708/747-4969
708/747-0424 - fax

Big N Little Shoes
3142 W. 111th
Chicago, IL 60655
773/239-6066

Dance & Mime Shop
643 W. Grand
Chicago, IL 60610
312/666-4406

Illinois Theatrical
P.O. Box 34284
Chicago, IL 60634
773/745-7777
800/745-3777
800/877-6027 - fax

Leo's Dancewear
1900 N. Narragansett
Chicago, IL 60639
773/745-5600
773/889-7593 - fax

Motion Unlimited
218 S. Wabash - 8th floor
Chicago, IL 60604
312/922-3330
312/922-7770 - fax

Costume Shops

All Dressed Up Costumes
150 S. Water
Batavia, IL 60510
630/879-5130
630/879-3374 - fax
www.alldressedupcostumes.com

Bead Different
214 E. Chicago Ave.
Westmont, IL 60559
630/323-1962

Beatnix
3400 N. Halsted
Chicago, IL 60657
773/281-6933

Beverly Costume Shop
11628 S. Western
Chicago, IL 60643
773/779-0068
773/779-2434 - fax

Broadway Costumes, Inc.
1100 W. Cermak
Chicago, IL 60608
312/829-6400
312/829-8621 - fax
www.broadwaycostumes.com

Cat'Ania's Hollywood Make-up & Hair
170th Torrence Ave.
2 River Place #L
Lansing, IL 60438
708/889-9800
708/889-9802 - fax

Costume Shops

Center Stage
497 Rt. 59
Aurora, IL 60504
630/851-9191

Chicago Costume Company
1120 W. Fullerton
Chicago, IL 60614
773/528-1264
773/935-4197 - fax
www.chicagocostume.com

Cindy Makes Things
2000 W. Carroll
Chicago, IL 60612
312/829-0099
312/829-0998 - fax
www.cindymakesthings.com

Dance & Mime Shop
643 W. Grand
Chicago, IL 60610
312/666-4406

Facemakers, Inc.
140 Fifth St.
Savannah, IL 61074
815/273-3944
815/273-3966 - fax

Fantasy Costumes Headquarters
(See our ad on page 116)
4065 N. Milwaukee
Chicago, IL 60641
773/777-0222
800/USA-WIGS
773/777-4228 - fax
www.fantasycostumes.com

Flashy Trash
3524 N. Halsted
Chicago, IL 60657
773/327-6900 • 773/327-9736 - fax

Hubba Hubba
3309 N. Clark
Chicago, IL 60657
773/477-1414
773/477-1412 - fax

Josie O'Kain Costume & Theatre Shop
2419B W. Jefferson St.
Joliet, IL 60435
815/741-9303
815/741-9316 - fax
www.josieokain.com

Leo's Dancewear
1900 N. Narragansett
Chicago, IL 60639
773/745-5600
773/889-7593 - fax

A Lost Eras Costumes & Props
Charlotte Walters
1511 W. Howard
Chicago, IL 60626
773/764-7400
773/764-7433 - fax

A Magical Mystery Tour
6010 W. Dempster
Morton Grove, IL 60053
847/966-5090
847/966-7280 - fax

Razzle Dazzle Costumes
1038 Lake St.
Oak Park, IL 60301
708/383-5962
708/383-0069 - fax

Show Off
1472 Elmhurst Rd.
Elk Grove Village, IL 60007
847/439-0206
847/439-0219 - fax

The Actor's Tools

Thrift Stores

Task Force Military
2341 W. Belmont
Chicago, IL 60618
773/477-7096

Victorian Emphasis
918 Green Bay Rd.
Winnetka, IL 60093
847/229-1227

Thrift Stores

Ark Thrift Shop
3345 N. Lincoln
Chicago, IL 60657
773/248-1117

Ark Thrift Shop
1302 N. Milwaukee
Chicago, IL 60622
773/862-5011

Chicago's Recycle Shop
5308 N. Clark
Chicago, IL 60640
773/878-8525

Sale Barn Square
971 N. Milwaukee
Wheeling, IL 60090
847/537-9886
www.salebarnsquare.com

Disgraceland
3338 N. Clark
Chicago, IL 60657
773/281-5875

Brown Elephant Resale
3651 N. Halsted
Chicago, IL 60657
773/549-5943

Brown Elephant Resale
3939 N. Ashland
Chicago, IL 60657
773/244-2930

Kismet Vintage Clothing and Furniture
2923 N. Southport
Chicago, IL 60657
773/528-4497

Little City Resale Shop
1760 W. Algonquin
Palatine, IL 60067
847/221-7130
847/358-3291 - fax

Ragstock
812 W. Belmont - 2nd floor
Chicago, IL 60657
773/868-9263
773/868-6819 - fax
www.ragstock.com

Right Place
5219 N. Clark
Chicago, IL 60640
773/561-7757

Salvation Army Thrift Store
General Number
773/477-1771
www.salvationarmy.org

Threads
2327 N. Milwaukee
Chicago, IL 60622
773/276-6411

Bookstores

Time Well
Consignment Furniture
2780 N. Lincoln
Chicago, IL 60614
773/549-2113
www.chicago-
antiques.com/timewell.htm

Unique Thrift Store
3224 S. Halsted
Chicago, IL 60608
312/842-8123

White Elephant Shop
Children's Memorial Hospital
2380 N. Lincoln
Chicago, IL 60614
773/883-6184

Libraries

Harold Washington Public Library
Chicago Public Libraries
400 S. State
Chicago, IL 60610
312/747-4300
www.chipublib.org

Newberry Library
60 W. Walton
Chicago, IL 60610
312/943-9090

North Suburban Library System
847/459-1300
www.nslsilus.org

Stock Montage
104 N. Halsted #200
Chicago, IL 60661
312/733-3239
312/733-2844 - fax
Library of stock stills

Bookstores

Act I Bookstore
2540 N. Lincoln
Chicago, IL 60614
773/348-6757 • 800/55PLAYS
773/348-5561 - fax
www.act1books.com

Act I Bookstore serves everyone from Chicago to Sao Paolo to Istanbul for its theatre and film book needs. You can find thousands of plays, acting books, screenplays, agent listings, monologues, musicals, audition notices, reading copies of shows currently auditioning, a professional resumé service, theatre games, and many other books for actors, directors, writers, producers, designers, teachers and filmmakers. Open Mon-Wed 10-8 and Thur-Sun 10-6. The best online bookstore for theatre and film is www.act1books.com.

Afterwords Bookstore
23 E. Illinois
Chicago, IL 60611
312/464-1110
www.abebooks.com/home/afterwords

Ch. 3 The Actor's Tools 123

Casting Hotlines

Barbara's Bookstore
1350 N. Wells
Chicago, IL 60610
312/642-5044
312/642-0522 - fax

Barbara's Bookstore
700 E. Grand
Chicago, IL 60611
312/222-0890

Barnes and Noble Bookstore
659 W. Diversey
Chicago, IL 60614
773/871-9004
773/871-5893 - fax
www.bn.com

Borders Books, Music & Cafe
830 N. Michigan
Chicago, IL 60610
312/573-0564
www.borders.com

Borders Books & Music
2817 N. Clark
Chicago, IL 60657
773/935-3909
www.borders.com

Feedback Theatrebooks
P.O. Box 220
Brooklin, ME 04616
207/359-2781
207/359-5532 - fax
Publishes books dealing with theatre.

Showfax
800/886-8716
www.showfax.com

Unabridged Books
3251 N. Broadway
Chicago, IL 60657
773/883-9119
773/883-9559 - fax

Casting Hotlines

The latest auditions are put on these hotlines first. The Audition Hotline is updated twice weekly.

Audition Hotline
312/409-9900

Illinois Filmboard Hotline
312/427-FILM

Talent and Casting Agencies

I've come for my 15%. Bwaahahahaha!!

Free Associates, "Back in the Shadows"

The Agent Biz

I speak not this, that you should bear a good opinion of my knowledge; insomuch, I say, I know you are; neither do I labour for a greater esteem than may in some little measure draw a belief from you, to do yourself good, and not to grace me. Believe then, if you please, that I can do strange things.

By Ben Winters

If you think being a performer is a tough gig, try being a talent agent for a day or two. For one thing, an agent is a person who spends all day interacting with advertising executives and actors, two professional classes not known for their equanimity. But the real tricky part is the business itself; as actors well know, entertainment is as stormy and variable an industry as they come.

"It's like a roller coaster, this business," testifies Elizabeth Geddes of the stalwart Geddes Agency, which first opened its door as a modeling agency back in 1967. "There's some really good years and some really awful years, and there's no way to tell what the next year is going to bring."

Agents

In 1970, the City of Chicago Yellow Pages included dozens upon dozens of listings for modeling agents (including the Playboy Agency, which lasted until the late 1980's) and a mere handful for screen and stage talent. By 1980 "theatrical agents"— as they are still, mostly inaccurately, classified— were on the upswing, with thirty or more in the business of finding performers for industrial films, television and radio commercials, and the odd TV show. (Plus the significant fraction of these who existed to represent performers in "belly dancing, strip tease and the exotic arts.")

What's interesting, as one charts the ebb and flow of the agencies over the years, is that the progression has never been a steady upward curve, with each subsequent year bringing more and more agents. The 1988 Sourcebook, an advertising industry bible that lists who's who in town, names fewer talent agents than were extant ten years earlier. By 2000, over a decade later, that number had remained about steady— until three agencies got out of the game late in the year.

The quantity and quality of talent agencies (like the quantity and quality of work available) is controlled by a zillion more or less knowable factors, from who's in the Mayor's office to what advertising theories are currently in fashion to the country and city's overall economic health. Agents, like the actors they seek to represent, are constantly at the mercy of an ever-changing marketplace.

This much is undeniable: Chicago's rise as a theatre town, accomplished in the later decades of the twentieth century, coupled with the tremendous importance of the local advertising business (with many of the world's most famous ad-game players located up and down Michigan Avenue) have created a singular atmosphere. With the possible exception of New York, there's nowhere else in the world where so many actors are in such close proximity to the people who need them to move product.

"I think Steppenwolf and some of the Remains [Theater] guys brought that here," says Geddes on how Chicago's explosion as a theatre scene helped court the attention of the commercial industry. "There's that reputation that just precedes the actor: If you have Steppenwolf or Remains or the Goodman on your resumé, people want to meet you, absolutely."

Nor is it just the actors who've been lucky enough to trod the boards at Steppenwolf who get in on that good fortune; with the rise to prominence of not only Steppenwolf and Goodman, but of Second City and other Chicago-based theatrical heavy hitters, the entire acting community developed a desirable sheen. And it was an acting community that was ever-growing: Actors in search of roles were (and are) drawn to the same well-reputed theaters as advertisers in search of talent.

Ch. 4 Talent and Casting Agencies

Agents

Chicago became known as a place with not only a lot of actors, but with a lot of very good actors.

"People come here because they know they're going to get really good, really honest actors," Geddes explains. "I think you bring this thread through in your work, and it's true, it's real, you're in the moment, it's really honest work."

It's a reputation that has only strengthened over the years.

"We're definitely known for it," says one local agent with several years of on-camera experience. "Especially in LA and New York, people look at Chicago actors as real people, really strong actors with not only industry experience, but really great theatre experience. We've also got some amazing schools, like Northwestern and DePaul, where a huge pool of...talent has come from."

"With our theatrical people and our Second City people who go out to LA [who] are repped by our LA office, I know [the LA office has] said how thrilled they are with how well our actors are trained," reports Debby Kotzen, formerly of CED and now president of her own voice-over agency, Naked Voices. "The actors who are trained in Chicago are generally of a higher caliber than those coming from LA."

Predating the solidification of Chicago as a center for acting talent (and arguably contributing to it) was the town's earlier establishment as a pillar of the advertising business. In the postwar ad boom of the 1950's, Chicago rose to prominence of the back of innovators like Leo Burnett (father of the so-called Chicago School of advertising) and Fairfax Cone of Foote, Cone and Belding. Such agencies remained relevant by holding on to their key customers as television became the key advertising mode. Local advertisers point to the famous "Where's the Beef?" spot of the early 1980's as pure Chicago: quirky, mildly bizarre, and incredibly catchy.

The talent agencies that sprang up over the 1970's, those that managed to survive, found their niche brokering between a growing talent pool and a growing pool of advertisers. Though the advertising business is overwhelmingly concentrated in New York, huge amounts of casting and shooting are done here in Chicago.

"The main [acting] industries in Chicago are commercial work and theatre, as opposed to industrials and film," says one local on-camera agent with several years in the business. "Commercials are the largest amount of work that we get here in Chicago, whereas in Los Angeles it's clearly film and TV, and in New York it's film, TV, and theatre. In Chicago, it's commercials, then industrials as well, and then theatre."

Within this general state of affairs there are the constant shifts and sea changes, inevitable in a business driven by the ever-changing needs of the advertising industry. Talent Agencies like ETA, Inc. and Salazar & Navas, which respectively specialize in representing African-American and Hispanic/Latin "types", found their place in the ad world as it gained respect for the non-white demographics.

Similarly, a late eighties to early nineties call in the market for non-traditional voice-over talent (meaning voices other than the game show/talk show booming male archetype) has meant a corresponding leap in interest from local performers who can fit the bill, and a need for agencies and agents to represent them. This has held particularly true for female voices, as it sank in to the advertising business that there was a new class of working wives with discretionary income, and who better to pitch to that market that women?

Kotzen notes another recent development in the voice-over demimonde:

"I know [in past years] the ad agencies did all of their auditions in-house, and they are not doing as many in-house any more," she explains. "They're all going to agents... they've cut back on their people. In New York they still have a fair amount of auditions that are done in the ad agencies, but here and in LA they don't."

Meanwhile, agents have responded to their client's desire to bring in more and more people for each potential gig— which means more work for the agent, and, not incidentally, a more frustrating situation for actors.

"It's a fiercely competitive market at every level," reports Lisa Lewis, a local actress and voice-over veteran. "There's a lot of competition....you used to go to an audition where there would be thirty people, and now there's a hundred. Everything is a cattle call."

Another, more painful example of the fickle nature of the agency game is the SAG/AFTRA strike that halted all union production for over six months in 2000. Union-franchised agencies had no choice but to wait it out until work could resume, and at least three— Harrise Davidson, Sa-Rah, and the local branch of CED, a national powerhouse— didn't make it.

Even without the strike, business has gotten tighter in recent years, thanks to a variety of unsettling trends summarized by longtime local standby Davidson, who closed her agency midway through 2000, in a farewell letter to PERFORMINK:

"I'd become increasingly frustrated by the eroding commercial, voice-over and industrial market here and the stagnated pay-scale for what little film and TV work we do get," wrote Davidson in a personal

Agents

address to actors and her fellow agents. "[And] the talent drain to LA; and watching good agents burn out and leave the business."

Davidson isn't the only one with doubts about the business's future:

"I'm definitely not one hundred per cent enthusiastically optimistic about it," says one agent, who asked not to be named, about the possibilities of recovering from the strike. "I'm going to be wary about what's going on."

Others are exhibiting a cautious optimism in the wake of the strike:

"I don't think we'll ever recover what we've lost; there's no way to recover [from] six months of not shooting commercials and voice-overs. It's a major part of this town's business," says Geddes. "Three companies went out of business, and that's a sad thing for the city...[but] we'll continue on absolutely. It's Chicago: That's what you do."

Of course, commercials aren't all you do: If you're a lucky agent, or a lucky actor, you occasionally dip your toes into the slightly more glamorous worlds of film and television. But in this arena, even more so than with commercials and industrials, fate can be cruel to agents and actors alike.

When movies and television were young, they never came to Chicago at all; their cameras were too big and unwieldy to go traipsing around, especially when they could toss up a vaguely-Chicagoesque skyline on a Hollywood backlot. By the mid-seventies things had started to open up, and occasional movies and episodic series were being shot in the real Chicago, creating a whole new field in which talent agents could operate.

"When Jane Byrne took over as mayor, that opened up the city for films," says Geddes, recalling the 1979-1983 mayor's welcoming attitude towards outside production, which precipitated the opening of the Chicago Film Office in 1980. "Prior to that there was not much film happening."

Films started to crop up, including landmark cultural pieces like "The Untouchables" and "Ferris Bueller's Day Off." Of course, such films showed off the glorious skyline; more importantly, they required the casting of hundreds of extras and cameos, which meant a boon for local agents and actors. (A famous example is the appearance of improv legend Del Close as a grafting city councilman in "The Untouchables.")

Once again, Chicago's reputation as a theatre town translated into a readiness on the part of producers to use local faces. The situation got even sunnier during the mid-nineties, when three weekly TV series— "Turks," "Early Edition," and "Cupid"— were briefly all working here at once. The success of Chicago agencies at landing actors on those shows (all of which were tragically short-lived) is evident in the number of resumés that now include spots on one or more.

"The reason for using Chicago talent is twofold," says Rick Moskal of the Film Office. "One is that [Chicago talent] has a great reputation, and two is that if it's going to be filmed in Chicago it doesn't make sense in terms of cost to audition people elsewhere and bring them in."

Local talent agencies were suddenly busy sending people to movie and film auditions— and not just for Chicago shoots.

"Chicago talent gets cast for shoots that don't even shoot here," says Moskal. "Chicago's reputation, built on its theatre, Second City and the like, has made Chicago that much more of an attractive place to film, and to cast out of for things being shot in other places."

Nowadays TV and film production is facing some of the same challenges as the commercial side, notably "runaway production," as more and more productions head to Canada, where filming is cheaper. Agents are weighing the pros and cons of the situation, developing strategies. Just as the commercial side of the industry must now recover from a six-month full-stop, the film and TV side must reshape itself to deal with new realities. Luckily, they're used to it.

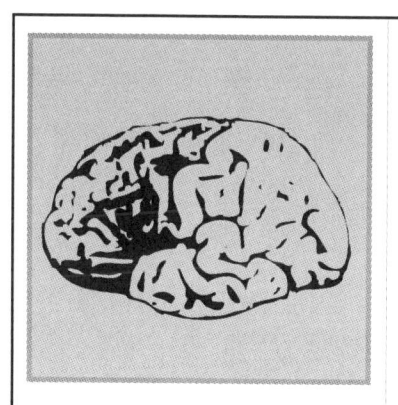

LEND US YOUR BRAIN

Great temp jobs
Great companies

Top Hourly Pay
Holiday and Vacation Pay
Referral Bonuses

Weekly Pay
Direct Deposit

An Inc. 500 Company

Smart Staffing, Inc.
WORKING SMARTER TOGETHER.

29 South LaSalle Suite 635
Chicago, IL 60603

Phone: 312.696.5306
Fax: 312.696.0317
www.smartstaffing.com

Getting an Agent Checklist

Dealing with your agent(s) is a full-time job, but if you do it well, it can be lucrative. Keep these steps in mind when seeking an agent:

1. Mailing

Materials
Your mailing should include a headshot and resumé, a cover letter and a self-addressed, stamped envelope. Refer to the checklists for headshots and resumés for more info.

Research
Different agencies do different things. Some focus on minority talent. Some are union, some aren't. Some handle theatrical bookings. Some have offices both here and in LA. Check them out through this book and Act I Reports before you start submitting.

2. Audition

I Should Bring...
Have at least 25 headshots and resumés with you and ready to go. If they want to represent you, you should be ready.

My Pieces
Have two or three pieces ready, even if they only want one. They'll probably put you on tape, so choose pieces that are suited to film. All these pieces should be contemporary; few agents care whether or not you can handle Shakespeare.

3. Relationship

Multi-Listing vs. Exclusivity
Most agents will not want to sign you exclusively at first. They'll wait until they've worked with you and decided that you're worth the commitment. In the meantime, you can sign with as many agents as you want. This is very different from LA or New York, where all talent is signed exclusively.

Checking In

132   The Book: An Actor's Guide to Chicago

Blah Blah

Every agency has different policies for checking in. Follow them. You want to remind your agents that you exist without irritating them. To this end, call with specific questions, not general chit-chat (e.g., "I was just calling to make sure you had enough pictures and resumés" is much more palatable than "Hey! How ya' doin'?"). Don't drop by, unless that's the specific preference of the agent. Remember, they're busy trying to get you work. There's fine line to follow here between keeping your face in their head and making them want to issue a restraining order. Use common sense.

Communicate

Let them know how an audition went. Keep them posted on the shows you do, the classes you take and the projects you're working on. Most importantly, let them know when you're going out of town (otherwise known as "booking out"). Nothing irritates an agent more than calling an actor and finding out they're on tour for the next month.

Union Status

It's up to you to keep track of your union status. If your next union job means you have to join, let your agent know.

Commission

An agent can only take 10 percent on a union job. They can take 20 percent for print work. If the gig is non-union, the agency can take more than 10 percent, and many do. Pay attention to the percentage your agent takes, particularly if you notice it changing. Incidentally, if an agent takes over 10 percent on a union job, they're breaking the law.

Ring, Damnit!

4. Booking

Be Available

Keep your pager or cell phone with you. If your agent wants to send you out, they may want to send you out right now.

Get the Info

Be sure you know where the audition is, when they're expecting you, whether there's copy, what you should wear, when it shoots, etc. Your agent may be in a hurry to get off the phone, but if you don't know these things you're going to look bad at the audition.

over ↘

5. Exclusivity

Benefits
Being exclusive is more prestigious, and you usually get more attention. The agency has invested in you, so they're more likely to try to get you work.

Problems
Be sure you like your agency and the people you're dealing with before you go exclusive. You're stuck with them. Also, inform other agencies that represent you of your decision promptly.

6. Collecting
It's your responsibility to collect from your agent. Keep track of what they owe you. This can be a difficult game to play, as many actors don't want to anger their agent by bugging them for money. However, they do have a responsibility to pay you. If you need to know what your legal rights are, you can start by calling Joyce Markmann at the Illinois Department of Labor. Also check out "Actors Don't Have to Be Victims" in the UNIONS chapter.

7. Scams
No agent should ever insist that you get headshots with a particular photographer or that you take classes from a particular studio. They can recommend, but they can't insist. Similarly, they shouldn't charge you a fee to sign with their agency. These are all scams designed to take advantage of inexperienced actors. If this happens, or if you're placed in any other situation that makes you uncomfortable, find another agent.

Need cash?

www.gotoppl.com

WHO SAYS YOU HAVE TO BE A STARVING ARTIST? We know you may have unusual hours, but this opportunity will allow you the flexibility to work your own business around your entertainment career. Visit us at **www.gotoppl.com** and see the exciting opportunities that await you at Pre-Paid Legal Casualty, Inc.

Success is all about timing! And your time is now. Regardless of your background, circumstances, education, or experience, we have the right opportunity for you. To learn more, visit us online or contact Andre' Andropolis, Independent Associate at **800-853-5240** or email **andres@prepaidlegal.com**.

"Forbes has just ranked Pre-Paid as #12 on the top 200 small companies of this year."

PPD
Listed
NYSE

Andre' Andropolis
Independent Associate
Pre-Paid Legal Casualty, Inc.
P 800-853-5240

Ch. 4 Talent and Casting Agencies

Talent Agencies

Ambassador Talent
333 N. Michigan #910
Chicago, IL 60601
312/641-3491
SAG/AFTRA/AFM franchised
Registration Policy: All ages. Send headshot & resumé. Agency will call, if interested.

Aria Model and Talent Management
333 N. Michigan #910
Chicago, IL 60601
312/641-3491
SAG/AFTRA/Equity franchised
Co-owners - Mary Boncher, Marie Anderson
On-Camera - Georgia Mindell, Bob Schroeder
Commercial Print - Vicki Fellner
Men's Print - Annette Navarro
Children - Amie Richardson
Runway - Nancy Tennicott
Registration Policy: Actors/models must submit resumé headshot/composite by mail. Agency will contact you, if interested.

Arlene Wilson Models
430 W. Erie #210
Chicago, IL 60610
312/573-0200
www.arlenewilson.com
AFTRA/SAG/Equity franchised
President - Michael Stothard
Agency Director - Dan Deely
Acting Division - Peter Forster
Women Fashion - Shea Spencer
Children, On-Camera, Commercial Print - Laura Alexander
On-Camera, Voice-Over, Commercial Print - Anna Jordan
Children - Lisa Goren
Men's Division - Amanda Lorenzen
Women's Division - Danielle Fotsch
Registration Policy: Submit headshot and resumé by mail first. The agency will contact you, if interested.

Baker & Rowley
1347 W. Washington #1B
Chicago, IL 60607
312/850-4700 • 312/243-4953 - fax
AFTRA/SAG/Equity franchised
On-Camera, Film, Print, Tradeshow - Diane Rowley
Commercial, Film, Voice-Over - Vanessa Lanier
Children - Justine O'Hara
Office Manager - Roberta Kablach
Registration Policy: Send five headshot/resumés and two voice demos with a S.A.S.E. Agents will contact you if interested. Multi-cultural representation. Open registration Tuesdays 12-2pm. No other drop-ins.

Big Mouth Talent
935 W. Chestnut #415
Chicago, IL 60622
312/421-4400
SAG/AFTRA/Equity franchised
Brooke Tonneman
Registration Policy: Send headshot and resumé with a S.A.S.E. Agency will call if interested. All ages.

ChicagoActors.com
(See our ad on page 105)
4933 W. Louise St. #1
Skokie, IL 60077
847/674-2277
www.chicagoactors.com

Concept Model Management, Inc.
1301 S. Grove Ave. #160
Barrington, IL 60010
630/686-6410
www.conceptmodels.com
Exclusive and non-exclusive talent. 17-24 years in age. No walk-ins. Send photo and resumé/composite card. Agency will call, if interested.

Talent Agencies

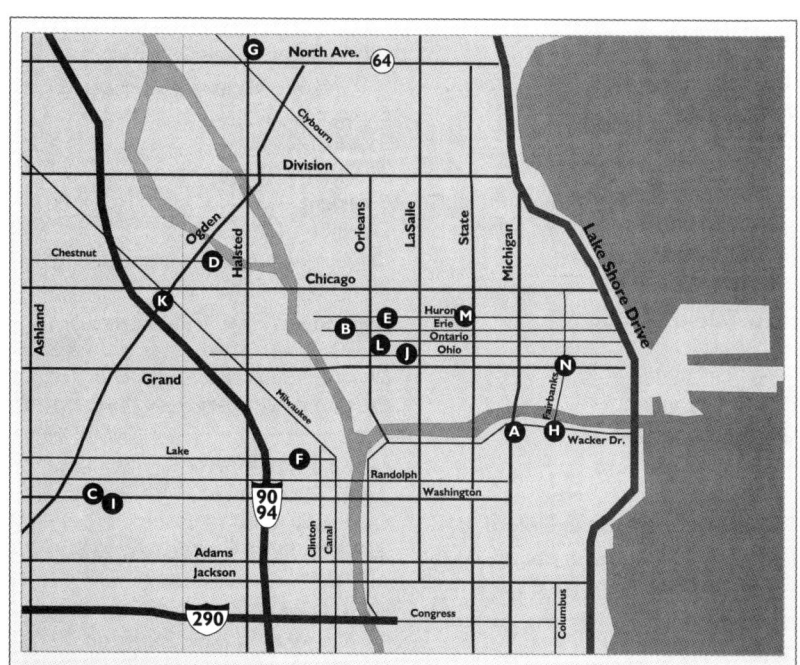

Agency Map

Your days of wandering around searching for an agency are over! Just keep *The Book* nearby with this handy reference to the downtown agencies.

A- Ambassador Talent
333 N. Michigan

A- Aria Model and Talent Management
333 N. Michigan

B- Arlene Wilson Models
430 W. Erie

C- Baker & Rowley
1347 W. Washington

D- Big Mouth Talent
935 W. Chestnut

E- Emilia Lorence Agency
325 W. Huron

F- Ford Talent Group
641 W. Lake

G- Geddes Agency
1633 N. Halsted

H- Karen Stavins Enterprises, Inc.
303 E. Wacker

I- Lily's Talent Agency
1301 W. Washington

J- Linda Jack Talent
230 E. Ohio

K- Salazar & Navas
760 N. Ogden

L- Shirley Hamilton Inc.
333 E. Ontario

M- Stewart Talent
58 W. Huron

N- Voices Unlimited
541 N. Fairbanks

Emilia Lorence Agency
325 W. Huron #404
Chicago, IL 60610
312/787-2033
AFTRA/SAG/Equity franchised
Owner - Fred Kasner
On-Camera, Print - Mark Nagel
On-Camera, Voice-Over - Jackie Grimes
On-Camera, Industrial, Feature Film - Judy Kasner
Convention, Trade Show- Vicki Karageianis

Open registration on Mon., Wed., Fri., 2:30pm- 4pm. Closed daily between 12:00 & 2:00. Actors should bring 3 headshots and resumés. Voice-over talent should submit a tape. Agency will call for reading at a later date, if interested.

Ch. 4 Talent and Casting Agencies **137**

Talent Agencies

ETA, Inc.
7558 S. South Chicago Ave.
Chicago, IL 60619
773/752-3955 • 773/752-8727 - fax
SAG/AFTRA franchised
Registration Policy: Mail composites and resumés to Joan P. Brown, who will contact you, if interested.

Ford Talent Group
641 W. Lake #402
Chicago, IL 60661
312/707-8700
AFTRA/SAG franchised
President - Katie Ford
On-Camera - Davia Lischer
On-Camera, Kids - Linise Belford
Registration Policy: Actors, please submit pictures and resumés to 3rd Coast Artists.

Geddes Agency
1633 N. Halsted #400
Chicago, IL 60614
312/787-8333 • 312/787-6677 - fax
AFTRA/SAG/Equity franchised
Film, TV, Theatre - Elizabeth Geddes, Paula Muzik
Commercial, Industrial - Holly Peterson
Voice-Over - Kathleen Collins
Agent Assistant - Erica Wilde
Registration Policy: Actors must submit headshot and resumé by mail only. Agency will call, if interested.

Karen Stavins Enterprises, Inc.
Three Illinois Ctr.
303 E. Wacker, Concourse
Chicago, IL 60601
312/938-1140
Registration Policy: Submit picture and resumé, composites or voice tapes. attn: New Talent. Agency will contact you, if interested. Non-union talent booked for commercials, industrials, TV/film, voice-over, trade shows, live shows. 17 years and older.

Lily's Talent Agency, Inc.
1301 W. Washington
Chicago, IL 60607
312/601-2345
AFTRA/SAG/Equity franchised
President - Lily Ho
Director - Tom Colby
On-Camera - Sara Strezepek
Print - Donna Roberts
Registration Policy: Actors must submit two headshots and resumés and S.A.S.E. by mail. Include phone number and statistics. Agency will respond, if interested.

Linda Jack Talent
230 E. Ohio #200
Chicago, IL 60611
312/587-1155 • 312/587-2122 - fax
AFTRA/ SAG Franchised
Voice-Over - Linda Jack, Brian Bragg
On-Camera - Mickey Grossman
On-Camera, New Talent - Stacy Shafer
Registration Policy: Submit by mail.

McBlaine & Associates, Inc.
(See our ad on page 139)
805 Touhy Ave.
Park Ridge, IL 60068
847/823-3877
President - Mary Poplawski
Voice-Over, Industrial, Commercial, Film, Children, New Faces, Print - Kristin Runfeldt, Paige Ehlman, Brett Ehlman
Registration Policy: No drop-ins. Send a headshot and resumé with a S.A.S.E.

Norman Schucart Enterprises
1417 Green Bay Rd.
Highland Park, IL 60035
847/433-1113
AFTRA/SAG franchised
TV, Industrial Film, Print, Live Shows - Norman Schucart, Nancy Elliott
Registration Policy: New talent should first submit headshot/composite and resumé with phone number by mail (include S.A.S.E. postcard). If interested, the agency will arrange to interview you in Chicago.

Talent Agencies

North Shore Talent, Inc.
454 Peterson Rd.
Libertyville, IL 60048
847/816-1811
847/816-1819
AFTRA/SAG franchised
On-Camera, Voice-Over, Print, Promotion, Convention - Sherrill Tripp, Shelley Hoselton

Registration Policy: Talent check-in line 847/816-1819. Submit headshot, resumé and any marketing materials (non-returnable). Agency will call, if interested. Registration by appt. only. No drop-ins.

Nouvelle Talent
P.O. Box 578100
Chicago, IL 60657
312/944-1133
AFTRA/SAG/Equity franchised
TV, Film, Trade Show - Ann Toni Sipka
Trade Show - Carlotta Young

Registration Policy: Send picture and resumé. Agency will contact you, if interested.

Salazar & Navas, Inc.
760 N. Ogden #2200
Chicago, IL 60622
312/666-1677
AFTRA/SAG franchised
On-Camera, Voice-Over, Film, Commercial Print, Children - Myrna Salazar
On-Camera, Voice-Over, Film, Commercial Print - Trina Navas
Children - Norma Martinez

Registration Policy: Hispanic/Latin types preferred, but all types considered and represented. New talent seen on Tuesday, 12-4pm.

McBlaine & associates INC

Leader in Non-Union Agencies

805 W. Touhy Ave.
Park Ridge, IL 60068
(847) 823-3877

See our registration policy in Agency

Ch. 4 Talent and Casting Agencies

Shirley Hamilton, Inc.
333 E. Ontario #302B
Chicago, IL 60611
312/787-4700
AFTRA/SAG/Equity franchised
President - Shirley Hamilton
On-Camera, Trade Show,
Voice-Over - Lynn Hamilton
TV, Film - Monica Campbell
TV, Film, Print - Laurie Hamilton

Registration Policy: Registration by mail only with S.A.S.E. Actors must submit headshot and resumé. Agency will contact by mail, if interested.

Stewart Talent
58 W. Huron
Chicago, IL 60610
312/943-3131
AFTRA/SAG/Equity franchised
TV, Stage, Film - Maureen Brookman, Maryann Drake, Todd Turina
Industrial Film - Nancy Kidder
Voice-Over - Joan Sparks
Commercial Print - Wade Childress
Print, Children - Kathy Gardner
Children - Kathy Gardner, Sheila Dougherty
Commercials, Children - Sheila Dougherty
Children - Jennifer Hall

Registration: Actors should mail or drop-off two pictures and resumés. The appropriate agent will contact you within six to eight weeks, if interested. No walk-ins.

Talent Group
1228 W. Wilson
Chicago, IL 60640
773/561-8814 • 773/728-5896 - fax

Registration Policy: No drop-ins. Send a headshot and resumé or voice-over tape addressed to Juliet Wilson. Adults only, please. Ages 18 and older.

Talented Kids, Inc.
6950 W. Windsor Ave.
Berwyn, IL 60402
708/795-1788
www.talentedkidsagency.com

Registration Policy: Representing children, infants to 16 years old. Please send photo and resumé. Agency will call, if interested. Auditions held periodically throughout the year.

Voices Unlimited
541 N. Fairbanks
Chicago, IL 60611
312/832-1113
AFTRA/SAG franchised
President - Sharon Wottrich
Voice-Over - Linda Bracilano

Registration Policy: Voice-over talent should submit commercial and/or narrative tape, two minutes or less with resumé. An agent will contact you if interested.

Talent Agencies – Milwaukee

Arlene Wilson Talent, Inc.
807 N. Jefferson #200
Milwaukee, WI 53202
414/283-5600 • 414/283-5610 - fax
www.mindspring.com/~arlene
AFTRA franchised
President - Michael Stothard
Agency Director - Catherine Hagen
Voice-Over, On-Camera, Broadcast Dir. - Carol Rathe

Registration Policy: Open call for actors Wed. 1:30-3pm. Must have current headshots and resumés or voice demo. May also send materials.

140 The Book: An Actor's Guide to Chicago

Jennifer's Talent Unlimited, Inc.
740 N. Plankinton #300
Milwaukee, WI 53203
414/277-9440
AFTRA franchised
President - Jennifer L. Berg

Registration policy: Actors must submit a headshot and resumé attn. Marna. Agency will contact you, if interested.

Lori Lins, Ltd.
7611 W. Holmes Ave.
Milwaukee, WI 53220
414/282-3500
AFTRA/SAG franchised

Booker - Lori Lins, Jenny Siedenberg, Betty Anthoine

Registration Policy: Actors must submit headshot and resumé. Agency will respond, if interested.

Tradeshow Agencies

Best Faces
1152 N. Lasalle #F
Chicago, IL 60610
312/944-3009
www.bestfacesofchicago.com

Registration Policy: Send materials attn: Judy Mudd. Agency will contact you, if interested.

Corporate Presenters
(A division of Karen Stavins Enterprises)
attn: New Talent
Three Illinois Center
303 E. Wacker, Concourse
Chicago, IL 60601
312/938-1140 • 312/938-1142 - fax

Registration Policy: Submit composite or headshot. Agency will contact, if interested. Narrators, hosts/hostesses and models booked for trade shows, conventions, special promotions and variety acts. 17 years and older.

Nouvelle Talent
P.O. Box 578100
Chicago, IL 60657
312/944-1133

Registration Policy: Send picture and resumé. Agency will contact you, if interested.

Temporary Professionals
Personnel Staffing Services
625 N. Michigan #600
Chicago, IL 60611
773/622-1202 • 773/622-1303 - fax
Gloria J-M Piecha - Director

Registration policy: Submit H/R. Will contact if interested.

Soon to be moving to a new location! Call for mailing address. Personnel staffing services for trade shows and promotions. Models - Talent - Costume Characters - Samplers - Temporaries - Bi Lingual Personnel

Member of the Chicago Convention & Tourism Bureau

Mail headshot and resumés. Agency will contact. No drop-ins.

Put your personality to work!

Out of samples?
See a movie!
page 304

Ch. 4 Talent and Casting Agencies 141

Casting Directors

Actors are generally welcome to submit one headshot and resumé and keep in touch with post cards. <u>Never</u> call a casting director; it will only hurt your chances of ever getting work through that individual.

All City Casting
attn: June Pyskacek
P.O. Box 577640
Chicago, IL 60657-7640
773/588-6062

Beth Rabedeau Casting
attn: Beth Rabedeau
920 N. Franklin #205
Chicago, IL 60610
312/664-0601

Big House Production
Voice Casting and Radio Production
2028 W. Potomac #2 & 3
Chicago, IL 60622
773/772-9539

Tenner, Paskal
attn: Rachel Tenner, Casting Director;
Mickie Paskal, Casting Director
20 W. Hubbard #2E
Chicago, IL 60610
312/527-0665
312/527-9085 - fax

CHICAGO CASTING
777 N. Green Street
Chicago, IL 60622
(312) 327-1904 phone
(312) 327-1905 fax
www.TheaterLand.com
Tina O'Brien and Janet Louer

New Listing!

Chicago Casting Center
attn: Janet Louer, Tina O'Brien, Siobhan Sullivan
777 N. Green
Chicago, IL 60622
312/327-1904

Simon Casting
attn: Claire Simon
1512 N. Freemont #202
Chicago, IL 60622
312/202-0124

Communications Corporation of America
Fred Strauss - Executive Producer
P.O. Box 14262
Chicago, IL 60614-0262
773/348-0001
773/472-6557 - fax
Casts entire productions
Specialized projects
Illinois Film Board member
Submission Policy: Will take submissions through mail. No walk-ins, no calls. Send to Fred Strauss Communciations

David O'Connor Casting
attn: David O'Connor,
Carrie Buhl, Sarah Reule
1017 W. Washington #2A
Chicago, IL 60607
312/226-9112

HollyRik & Heitz Casting
attn: Rik Kristinat or Hal Watkins
920 N. Franklin #205
Chicago, IL 60610
312/664-0601
312/664-3297 - fax
www.HollyRik.com

Holzer & Ridge Casting
773/549-3169

142 The Book: An Actor's Guide to Chicago

Extras Casting

Jane Alderman Casting
attn: Jane Alderman
c/o Act One Studios
640 N. LaSalle #535
Chicago, IL 60610
312/397-1182

JAZ Casting
attn: Jennifer Rudnicke, Cathy Kul
3617 N. Kedvale
Chicago, IL 60641
312/343-8111

Kordos & Charbonneau
attn: Richard Kordos or Nan Charbonneau
P.O. Box 420
Wilmette, IL 60091
847/674-4775

K.T.'s
P.O. Box 577039
Chicago, IL 60657-7039
773/525-1126

ReginaCast
P.O. Box 585
Willow Springs, IL 60480
312/409-5521
www.reginacast.com

Segal Studio
attn: Jeffrey Lyle Segal
1040 W. Huron
Chicago, IL 60622
312/563-9368

Talking Headshots Casting
Ted Sarantos
2857 N. Halsted
Chicago, IL 60657
773/528-7114
773/528-7153 - fax

TrapDoor Casting
Beata Pilch and Nicole Wiesner
Independent Casting Directors
1655 W. Cortland
Chicago, IL 60622
773/384-0494
www.trapdoortheater.com

Casting Directors Beata Pilch and Nicole Wiesner specialize in diverse talent for film, television commercial, and theatrical productions. Past credits: Carsey-Werner Productions, Nickelodeon, and various independent films, print and industrials. We've been sought by the best, now we're available for you!
Actors send headshots. Unique character types encouraged.

Extras Casting

Casting by McLean/For Extras
P.O. Box #10569
Chicago, IL 60610
Registration Policy: Send headshots and resumés by mail. Include phone number, social security number and all sizes on resumé.

Holzer & Ridge Casting
773/549-3169

McCall Model & Talent
6930 South Shore Drive, #1
Chicago, IL 60649
773/256-1264 • 773/256-1279 – fax

Karen Peake Casting
1212 S. Michigan #1002
Chicago, IL 60605
312/360-9266
Registration Policy: Send S.A.S.E to get registration information.

Literary Agents

K.T.'s
P.O. Box 577039
Chicago, IL 60657-7039
773/525-1126
Registration Policy: Send 6 pictures or composites. Include on resumé phone number, address, social security number, height, weight, hair and eye color, age (or age range), car color and make.

ReginaCast
P.O. Box 585
Willow Springs, IL 60480
312/409-5521
www.reginacast.com
Registration Policy: Send a current photo with your age and height, phone numbers and email address to both locations. If possible, please email before mailing.

Literary Agents

Austin Wahl Agency
1820 N. 76th Ct
Elmwood Park, IL 60070
708/456-2301
Submission Policy: Write letter of interest, describing material. Include synopsis, publication history, and sample of writing.

International Leonards Corporation
3612 N. Washington Blvd
Indianapolis, IN 46205
317/926-7566
Submission Policy: Write letter of interest, include queries and SASE. Agency will contact, if interested. Accepting submissions for TV, Film. NO BOOKS.

Stewart Talent
58 W. Huron
Chicago, IL 60610
312/943-3131
Literary Submissions: Send 2 page synopsis/summary and letter of inquiry with S.A.S.E. to Stewart Talent, sttn: Literary Division. Agency will contact you, if interested.

Need inspiration?
Check out the Libraries on page 123

144 The Book: An Actor's Guide to Chicago

Film, TV and Industrials

I finally broke in! Now how do I break out?!

Chicago Human Rhythm Project, Fool Moon

Cutting a Demo Tape

Shall we clap into 't roundly, without hawking, or spitting, or saying we are hoarse; which are the only prologues to a bad voice?

By Julie Daly

Demo tapes are essential for voice-over work. The tape represents your talent. And, the professionals listening to your tape are busy and have just about two minutes for you to impress them. Your demo has to pop, it has to be tight and it has to sound professional.

More importantly, your demo tape should represent you. Know your demographic and know your skill set, then layer it into your product. Most coaches agree that the demo tape should run a maximum of two minutes. (Voice Over U's Sherri Berger notes that the current trend in LA is an even zippier one to one and a half minute tape.) The demo should consist of actual or virtual national or regional radio ads, not your cousin Eddie's made up copy of a car dealer's sizzling sale; professional product is the key here.

Catching an Agent

You've rolled up your sleeves and produced a dynamo demo tape. Now you want an agent to hear it, pick up the phone and beg you to let them represent you. Better yet, you want to be on their CD. The agent's CD is ground zero. It is a compilation of their best talent. The precious CD gets sent to the ad agencies who then say, "We'll take track number three. Here's a bazillion dollars."

Before your eyes glaze with images of paying off your student loans, let's backtrack to getting an agent.

"We do, eventually, listen to all of the tapes that we get," says Debby Kotzen, a former voice-over agent with the now closed CED. "It should be professionally produced. If we like them we call them in, talk to them, find out where they are. We audition them. Cold reads are crucial," continues Kotzen.

That last sentence echoes in every discussion we have about voice-overs. CED likes the demo to be no more than one and a half minutes, which is the trend in LA. And on the controversy over head shots: "No headshots unless you're submitting for on-camera as well."

Talent agent Linda Jack advises, "Actors need to remember that for voice-over work they need to concentrate on communication coming through the voice, not the body." Length of tape? "A minute to a minute and a half." Headshots? "Headshots are worthless to me."

Linda Bracilano, talent agent with Voices Unlimited, stresses the importance of the cold read. "We are looking for incredible cold readers. If you can't produce in the studio...well, that's not good," she says. The agency listens to all of the demo tapes. "No priority, we just go through the pile." Length of tape? "Less is more. Voice-over demo tapes are only used to get an agent. You really have to be on the agent's CD now."

Bracilano cautions actors to really think before making the tape. "Demo tapes are so expensive, you have to know that you're good. It has to be something that you have to do, not just something to make extra money or you won't make it," she stresses. Headshots? "No."

"Have some training first," advises Jackie Grimes of Emilia Lorence. "The market is inundated with with unmarketable voices." Length of demo? "As long as it's not more than two minutes, I'll listen to it. We want variety on the tape, if they can do it," she stresses.

Demo Tapes

Audio One, Inc.
(See our ad on this page)
325 W. Huron #512
Chicago, IL 60610
312/337-5111
312/337-5125 - fax

Bobby Schiff Music Productions
363 Longcommon Rd.
Riverside, IL 60546
708/442-3168
708/447-3719 - fax

Bosco Productions
(See our ad on page 149)
160 E. Grand - 6th floor
Chicago, IL 60611
312/644-8300

Dress Rehearsals Studios, Ltd.
312/829-2213
312/829-4085 - fax
www.chicagostudios.com

Music Workshop
Bob Kalal
4900 W. 28th Pl.
Cicero, IL 60804
708/652-4040
members.xoom.com\musicwkshop

Rainbow Bridge Recording
117 W. Rockland Rd.
Libertyville, IL 60048
847/362-4060
847/362-4653 - fax

Renaissance Video
130 S. Jefferson
Chicago, IL 60661
312/930-5000
312/930-9030 - fax
www.whateverwerks.com

AUDIO ONE
LEARN HOW TO SELL YOUR VOICE
for fun and $$$
from the most experienced voice acting coach in Chicago
Beginning to Advanced
ALL TYPES - ALL AGES
Demo tapes - Auditioning - Marketing and Free Lifetime Guidance
FREE INFO PACK   Toll Free 24 hrs
1-877-670-4300

Demo Tapes

VOICE OVER DEMO TAPES

*Private Coaching & Directing
*Full service professional recording studios
*Scripts   Cassette and CD Duplication   J-cards

BOSCO PRODUCTIONS

(312) 644-8300
160 E Grand   Chicago IL 60611
Fax (312) 644-1893   E-mail radioact1@aol.com
www.BoscoProductions.com

Film, TV & Industrials

Ch. 5 Film, TV, Industrials **149**

Demo Tapes

Sound Advice
(See our ad on page 63)
Kate McClanaghan, Gina Mazza, Tyrone Dockery
2028 W. Potomac #2 & 3
Chicago, IL 60622
773/772-9539
www.voiceoverdemos.com

Sound Advice is the most complete, start-to-finish voiceover demo production service. We maintain no one does what you do. The copy is written/selected specifically for you by Professional Producers. Our mailing list and marketing plan is unparalleled. We coach, direct and produce you to get you completely poised to work. Get trained and produced by two of Chicago's top former Talent Agents, Gina Mazza (CED) and Tyrone Dockery (Stewart) and Kate McClanaghan, Producer at top Ad Agency (DDB Worldwide).

Sound/Video Impressions
110 S. River Rd.
Des Plaines, IL 60016
847/297-4360
847/297-6870 – fax

VoiceOver 101
Ray Van Steen
325 W. Huron #512
Chicago, IL 60610
312/587-1010
312/337-5125 - fax

Private, individual coaching sessions in voicing TV/Radio commercials, narrations. Employs record/playback method in recording studio environment. Basics through production of voice-over demo. Van Steen is a published writer on the subject, and has voiced thousands of commercials. Phone for free, no-obligation brochure.

Voice Over U
Sherri Berger
773/774-9559
773/774-9555 - fax
sherriberger.voicedemo.com

Voices On
Thomas Test
773/528-7041

Your demo needs cutting-edge scripts and production values to stand out from the crowd. EVERY demo I've produced has resulted in agent representation for my students. Call Telly award-winning v/o talent Tom Test of "Voices On" at 773/528-7041 for private coaching, in-studio audition workshops, and demo production.

Need a start?
Check out voice classes starting on page 62

To Reel, or not to...

"I will tell you the beginning; and if it please your ladyships, you may see the end; for the best is yet to do."

By Julie Daly

Honestly, in Chicago do you really need a reel? If you haven't done any on-camera work yet, then no. If you have, then maybe. Georgia Mindell of Aria says reels are more standard in LA and New York. Clients (ad agencies, production houses) in Chicago don't normally ask for one, but if you're seeking representation it's a good idea to bring along a sample of your work. Having a reel is just icing on the cake. A good quality tape approximately 2-5 minutes long is all you need to show your agent what you've got. Don't go out and spend a ton of cash yet—you can compose your own reel of selected works if you're only giving it to your agent. A professional reel is another matter—read on.

Reels

The reel doesn't have to be broken down into categories like industrial, commercial or theatrical, it can be a general reel showcasing your best moments. Say you have 10 minutes of a really great scene. Don't put the whole scene onto the tape; use only the best bits. Make sure your tape demonstrates your versatility. Put only put one example of each character-type you've done. You want it to be quick and painless to watch, not a constant repetition of the same character. The viewer should see someone who can act, react and think.

Once you've aquired an agent and are working you may consider having a professional reel done. This is a big expense, and you should put a lot of thought into it. Consult with your agent, and ask to see other actor's reels. With good research you're more likely to get what you want when you shell out the dough.

You're out there working, dreaming of being on the big screen someday. Make sure you get a copy of all the work you do, from commercial to student film. Before you leave the set, get the name and number of the person you should contact in order to get a copy of the project. The time it takes to get a copy varies from job to job, and you usually have to be charmingly aggressive in obtaining them. But remember, you need the copy as much as the paycheck. Someday the spot may appear on your professional reel, so make sure you know the format you'll need it in. Check out www.videouniversity.com to educate yourself on the world of filmmaking. The better the quality going in, the better the final product. Some production companies will put the copy on anything you ask for without charging, others will charge a fee for higher quality. Pay for the higher quality now; you don't want to compromise the final product.

OK, so you've done enough work to have a professional reel done. According to Kevin Chatham, manager of FTV labs here in Chicago, an actor should bring in copies of their work on 3/4 inch, digital beta cam or high 8. You can bring in a VHS tape, but try to obtain a copy of your work on a higher quality medium; a lot is lost in duplication, so you want to start with the best you can. Also, Chatham suggested having the master demo done on the highest quality format you can afford. This way the final copy, the one that you will be sending to those studio execs, is the best it can be.

Studios like FTV charge by the hour. They will be more than happy and are quite capable of sitting with you and consulting about what your reel should look like, but if you have a good idea of what you want before you walk in the door you will cut your costs considerably. Sit down with your agent and discuss what your reel should look like;

again 3-5 minutes is all that is needed, but assume the client's not going to watch more than 60 seconds. You'll want to move in and out of scenes as fast as possible. If you can, make a rough-draft and bring it to show the editing house what you have in mind. At least have an idea of how the reel should move, think about what type of music should be behind it, and know what you want. At $100-150 an hour, it's in your best interest to be prepared.

Once your master reel is done, you'll have to get copies made. Have them done on VHS or Super VHS—most casting directors won't be able to play a 3/4 inch reel. Duplication will cost $3-8 per cassette. Make sure that the cassette itself as well as the case has your contact information. Just like your headshot, the reel will do you no good at all if someone loves you but can't reach you. Also, don't waste your money by sending out unsolicited tapes to everybody here in Chicago. The tape is a tool that your agent uses to submit you for out-of-town work. Here in Chicago, casting directors like to see the person, not the tape.

Reels

Absolute Video Services, Inc.
715 S. Euclid
Oak Park, IL 60302
708/386-7550
708/386-2322 - fax
www.absolutevideoservices.com

Allied Digital Technologies
1200 Thorndale Ave.
Elk Grove Village, IL 60007
847/595-2900
847/595-8677 - fax

Argonne Electronics
7432 N. Milwaukee
Niles, IL 60714
847/647-8877

Cinema Video Center
211 E. Grand
Chicago, IL 60611
312/644-0861
312/644-2096 - fax
www.networkcentury.com

ELB's Entertainment, Inc.
Eugene Barksdale
2501 N. Lincoln Avenue #198
Chicago, IL 60614-2313
800/656-1585
800/957-3527 - fax
www.elbsentertainment.com

Ch. 5 Film, TV, Industrials 153

Reels

Film to Video Labs
5100 N. Ravenswood #200
Chicago, IL 60640
773/275-9500
773/275-0300 - fax
www.ftvlabs.com

Golan Productions
1501 N. Magnolia
Chicago, IL 60622
773/274-3456
312/642-7441 - fax
www.atomicimaging.com

Rainbow Bridge
117 W. Rockland Rd
Libertyville, IL 60048
847/362-4060
847/362-4653 - fax

Intervideo Duplication Services
3533 S. Archer
Chicago, IL 60609
773/927-9091
773/927-9211 - fax
www.historicvideo.com

Master Images Video Duplication
112 Carpenter Ave
Wheeling, IL 60090
847/541-4440

Northwest Teleproductions
142 E. Ontario
Chicago, IL 60611
312/337-6000
312/337-0500 - fax
www.nwtele.com

Rainbow Bridge Recording
117 W. Rockland Rd.
Libertyville, IL 60048
847/362-4060
847/362-4653 - fax

Renaissance Video
130 S. Jefferson
Chicago, IL 60661
312/930-5000
312/930-9030 - fax
www.whateverwerks.com

Sound/Video Impressions
110 S. River Rd.
Des Plaines, IL 60016
847/297-4360
847/297-6870 - fax

Video Replay, Inc.
118 W. Grand
Chicago, IL 60610
312/467-0425
312/467-1045 - fax
www.videoreplaychicago.com

Technique acting up?
Catch a refresher in Acting Classes on page 47

Using an Ear Prompter

> I pray you, mar no more of my verses with reading them ill-favouredly.

By Julie Daly

Ah, the ear-prompter! You've heard of it, you know people who make their living with it, but is it for you?

An ear prompter is a device that fits in your ear and feeds you your lines. They can be either wired or wireless and are connected to a tape recorder into which you have recorded your copy. The trick to using one is to be a step behind the copy. You need to be listening and speaking at the same time—it's a bit tough at first, but like any technique it can be artfully mastered with the proper amount of practice.

An ear-prompter is essential for the actor who plans to work in industrials. Industrials (both on-camera and live) have been and continue to be the bread and butter for many Chicago actors. Clients that produce

Ear Prompter

industrials prefer to hire people who are ear-prompter proficient; it allows them to change copy at the last minute without worrying whether an actor will have time to memorize. Generally an ear-prompter is used for narration rather than scene work. But when it's necessary for a scene, especially if the script isn't available until the day of the shoot, the actors have to be wonderful at it to make it work well. You should make sure that you can both narrate and speak dialogue with an ear-prompter before you claim proficiency on your resumé.

According to Ann Jacques of Act One Studios, you should ask yourself three important questions before you before you run out and buy one (and they're expensive, costing $300-600).

Will your agent be submitting you for industrials which require an ear-prompter (i.e. spokesperson/narration)? This is a question you must ask your agent. If so, be sure you have a good industrial headshot for your agent to submit.

Are you really good at it? Can you deliver the copy in a natural, conversational way? Don't trust yourself, get a second opinion: take a class or work out with other actors. If you don't look like you're listening to yourself, or reading off the inside of your eyeballs, it's working.

Are you comfortable with it? Can you get past the technology to the really communicate with the camera or the other character? The ear-prompter is just a tool; the goal is the same as with any acting scene—honest communication.

If you answered yes to all three questions then it's time to purchase an ear-prompter.

Do you really need to take a class to learn how to use the ear-prompter? No, of course not. Is it a good investment? Yes. There are many classes out there that you can take. Here's the low-down.

Act One Studios for example, offers two classes for the ear-prompter: Basic Industrial Film and Ear-Prompter class. This class is nine weeks long, and you'll leave knowing everything you ever wanted about industrials and the use of the ear-prompter. The first four weeks are without the prompter. You start with basic scene-work for industrial film copy. Remember, this is still acting. You then move onto narration – again without the ear-prompter, focusing on text analysis. Jaqcues believes wholeheartedly that the requirements of an industrial text are the same as those of a Chekhov text. Who am I? Where am I? Who am I talking to? Why? The extra step (and probably the biggest hurdle for most of those trained in the theatre) for text analysis of an industrial narration is "How can I dig out the meaning when I don't know any-

Ear Prompter

thing about the subject matter?" i.e., we're not all chemical engineers. In the fifth week the ear-prompter is introduced (Act One has the equipment), using narration script for the first few weeks and then advancing to scenework.

Advanced Ear-prompter is a five-week brush-up course, designed for students who are out there auditioning and or working to come back with questions that arise during the work.

Another option is to take Michael Colucci's two hour intensive one-on-one private session. Colucci also has equipment that you can use before you invest in your own ear-prompter.

Colucci only accepts actors with basic script analysis skills and some experience. He believes you have to work extra hard as an actor to make a dry industrial script come to life. His program can be summed up in three steps, the "Holy Trinity of the ear-prompter."

Put a polished performance on the tape – this is the cornerstone of his whole concept. Make sure the copy reflects your own rhythms, that way you can lock into the script naturally, and reproduce a strong take for the camera.

Have one hundred percent of your focus on listening. If rule number one has been followed, the ear prompter should be feeding you a Xeroxed copy of a strong reading. Listen to it! You shouldn't be worried about your performance, rule one takes care of that.

The vocal juggle – you have to be comfortable speaking while you're listening, so you can speak half a phrase behind the tape. According to Colucci, this is the most difficult part, and just takes practice.

Two common pitfalls Colucci teaches you to avoid:

Be careful not to "step on your own feet" i.e., make sure you give yourself some breathing room. You need to be confident enough to let the words come to you before you speak them. Don't be afraid to fall behind, that's where you should be! Otherwise, you'll end up waiting for words, which will ruin that polished performance that is on your tape. Be careful not to get ahead of your rhythm. This happens to everyone in the beginning – trust yourself, you'll get it.

You WILL often get behind on technical scripts because the words are mouthfuls, They're challenging. Don't be too slow. Hence the importance of a polished performance on the tape. Listen to it carefully and lock into your own rhythm. Stay true to it.

Just like Jaqcues, Colucci can't stress the importance of practice enough. When practicing, take your materials from more technical

Ear Prompter

sources such as a computer magazine or an instruction booklet. The Monday edition of the business section in the Chicago Tribune is a great source. Remember that 50-75 percent of the industrial work you'll be doing will be technical.

For more information on Michael Colucci's class, call 888-Colucci.

The people Ann Jaqcues has seen excel at the ear-prompter workout with other actors on a regular basis and make practice a priority. "Students will say to me, you make this look easy, but you do it all the time. I tell the students the only difference between me doing it all the time and you doing it all the time is a paycheck. If you will commit to practicing, it'll become easy for you and then you'll get those jobs."

Ear Prompters

Instant Memory™ Ear Prompting Systems
Credible Communication, Inc.
155 Little John Trail NE
Atlanta, GA 30309
404/892-0660
www.ear-prompter.com

Sargon Yonan
67 E. Madison #1415
Chicago, IL 60603
312/782-7007
312/782-7529 - fax

NEW EAR-PROMPTER OPTIONS?

Yep. Not only are INSTANT MEMORY ear-prompters smaller, louder, tougher, and less expensive, *now* they're available in both wireless (w/35-minute video) *and* hardwire models. New this year, our "Touch/Pause" remote micro recorder. Lowest prices. Satisfaction guaranteed. Check www.ear-prompter.com, or free brochure from INSTANT MEMORY
155 Little John Trail, NE✦ Atlanta, GA 30309✦ (404)892-0660

Getting Paid

Besides this nothing that he so plentifully gives me, the something that nature gave me, his countenance seems to take from me.

By Ben Winters

If you're an actor who wants to make a living, there's plenty of reasons a Screen Actors Guild (SAG) card can be worth more in your wallet than a Visa Platinum. The vast majority of paying gigs in Chicago aren't in the theatre, they're in commercials and industrials. For folks doing that kind of work, the union offers a certain set of protections: a guaranteed pay scale and working conditions, not to mention the peace of mind that comes from the protection of union muscle.

Alas, it takes time and toil (and that pesky entrance fee) to gain entry into SAG (or the Association of Film, Television and Radio Artists, SAG's oft-overlooked sister union). In the meantime, there's plenty of paying non-union work to be had, from industrial videos to local commercials to passing out detergent samples at your local Jewel-Osco. While some local agencies work exclusively with union clients, many specialize in non-union gigs. Even SAG-franchised agencies can do non-union work—provided they don't send union actors to non-union jobs.

But there's a major pitfall: a non-union actor is a one-man or one-woman show. You've got to be ready to hustle, not only to get your headshots in the mail, nail the audition and nail the gig, but to collect your payment afterwards. As any non-union actor who's been around the block a time or two can tell you, sometimes the hardest part of the job isn't memorizing the lines, it's getting the fee.

Ch. 5 Film, TV, Industrials

Getting Paid

Here's how it works when all goes smoothly: The client hires the agency and the agency hires the talent (that's you). Talent and agent have a contract, signed in advance, affording the agency a certain percentage of the fee; after the work is completed the client sends along two checks, one for your share and one for the agency. (Under a SAG contract, the agency gets 10 percent from the actor's cut and another 10 pecent from the client; non-union fees are higher, ranging from 15/15 upwards.)

It is the agent's responsibility to forward your payment to you, and any agent will say they always do so immediately upon receiving it. And yet the city is full of actors with horror stories to tell of waiting anywhere from "months and months" to "over a year" to "forever" to get their cash from a gig.

Without the union behind you, keeping yourself from the ranks of the unpaid, is your own responsibility, and it can be a daunting task. But with a little savvy and a little patience, it's not impossible.

The first steps to ensuring timely payment are taken before the job even starts, indeed before the audition even takes place.

The city is full of agencies, and most are fully licensed, reputable operations. But though clip joints are getting rarer (knock on wood), the talent agent business, like any industry with a lot of cash sloshing around, will always have its share of fly-by-night operations and rip-off artists ready to prey on starry-eyed would-be actors. Part of your responsibility when pursuing the work is to be smart: By staying alert for certain tell-tale signs of the scam artists, you can avoid trouble when it comes time to get paid.

Suzanne Davis works the agent-client beat at the Illinois Department of Labor, and she's a font of information about who the bad guys are. Though reluctant to talk on record (partly because so many of her examples come from real-life situations), she walked me through some of the ways a wary actor can avoid a bad apple agent— the ones likely to drag their feet on payment, if they ever intend to pay at all.

For example, if an agency starts giving you a long list of charges, you know you're in the wrong place. State law dictates that under no circumstances can a talent agency insist an actor use a particular photographer for their headshots, or demand you sign up for some sort of audition newsletter (for a nominal fee, of course...). No mandatory classes, or no asking you to come in and answer the phones. An agent is licensed to send you out on potential employment as a performer; any of the extras are not only against the law, they're a sure tip-off that this particular agent is in the game to make as much dough as possible at your expense.

Getting Paid

If you're unsure about a particular agency, trust your instincts, and do a little background work. Ask your fellow actors if they've heard anything. Or call Davis, a straight shooter and a friend to actors. Any non-sketchy agency will have their license (along with a $5,000 bond) on file with the Department of Labor, and she's the one to ask.

Illinois Department of Labor
Suzanne Davis
160 N. LaSalle, 13th floor
Chicago, IL 60601
312/793-1804

But what if all goes well—it's a seemingly decent agency, you have a good audition, and you do the work—and you end up sitting around waiting for that precious check? Here's a few pointers on what to do next:

1. Wait

The Private Employment Agency Act of the State of Illinois Compiled Statutes (that's 225 ILCS 515/0.01, available online at www.legis.state.il.us/ilcs) dictates no maximum or minimum time by which a client must pay an agent. In other words, under the law, an advertiser or other employer of actors has no particular obligation to get your money to your agent within any duration of time whatsoever.

Where there is no law, however, there is common practice. As a rule of thumb, an actor on a non-union job can expect to wait between two weeks and a month for a check to be issued and sent along.

So don't call your agent the day after the shoot and demand your cash. Jumping the gun isn't just rude—it's potentially deadly to your career. Pestering an agent about money prematurely is like sending a letter telling them in no uncertain terms that you're irresponsible and unprofessional, and they'll be less and less inclined to send you out on further auditions.

Hard as it may be, the first step is to hang tight. Borrow a little more scratch from mom and dad and wait at least a few weeks before getting worried.

2. Wait some more

The truth is, agents are exceptionally busy people, and they don't need cash-poor actors banging the door before there's any good reason. The most likely cause for any delay in your payment is that the agency hasn't

Getting Paid

yet been paid by the client. The hard truth is that—according to the Private Employment Agency Act—the agent doesn't owe you a cent until they've gotten the checks from the client.

(That PEA Act is a treasure trove of fascinating information. Did you know that agents can't send female performers to "any questionable place, or place of bad repute, house of ill-fame or assignation house, or to any house or place of amusement kept for immoral purposes, or place resorted to for the purpose of prostitution or gambling?" Also, those known to be "questionable characters, prostitutes, gamblers, intoxicated persons, or procurers" aren't even allowed inside an agency).

Give your agent the benefit of the doubt. But when more than a month has elapsed and you're still looking down the barrel of an empty mailbox, it's time to take action.

3. Call your agent or pay them a visit

"The check was always sitting up there and it's just that nobody knew it was there," says one non-union actor of an elusive payment. "I went up there and I said, 'I did work for you all on such and such date, on such and such contract, now where's my money?'"

Lo and behold, the money was indeed there, waiting patiently to be retrieved.

"Apparently it just wouldn't happen over the phone," he says. "I had tried like three times...when I went up there, they looked and found it. It was in their files."

A local voice-over agent suggests that, if after thirty days a check is still not forthcoming, it's perfectly reasonable to call and inquire as to its whereabouts—it's always possible that (as in the above case) the check has arrived and been mislaid or overlooked.

"Thirty days after the job is an industry standard," says this agent. "It's completely appropriate for the actor to give their agent a call and say, 'I just want to give you a head's up.' Trust me, we want to get [checks] out as quickly as possible."

Sometimes a quick phone call is all it takes to get things straightened out, whether the problem is at the agency or (as is more common) with the client. "Usually the actor will call you and say, 'Where's my money, this project happened a while ago?' That's when I would call the client and say, 'This actor worked on this day, when can we expect payment?' And then [the client] is usually really nice about it. Either they're behind in their paperwork, or the actor is jumping the gun and it felt like a month but it's only been two weeks."

Getting Paid

Make sure of your dates, and then call. Try to be polite, but not timid. Remember that as intimidating as it can be to talk with someone who can control your destiny (in whatever way), the truth is that agents work for you, not the other way around. Part of their job is making sure that you get paid. If you start to sense you're being blown off, be persistent and find out what's going on. Hey, it's your money.

4. Drastic Measures

If your series of phone calls to the agent proves fruitless, it may be time for the big guns.

One possibility is to call up the client directly and ask what's going on: a rare, but not unheard of, action according to Davis. (Here's another reason to check your contract before doing the job. Some agreements specifically stipulate that an actor may not contact the client in these circumstances.) If they tell you they sent out checks to the agency a month ago, you know something is fishy.

At the very least, you remind them of your existence, something your agent may have been too busy to get to, and hopefully hurry the check along.

Another, less palatable option is to sue the agent in small claims court for non-payment, either by hiring a lawyer or by going after them by yourself ("pro se" is the technical term, Latin for..."by yourself"). If you've always wanted to play Clarence Darrow, this might be fun, but more likely it would be an aggravating, expensive waste of time.

The smart move is to call the Department of Labor and chat with Davis, who handles these kinds of things for a living. An agent late on payment will be much more affected by a call from Davis, who comes with all the weight of the State of Illinois, than from you and your non-union.

Davis most likely has a relationship with the agency, probably with your specific agent, and is in a position to find out exactly what's going on with your money. If she's not satisfied with their answers, she can take steps, not only to recover your fee but to land the agency in hot water for their delinquency.

5. Learn... Move on... Join the Union

If there's no other lesson to be learned from being jerked around by an agent, or simply from suffering through the occasional unavoidable delays, it's that SAG/AFTRA membership is to be coveted and strived towards. Union membership is more than a feather in your cap; it means minimizing exactly this sort of aggravation.

Ch. 5 Film, TV, Industrials

Acting on Film

"I am not a slut, though
I thank the gods I am foul.

By Adrianne Duncan

So…you wanna be in the movies? So do I, and I hope to give you some tips on how to do a good job once you are cast. I'd like to share what I learned while working on *The Chameleon*, the independent SAG feature shot last October in Michigan.

Even though I had been on sets many times, I knew I would need to learn about preparing for a lead role, and so I read. A lot. Three of the books I highly recommend, and from which much of this article is drawn, are *Acting in Film* by Michael Caine, *The Camera Smart Actor* by Richard Brestoff and *Secrets of Screen Acting* by Patrick Tucker.

"Acting in Film" is a series of observations and advice by Caine, the actor who starred in such films as *Alfie, Sleuth* and *Educating Rita*—to name three out of over 100. "The Camera Smart Actor" takes the reader through a typical first day on a set and explains the various functions of the crew, which is immensely helpful. "Secrets of Screen Acting" is one of the best books on film acting technique I've ever read. Tucker is a British director and tends to work more technically. Some of his advice sounds as though it would produce artificial results, but it is invaluable and works in practice.

Acting in film is about preparation. Too many actors expect that they will get on a set and be told what to do and how everything works. Most likely, you won't. You are a freelance professional who has been hired to do a specific job, and you should know what that job entails and how it fits into everyone else's jobs.

Don't expect that the director will give you some magical insight about how to play the character. That's not really their job. Most of what they will tell you is technical— and remember, the director is thinking in terms of the story and how you fit into it, not just about you. Any acting direction you get on a set is GRAVY.

Part of your job as an actor is to make everyone else's life easier: the director by knowing your lines and having explored your role and made strong choices before getting on the set; the editor by making sure your continuity is as perfect as it can be; the first AD (assistant director) by making sure they know where you are at all times.

There are two types of continuity—technical and emotional—and both are important. Technical continuity involves doing the same thing in the same way on every take. In *The Chameleon*, there is one scene in which I had to eat a bagel and drink orange juice. I choreographed for myself on which syllables I would take a bite of bagel, pick up the glass, take a sip of juice, put the glass down and so on. This helps the editors, who like to cut on a movement so that the audience will be distracted by the motion and not notice the abruptness of the cut. If you're constantly doing different actions or are moving differently, it limits the editor's options. Again, you are trying to make their lives easier. A fringe benefit is that better continuity for you means more chances of you being the one they cut to and stay on.

Emotional continuity involves matching your emotions and mood from scene to scene. This is important as scenes are shot out of sequence. You should get something on the set called a "day out of days," which is a schedule of which scenes are being shot on which days (which is always subject to change.) Make a time frame for yourself, both as an actor to stay organized and as a character to stay chronologically in the story. As a lead character, this is even more important since you will be carrying a large portion of the story and you need to make sense. You as the

Acting on Film

actor need to be flexible and ready for any change—that's why the timeline and any notes you can make to help yourself are such great tools.

A common misconception is that film acting is always smaller and more subtle than stage acting, when in fact the opposite is often true. Sure, in a close-up you can do a lot of acting with your eyes alone, but in a wide or a master shot you need to use your entire body to act—any less and your performance will be missed. In those types of shots you need to physicalize, not internalize. Adjusting to size of shot is an area that Patrick Tucker elaborates upon in "Secrets of Screen Acting." Always ask the DP (director of photography) or director what the size of the shot is. You can also tell the size of the shot by how far away the boom operator is holding the mike. The boom operator wants to keep the mike right over the edge of the frame—as close as possible to pick up the sound but not to enter into the picture. You should always be aware of the size of the shot so that you can adjust your acting accordingly.

You need to adjust vocally according to size of shot as well. Remember the principle of the boom moving farther away as the shot gets wider? Your voice should follow this principle as well. In film, you do not want to over-project. Nothing sounds more artificial than a loud, over-articulated performance. Think of sucking the mike into you, rather than pushing your voice out toward the mike. Yes, in post-production they can take your voice down if you're too loud, but you will lose the intense emotional qualities you can gain by pulling in vocally.

Another area to be aware of that also goes against the "less is more" principle is reaction shots. The footage that most likely will wind up as a reaction shot is of you listening while the other character in the scene is talking. However, you have to give some kind of reaction to cut to. Even though you may feel like you are listening and reacting, it may not necessarily look like it. You have to do *more* with your face, not less. Listen with all of your senses and your whole body. Physicalize your reactions, but don't let your acting show.

Another great trick that Tucker gives in "Secrets of Screen Acting" is bringing your hands up into the shot. Again, this sounds artificial, but be aware of the communicative powers of your hands. If you can motivate your hands up into the frame (at key points, not all the time), the shot (and you) will be far more compelling.

Every film set is different. Depending upon the people involved, you will probably be treated according to the atmosphere on the set and the size of your role. My advice is to be nice to everyone all of the time, no matter how you are treated. Be professional and prepared. Bring wardrobe that could be used for your character— you never know how good or bad the wardrobe person can be, or how big the wardrobe budget is. Be proficient at doing your own makeup—again, you may be better than the makeup artist. This goes for men too—bring powder for shine and foundation or concealer for skin tone. Bring a portable alarm clock—you never know when the power could go out. Bring a book. Work out if you can. Calls tend to be early in the morning—try to get up half an hour early and warm up physically and vocally. Get sleep and eat right.

While you are shooting, you may be asked if you want to watch dailies. Dailies, or rushes, are rough cuts of the scenes that have already been shot and which many directors watch every day. As far as watching dailies goes, this is an issue on which actors feel differently. I didn't watch my dailies and I'm not sure if I ever would. It is hard to be objective about your work and when you are in the middle of the process, self-criticism could hamper your performance.

Finally, once you have done your preparation, familiarized yourself with technical terms, done your reading and research, gotten healthy and physically fit—relax! Be in the moment and concentrate on the other actors in the scene with you. Listen. React. Work moment-to-moment. The camera can read anything false. Concentrate on the relationship you have with the other character in the scene—that's what will be interesting. Know how to work with the camera, but ultimately forget about it. And try not to put too much pressure on yourself.

I read a great quote from Al Pacino in which he talks about "the courage, not just to fail, but to be utterly boring, like Brando did. They're not called 'keeps', they're called 'takes'. Actors think you have to keep everything!" Acting in film is a blast. Take pride in your ability and your craft; treat yourself as a professional and others will return the favor.

Heading West

Therefore devise with
me how we may fly,

Whither to go, and
what to bear with us.

By Adrianne Duncan

When the good folks at PERFORMINK Books asked me to write this article, I considered calling it "How To Move To Hollywood And *Not* Work As An Actor," because that's what most people (including myself) do. I'm only sort of kidding. Hopefully the following article will give you some tips on how to proceed, and some advice on how to keep it all in perspective.

The Decision

I am relatively biased about the merits of moving to L.A. versus staying in Chicago. As I write this from my apartment in Hollywood, I only wish I had moved out here sooner. Let me qualify that. First of all, Chicago is an incredible training ground and theatre city. You can do things in Chicago that you simply cannot do in L.A. (like have a sense of integrity, for example). Seriously, if you are new to the profession, stay in Chicago and get trained. Do as much theatre as you can. You will be much more likely to develop a good relationship with an agent (and more likely to get an agent at all) in Chicago than you will be in L.A. Use the commercial and industrial work that is available in Chicago to get experience on a set. But when you start itching for that film and television career, move. Do not fret. Do not hesitate. Chicago will still be there. If you hate L.A., you can move back. Your friends will still remember you. The reality is that, if you want to have a career above a certain level, you need to be in L.A.

The one thing you will have going for you in Hollywood, besides your amazing talent, is your age. L.A. is in love with youth. An agent here would much rather take a chance on an inexperienced 22-year-old than a 40-year-old with Royal Shakespeare Company credits. Now, if you're not 22, do not panic. There is room for everyone, and there are exceptions to every rule. There are wonderful, intelligent and human agents and casting directors here who will be more than willing to put their reputations on the line for actors they believe in, regardless of age. What you need to have above all else when you come here is a sense of tenacity. Many of the hopefuls that flock to Hollywood every year leave at the end of that year in defeat. A year is not enough time to determine whether you will make a career here. You need to stick it out and have a sense of perspective.

Preparing for your move

Okay, you've decided to make the leap. There are many things you will need to do, including throwing yourself a fabulous going-away party.

Research the city. Any Chicago bookstore will have books on L.A. I found a great one called "Moving To Los Angeles" published by "Backstreet Guides." There is one indispensable book you should own that you can find at Act I Bookstore called "The Working Actor's Guide to L.A". (also known as *WAG*). *WAG* is L.A.'s version of "The Book" and contains loads of practical information about the city as well as industry information. Buy some street maps at Rand McNally (you'll need them anyway) and familiarize yourself with the neighborhoods, major streets and the notorious L.A. freeway system.

Get *BackStage West*. *BSW* is L.A.'s PERFORMINK. It is primarily a theatre paper, but contains ads for photographers, demo reel duplication services, and the like. I suggest you start a subscription (or at least buy one) before you leave Chicago to familiarize yourself with the scene. *BSW* also has audition listings for film, theatre and some television. When you get to L.A., you can submit yourself for some very legitimate low-budget SAG independents that are looking for new talent, as well as for both Equity and non-Equity theatre. Most Equity theatre in L.A. is Equity-waiver (also known as 99-seat) theatre. Equity-waiver theatre is produced through a special arrangement with Equity whereby Equity actors can perform for free if the size of the house is 99 seats or less. Non-Equity performers can also be in those shows without affecting their union status. Most productions in L.A. are either outright showcases (evenings of scenes performed for agents and casting directors) or might as well be—the only intent of the many productions is to get the actors up in front of industry people. However, there is a lot of great, legitimate theatre in L.A.

Get familiar with the Breakdowns. The Breakdowns are a daily service provided to agents that let them know which roles are being cast for what shows and films. The Breakdowns come out early every morning and are either faxed or emailed out. Have your agent in Chicago show you the Breakdowns so that you can get an idea of what they are. It is not at all kosher for actors to get the Breakdowns, but every actor in L.A. does, and every agent and casting director knows about it. Once you move to L.A. and find your connection, you can have them either faxed or mailed to you and can expect to pay anywhere between $15 to $100 a month for the privilege. Remember, technically these aren't meant for actors, so be discreet. Once you start getting the Breakdowns, you can submit yourself for projects, even without an agent. Just don't expect to be called in for 90 percent of what you submit yourself for. And be aware of the rapidity with which most television shows cast.

The Move

Give yourself plenty of time with your move. Expect to backslide a little bit from where you were Chicago. Give yourself a cushion of at least a few weeks to get settled and attend to practicalities before you try to get an agent or manager or try to start auditioning.

Decide on a time frame. Pilot season (January through April/May) is probably the absolute worst time for you to go and expect to start working. It is the busiest time of year in L.A. (this is when multiple pilots for new television shows cast and shoot, and the agencies and casting directors are swamped). Some people suggest moving in the fall, which is not a bad time – but then you run up against the holidays, and pilot season is looming around the corner. I suggest summer or

Heading West

early fall. Summer is hiatus (meaning that the television shows are not shooting) and agents are much more free to see new talent.

I highly, highly, highly recommend that you visit L.A. for an extended period of time before you decide to move here. Make your visit about practical things. I would, in fact, recommend planning a trip immediately before your move to check out neighborhoods and rent an apartment. If you want to do career work, perhaps your Chicago agent can set up meetings with L.A. agents or casting directors. However, be prepared to have a wonderful conversation and then hear "Great, let us know when you move." Industry people here are wary of non-L.A. residents. They don't want to call you in last-minute for an audition for a show that shoots the next day only to discover you have returned home.

Find an apartment. I recommend that you do this before you move, if at all possible. There are several safe, convenient areas to consider. One is Hollywood and West Hollywood, which border each other and are centrally located. You'll be close to all the studios, minutes away from the Valley as well as the 10 freeways to take you to the ocean. Some areas in the Valley also have a nice, if more suburban feeling, such as Burbank and Sherman Oaks. If you prefer to live by the ocean, try Santa Monica or Venice, but expect crowds and high rent. There are two quirks about L.A. apartment rentals. One is that, in general, the financial and credit check you must pass in order to be approved is much more stringent than it is in Chicago. The other is that, for God knows what reason, most apartments in L.A. do not come equipped with refrigerators. Be prepared to buy (about $400 for a decent full-size) or rent (roughly $35 per month).

Buy a car. This is *mandatory*. You cannot exist as an actor in L.A. without a car. You know how quickly auditions and bookings can come up in Chicago; multiply that by 100 and factor in the non-existent subway system, inconvenient buses and expensive taxis that you have to pick up the phone and order, not hail in the street. If you decide to buy in California and want to check out used cars, the L.A. RECYCLER is an excellent place to start. This is a weekly newspaper devoted strictly to classifieds. They also have a free Web site with thousands of cars, photos included, at www.larecylcer.com.

Get a job (unless you're independently wealthy). Waiting tables in L.A. is a profession. I can't in good conscience recommend, but there are plenty of places to work and you will be in good company. Temping is an option I have found to be most flexible and relatively lucrative. Look in *WAG* for temp agencies; there is also a free magazine available in street kiosks called *Working World* that has ads from every temp agency in L.A. Other options include PA work (long hours and little glory), retail, dog walking (believe me, there's a lot of it), substitute teaching, tutoring for the SAT at one of the major centers like Kaplan or The Princeton Review, being a guide at the studios or being a personal assistant. Be creative. Don't pick a job that is inflexible time-wise, or that stifles you. You will have enough frustration in your chosen career.

Your SAG Card, Demo Reel and Resumé

Having your SAG card and some evidence of your work on tape are two great things to have in hand before beginning your journey west. They can, however, be obtained in L.A. as well. It is easier to get your SAG card in a smaller market like Chicago, and having it will set you apart from thousands in L.A. who do not. When casting directors have two days to cast a two-line co-star role, for example, they are not going to spend time looking at non-union actors who they will have to Taft-Hartley (basically, explain to SAG why Susie non-union is the only actor who could possibly do this two-line role out of the thousands already in the union who would kill for said small role). They are going to look in the already enormous pool of union actors and avoid the red tape of having to Taft-Hartley someone (though non-union actors do get the Taft-Hartley all the time).

Another way into SAG, which many non-union actors in L.A. opt for, is by getting three "vouchers" by being an extra. SAG members are none too happy about the voucher system, since essentially it lets people into the union who have not yet proven their worth (i.e. actually acted). But whatever works.

The demo reel is also a handy tool to have. The demo reel serves two purposes: (1) to show people that you can act and (2) to show that you have been "bought" (i.e. cast in a recognizable show or film with recognizable actors). Number two is vastly more important than number one here in good old L.A. You can have the most spectacular performances in 10 student films on your reel, and it will not carry as much weight as co-starring roles on *Buffy, The Vampire Slayer* and *That 70's Show*. Any roles in Chicago productions that are either recognizable or have recognizable actors in them are worth their weight in gold. However, as we all know, it's difficult to get cast in those shows. So don't worry about it. Get what you can of yourself on tape, but if you're itching to get moving, don't sit around Chicago waiting to improve your demo reel. Every day you wait, umpteen shows and films shoot in L.A. that you could potentially be a part of. You can get tape on yourself here as well. The dichotomy is that it's easier to get an agent and auditions in Chicago, but there is so much more production in L.A., even if it is harder to be seen for it.

As far as your resumé goes, there's not that much difference between an L.A. resumé and a Chicago one (as long as your Chicago resumé is set up correctly). Use terms like "co-star" and "principal" as opposed to the name of your character. List television and film first, before theatre. Don't list industrial film (unless you have nothing else). Don't list extra roles (unless they're very creatively camouflaged). By that I am not advocating lying. If you did not get cast on *Cupid*, don't put that you did.

Agents, Managers and Casting Directors

When you move to L.A., regardless of how wonderful your agency or audition situation was in Chicago, do not expect the same treatment unless you are extremely lucky. People do move out here and get set up with an agent or manager right away, but the opposite is more often the case. Even if you are one of the lucky few, don't expect as many auditions as you had in Chicago. There are hundreds more casting directors here than in Chicago, and you need to give them time to get to know you.

Unlike Chicago, L.A. is an exclusive town. That means you can only be signed with one agency (unlike Chicago's "multi-listing" system). There is also another major difference between L.A. and Chicago – commercial agencies and theatrical (meaning television, film and theatre) agencies are two distinct entities. Some theatrical agencies do have a commercial department and vice versa, but you will probably wind up with one commercial agent and a different theatrical agent. Needless to say, it is far, far easier to get a commercial agent than it is to get a theatrical agent.

There are several roads you can take to try to get an agent if you can't get any help from your Chicago agent. One is doing a mailing. Many will tell you that this is a waste of time; however, it definitely can work. Get a copy of *The L.A. Agent Book* by K. Callan, as well as a copy of a book (such as Ross Reports or the one published by Breakdown Services) that lists all the L.A. agents. The *L.A. Agent Book* is great in that it gives you a detailed perspective on each agency it lists, as well as some helpful advice. It does not list every agency in L.A., however. You need to figure out which agents you are targeting

Heading West

and do a mailing to a select few of 20 or 30. Target respectable, small to mid-sized agencies. Make sure they are SAG franchised and that they will look at developmental talent (that's everyone other than Tom Cruise and Halle Berry). Don't submit yourself to the big boy—that means ICM, William Morris and CAA. They will laugh at you (unless you're 19 and devastatingly beautiful).

There is a phenomenon in L.A. that often happens at the larger agencies known as "hip-pocketing" – that occurs when an agent (usually at one of the larger agencies) agrees to take on an actor without signing them. The agent will send you out on a few auditions and, depending on how you do, may agree to represent you from there. Obviously, if you book a series, they'll sign you. "Hip-pocketing" occurs when an agent likes an actor but doesn't want to stake their reputation on them, or risk overloading their client list.

Another way to try to get an agent is through a showcase or workshop. A showcase, as mentioned previously, is where scenes are performed for agents and casting directors. You can either pay to get into one or you can get a group of actors together yourself, rent a space, and organize the evening. Workshops happen more frequently and are for usually just one or two agents and/or casting directors. Workshops generally consist of 25 or so actors who are given scenes to cold read and can then participate in a question-and-answer session with the industry person. They are commonly referred to as "paid auditions," and, in a sense, they are. However, you can get some great advice and sometimes even great coaching from them, and people book roles and get agents from them all the time.

The best way to get an agent, though, is through a referral. Use your creativity and start spreading your feelers. Ask your friends to recommend you to their agents. If you create a relationship with a casting director in which it would be appropriate to ask a favor, ask if they have relationships with particular agents to whom they can recommend you.

Once you start getting meetings with agents, you may easily get turned down with the phrase "Oh, we already have several people like you." Like me, you think? But I'm different and unique! Not so to Hollywood. Hollywood is all about stereotypes, and the smaller the role is, the more stereotypically it will be cast. Just think of the scene in *Hollywood Shuffle* where the casting directors ask Robert Townsend if he can "be more black." An agent may even want you to take several headshots, each giving an idea of a different type of role—the tough girl, the timid secretary, the lawyer, the runaway, the hoodlum, the homeless man. Every day, casting directors receive thousands—that's right, *thousands*—of submissions for roles. They need to be able to flip through pictures and call in whoever most closely resemble the part they are casting. The bigger the role, the more extensive your resumé and the more clout your agent has, the less this phenomenon will exist. But it still exists, even in the upper echelons.

Another topic that may be confusing to Chicago actors is the one of managers. Many actors, even non-famous and non-working ones, have both an agent and a manager. Managers are not union-franchised, like agents are. Managers can also take up to 15 percent of whatever work they get for you, as opposed to an agent's 10 percent. If you have both an agent and a manager working on the same booking, you will give away 25 percent off the gross of that booking. So why get a manager, you ask? In my opinion, you should have as many people in your corner pushing to get you work. When you book something, trust me, you will be more than happy to give away 25 percent of it.

Avoid agents and managers who charge you some sort of a "fee" to be represented by them. Also avoid agents and managers who might not charge you a fee, but insist that you have your pictures taken by a specific photographer or take a specific class before they will represent you (trust me, they're getting a kickback). These people are not legitimate—it's better to fly solo than to hook up with one of these bozos. Also dodge auditions that require nudity and casting directors that ask you out (unless you're comfortable with them and it's not sleazy). This town is full of vultures just waiting to feed on corn-fed Midwesterners fresh off the bus.

If you are depressed after reading this article and finding out just how difficult Hollywood really is, don't be. I could spend hours telling you all the negative things about the business and you could easily be one of the lucky ones who hit L.A., get an agent and book a series within two weeks. As a highly successful actor friend of mine said, "You're probably not going to book this show or that movie tomorrow, statistically speaking. But if you did, and you were famous tomorrow, it wouldn't be that weird." There are multiple exceptions to every rule. There are nice people out here in positions of power who are genuinely interested in good actors and would love to further someone's career. The town is an exciting place to be in—it is steeped in Hollywood tradition and the business is all around you. If you genuinely love the craft, come. Just be prepared to work your ass off, smile bravely in the face of absurdity and fear and hang on tight. Perseverance will get you everywhere.

Looking for an opening night gift?

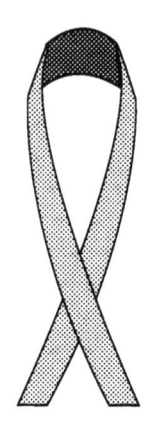

Donate to
Season of Concern
in your cast member's name.

Season of Concern
The Theatre Community's
AIDS Care Charity

Call 312/332-0518

Unions and Organizations

Didn't you guys hear? The strike's over!

Rivendell, Factory Girls

Actors Equity Association

> Now my co-mates, and brothers in exile, Hath not old custom made this life more sweet Than that of painted pomp?

By Carrie L. Kaufman

If you're at all familiar with theatre in New York or Los Angeles, you know that getting your Equity card is the first and foremost priority on young actors' minds. People do summer theatre as much for the Equity points as for the experience. They will find anything to get that Equity card.

Not in Chicago.

Non-Equity theatre rules in Chicago. There are, at any given time, over 200 theatres in this city and only 40 or so are Equity. Of those, over 40

Actors Equity

percent are Tier N, which is, for all intents and purposes, the stage between Equity and non-Equity.

This is not to say that actors can't, or shouldn't, join **Actors Equity Association.** But you must be wise about where your career is going and if you are ready to make the commitment. Once you join, you cannot do non-Equity theatre again unless you drop out of the union, forfeiting your dues and entrance fee and any benefits you may have accrued.

Actors need to consider the types of roles they can realistically be cast in. If you're a quirky, specialty character type, would it be wise to take that Goodman Equity contract and shut off the few future roles available by closing the non-Equity door? On the other hand, are there millions of people just like you who could be offered a non-Equity contract for less money in an Equity show and still be available to do non-Equity theatre?

While you're talking to yourself, consider this: In the last decade, Actors Equity in Chicago has bent over backwards to embrace small theatre companies, giving their members many more opportunities to work. The Chicago Area Theatre (CAT) contract has seven tiers with, among other things, different salary structures and casting requirements. Most exciting is the Tier N contract, which has made it possible for small, low-budget theatres to hire Equity actors on a show-by-show basis. (See below for a complete rundown of Equity contracts frequently used in the Chicago area.)

If you are faced with the decision whether or not to join Equity, remember— if a company thinks you're good enough to turn Equity, they'll probably think you're good enough to cast in the future.

Membership

There are three ways to join Actors Equity Association:

1) Get cast in an Equity show and sign an Equity contract.

2) Be a member in good standing of one of the eight unions that make up the 4-A's (Associated Actors and Artists of America). The sister unions are: **AFTRA** (the American Federation of Television and Radio Artists), **SAG** (the Screen Actors Guild), **AGMA** (the American Guild of Musical Artists), **AGVA** (the American Guild of Variety Artists), **SEG** (Screen Extras Guild), **HAU** (the Hebrew Actors Union), **APATE** (Association of Puerto Rican Artists and Theatrical Employees) and

Actors Equity

IAG (the International Artists Guild).

3) Join the Equity Membership Candidate Program.

The first avenue is possible, but rare.

The second is up to the other unions.

The **Equity Membership Candidate Program** (EMC) gives non-Equity actors the chance to work in Equity theatres and earn points toward Equity membership. The first step is getting cast for a non-Equity role by an Equity theatre who participates in the program. That's where summer theatre comes in.

Once you enroll and pay your $100 fee (which will go toward your initiation fee once you join the union), you earn points for each week you work in an Equity show until you reach 50 weeks, when you can join the union. At that point, you cannot be hired by an Equity theatre unless they sign you to an Equity contract. It is not unusual for a non-Equity actor to reach 50 weeks and then drop out of the EMC program so they don't have to join Equity. At that point you can re-join EMC, but you have to pay another $100 and start again from scratch.

The **initiation fee** for joining Actors Equity Association is $800. Members also must pay **semi-annual dues** totaling $78 and pay 2 percent of their gross salary for each Equity contract they sign.

Benefits

Equity members have access to a **health plan**, a **vision care plan** and **dental plan**. Equity actors can be eligible for one year of health benefits if they complete 10 Equity work weeks in a 12 month period. They have to keep working 10 weeks or more each following year to maintain health benefits.

Other benefits are a bit less tangible, but make up the backbone of Equity's existence. All producers must post a **bond**, for instance, for each show so Equity members can get paid if the show closes early. The union also administers a **pension plan** and provides **workers' compensation**. Actors under Equity contracts must be given certain breaks at certain periods of time, and the work space must be of a certain standard. Actors also can't work more than so many hours in a day or week. If you supply a costume piece you must, under Equity rules, be paid rental for that costume by the theatre.

I could go on. It's a union.

Contracts

Equity theatres in the Chicago area work under four basic types of contracts: **CAT** (Chicago Area Theatre), **LORT** (League of Resident Theatres), **Dinner Theatre** and **Children's Theatre**.

CAT

The Chicago Area Theatre contract came to being in the mid-1980's as a more flexible alternative to other Equity contracts. It is divided into seven tiers which specify, among other things, different salary arrangements and shows per week. Each tier has a standard minimum salary and benefits, but often theatres negotiate their own. Every tier but Tier N requires at least one Equity actor and an Equity stage manager. Tier N requires the stage manager be an Equity Membership Candidate. Tiers 2 - 6 require understudies, though the understudies do not have to be Equity members. An Equity understudy who is required to be there all the time would be paid the same as an Equity actor. An understudy who is hired on a "stand-by" basis would be paid a salary equivalent to three tiers down from the tier the show is working under. For instance, a stand-by understudy for a Tier VI theatre would be paid a Tier III salary, which would go up when the understudy went on. CAT theatres can be for-profit or non-profit.

Here is a brief rundown of the CAT tiers and their weekly salaries:

Tier 6: up to eight performances a week with a minimum salary of $609.50 for actors and $728.75 for stage managers.

Tier 5: up to eight performances a week with a minimum salary of $507.75 for actors and $594.25 for stage managers.

Tier 4: up to seven performances a week with a minimum salary of $429.75 for actors and $493.00 for stage managers.

Tier 3: up to six performances a week with a minimum salary of $298.25 for actors and $346.75 for stage managers.

Tier 2: up to five performances a week with a minimum salary of $217.55 for actors and $250.75 for stage managers.

Tier 1: up to four performances a week with a minimum salary of $141.75 for actors and $173.50 for stage managers.

Tier N: up to four performances a week with a minimum salary of $140.75 for actors, with no requirement to hire understudies or contribute to the health insurance fund. An Equity stage manager isn't

Actors Equity

required either, unless the show has three or more Equity actors. If a stage manager is hired under Tier N, it will cost $172.50 a week. In addition, Tier N theatres must do 50 percent of their season as Equity shows. Tier N work weeks do not count towards an actor's eligibility for health care benefits.

In addition, CAT contracts offer a "**More Remunerative Employment**" (MRE) clause. Essentially, if an actor gets a higher paying job — say a national commercial — then the theatre is required to let the actor do the commercial and put on an understudy in his stead until the job ends. This was a recognition that actors in Chicago earn their bread and butter from on-camera work and that if theatres wanted to attract actors who might earn more, they needed to promise them time off when the opportunities came up. The MRE is applicable to all CAT contracts, including CAT N. It is not applicable to many other Equity contracts. LORT and Dinner Theatre contracts, for instance, don't have MREs.

LORT

The **League of Resident Theatres** is a membership organization of non-profit regional theatres around the U.S. Guthrie is LORT. Arena Stage is LORT. Basically, the anchor regional theatre in any city is probably a member of LORT and therefore under a LORT Equity contract. LORT contracts with Equity permit touring and cover musical and non-musical theatre. Salary and contract requirements are based on the theatre's budget and box office grosses. There are five levels: A, B+, B, C & D. Theatres may employ a resident company but are not required to do so. Chicago has three LORT contract theatres: **Goodman**, **Northlight** and **Court**.

Dinner Theatre

Chicago is the birthplace of dinner theatre. Over 35 years ago, William Pullinsi took some inheritance money and started Candlelight Dinner Playhouse, inventing the concept of dinner theatre. Candlelight, sadly, closed its doors in 1997, but the concept lives on all over the country. Most of the dinner theatres in the Chicago area are in the suburbs and most focus their attention on musical theatre. Happy is easier to digest. There are six tier structures under the Dinner Theatre contract. Salary is based on seating capacity. Actors Equity must approve any dinner theatre in Chicago (and New York City, Los Angeles County or San Francisco). Dinner does not have to be served in the same room as the show. This puts theatres such as **Marriott Theatre at Lincolnshire** — which often sells restaurant/theatre packages — under this contract.

AFTRA & SAG

By Carrie L. Kaufman

Actors can get pretty steady work in commercials, industrials, voice-over and film in Chicago. Most of it's paid. Some of it's paid well. Almost all of it is union.

The **American Federation of Television and Radio Artists** (AFTRA) and the **Screen Actors Guild** (SAG) are the other two performer unions. They are closely related. In fact, in Chicago, AFTRA and SAG are run out of the same office under one executive director. They are, like all unions, run by an elected board of members.

Whether or not a production is covered by AFTRA or SAG is quite complicated and is one of the reasons union members have been clamoring for a merger for decades.

SAG covers all movies and all animation, regardless of the medium. If a movie is shot on film, it's SAG. If it's shot on digital video, it's still SAG. It's SAG even if it is only released on TV.

AFTRA covers radio and vocal recording, as well as broadcast news people. It also covers awards shows and soap operas.

Union jurisdiction gets murky when it comes to commercials, industrials (workplace videos), basic cable and non-prime-time programming or syndicated programming. Officially, it's up to the producer to decide which contract to use. In cities where AFTRA and SAG are administered out of the same office, jurisdiction over television commercials and industrials is determined by the medium used. Commercials and industrials in Chicago, for instance, are SAG if they are shot on film and AFTRA if they are shot on video.

Membership

Joining AFTRA and SAG is fairly easy, though not cheap. You can join AFTRA at any time by simply paying the initiation fee and half a year's

AFTRA & SAG

dues. For SAG, you first have to get cast under a SAG contract. That means you land your first big commercial (for convenience sake, let's say it's shot on film and is SAG), or even local SAG commercial, or you get the role of the young doctor who comes into the hospital room and says, "It's late. Everybody out," in the latest Bruce Willis flick. Once you get that contract, you are eligible to join SAG. But you don't have to join right away.

As you're signing that contract, you will likely hear — from your agent or the casting director, or even the production coordinator — two words: **Taft-Hartley.** "You're Taft-Hartley now, so you'd better call the union," the production coordinator will say as she bumps you up from an extra to a speaking role.

The Taft-Hartley Act is one of the laws that covers unions and is also known as the National Labor Relations Act. Essentially, it says that a union can't require somebody to join until 30 days after their first day of employment. For a steel worker, that's a month after they're hired. For an actor, that could be years after they get their first job.

Once you get that first SAG job, you have 30 days to take as much union work as you can land without joining the union. If you land a union job 31 days after your first, though, you immediately have to join the union.

This is when actors get in trouble. **The initiation fee for SAG is currently $1,234.00.** That number is the equivalent of two day rates in a theatrical film or television show. Minimum yearly dues are $100, to be paid in twice yearly installments — the first in addition to the initiation fee when you join. The initiation fee for AFTRA is currently $1,000. Minimum yearly dues are $116, to be paid in twice yearly installments. Dues for both unions are based on an actor's earnings.

So, you've spent all the money you made two years ago doing SAG jobs under the Taft-Hartley 30-day protection. Now you have to fork over $1,234 to the union *before you even step on the set.* Don't have it? Too bad. You should have put it away two years ago in anticipation of having to join. You either come up with the money or lose the job— and possibly your agent's good will. SAG and AFTRA do offer payment plans, but you have to be ready to fork over something.

Contracts

There are multiple SAG and AFTRA contracts for various aspects of the business. Under some contracts, you might just get paid a session fee. Under others, you might get paid a session fee plus residuals, with more to be negotiated after the sale of the production. SAG and AFTRA have books on this.

As many of you know, in 2000 AFTRA and SAG held a six-month long strike against the advertising industry and, more specifically, the corporations that use actors to advertise their products. They came away with a mix of a contract with residuals and without; but they got a significant pay raise in lieu of residuals. Most SAG or AFTRA members in Chicago make most of their acting money by doing commercials, so here's a basic run-down.

If you make a commercial for radio or TV, you will be paid a $500 session fee. Above that, if your commercial runs on network TV — ABC, NBC, CBS, FOX — then you will get paid every time that commercial runs. If the commercial runs on cable, you will get paid a flat rate above the session fee for 13-weeks of use. Most commercials will have a combination of cable and network runs. SAG and AFTRA didn't satisfactorily resolve tracking when ads ran on which medium.

But they did get some satisfaction on rates for the Internet. SAG and AFTRA have limited jurisdiction on Internet commercials. Commercials made for broadcast and moved to the Internet will earn actors $1,500, or three session fees, for each 13-week period of use. Ads made directly for the Internet are subject to negotiation by the actor and his agent and the ad agency.

For more comprehensive information on the SAG/AFTRA commercials contract, head to www.performink.com. You will also find updates there on the TV and movies contract that is up for negotiation — and some say heading for another strike — in June.

Product Conflict

If the ad agency stops running a commercial, they still might have to pay you. Under rules governing **product conflict,** an actor under contract to do a commercial for one type of product — such as a Nissan — cannot turn around and do a commercial for a competitive product — such as the Ford F150. Remember, image is everything, and neither ad agencies nor their clients want that cuddly, yet enigmatic man the public is so identifying with to show up selling a competitive product.

In that case, the advertiser must pay the actor a **holding fee** to keep the actor from being in a competitive commercial. The holding fee, paid every 13 weeks, is equivalent to the session fee. For nice national campaigns, the agency and client might pay the fee for a few years.

Now, suppose you did a non-union commercial for the MaidRite Hamburger Shack back in your hometown of Waterloo, Iowa in the summer of 1990. Then you get cast in a national Burger King commercial. Great, right? Sorry. You're out of luck. That MaidRite commercial was non-union. Unless your contract specified otherwise, they may still be running the commercial. Even if they aren't, they don't have to pay you anything to hold the commercial, and they could run it any time. In fact, if the owner of the store sees your face coming across his TV screen every hour or so, he might decide to take your old commercial out of the can and exploit your newfound familiarity.

Chances are, if you make a non-union commercial, you can never do a union commercial for the same type of product. Period. You may, if you want to pay the legal bills, go back and draw up a contract with the non-union client to not use the commercial again. You may have to pay the non-union client a hefty sum in order to do so.

If you ignore that MaidRite commercial and take the Burger King job, then someone from Burger King notices your younger face on a local TV station in Iowa, the trouble you can get into is enormous. The production company may simply be able to cut you out of the Burger King commercial and you'll have to forfeit any fees you may have earned. If they can't do that, and the Burger King bigwigs and the ad agency decide to pull the commercial, *you could be liable for all of the expenses incurred to put that commercial together.* Everything. The entire production — hundreds of thousands of dollars — could be charged to you.

Similar consequences can ensue if you did a union commercial for McDonald's in 1990 and have simply "forgotten" about those checks McDonald's is still paying you in holding fees.

That said, if you do a union commercial for McDonald's and they stop paying you holding fees, they cannot run that commercial again without hiring you again. Then you are free to do the Burger King commercial. This is one obvious advantage of working under a union.

Benefits

AFTRA and SAG are unions and give their members the same benefits as any union, including pension, retirement and health plans.

Actors must earn $7,500 in a 12-month period to get one year of health insurance. To keep it, they have to make at least $7,500 per year thereafter.

AFTRA & SAG

On a set, AFTRA and SAG negotiate everything from meals and bathroom breaks to overtime. There are myriad rules, and it would behoove any actor to call the AFTRA/SAG office to find out what they are.

If an actor is on a shoot and something comes up that is questionable — say the production manager says everybody is working overtime and not getting paid overtime rates — it's not a union actor's responsibility to argue. Tell the production manager that it's all right with you if it's all right with your union and your agent, then get on the horn and call either one. Let them do the arguing for you.

Joining a union is never an easy process. There are rules and regulations galore. Sometimes it might seem as if they get in the way. But all the rules are there to protect the members, and actors need all the protection they can get.

Need personal protection? Check out the Attorneys on page 303

Unions

Actors Equity Association
203 N. Wabash #1700
Chicago, IL 60601
312/641-0393
312/641-6365 - fax
www.actorsequity.org

American Federation of Television & Radio Artists (AFTRA)
1 E. Erie #650
Chicago, IL 60611
312/573-8081
312/573-0318 - fax
www.aftra.org

Directors Guild of America
400 N. Michigan #307
Chicago, IL 60611
312/644-5050
312/644-5776 - fax
www.dga.org

Screen Actors Guild (SAG)
1 E. Erie #650
Chicago, IL 60611
312/573-8081
312/573-0318 - fax
www.sag.org

Ch 6. Unions & Organizations 187

Resources

Legal Resources

As actors, we are often left to fend for ourselves, particularly if we are not in a union. Fortunately, the government provides a number of agencies that will help you deal with disputes of hiring or payment. Following is a list of the main ones.

Employment Issues

Illinois Department of Labor
160 N. LaSalle - 13th floor
Chicago, IL 60601
Wage Claim Division (for employment compensation)
312/793-2808

If your dispute is directly with an employer and it deals with your pay, call the **Wage Claim Division** of the Department of Labor. They step in when an actor is paid less than they were hired for or when an actor is not paid at all (if, in fact the theatre or production company has agreed to pay in the first place).

If you feel you've been wronged in your pay, file a complaint with the Wage Claim Division. They will send a letter to the employer. When they get the employer's response, they will compare your claim to their response and either dismiss it or send it to the next level—a hearing. If the employer is found liable in the hearing, he or she has a certain amount of time to pay. If the employer still doesn't pay, Wage Claim then sends it to the Attorney General's office, where legal proceedings are begun. For this last phase to take place, actors need to stay in touch with the Department of Labor after an employer is found liable. The department has no way of knowing if the employer has fulfilled his or her obligations unless you tell them.

The Equal Opportunity Employment Commission

National Office	Chicago District Office
1801 L Street, N.W.	500 West Madison #2800
Washington, D.C. 20507	Chicago, IL 60661
202/663-4900	**312/353-2713**
TDD: 202/663-4494	TDD: 312/353-2421
www.eeoc.gov	

The **EEOC** protects against discrimination in the workplace. If you feel you've been sexually harassed, call the EEOC and make a complaint. If you feel you've been dismissed because of your race, call the EEOC.

There are laws that protect you and the commission will check out your story. Chances are, you aren't the only one who has complained.

In cases of sexual discrimination—including harassment and pregnancy—you can also call the **Women's Bureau,** which has regional offices all over the country. The Chicago office of the Women's Bureau is at 312/353-6985. They cover the Illinois, Indiana, Michigan, Minnesota, Ohio and Wisconsin areas.

The Women's Bureau is not an enforcing agency. They are a resource for information and statistics on women in the workplace. But they can give you advice or point you in the right direction if you feel you've been wronged.

Department of Human Rights
100 W. Randolph #10-100
Chicago, IL 60601
312/814-6200
www.state.il.us.dhr

The Illinois Department of Human Rights deals with any sort of discrimination in the work force. They are essentially the state alternative to the EEOC. If you've been fired because you're pregnant, call them. If you've been fired because you're over 40, they can help. If you've been fired or not hired because you're African-American or Hispanic or have an unfavorable military discharge or an arrest record, call them. They are also the place to call if you've been the victim of sexual harassment.

Consumer Issues

Illinois Attorney General
100 W. Randolph
Chicago, IL 60601
312/814-3000
(Check the white pages for specific departments.)

The Office of the Attorney General deals with consumer issues. If you pay to get your headshots reproduced and the company goes bankrupt after it's cashed your check, call the Attorney General's office.

Better Business Bureau
Chicago Office
330 N. Wabash
Chicago, IL 60611
312/832-0500

Resources

The Better Business Bureau deals with contracts and obligations. If you paid a photographer to take your headshot but the film came out totally black, and he won't give you your money back, call the Better Business Bureau. (As well as the Attorney General's office).

If, however, that same photographer asks you to pose nude or if an agent starts yelling and screaming obscenities at you, the Better Business Bureau will be of no help. They may be sympathetic, but they do not deal with matters of behavior.

Similar Organizations

The Actors' Fund
203 N. Wabash #2104
Chicago, IL 60601
312/372-0989 • 312/372-0272 - fax
www.actorsfund.org

Chicago Access Corporation
322 S. Green #100
Chicago, IL 60607
312/738-1400 • 312/738-2519 - fax
www.cantv.org

Chicago Dance Coalition
410 S. Michigan #819
Chicago, IL 60605
312/419-8384

Chicago Film Office
1 N. LaSalle #2165
Chicago, IL 60602
312/744-6415 • 312/744-1378 - fax
www.ci.chi.il.us/wm/specialevents/filmoffice/

Chicago National Association of Dance Masters
5411 E. State St. #202
Rockford, IL 61108
815/397-6052 • 815/397-6799 - fax
www.cnadm.com

Illinois Film Office
100 W. Randolph - 3rd Floor
Chicago, IL 60601
312/814-3600
312/814-8874 - fax
www.commerce.state.il.us

National Dinner Theatre Association
P.O. Box 726
Marshall, MI 49068
616/781-7859
616/781-4880 - fax
www.ndta.com

University/Resident Theatre Association (U/RTA)
1560 Broadway #414
New York, NY 10036
212/221-1130
212/869-2752 - fax
www.urta.com

Women in the Director's Chair
941 W. Lawrence #500
Chicago, IL 60640
773/907-0610
773/907-0381 - fax
www.widc.org

Theatres

The audition notice said they were looking for character actors. What the hell?

Chicago Shakespeare Theater, "Two Gentlemen of Verona"

Director's Directing

All the world's a stage, And all the men and women merely players: They have their exits and their entrances, And one man in his time plays many parts.

By Carrie L. Kaufman

Directing is trusting. Directing is giving in to the play. Directing is sculpting. Every director will say that their prep depends on the play, but in talking to them some patterns emerge. And, strangely, even those who say they don't prep well usually walk into the play with an overall metaphor—if not for the play itself, then certainly for their directing approach. Many of these directors take similar approaches, yet they highlighted different things when interviewed. Some gave more details about the overall esthetic and their overriding metaphor. Some gave nitty gritty details about the task of working with actors. It doesn't mean the director who talked more about esthetic doesn't do those same nitty gritty details or that the detail person doesn't have a clear esthetic. It just means that they, as directors, tend to see their craft through a particular lens.

Directors

For **Cal MacLean,** it's text and rhythm. He immerses himself in the text, often rewriting it or, to be more precise, re-translating. When the text work is done, when he's sure he has the right theatrical piece for the budget and space and group of actors he's working with, he lets go and lets the rhythm of the piece take over.

That approach has garnered MacLean critical acclaim and awards in Chicago for much of the past decade. An ensemble member at Famous Door, MacLean has directed some of that theatre's turning point productions, including *Salt of the Earth* in 1991, *Conquest of the South Pole* in 1992 and last season's *Ghetto,* which recently won him a Jeff Award.

One can look at *Ghetto* as a case study of how MacLean works.

"There were a lot of ideas from a lot of the various versions of that play that I read that became our version." Essentially, he says, the *Ghetto* Chicago audiences saw for almost six months was an adaptation of Joshua Sobel's translation. The original play called for almost 60 actors and for scenes that took place in many different places in the ghetto. MacLean distilled all of the scenes to take place in the Yiddish theatre the Jews of the ghetto had been forced to recreate. But the scenes didn't just take place in the theatre, they took place in the theatrical style common to Yiddish theatre at mid-century.

"The set was a theatre and we tried to encapsulate the life of the entire ghetto within the walls of that theatre," says MacLean. "The things that happened elsewhere were in some way imagined as if the company of actors had turned that piece of life into a skit, a scene, a dance, a debate. We weren't seeing this actually happen, we were presenting it as if the ghetto theatre had turned it into a scene."

The audience didn't necessarily see it, but the actors knew and MacLean knew. "It was not meant to be a solution that explained what all this was, it simply guided our approach," he says.

MacLean uses that approach in many of his plays, a sort of underlying metaphor akin to the actor's psychological gesture. Nobody knows it's there, but it informs the choices made by everyone involved.

The Yiddish theatre approach fit in with another oft-used theme in a Cal MacLean directed play—the hyper-theatrical.

"The theatre that I tend to like has that theatrical element to it," says MacLean. "It is much more interesting to me to watch performers who are able to not only inhabit the internal guts of the play and the charac-

Directors

ters in the play, but who are also conscious of the skill in performance."

Often, MacLean breaks through the fourth wall by connecting the audience and actors through the rhythms of the piece. It might, indeed, be a piece of music that sets the tone. It might simply be a phrase or idea repeated by the actors, but just like good music, audiences tend to feel as much as see a Cal MacLean-directed play. The son of a musician, MacLean sees rhythm as a key element in communicating with actors, so it's not surprising that rhythm translates into the actors' communication with the audience.

"I often work through trying to encourage [actors] to feel the rhythmic pulse of the language," he says. Sometimes that entails giving an actor a line, but he's not trying to force an imitative line reading. "I just want them to get the pulse and do with the pulse what they feel."

MacLean approaches blocking in the same way. Unless the scene needs to be choreographed—like the orgy scene in *Ghetto*—he doesn't come into rehearsal with a master plan detailing exactly where each person should move at a given moment. He often comes in with an idea, then lets the actors trust their impulses. But he doesn't let them go too far.

"Most of the time it will start out organically and we'll pursue many different possibilities and everybody's instincts, and then I'll say this, this, this and this," he says.

If you're cast by MacLean, be prepared to read. It depends on the play, but he usually starts rehearsals with a few days of table work in which the actors and designers are not only reading the text, but also reading the dramaturgical material MacLean has spent the last few months collecting.

With all the planning MacLean walks in with, he says it's easy to get bogged down in the rhythm and style, for instance, and forget about getting to the nub of what the characters want from each other. This is one of the things he talks about with his directing students at Illinois State, where he is head of directing.

"When you're in a rehearsal process, you have many different stages: foundation, structure, surface and detail. It's important not to get those things mixed up," says MacLean. When a director walks into rehearsal, he or she has to not focus on all of the prep work and just "be clear on what it is we're exploring today. I try not to get bogged down by being clear of what the goal of rehearsal should be," says MacLean.

MacLean's work in Chicago can almost exclusively be seen at Famous

Directors

Door. He is also the artistic director of the Illinois Shakespeare Festival and directs many of that theatre's projects.

The first thing **Gary Griffin** deals with in rehearsal is fear. No, he doesn't walk in with his knees shaking, but a play for Griffin is a block of granite that needs to be sculpted to uncover its form. The fear lies in where to make the first blow with the chisel and what choices to make next.

"It's good to just right from the beginning look at the things that scare us and tackle them head on," Griffin says of his early rehearsal process. Like a sculptor, he says, he needs to "make a big mess," out of which comes "the power of exploration." He has actors overdo moments, ham it up as it were. He encourages them to explore choices that are the opposite of the obvious ones. That gives them a freedom, more room for maneuver. Having struck the stone from sides they never thought possible and seeing not its disintegration but its form emerge, they are not afraid to strike from other sides.

As with all the other directors interviewed, Griffin stresses that his approach tends to be different with each play. He's not afraid of table work in rehearsal, but he doesn't want to keep actors sitting and thinking for longer than is necessary for the piece.

"It's in your body," he says. "The act of really doing a play isn't an act of literary criticism." Actors can talk about why someone does or says something, but Griffin believes, "You have a better sense of that if your body's engaged."

Griffin comes into rehearsal with some rough blocking in his head, but, he says, "hopefully, blocking evolves through behavior." Stage movement for him isn't really an actor problem anyway.

"I find that blocking and staging decisions are more things you do in pre-production with your set designer," Griffin says. A good design creates good blocking patterns. "Hopefully your design encourages strong diagonals, strong vantage points [and] behavior" that the actors will naturally fall into.

Griffin likes the actors he casts to be off book as soon as possible, though he's mindful of those who need to wrestle with the words and the characterization as one piece. "Some actors just can't say a line until they mean it," he says.

"First run-throughs are just terribly painful experiences," Griffin says. "I think actors need to get a grasp on the big picture. You learn a lot

Directors

about how moments flow in and out of each other." He does at least three run-throughs before tech, then he expects actors to keep working when the design elements are integrated.

"I like the actors to give me as much of their performance as possible and not just mark their way through it," Griffin says.

The kinds of actors Griffin likes to work with are those "who have that sense of play and mischief," he says. "I tend to connect best with people who love the process of discovery and who like to continually challenge the play and don't like to set things right away and are real explorers and learners." He finds it hard to work with actors who are too result-oriented.

For Griffin, a good play as well as a good process is about change and discovery. "In the theatre we get this opportunity to pay attention better," he says. "We observe people who clearly in some way have blinders on. We watch them go from a place where they're not paying attention to a sense of heightened awareness as they go through the story." Figuring out what the characters are blind to and then discovering how they attain sight is one of the thrills of directing for Griffin.

Another thrill is that he directs so often. He has directed such diverse pieces as *Gross Indecency,* based on the life of Oscar Wilde, at Court theatre; the American premiere of Stephen Sondheim's unearthed first musical *Saturday Night,* with completely new musical arrangements and even an extra song; Famous Door's acclaimed 1999 production of the British coming-out play *Beautiful Thing,* which transferred to New York for a short run; and Chicago Shakespeare's 2000 production of Peter Whelen's *The Herbal Bed,* about a scandal involving Shakespeare's daughter. As of this writing, he is preparing for Court Theatre's *Hay Fever,* a 1930's musical. Griffin directs an average of six shows a year, which makes him one of the most in-demand directors in town, and most of the shows he directs get critical, as well as audience, acclaim, which also makes him one of the most successful.

Griffin often goes from opening night right into a rehearsal for another play, but he doesn't lament the lack of prep time. He puts in his dramaturgical work, then lets the play sit in the back of his head, and things that happen in his life inform the piece. Being busy helps in this process. "When you have something else to think about when you're working, it's often really positive because you can't obsess."

Gary Griffin is currently the associate artistic director at Chicago Shakespeare Theatre and a company member at Famous Door. He has been directing in Chicago for 12 years.

"For me, the art of directing is the art of listening," says **Abigail Deser**. "That might mean listening to the text, it might be listening to what's underneath or between the words, it might be listening to the actors, it might be listening to the music. It is not a skill that you learn, it is something you give into."

In other words, to paraphrase Sanford Meisner, you can't do directing, you have to let the play show you how to direct.

Deser directs much like she was taught to act, by focusing on full-body listening and exploring incessantly what the characters want. She came to directing, she says, in the midst of a two-year Meisner intensive she was taking in New York. She would direct scenes for class and found she could apply what she was learning to directing as well as acting.

To be in an Abigail Deser directed play is to be continually focused on the point. She likes her actors to have the freedom to explore—she does virtually no blocking, for instance—but their exploration can't be ambiguous.

"It's my job to help the actors clarify what it is they're doing, what it is they want and whether they're getting it," says Deser. "I ask them to check in all the time [asking themselves] are you getting what you want. One of the things I watch for is when things become vague," she says. "Usually it's because the actor doesn't know what they want."

For Deser, a "singular clear action makes for good acting. I believe you can't play more than one thing at any given moment."

Deser does a lot of research before rehearsals begin. She closely scrutinizes the text, making sure she know what every line means. She'll listen to music that lends itself to the piece. She'll read about the life and times of the period. She'll do whatever the play dictates and whatever comes to her as she's churning through it. Then she lets it go.

"I do homework so I know absolutely everything, and then I walk into the room and I try to forget everything I know," she says, adding, "Half the time, what the actors discover is more interesting or more truthful or more alive than what I would bring."

In fact, even with all of her preparation, Deser doesn't really know the characters until she meets them in the bodies of the actors she has or is about to cast.

"I know the story intimately, and I have an impression of the charac-

Directors

ters, like one would an impression of the person," she says.

Her rehearsal process works on the same pattern as her pre-rehearsal preparation. She spends the first day of table work describing for the cast the world of the production of the particular play they are about to embark on. Then, Deser and the cast will often spend days combing through the text, posing questions line by line and occasionally word by word, closely examining the plot of the play and intentions of each character, often through different perspectives. After that, they get on their feet and "stop thinking the script and start working to get it in our bodies.

"With the script in hand, we begin to create a world, physically and emotionally using the words we have."

Deser might let the actors go for a few minutes and see what they come up with. She is also apt to interrupt them after a couple of lines.

"Two actors might begin a scene with the first line of that scene, and I might stop them and say, okay what are the existing conditions that you come into the room with?" Deser explains. Are they late? Are they coming in with good news? Bad news? She asks the actors what their expectations are when they walk in and how that changes with what they discover. She asks them simply if they believe the other actor.

"I have them act these various scenarios out rather than talk them out until we find one that seems to work," she says. Then she lets the actors go on again, until they get stuck or start to wander into vagueness. Then she asks them more questions, including whether or not what they've decided is a helpful choice. She doesn't give them the choice, or even the verb. She asks the questions that will make them choose the right action for themselves.

"I can't say act devastated, what I can say is where were you and if they've hit on the right thing, it will create the right condition," says Deser. "I don't have a stake in whether they're coming from the grocery store or visiting their dying friend. I care about the life they walk into the room with."

In terms of blocking, she does shape the piece towards the end, but she finds that the actors usually do most of the work. "Anxiety that manifests itself about where should they go is really anxiety about what should they do," she says. Once those questions are answered, the blocking usually takes care of itself.

"Ultimately what I strive for is an intuitive way of working when I'm in rehearsal," Deser says. "I try to give in to the possibilities as opposed to hold on tightly to some design."

Abigail Deser is a company member and resident director at Roadworks. She has also directed for Steppenwolf, Famous Door and other theatre companies.

A **Mary Zimmerman** play is like no other. People hang upside down on pipes or slog through water. Whole relationships are indicated with a dance or a roll on the floor. Sometimes they don't even take place on a stage. But in each and every one, actors are connecting with each other in vital ways and mesmerizing stories are being told.

Mary Zimmerman works like no other director in Chicago. She writes all of her plays, but she doesn't write them until rehearsal. Often, she doesn't have the entire text set until just a few days before tech. She does very little research beyond reading the original text from which her stories will come.

"I make the thing in rehearsal and I don't know what it is before I start," she says. "I don't know anything except it opens on a certain date and it's based on a certain text."

She doesn't have elongated rehearsal periods, either. Mostly, she rehearses for four weeks. She says she has virtually no other thoughts in her life during that period. She doesn't even write on a regular basis. It could be after rehearsal, when she's sparked by something she has seen.. It could be before rehearsal. It could be in the middle of the night.

She doesn't even know which stories, or parts of stories, she'll pursue. She says she takes that from who she casts.

"I'm looking for the most graceful and intelligent people I can find," she says of the actors she casts. Zimmerman pieces are very balletic. Movement tells the story as much as—maybe more than—words.

She does not have her actors improvise. They do not work through stories that she simply writes down.

She does know—vaguely—which parts actors will play when she casts them. Often, she'll know within the first week, after she's had a chance to write some material.

Sometimes she'll come into the auditions with sides, but they don't necessarily make it into the play. On the first day, she'll talk with the cast about the original text, which they will have already read. From that discussion, she will begin to get a sense of which stories to write for which actors. Sometimes she'll come in with an image on that first day—like

Directors

building a camel—and work with the cast on making it happen.

"I'm sort of stalling a little bit until I can write," she says.

By the second day of rehearsals, she usually has a few scenes.

The design process is her favorite part about directing. "It's a dreamy collaborative process where you get to make something solid," she says. "It's like creating a little diorama."

Often, the design will shape the script and sometimes even dictate the adaptation.

For the 1999 Lookingglass production of *Metamorphoses,* all she knew was she wanted it to be in water. That's what she started with. "The idea of doing a show in water preceded what show it was going to be," she says. "The idea of water determined what myths I picked."

With last season's Lookingglass production of *11 Rooms of Proust,* Zimmerman says her designers were with her and the cast every day. *Proust* took place in 11 different rooms, with no set stage.

"Literally [*Proust*] was being designed as I was staging it," she says. Lighting designer John Culbert would put up a light and Zimmerman would stage into that.

Zimmerman tends to work with the same designers: Lookingglass artistic associates Mara Blumenfeld for costumes and Dan Ostling for sets. Culbert lit *Proust* and *SM.* She works more with lighting designer T.J. Gerckens, who just won a Jeff for *The Odyssey* and who also lit *Journey to the West* and *The Notebooks of Leonardo daVinci,* among others.

"My designers and I tend to have a vocabulary built up. They know how I think, and I know how they think."

And while she is introducing new scenes right up to tech, she stresses "There are scenes that have had way more attention than the average play thing because there's been nothing else to rehearse."

Her metaphorical approach to her work has changed over the years. "I used to have an architectural metaphor—there was nothing and we built this thing," she says. "Now it's archeological. The thing is complete and it's waiting for us and it's lying under the ground and all we have to do is uncover it. If we work with fear and work too fast, we will damage it and if we work too slow, we will never fully unearth the treasure".

Audition Nightmares!

He that escapes me without some broken limb, shall acquit him well.

By Kevin Heckman

Audition horror stories make up the bread and butter of many a barroom conversation. We've all had those terrible experiences, either because we did something stupid, the theatre did something unprofessional or the power went off in the middle of our monologue. Following are a mere sample of dozens of audition horror stories from actors and directors throughout town, and, because we simply can't help ourselves, a little advice to go with them.

Preparation

Many were the tale of the unprepared auditionee. If you haven't practiced or aren't ready for an audition, you run the risk of being memorable for all the wrong reasons.

Some time ago we were auditioning for a show wherein the director required a two-minute monologue. A person showed up with no monologue prepared but offered to read a speech from the script. The script was a new one and not published. The director had a copy in front of him. The director informed the person that reading from the script was NOT acceptable and he wanted a two-minute monologue. The person insisted they could read from the script, picked up the director's copy and began searching for a speech. The director tried to pull the script away and the person and the director actually had a struggle over the script. Finally, the director pulled it away and told the person to do a prepared monologue or leave. The person came up with some half-baked monologue and then left.

A woman came in to audition, and we thought she was shy. During the monologue it became clear that English was her second language, which was fine. Her acting was okay but the singing part is what I'll always remember. Rather than bring sheet music, she asked to sing *a capella*. Her choice was Madonna's "Like a Prayer." The choice was bad, but what was worse was that she sang while holding the liner notes from the tape cassette packaging. It was like watching a car accident in slow motion.

Appropriate Behavior

More than anything else, inappropriate behavior will plant your headshot firmly in the "Do Not Call—Ever!" file. This means knowing who you're auditioning for, what they produce and not assaulting anyone, among other things.

During one audition, a well-endowed woman in a very loose white blouse delivered a dramatic monologue. While at no point in the monologue does the character say "I think I'll get down on all fours now. I think I'll bend this and then that way. Watch me arch my back," that was exactly what she did. And every move seemed to be calculated to reveal more and more cleavage. It was mesmerizing. I can't remember her monologue or song and her face is a faint memory, but I'll always remember the audition. At the time I began thinking, "screw theatre, let's just charge for this." The others who were there tell me she was a good actress, a little unpolished, but good. She so distracted me I could not tell. I guess the whole thing wouldn't seem so odd to me if it weren't for the fact that she was auditioning for Cinderella for a family theatre.

While I was casting for About Face, an actor who was reading an angry, but not violent, scene grabbed the reader (who just happened to be the artistic director) by the shirt and shoved him through the first and into the SECOND row of the audience. Oddly enough, he is not an actor who I felt needed to be seen by any of the other theatres where I have worked.

One of the worst was the actor with the heavy Berwyn dialect who showed up and introduced "this thing I wrote" as his audition piece. He then proceeded to do Sean Connery's "You want to get Capone?" monologue from *The Untouchables*. Since the guy wasn't David Mamet, it made for a generally uncomfortable feeling—incompetence and dishonesty all wrapped into an interminable two-minute package.

We once had a policeman (not Chicago--we weren't sure by the uniform where he was from, and wondered if he was truly a cop) show up for an audition for one of our shows--we weren't looking for a cop at all. He spent his entire audition time showing us his loaded gun. When he was finished, we thanked him. And that was that.

On a less violent note, we once had an actor ask us the following, just as he was about to do his monologue: "Oh, can I ask a question first . . . How much do you pay. Because if it's not a lot, I don't want to audition." Keep in mind that he already had made his appointment and was now there, auditioning in his allotted time slot.

Don't Lie on Your Resumé

Hopefully everyone realizes that lying on their resumé about a local show is a BAD idea.

A young man came in to audition for me at a theatre where I had directed several plays. I was looking at his resumé, and I see a show listed that I know was done here at this theatre. "So, you were in ___, huh?" "Yes, it was a great experience," he replies. I said, "I know, I directed it and it was wonderful. You can leave now."

The famous audition story at Second City is when an actor was auditioning in LA for a small theatre production and had a credit on his resumé for Second City in Chicago. The woman running the audition was an alum of the theatre and said "You know, I was at Second City during that time and I don't remember you." He continued to claim that he was in the resident company there. She said, "Do Bernie" - meaning, do an imitation of Second City co-founder Bernie Sahlins, which every staff or cast member of the theatre could do— the guy said "Whose Bernie?" He was asked to leave the audition.

X-Files

Some stories didn't necessarily lend themselves to morals, but are part of Chicago theatrical lore, or at least should be.

Auditions

A man attended the Unifieds auditions a few years ago. He came in and did his two pieces and was promptly arrested as he left the stage by a pair of Chicago policemen. Apparently, he was wanted for credit card fraud, and the cops had tracked him down at the Unifieds because he'd reserved a spot using his real name. He didn't get any call backs.

Only in Chicago...

Just a few days after I'd moved to Chicago, I got kind of lost and was squeaking in just barely on time to an audition. There was one other woman in the waiting area. I really didn't pay any attention to her at all since I'd been running to get there on time. About a minute later, she was called in to the audition room. I was glad to have a minute to myself to get my head on straight. I could hear her audition through the door... she was singing "How much is that doggie in the window" complete with barking and then the sound of metal chairs crashing. I heard the auditor say, "WHAT IN THE HELL WAS THAT?!?!" A minute later the actress came back out into the waiting area and I notice she was wearing a tutu, with striped Raggedy-Ann type stockings, one black canvas high-top sneaker and one toe shoe and was carrying one of those "invisible dog" leashes!

Fantod Theatre Company held auditions for an original, brand new play a while back. Midway through the first evening of auditions, wherein we were watching people's modern, comedic monologues (*a ppropos* to the play), a gentleman walked into the theatre. His dress immediately raised some eyebrows; it seemed he had stepped out of the corporate world of the sixties in his natty, rumpled suit and Sam Spade-looking hat. He then proceeded to launch into a dramatic monologue pulled from Clifford Odett's *Awake and Sing*. He was truly wonderful, but after he left we were like, "Wrong audition, pal." It was then we looked at his audition sheet. He noted that the role he was seeking in our show was that of "Happy". There was no character in the show we were doing with that name, but of course that was the name of the son in *Death of a Salesman,* which first came out in 1949. Furthermore, the person running the auditions did not have the gentleman on her list nor could she recall seeing him in the course of the evening, even though his dress was so remarkable. We all have arrived at the belief that we must have seen a ghost that evening, a ghost from the past who had simply wandered across decades into the wrong audition.

Audition Checklist

The audition is the one constant of an actor's life. We're always looking for new work, and no one's come up with a better way to hire actors. It's unfair and inaccurate and a fact of life. All we can do is give the best audition we can at all times. Here's some advice on how.

1. Finding a Piece

Monologue Books
These have their ups and downs. On the up: The monologue is cut and ready to go. On the down: The monologue is convenient, so someone else has probably already used it.

Plays
Many fantastic writers have monologues to be found in their lesser-known works. That means you need to read those obscure works. Of course you should be reading plays all the time anyway, right? Right.

Other Sources
There are monologues to be found in literature, poetry, movies, biographies, soup cans, etc. Some directors prefer pieces from traditional sources, but, generally speaking, if it's a good piece it doesn't matter where it's from.

Write Your Own
This is a controversial possibility. Most directors seem to be opposed to this route because generally, actors aren't strong writers. If it's a good monologue, you might get away with it, but you probably shouldn't admit the pieces are original.

Cross-Gender Pieces
If you're going to do a piece intended for the opposite gender, make sure it's good. Auditors sometimes find these pieces distracting, so if you go for it, it had better be strong enough to overcome that possible reaction.

2. Preparing a Piece

Choosing a Piece
A good piece shows your strengths. If you're a physical actor, choose a piece that allows you to be physical. If you have great emotional range, find an emotionally charged piece.

Practice, Practice, Practice
Try the piece out for your friends; don't let your first performance of a piece count.

Over ⟶

3. What Should I Wear?!

Suggestions
You don't want to wear a costume. This would be bad. However, wearing a long skirt when you audition for a period piece can be worthwhile.

Don't Limit
Tight clothing, uncomfortable shoes or anything that limits your movement should be avoided.

4. Getting There

Leave Time
When you make the appointment, be sure you know how to get to the audition location. Be sure to leave more than enough time for travel. If you're late, the auditors won't care that the eL was running slowly or your car had a flat. They only care that you've upset their schedule, and they won't be sympathetic.

Call Ahead
If you can't make an audition, CALL. Nothing will anger an agent or director more than a missing actor. What's more, many of them have long memories.

5. On Site

Arrival
Be kind to everyone. The audition monitor isn't necessarily a mere peon for you to abuse. They can, and often do, let directors know about abusive or rude actors, and those people won't get work. Your audition begins the moment you enter the building.

The Walls Have Ears
Before and after your audition, be wary of voicing loud opinions. The walls are thin, and you never know who's listening.

Conflicts
Be honest in listing your conflicts. If you try to introduce them after being cast, you'll only anger the director/producer/whomever. If you have to be out of town for a wedding, let them know. If a conflict is negotiable, let them know that. Keep communicating, though, or you'll alienate someone.

6. The Audition

Choose a Focal Point
Be sure you're going to be performing at least three-quarters front. No profiles. Most auditors seem to prefer you not act to furniture. Above all, don't focus on the person for whom you're auditioning. They want to watch your piece, not be a part of it.

Make Strong Choices
Strong choices are key—both in monologues and cold readings. The auditors see dozens of auditions; don't let yours blend in with the rest.

Take Direction
If the director asks for a new take on a piece, do it. This is a good thing. It means the director is interested and wants to see if you can take direction. Take it.

Get In, Get Out
Enter with confidence, perform with confidence, leave with confidence.

Don't Apologize!
Never, ever, ever. The audition you feel was poor may have seemed fine to the director. Let them decide how you did.

7. Musical Auditions

Make Your Music Friendly
Put it in a three-ring binder on sturdy paper that's easy to handle. The accompanist is sight reading and turning pages, so make seeing and handling the music easy.

Keep It Playable
Don't expect your accompanist to transpose for you. You'll just piss them off. Also, choose songs with easy accompaniments. You don't want your audition destroyed because the accompanist can't play your song.

Set a Tempo
Let them know how you like it.

Don't Shoot the Piano Player
Your accompanist is doing his/her best. Don't blame the accompanist when they screw up. Even if it's awful, keep the beat, keep singing and let the accompanist follow you. The auditors know when the accompaniment is a mess, but they won't appreciate you pointing it out in word or gesture. Keep a smile on your face.

8. Afterwards

Send a Card
Particularly after a call back or after being called in from a general, send a postcard saying thanks. Don't ask about the decision; just say "Hi."

Don't Be Rude
If you're offered a part you don't want or can't take, call back and let them know. Someone else is waiting on your decision, so make it and make the call.

Thank You!

Equity Theatres

There are scores, even hundreds, of theatres in Chicago, as any glance at the Theatre Listings in PERFROMINK or the READER aptly demonstrates. Nowhere will you find so many of them listed in one place, as you will in these listings.

Be aware of the union status, mission and contact names of theatres to which you send headshots. Casting Directors hate nothing so much as wasting time with actors who haven't done their research. Especially note the name to whose attention headshots should be sent. It's not always the artistic or managing director.

Finally, all this information comes from the theatres themselves. In compiling this information, some theatres did not choose or were not able to release all information. If something here turns out to be completely in error, please let us know. Break a leg!

The Aardvark
Ann Filmer - Artistic Director
1539 N. Bell
Chicago, IL 60622-1854
773/489-0843
www.aardvarktheatre.com
Send headshots to the attention of **Ann Filmer.**
Equity – CAT N – Itinerant
Founded in 1995. Starting non-Equity pay is $10-12/performance. They attend the Unifieds.

The Aardvark is a theatre collective of working artists reaching out to our community in Chicago from the north side to the southside with our productions, city programs and youth outreach.

Their 1999-2000 season included:
 Descent - Jeff Recommended
 Estrogen Fest - Jeff Recommended

They accept unsolicited synopses from playwrights and project proposals from directors.

About Face Theatre
Kyle Hall & Eric Rosen - Artistic Directors
3212 N. Broadway
Chicago, IL 60657
773/549-7943
773/549-3290 - box office
www.aboutface.base.org
Send headshots to the attention of **Kyle Hall & Eric Rosen.**
Equity – CAT N – Resident
Founded in 1995. Starting non-Equity pay is $85/week. The nearest eL stop is Belmont on the Red/Brown/Purple lines.

About Face is a collection of artists who, regardless of their sexualities, are committed to the creation of performances that examine and participate in the development of the gay, lesbian and bisexual communities.

Their 1999-2000 season included:
 Dancer from the Dance
 Xena Live!
 Four - Jeff Recommended
 Eleven Rooms of Proust - Jeff Recommended
 Raising Voices - Jeff Recommended

They accept unsolicited synopses from playwrights and project proposals from directors.

208 The Book: An Actor's Guide to Chicago

Theatres—Equity

American Theater Company
Brian Russell - Artistic Director
Gregory Werstler - Managing Director
1909 W. Byron
Chicago, IL 60613
773/929-5009
773/929-1031 - box office
www.atcweb.org
Send headshots to the attention of **Brian Russell**.
Equity – CAT II – Resident
Founded in 1985. Starting non-Equity pay is $50-75/week. The nearest eL stop is Irving Park on the Brown line.
American Theater Company is an ensemble of artists committed to producing new and classic works that have contemporary relevance and engage the imagination of our audience. We foster and encourage freedom of expression, imagination, creativity, community, and personal responsibility as we explore and celebrate human potential.
Their 1999-2000 season included:
 The Skin of our Teeth
 American Buffalo
 Medea
 The Mineola Twins
They accept unsolicited synopses from playwrights and project proposals from directors.

Apollo Theater
Rob Kolsen - Artistic Director
916 S. Wabash #503
Chicago, IL 60605
312/461-9292
773/935-6100 - box office
www.apollochicago.com
Send headshots to the attention of **Rob Kolson**.
Equity – Resident
Founded in 1991. Starting non-Equity pay varies. The nearest eL stop is Fullerton on the Red/Brown/Purple lines.
They accept unsolicited synopses from playwrights and project proposals from directors.

Apple Tree Theatre
Eileen Boevers & Ross Lehman - Artistic Directors
Todd Schmidt & Brigid Ann Brown - Managing Directors
595 Elm Pl. #210
Highland Park, IL 60035
847/432-8223
847/432-4335 - box office
www.appletreetheatre.com
Send headshots to the attention of **Casting**.
Equity – CAT III – Resident
Founded in 1983. Starting non-Equity pay is $175/week. They hold season auditions in June. The nearest Metra stop is in Highland Park.
Apple Tree is committed to producing works that illuminate the human condition, celebrate the tenacity of the human spirit and expand the vision of artists and audiences alike.

Auditorium Theatre Council
Marc Robin - Artistic Director
Jan Kallish - Executive Director
50 E. Congress
Chicago, IL 60605
312/922-2110
312/559-1212 - box office
Send headshots to the attention of **Mark Robin**.
Equity – Production – Resident
Founded in 1998. They do not hire non-Equity actors. The nearest eL stop is the Library stop on the Brown line.

Ch. 7 Theatres 209

Theatres—Equity

Bailiwick Repertory
David Zak - Artistic Director
Debra Hatchett - Managing Director
1229 W. Belmont
Chicago, IL 60657
773/883-1090
www.bailiwick.org
Send headshots to the attention of **David Zak.**
Equity – CAT N – Resident
Founded in 1982. Starting non-Equity pay is $10/performance. They attend the Unifieds. The nearest eL stop is Belmont on the Red/Brown/Purple lines.

Bailiwick has been the Off-Loop leader in works that represent our diverse community on stage, and are daring and provocatively relevant for today's audience - no matter if the work is a re-envisioned classic or world premiere.

Their 1999-2000 season included:
 The Deep Blue Sea
 42 Riverside Drive
 Stones
 Dear Friends and Gentle Hearts
 Now, Then, Again - Jeff Citation: New Work (Penny Penniston), Light Design (Michael Rourke) - Jeff Recommendation: Original Music (Joe Fosco)
 Mrs. Coney
 The Christmas Schooner
 The Whole World in Our Hands
 MotherSON
 Party
 Q
 Relative Comfort
 Brave Smiles: Another Lesbian Tragedy
 Endless Night, Sweet Delight
 Patience and Sarah
 The Trick
 Sir
 Naked Will
 Angels Into Dust
 Bare
 Preaching to the Perverted
 Workout!

They accept unsolicited scripts from playwrights and project proposals from directors.

Black Ensemble Theater
Jackie Taylor - Artistic Director
4520 N. Beacon
Chicago, IL 60640
773/769-5516
773/769-4451 - box office
www.blackensembletheater.org
Send headshots to the attention of **Jackie Taylor.**
Equity – CAT I – Resident
Founded in 1976. Starting non-Equity pay is $30/performance. The nearest eL stop is Wilson on the Red line.

Black Ensemble Theater produces theater that reaches across racial barriers.

Their 1999-2000 season included:
 The Jackie Wilson Story (My Heart is Crying, Crying) - Jeff Recommended
 Moms (Jackie "Moms" Mabley Story) - Jeff Recommended

They accept project proposals from directors.

Bog Theatre
515 E. Thacker St.
Des Plaines, IL 60016
847/296-0622
www.chicagotribune/link/bogtheatre.com
Equity – CAT N

Theatres–Equity

Brittany Productions, Inc.
Susan Haimes & Susan Harland - Artistic Directors
975 Brittany Rd.
Highland Park, IL 60035
847/432-0048
They do not accept unsolicited headshots.

Equity – Itinerant
Founded in 1998.
Brittany Productions is an independent producer of commercial theatre.
They accept unsolicited synopses from playwrights and project proposals from directors.

Center Theater
1346 W. Devon
Chicago, IL 60660
773/508-0200
Send headshots to the attention of **Dale Calandra - Founding Director.**
Equity – CAT I – Resident

Starting non-Equity pay varies. The nearest eL stop is Loyola on the Red line.
Center Theater is a professional Equity theatre providing quality theatrical productions on the cutting-edge of modern drama and training for actors, directors, playwrights and singers of all levels that inspires growth both personally and professionally.

Chicago Dramatists
Russ Tutterow - Artistic Director
Ann Filmer - Managing Director
1105 W. Chicago
Chicago, IL 60622
312/633-0630
Send headshots to the attention of **Russ Tutterow.**
Equity – CAT I – Resident

Founded in 1979. Starting non-Equity pay varies. They hold season auditions in January. The nearest eL stop is Chicago on the Blue line.
Chicago Dramatists is dedicated to the development and advancement of playwrights and new plays.
They accept unsolicited synopses from playwrights.

Chicago Shakespeare Theater
Barbara Gaines - Artistic Director
Criss Henderson - Managing Director
800 E. Grand
Chicago, IL 60611
312/595-5656
312/595-5600 - box office
www.chicagoshakes.com
Send headshots to the attention of **Casting.**

Equity – CAT V – CAT III – Resident
Founded in 1986. Starting non-Equity pay was not revealed. They hold season auditions in the fall and spring.
Their 1999-2000 season included:
  Antony & Cleopatra
  A Midsummer Night's Dream
  All's Well That Ends Well

Chicago Theatre Company
Douglas Alan Mann - Artistic Director
Luther Goins - Managing Director
500 E. 67th
Chicago, IL 60637
773/493-0901
773/493-5360 - box office
www.chicagotheatrecompany.com
Equity – CAT I – Resident

Founded in 1984. Starting non-Equity pay is $75/week. The nearest eL stop is 69th on the Red line.
Chicago Theatre Company was founded to present compelling and universal themes from an African-American perspective.
They accept unsolicited synopses from playwrights and project proposals from directors.

Theatres—Equity

Court Theatre
Charles Newell - Artistic Director
Diane Claussen - Managing Director
5535 S. Ellis
Chicago, IL 60637
773/702-7005
773/753-4472 - box office
www.courttheatre.org
Send headshots to the attention of **Casting**.

Equity – LORT D – Resident
Founded in 1955. Starting non-Equity pay is $225/week. The nearest eL stop is Garfield on the Red line.
Court Theatre exists to celebrate the immutable power and relevance of classic theatre. We share a collective aspiration to create a national center for classic theatre.

Division 13 Productions
Joanna Settle - Artistic Director
Katie Taber - Managing Director
601 S. LaSalle T463
Chicago, IL 60605
773/252-2510
Send headshots to the attention of **Casting**.
Equity – CAT N – Itinerant
Founded in 1995. Starting non-Equity pay is $200-500/run.

Division 13's mission is to produce vital and contemporary works for the theatre, including the classics, new scripts, premiere translations and original stage adaptations.
Their 1999-2000 season included:
Play
The Mustache
Tragedy: a tragedy
They accept project proposals from directors.

Drury Lane Theatre Evergreen Park
Marc Robin - Artistic Director
John Lazzara - Managing Director
2500 W. 95th
Evergreen Park, IL 60805
708/422-8000
708/422-0404 - box office
www.drurylane.com
Send headshots to the attention of **Marc Robin**.
Equity – Dinner Theatre – Resident
Founded in 1959. Starting non-Equity pay is $300/week. The nearest eL stop is

95th on the Red line.
Drury Lane produces family entertainment in musicals and ice shows. They do farces and straight plays and many star concerts.
Their 1999-2000 season included:
All Night Strut - Jeff Nominated: Director (Terry James) - After Dark: Revue, Ensemble
La Cage Aux Folles - Jeff Nominated: Actor (Jim Harms)
They accept unsolicited synopses from playwrights and project proposals from directors.

European Repertory Co.
Dale Goulding & Yasen Peyankov - Artistic Directors
P.O. Box 578220
Chicago, IL 60657
773/248-0577
Send headshots to the attention of **Rick Frederick - Casting Director**.
Equity – CAT N – Itinerant

Founded in 1992. Starting non-Equity pay was not revealed.
European Repertory Company is committed to bringing classical and contemporary European theatre to Chicago.
Their 1999-2000 season included:
Zoyka's Aartment
Slavs!
They accept unsolicited synopses from playwrights.

212 The Book: An Actor's Guide to Chicago

Theatres–Equity

Famous Door Theatre Company
Karen Kessler - Artistic Director
Jeffery Anderle - Managing Director
P.O. Box
Chicago, IL 60657
773/404-8283
773/327-5252 - box office
famousdoortheatre.org
Send headshots to the attention of
Hanna Dworkin - Casting Director.

Equity – CAT I
Founded in 1987. Starting non-Equity pay is $15-25/performance. They hold season auditions in May.
Their 1999-2000 season included:
Ghetto - Jeff Recommended
The Homecoming - Jeff Recommended
This Lime Tree Bower
They accept unsolicited synopses from playwrights.

Festival Theatre
Dale Calandra - Artistic Director
Deborah Stewart - Managing Director
P.O. Box 4114
Oak Park, IL 60303
708/524-2050
www.oprf.com/festival/
Send headshots to the attention of **Dale Calandra.**
Equity – CAT III – Resident

Founded in 1974. Starting non-Equity pay is $100/wk. They hold season auditions in January or February. The nearest eL stop is Harlem & Lake on the Green line.
Illinois' oldest professional outdoor theatre, Festival Theatre produces the classic works of western drama (usually Shakespeare).
Their 1999-2000 season included:
Macbeth
12th Nite

First Folio Shakespeare Festival
Alison C. Vesely - Artistic Director
David Rice - Executive Director
146 Juliet Ct.
Clarendon Hills, IL 60514-1226
630/986-8067
www.firstfolio.org
Send headshots to the attention of **Alison C. Vesely.**
Equity – CAT III – Resident

Founded in 1996. Starting non-Equity pay is $75/week on the mainstage or $50/performance for touring. They hold season auditions in January or February.
First Folio is a summer theatre specializing in producing Shakespeare-under-the-stars and educational programs.
Their 1999-2000 season included:
Romeo and Juliet
Much Ado About Nothing

Goodman Theatre
Robert Falls - Artistic Director
Roche Schulfer - Executive Director
170 N. Dearborn
Chicago, IL 60601
312/443-5151
312/443-3800 - box office
www.goodman-theatre.org
Send headshots to the attention of
Tara Lonzo - Casting Director.
Equity – LORT B – LORT D – Resident
Founded in 1925. Starting non-Equity pay is $275/week.

Their 1999-2000 season included:
Morning, Noon, and Night
The Odyssey
A Christmas Carol
A Moon for the Misbegotten
Boy Gets Girl
A Raisin in the Sun
Zoot Suit
Jacob Marley's Christmas Carol
Millennium Mambo
Schoolgirl Figure

Ch. 7 Theatres 213

Theatres—Equity

greasy joan & co.
P.O. Box 13077
Chicago, IL 60613
773/761-8284
www.greasyjoan.org
Send headshots to the
attention of **Karm Kerwell**.
Equity – CAT N – Itinerant

Founded in 1995. Starting non-Equity pay was not revealed.
greasy joan is dedicated to plays classical in scope and focuses on pieces rarely produced.
They accept unsolicited synopses from playwrights and project proposals from directors.

Illinois Shakespeare Festival
Calvin MacLean - Artistic Director
Fergus G. Currie - Managing Director
Campus Box 5700
Normal, IL 61790-5700
309/438-8974
309/438-2535 - box office
www.thefestival.org
Send headshots to the
attention of **Calvin MacLean**.
Equity – Resident

Founded in 1978. Starting non-Equity pay is $1,750/run.
Illinois Shakespeare Festival is the Midwest's leading outdoor summer Shakespeare festival.
Their 1999-2000 season included:
  The Taming of the Shrew
  King John
  The Three Musketeers
They accept project proposals from directors.

Illinois Theatre Center
Etel Billig - Artistic Director
P.O. Box 397
Park Forest, IL 60466
708/481-7914
708/481-3510 - box office
www.ilthctr.org

Send headshots to the attention to the attention of **Pat Decker – Casting**.
Equity – CAT III – Resident
Founded in 1976. Starting non-Equity pay is $200/week. They hold season auditions in the summer.
They accept unsolicited synopses from playwrights.

Irish Repertory
5875 N. Lincoln
Chicago, IL 60659
773/275-2600
773/275-2650 - box office
www.irishrep.com
Send headshots to the attention of
Matt O'Brien - Producing Director.
Equity – CAT III – Itinerant
Founded in 1991. Starting non-Equity pay was not revealed. Season auditions are in September.

Irish Repertory is the professional theatre devoted exclusively to Irish and Irsh-American playwrights.
Their 1999-2000 season included:
  The Main
  Long Day's Journy into Night
  Buckets o' Beckett
They accept unsolicited synopses from playwrights.

Theatres—Equity

The Journeymen Theatre Company
Frank Pullen - Artistic Director
3915 N. Janssen
Chicago, IL 60613
773/529-5781
312/494-5720 - box office
www.TheJourneymen.org
Send headshots to the attention of **Frank Pullen.**
Equity – CAT N – Itinerant
Founded in 1994. Starting non-Equity pay was not revealed.
The Journeymen seek to draw upon humanities in a way that helps the general public understand a topic of public concern.
Their 1999-2000 season included:
    Edward II - Jeff Citation: Original Music
    In the Belly of the Beast -
        Jeff Nominated: Actor
    for colored girls... - Jeff Nominated:
        Supporting Actress
They accept unsolicited scripts from playwrights.

Light Opera Works
Lara Teeter - Artistic Director
927 Noyes St.
Evanston, IL 60201
847/869-7930
847/869-6300 - box office
www.light-opera-works.org
Send headshots to the attention of **Lara Teeter.**
Equity – Guest Artist – Resident
Founded in 1980. Starting non-Equity pay varies. The nearest eL stop is Foster on the Purple line.
Light Opera Works produces music theatre form a variety of world traditions.
They accept unsolicited synopses from playwrights.

Live Bait Theater
Sharon Evans - Artistic Director
Lotti Pharriss - Managing Director
3914 N. Clark
Chicago, IL 60613
773/871-1212
www.livebaittheater.org
Send headshots to the attention of **Lotti Pharriss.**
Equity – CAT N – Resident
Founded in 1987. Starting non-Equity pay is $20/performance. They attend the Unifieds. The nearest eL stop is Sheridan on the Red line.
Live Bait Theater was founded to produce new work by emerging Chicago playwrights and solo artists.
Their 1999-2000 season included:
    The Tall Ships - American Theatre Critics
        Association Osborn Award for New
        Work: Runner-up
    Best of Fillet of Solo
    True Life Tales
They accept unsolicited scripts from playwrights and project proposals from directors.

Lookingglass Theatre Company
Laura Eason - Artistic Director
2936 N. Southport
Chicago, IL 60657
773/477-9257
773/477-4088 - box office
www.lookingglasstheatre.org
Send headshots to the attention of **Laura Eason.**
Equity – CAT III – Itinerant
Founded in 1988. Starting non-Equity pay was not revealed. The nearest eL stop is Wellington on the Brown line.
Lookingglass is an ensemble-based company dedicated to the development of highly visual, physical, innovative works and continued experimentation for the American stage.

Ch. 7 Theatres

Theatres—Equity

Marriott Theatre
Dyanne Earley - Artistic Director
10 Marriott Dr.
Lincolnshire, IL 60069

847/634-0204
608/266-9055. - box office
www.MarriottTheatre.com

MPAACT
P.O. Box 10039
Chicago, IL 60610
773/324-0757
www.mpaact.org
Send headshots to the attention of **Carla Stillwell - Director of Artist Development.**
Equity – Itinerant
Founded in 1990. Starting non-Equity pay is $500/run. They hold season auditions in October.

MPAACT exists to develop, nurture and sustain Afrikan Centered Theatre. ACT is an artistic expression which is grounded in the many cultures and traditions of the Afrikan continent and its diaspora.

Their 1999-2000 season included:
    The Glow of Reflected Light
    Exoskeletal Blues

They accept unsolicited scripts from playwrights and project proposals from directors.

New American Theater
Carl Balson - Artistic Director
Mary Beaver - Managing Director
118 N. Main St.
Rockford, IL 61101
815/963-9454
815/964-6282 - box office
www.newamericantheater.com
Send headshots to the attention of **Miki Thiessen - Marketing Director.**

Equity – Resident
Founded in 1971. Starting non-Equity pay varies. They hold season auditions in June.
New American Theater is the only Equity theatre in Rockford.
They accept unsolicited synopses from playwrights and project proposals from directors.

Next Theatre Company
Kate Buckley - Artistic Director
Robert Scogin - Managing Director
847/475-6763
847/475-1875 - box office
www.nexttheatre.org
Equity – CAT N – Resident
Founded in 1981. Starting non-Equity pay

varies. They hold season auditions in the fall. The nearest eL stop is Noyes on the Purple line.
The Next Theatre is dedicated to the production of innovative twists on the classics and the presentation of contemporary plays that entertain and challenge the intellect and heart of its audience.

Northlight Theatre
B.J. Jones - Artistic Director
Richard Friedman - Managing Director
9501 Skokie Blvd.
Skokie, IL 60077
847/679-9501 x8
847/673-6300 - box office
www.northlight.org
Send headshots to the attention of **Janet Mullet - Associate Producer.**

Equity – LORT D – Resident
Founded in 1974. Starting non-Equity pay was not revealed. The nearest eL stop is Skokie on the Yellow line.
They accept unsolicited synopses from playwrights and project proposals from directors.

Theatres—Equity

Organic Theater Company
Katie Klemme - Artistic Director
1420 Maple
Evanston, IL 60201
847/475-0600
847/475-2800. - box office
www.organictheater.com
Send headshots to the attention of **Ina Marlowe.**
Equity – CAT II – Resident

Founded in 1974. Starting non-Equity pay varies. They hold season auditions in late summer. The nearest eL stop is Dempster on the Purple line.
Organic Theater Company believes that true theater should illuminate the human condition and enrich the spirit.
Their 1999-2000 season included:
The Old Settler
The Food Chain
Goodnight Children Everywhere

Phoenix Theatre
749 N. Park Ave.
Indianapolis, IN 46202
317/635-2381
317/635-7529 - box office
Send headshots to the attention of **Bryan Fonseca - Producing Director.**
Equity – SPT – Resident
Founded in 1983. Starting non-Equity pay is $100-125/week.
Phoenix Theatre is a contemporary theatre company with an emphasis on newer plays and original works.

Their 1999-2000 season included:
Three Days of Rain
The Woman in Black
The Millennium Game Show
The Most Fabulous Story Ever Told
Jackie: An American Life
The Beauty Queen of Leenane
Wit
Beautiful Thing
The Journal of Ordinary Thought
Resident Alien
They accept project proposals from directors.

Piven Theatre Workshop
Joyce Piven & Byrne Piven - Artistic Directors
927 Noyes St.
Evanston, IL 60201
847/866-6597
847-866-8049 - box office
www.piventheatreworkshop.com

Send headshots to the attention of the **Production Manager.**
Equity – CAT N – Resident
Founded in 1971. Starting non-Equity pay was not revealed. The nearest eL stop is Noyes on the Purple line.
Piven is a theatre that teaches - a workshop that produces theatre.

Prop Thtr
Scott Vehill - Artistic Director
Jonathan Lavan - Managing Director
2621 N. Washtenaw
Chicago, IL 60647
773/486-PROP
www.viprofix.com/proptheatre.html
Send headshots to the attention of **Jonathan Lavan.**

Equity – Guest Artist – Itinerant
Founded in 1981. Starting non-Equity pay is $200/run.
Prop is an edgy company that produces exclusively new works or new adaptations of historical or counter-cultural literature.
They accept unsolicited scripts from playwrights and project proposals from directors.

Theatres—Equity

Red Hen Productions
Elayne LeTraunik - Artistic Director
2944 N. Broadway
Chicago, IL 60657
773/728-0599
312/409-8123 - box office
www.redhenproductions.com
Send headshots to the
attention of **Elayne LeTraunik.**
Equity – CAT I – Resident
Founded in 1997. Starting non-Equity pay is
$100/run. The nearest eL stop is Berwyn on the Red line or Damen on the Brown line.
Red Hen seeks out plays that are artistically worthy but rarely produced as well as new plays by primarily but not exclusively Chicago playwrights.
Their 1999-2000 season included:
 Class Enemy - Jeff Recommended
 A Dybbuk - Jeff Recommended
They accept unsolicited scripts from playwrights and project proposals from directors.

A Red Orchid Theatre
Guy Van Swearingen - Artistic Director
1531 N. Wells
Chicago, IL 60610-7752
312/943-8722
www.a-red-orchid.com
Send headshots to the
attention of **Guy Van Swearingen.**
Equity – CAT N – Resident
Founded in 1993. Starting non-Equity pay varies. The nearest eL stop is Sedgwick
on the Brown line.
A Red Orchid stretches their artists and audiences and celebrates the uniqueness of theatre.
Their 1999-2000 season included:
 Kharma Talk
 Place of Angels - Jeff Recommended
 Mr. Bundy - Jeff Nominated:
  Supporting Actress
They accept unsolicited synopses from playwrights and project proposals from directors.

Remy Bumppo
James Bohnen - Artistic Director
433 Melrose #2
Chicago, IL 60657
773/528-8762
773/871-3000 - box office
Send headshots to the
attention of **James Bohnen.**
Equity – CAT II – Itinerant
Founded in 1996. Starting non-Equity pay
was not revealed. Season auditions are held in September.
Remy Bumppo is dedicated to giving the best actors in Chicago the opportunity to perform the works of great playwrights. We pride ourselves on delivering high production quality and creating an atmosphere of comfort and professionalism for these artists to thrive in.
Their 1999-2000 season included:
 The Road to Mecca

Wanna Write a Musical?
Join the New Tuners Workshop!

* The only group of its kind dedicated to developing and producing NEW MUSICALS - right here in Chicago!
* If you're an aspiring composer, lyricist or writer interested in writing for musical theatre, the New Tuners Workshop is for YOU!

Call John Sparks for more information
at 773/929-7367, x22

---

218 The Book: An Actor's Guide to Chicago

Theatres—Equity

Renaissance Theatre
Marie Kohler & Raeleen McMillion - Artistic Directors
Liesl Jeffery - General Manager
342 N. Water St. #400
Milwaukee, WI 53202
414/273-0800
www.r-t-w.com
Send headshots to the attention of **Jennifer Rupp - Production Manager.**
Equity – SPT – Resident.
Founded in 1993. Starting non-Equity pay is $300/week. They hold season auditions in May.
Renaissance Theatre was founded and is operated by women interested in theater with a uniquely feminine voice.
Their 1999-2000 season included:
Full Gallop
Midnight and Moll Flanders
Eleemosynary
They accept unsolicited synopses from playwrights and project proposals from directors.

Rivendell Theatre Ensemble
Tara Mallen - Artistic Director
Sharon Furiya - Managing Director
1711 W. Belle Plaine #3B
Chicago, IL 60613
773/472-1169
Send headshots to the attention of **Tara Mallen.**
Equity – CAT 1 – Itinerant
Founded in 1995. Starting non-Equity pay is a small stipend.
Rivendell Theatre Ensemble is a professional Equity company whose mission is to create an intimate theatre experience that explores new voices and reflects personal human journeys in an engaging salon environment.
Their 1999-2000 season included:
The Clink
Cyrano de Bergerac - Jeff Recommended
The Factory Girls - Jeff Recommended
They accept project proposals from directors.

Roadworks
Shade Murray - Artistic Director
Jennifer Avery - Managing Director
1144 W. Fulton Market #105
Chicago, IL 60607
312/492-7150
www.roadworks.org
Send headshots to the attention of **Shade Murray.**
Equity – CAT N – Itinerant
Founded in 1992. Starting non-Equity pay is $75/week. They hold season auditions in late July. The nearest eL stop is Ashland on the Green line.
Roadworks Productions has successfully cultivated the next generation of theatre patrons through innovative, ground-breaking productions.
They accept unsolicited synopses from playwrights.

Seanachai Theatre Company
5108 N. Ashland #2
Chicago, IL 60640
773/878-3727
www.seanachai.org
Send headshots to the attention of **Michael Grant** - Artistic Director.
Equity – CAT N – Itinerant
Founded in 1995. Starting non-Equity pay is not enough.
Seanachai Theatre Company is an ensemble of actors and playwrights that specialize in new plays and Irish works.
Their 1999-2000 season included:
Translations - After Dark: Ensemble, Technical Excellence
Marked Tree - After Dark:
New Play (Coby Goss),
Director (Scott Cummins)
They accept unsolicited scripts from playwrights and project proposals from directors.

Theatres—Equity

Second City
1616 N. Wells
Chicago, IL 60614
312/664-4032
312/337-3992 - box office
www.secondcity.com
Send headshots to the attention of **Casting.**
Equity – Special Agreement – Resident

Founded in 1959. Starting non-Equity pay is nothing. The nearest eL stop is Sedgwick on the Brown line.

The Second City is the foremost improv-based comedy theatre in the country.

Shakespeare on the Green
700 E. Westleigh Rd.
Lake Forest, IL 60045
847/604-6344
www.sotg.pac.barat.edu
Send headshots to the attention of **JoAnne Zielinski – Producer.**
Equity – CAT I – Resident

Founded in 1990. Starting non-Equity pay is $300/run. They hold season auditions in April. The nearest Metra stop is Ft. Sheridan.

Shakespeare on the Green offers one play by Shakespeare each summer on the front lawn of the Barat College campus.

Their 1999-2000 season included:
 King Lear

Steppenwolf Theatre Company
758 W. North - 4th floor
Chicago, IL 60610
312/335-1888
312/335-1650 - box office
www.steppenwolf.org
Send headshots to the attention of **Phyllis Schuringa - Casting Director.**
Equity – Resident

Founded in 1975. Starting non-Equity pay is $250/week. They hold season auditions from May-July.

Steppenwolf was founded on a commitment to the principles of ensemble collaboration and artistic risk.

Their 1999-2000 season included:
 Side Man
 Hysteria
 Valparaiso
 One Flew Over the Cuckoo's Nest
 Closer
 The Infidel
 Orson's Shadow
 Detail of a Larger Work

They accept unsolicited synopses from playwrights.

Strawdog Theatre Company
Mike Dailey, Jennifer Avery & Sarah Stray - Artistic Directors
Tim Zingelman - Managing Director
3829 N. Broadway
Chicago, IL 60622
773/528-9889
773/528-9696 - box office
www.StrawDog.org
Send headshots to the attention of the **Casting Director.**
Equity – CAT N – Resident

Founded in 1987. Starting non-Equity pay varies. The nearest eL stop is Sheridan on the Red line.

Strawdog strives to inspire and provoke through ensemble based works.

Their 1999-2000 season included:
 Manufracture
 Measure for Measure - Jeff Citation:
  Original Music, Sound Design
 Return to the Howard Bowl

They accept project proposals from directors.

Theatre at the Center

Michael Weber - Artistic Director
907 Ridge Rd.
Munster, IN 46321
219/836-0422
219/836-3255 - box office
Send headshots to the attention of **Michael Weber.**

Equity – CAT III – Resident

Founded in 1991. Starting non-Equity pay is $200/week. They hold season auditions in February.

Theatre at the Center does Chicago premieres and revivals of both plays and musicals.

They accept unsolicited scripts from playwrights.

Victory Gardens Theater

2257 N. Lincoln
Chicago, IL 60614
773/549-5788
773/871-3000 - box office
www.victorygardens.org
Send headshots to the attention of the **artistic staff.**
Equity – CAT IV – Resident

Founded in 1974. Starting non-Equity pay is $214.88/week. The nearest eL stop is Fullerton on the Red/Brown/Purple lines.

Since 1974, Victory Gardens has stayed true to an undeniably challenging mission - developing and producing new plays by Chicago writers.

Their 1999-2000 season included:
  Bluff
  Door to Door
  Knock Me A Kiss
  Voice of Good Hope
  Cahoots

They accept unsolicited scripts from playwrights.

Writers' Theatre Chicago

Michael Halberstam - Artistic Director
Judi Jeroslow - Executive Director
c/o Books on Vernon
664 Vernon Ave.
Glencoe, IL 60022
847/835-7366
847/835-5398 - box office
www.illyria.com/writers.html
Send headshots to the attention of **Casting.**
Equity – CAT V – Resident

Founded in 1992. Starting non-Equity pay is $125/week. They attend the Unifieds. The nearest Metra stop is Glencoe.

Writers Theatre uses the word and the artist as their primary focus. In our intimate space, we bring our audiences face to face with literature's greatest creators and creations.

Their 1999-2000 season included:
  Incident at Vichy - Jeff Recommended
  Fallen Angels - Jeff Recommended
  Nixon's Nixon - Jeff Recommended
  Loot

Just sent out your last headshot?

Check out the Photographer listings on page 87

Non-Equity Theatres

Alchymia Theatre
Scott Fielding - Artistic Director
4249 N. Lincoln
Chicago, IL 60618
773/755-6843
773/250-7262 - box office
www.alchymia.org
Send headshots to the attention of **Scott Fielding**.
Non-Equity – Resident
Founded in 1999. Starting pay varies. They hold season auditions in the summer. The nearest eL stop is Montrose on the Brown line.
Alchymia strives to create theatre capable of awakening people to an experience of their deepest being; our approach is based in large part on the theatre legacy of Michael Chekhov and the principles on which he developed his art.
Their 1999-2000 season included:
  The White Princess
  Rosmersheln
They accept unsolicited synopses from playwrights and project proposals from directors.

Alphabet Soup Productions
Susan Holm - Artistic Director
Mark Pence - Managing Director
P.O. Box 85
Lombard, IL 60148
630/932-1555
Send headshots to the attention of **Mark Pence and Susan Holm**.
Non-Equity – Itinerant
Founded in 1987. Starting pay is $20/performance. They hold season auditions in August and January.
Alphabet Soup is a children's theatre company with a fractured fairytale approach. We respect our actors as well as our audiences.
Their 1999-2000 season included:
  Alice in Wonderland
  The Christmas Toyshop
  A Christmas Carol in HogPatch Holler
  Beauty and the Beast - Children's Theatre Festival at the Miracle Theatre
    (Coral Gables, FL): Best Musical

American Girl Theater
Scott Davidson - Artistic Director
111 E. Chicago
Chicago, IL 60611
312/787-3883 x2081
877/AG PLACE - box office
www.americangirl.com/
Send headshots to the attention of **Scott Davidson**.
Non-Equity – Resident
Founded in 1986. Starting pay was not revealed. The nearest eL stop is Chicago on the Red line.
American Girl Theater is a live musical theater featuring a musical and programs for girls and their families.
They accept unsolicited synopses from playwrights.

Attic Playhouse
Kimberly Loughlin - Artistic Director
410 Sheridan Rd.
Highwood, IL 60040
847/433-2660
www.atticplayhouse.com
Send headshots to the attention of **Kimberly Loughlin**.
Non-Equity – Resident
Founded in 1998. Starting pay is nothing. They hold season auditions in the summer.
Attic Playhouse is a professional theatre that strives to showcase a variety of theatrical plays/musicals.
They accept unsolicited scripts from playwrights and project proposals from directors.

Theatres—Non-Equity

Azusa Productions
Maggie Speer - Artistic Director
Stephen Dunn - Managing Director
1639 W. Estes
Chicago, IL 60626
312/409-4207

They do not accept unsolicited headshots at this time.
Non-Equity – Itinerant
Founded in 1996. Starting pay is $0-100.

Beverly Theatre Guild
9936 S. Harnew Rd. East
Oak Lawn, IL 60453
312/409-2705
www.beverlytheatreguild.org
Send headshots to the attention of **Ed Fudacz – President.**
Non-Equity – Resident
Founded in 1963. Starting pay in nothing. The nearest eL stop is 95th Street on the Red line.

Beverly Theatre Guild does a full complement of theatre, musicals, comedies & dramas.
Their 1999-2000 season included:
Guys & Dolls
Curious Savage
Lend Me A Tenor
They accept unsolicited synopses from playwrights and project proposals from directors.

Borealis Theatre
Jeffery Baumgartner - Artistic Director
P.O. Box 2443
Aurora, IL 60507
630/844-4928
www.borealis-theatre.org
Send headshots to the attention of **Casting.**
Non-Equity – Resident
Founded in 1990. Starting pay is $200-300/run. They hold season auditions at the end of August. The nearest Metra stop is Aurora.

Borealis Theatre Company and Fox Valley Shakespeare Festival are dedicated to presenting a balanced season in an entirely bold, creative and exciting fashion, which engages our audiences and artists alike.
Their 1999-2000 season included:
Noises Off
Man and Superman
Vincent
They accept unsolicited scripts from playwrights.

Bowen Park Theatre Co.
Maggie Speer - Artistic Director
39 Jack Benny Dr.
Waukegan, IL 60085
847/360-4741
Send headshots to the attention of **Maggie Speer.**

Non-Equity – Resident
Starting pay is $0-500/run.
Bowen Park's goal is to creat a new venue for well-produced theatre that can offer theatre artists paid opportunities.

Boxer Rebellion Theater
Steve Young - Artistic Director
1257 W. Loyola
Chicago, IL 60626
773/465-7325
www.boxerrebellion.org

Ch. 7 Theatres 223

Theatres—Non-Equity

Breadline Theatre Group
Paul Kampf - Artistic Director
1802 W. Berenice
Chicago, IL 60613
773/327-6096
www.breadline.org
Send headshots to the
attention of **Paul Kampf**.
Non-Equity – Resident
Founded in 1993. Starting pay is nothing. The nearest eL stop is Irving Park on the Brown line.
Breadline produces only world premiere productions that emphasize the theatrical and believe in the ensemble as a creative tool.
Their 1999-2000 season included:
 The Chorus Rebellion
 The Irish Drummer Girl
They accept unsolicited scripts from playwrights.

CenterLight Sign & Voice Theatre
Patti Lahey - Artistic Director
3444 Dundee Rd.
Northbrook, IL 60062
847/559-0110 x237
847/559-9493 TTY - box office
www.centerlighttheatre.com
Send headshots to the
attention of **Patti Lahey**.
Non-Equity – Resident
Founded in 1974. Starting pay is $15-20/show. The nearest Metra stop is Fox Lake.
Their 1999-2000 season included:
 Nunsense
 Annie
 Crimes of the Heart
 Rhythms 2000
 The Velveteen Rabbit
They accept unsolicited scripts from playwrights and project proposals from directors.

Chicago Kids Company
Jesus Perez - Artistic Director
Paige Coffman - Managing Director
3812 W. Montrose
Chicago, IL 60618
773/539-0455
Send headshots to the
attention of **Jesus Perez**.
Non-Equity – Resident
Founded in 1992. Starting pay is $25/performance. They hold season auditions in August and January.
Chicago Kids Company offers theatre for children who would not normally get the chance to see a live play.
Their 1999-2000 season included:
 Goldilocks and the Three Bears
 Cinderella
 Mrs. Claus
 The Three Little Pigs
 The Easter Bunny

Circle Theatre
Greg Kolack, Alena Murguia and Todd Cornils - Artistic Directors
7300 W. Madison
Forest Park, IL 60130
708/771-0700
Send headshots to the
attention of **Alena Murguia**.
Non-Equity – Resident
Founded in 1985. Starting pay is $100/run. The nearest eL stop is Harlem on the Green line.
Circle is an artist-based company whose mission is to produce exciting theatre accessible to a widely diversified city and suburban audience.
Their 1999-2000 season included:
 Earth and Sky
 The Crime of the Century - Jeff Citation
 Candida
 The Cover of Life - Jeff Citation
 The Life
 American Buffalo
They accept unsolicited synopses from playwrights and project proposals from directors.

Theatres—Non-Equity

City Lit
Mark Richard - Artistic Director
Paige Hearn - Managing Director
1020 W. Bryn Mawr
Chicago, IL 60660-4627
773/293-3682
members.aol.com/citlitpage
Send headshots to the attention of **Mark Richard**.
Non-Equity – Resident
Founded in 1979. Starting pay is $10-15/performance. The nearest eL stop is Bryn Mawr on the Red line.

City Lit is the city's premier company devoted to the adaptation of literature to the stage.

Their 1999-2000 season included:
  20/20 Hindsight
  Alice's Adventures in Wonderland

They accept unsolicited synopses from playwrights and project proposals from directors.

cobalt ensemble theatre
Katherine Condit-Ladd - Artistic Director
Eric Dansen - Managing Director
PMB 225
5315 N. Clark
Chicago, IL 60640
312/458-9182
www.cobaltensemble.org
Send headshots to the attention of **Katherine Condit-Ladd**.
Non-Equity – Itinerant
Founded in 1997. Starting pay is $5/show.

They hold season auditions in the summer.

cobalt ensemble is an ensemble based group that strives to present fresh works that offer a potent interchange between performers and audience.

Their 1999-2000 season included:
  Dream of a Common Language
  Raised in Captivity
  The Architect

They accept unsolicited scripts from playwrights and project proposals from directors.

CollaborAction Theatre Company
Anthony Moseley - Artistic Director
1945 W. Henderson
Chicago, IL 60657
312/409-2741
www.collaboraction.org

ComedySportz
Tim Chidester - Artistic Director
Steph DeWaegeneer - Managing Director
2851 N. Halsted
Chicago, IL 60657
773/549-8080
773/549-8080 x21 - box office
www.comedysportzchicago.com
Send headshots to the attention of **Jed Resnik**.
Non-Equity – Resident

Founded in 1987. Starting pay was not revealed. They hold season auditions in January and June. The nearest eL stop is Diversey on the Brown line.

ComedySportz is America's #1 comedy competition featuring professional improvisers performing a series of short games, scenes, and songs all based on audience suggestions.

They accept project proposals from directors.

Ch. 7 Theatres 225

Theatres—Non-Equity

Common Ground Theatre
D. Leader - Artistic Director
18120 Mary Ann Ln.
Country Club Hills, IL 60478
708/647-1319
www.commongroundtheatre.org
Send headshots to the attention of **D. Leader.**
Non-Equity – Resident

Founded in 1994. Starting pay varies. Common Ground is dedicated to attracting a new generation of audiences and performers to the arts using innovative productions that explore relevant themes.

They accept unsolicited scripts from playwrights and project proposals from directors.

Congo Square Theatre Company
Derrick Sanders - Artistic Director
Anthony A. Edwards - Managing Director
1156 W. Grand #2R
Chicago, IL 60622
312/243-9055
www.congosquaretheatre.org
Send headshots to the attention of **Derrick Sanders.**

Non-Equity – Itinerant
Founded in 1999. Starting pay varies. Congo Square is an ensemble dedicated to artistic excellence. In producing definitive and transformative theatre spawned from the African Diaspora, as well as from other world cultures, Congo Square seeks to establish itself as an institution of multcultural theatre.

They accept unsolicited synopses from playwrights and project proposals from directors.

Corn Productions
2620 N. Lawndale
Chicago, IL 60647
312/409-6435
www.TheaterChicago.com/Corn

Defiant Theatre
Jim Slonina and Christopher Johnson - Artistic Directors
Jennifer Gehr - Managing Director
3540 N. Southport #162
Chicago, IL 60657-1436
312/409-0585
www.defianttheatre.org
Send headshots to the attention of **Jim Slonina.**
Non-Equity – Itinerant
Founded in 1993. Starting pay is nothing. Defiant strives to subvert the social, moral, and aesthetic expectations of mainstream artistic expression. Honoring a wide range of theatrical traditions, including farce, naturalism, kabuki, vaudeville, and puppetry, Defiant seeks to revivify the conventions of each form through irreverent explorations of its contemporary function.

Their 1999-2000 season included:
   The Love Talker
   Godbaby
They accept unsolicited synopses from playwrights and project proposals from directors.

Theatres—Non-Equity

Dolphinback Theatre Company
Matt Wallace - Artistic Director
1710 W. Belmont #2F
Chicago, IL 60657
312/409-7980
www.dolphinback.com
Send headshots to the
attention of **Matt Wallace.**
Non-Equity – Itinerant
Founded in 1993. Starting pay varies.

Dolphinback is dedicated to developing and producing original works, as well as presenting Chicago premieres and plays rarely performed in the Chicago area.
Their 1999-2000 season included:
  Anna Weiss
  Dogs By Seven
  The Sound of One
They accept unsolicited synopses from playwrights and project proposals from directors.

Eclipse Theatre Company
Anish Jethmallani - Artistic Director
Katie Bandehey - Managing Director
P.O. Box 578960
Chicago, IL 60657
312/409-1687
www.eclipsetheatre.com
Send headshots to the
attention of **Gary Simmers.**

Non-Equity – Itinerant
Founded in 1990. Starting pay is $50/run.
Eclipse produces one playwright per season.
Their 1999-2000 season included:
  Watch on the Rhine - Jeff Recommended
  The Lark - Jeff Recommended
  Another Part of the Forest

Emerald City Theatre Co.
Karen Cardarelli - Artistic Director
Beth Klein - Managing Director
2936 N. Southport
Chicago, IL 60657
773/529-2690
773/935-6100 - box office
www.emeraldcitytheatre.com
Send headshots to the
attention of **Casting Director.**
Non-Equity – Resident
Founded in 1996. Starting pay is $10/performance plus $50 rehearsal pay. They

hold season auditions in August and December. The nearest eL stop is Diversey on the Brown line.
Emerald City produces high quality productions aimed at the entire family for an affordable price.
Their 1999-2000 season included:
  Green Eggs & Ham
  Frosty
  Rapunzel
  The Wizard of Oz
They accept project proposals from directors.

ETA Creative Arts Foundation
7558 S. South Chicago
Chicago, IL 60619
773/752-3955
www.etacreativearts.org
Send headshots to the attention of
Abena Joan Brown – President.
Non-Equity – Resident
Founded in 1971. Starting pay is $30/performance. The nearest eL stop is 69th on the Red line.

ETA Creative Arts tells the African/African-American story in the first voice.
Their 1999-2000 season included:
  Get Ready - Jeff Citation:
    Supporting Actor (Woody Bolar)
They accept unsolicited scripts from playwrights and project proposals from directors.

Theatres—Non-Equity

Excaliber Shakespeare Company
Darryl Maximilian Robinson - Artistic Director
The Harrison Street Galleries Studio Theatre
208 W. Harrison St.
Oak Park, IL 60304
708/366-7832
773/533-0285 - box office
Send headshots to the attention of **Darryl Maximilian Robinson.**

Founded in 1987. Starting pay is $5-10/performance. They hold season auditions in spring and summer. The nearest eL stop is Austin on the Blue line.
The Excaliber Shakespeare Company is Chicago's only theatre, sans grants, sans corporate sponsorship, that is truly committed to high art and racial harmony.
Their 1999-2000 season included:
 The Blood Knot - Jeff Recommended, Black Theatre Alliance: Director-Ensemble (Darryl Maximilian Robinson)

Factory Theatre
Jenny Kirkland and Steve Walker - Artistic Directors
Wendy Tregay - Managing Director
P.O. Box 408679
Chicago, IL 60640
312/409-3247
www.factorytheater.com
Non-Equity – Itinerant
Founded in 1991. Starting pay is nothing.
Factory Theater has produced over 45 original plays, all written by members of its ensemble.

Their 1999-2000 season included:
 Endzone
 Herb Stabler: Wandering Spirit - Jeff Nominated: Original Work
 Surface Dwellers
 Dragon Tales
 Dancing With the Past
 Vinyl Shop - Jeff Nominated: Adaptation, Supporting Actor (Matt O'Neill), New York Fringe Festival: Excellence in Performance (Matt O'Neill)
They accept unsolicited scripts from playwrights.

Fantasy Orchard Children's Theatre
Dana Low - Artistic Director
P.O. Box 25084
Chicago, IL 60625
773/539-4211
www.kidtheater.com
Send headshots to the attention of **Dana Low.**
Non-Equity – Resident
Founded in 1990. Starting pay is $20/per-

formance. They hold season auditions in the fall. The nearest eL stop is Wellington on the Brown line.
Fantasy Orchard produces folk and faerie tales from round the world highlighting various cultures found in the Chicago area.
Their 1999-2000 season included:
 Rapunzel and the Witch
 The African Cinderella
They accept unsolicited scripts from playwrights and project proposals from directors.

Fantod Theatre
Kelly Cooper - Artistic Director
Annie Joseph - Executive Director
P.O. Box 268951
Chicago, IL 60626
773/761-7220
773/296-2805 - box office
Non-Equity – Itinerant
Founded in 1998. Starting pay is $50/run.

Fantod Theatre Co. is bent on keeping the "play" in plays and operates on this bent both on and offstage. We are keen on plays that are both fantastic and humorous.
Their 1999-2000 season included:
 Pond 7
 The Major
They accept unsolicited scripts from playwrights and project proposals from directors.

Theatres—Non-Equity

The Feast of Fools Cabaret
1420 Winnemac #2E
Chicago, IL 60640
773/784-3397
312/962-9708 - box office
www.thefeastoffools.com
Send headshots to the
attention of **Fausto Fernes.**
Non-Equity – Resident

Founded in 1969. Starting pay is nothing. The Feast of Fools Cabaret presents eclectic self-made theatrical works-of-art in a variety/talk show format, where an emphasis is placed on costume, sexuality, history, and a casual atmosphere.

They accept unsolicited scripts from playwrights and project proposals from directors.

Firstborn Productions
Gregory Gerhard - Artistic Director
1618 W. Fargo #1
Chicago, IL 60626
773/728-2814
www.firstborn.org
Send headshots to the
attention of **Gregory Gerhard.**
Non-Equity – Itinerant
Founded in 1996. Starting pay is nothing

Firstborn operates with the intent to combine elements of core ensemble acting with heightened non-realistic elements to provide an unique theatrical experience.

Their 1999-2000 season included:
 The Secret Rapture - Jeff Recommended
 Cyber:/womb

They accept unsolicited scripts from playwrights and project proposals from directors.

Fleetwood-Jourdain Theatre
2100 Ridge Ave.
Evanston, IL 60201
847/328-5740

The Free Associates
2936 N. Southport #210
Chicago, IL 60657
773/296-0541
773/975-7171 - box office
www.thefreeassociates.com
Non-Equity – Resident
Founded in 1991. Starting pay was not revealed. The nearest eL stop is Wellington on the Brown line.

Free Associates is an ensemble-based theatre company that specializes in presenting original, unscripted parodies of film, theatre. literature and television as well as traditional scripted shows.

Their 1999-2000 season included:
 MedeaMorphosis: Greek Tragedy to Go
 Charlie and the Fiction Factory
 Back in the Shadows Again:
  the Lighter Side of "Dark Shadows"

They accept unsolicited scripts from playwrights and project proposals from directors.

Need more income?
Check out the Temp Agencies on page 29

Theatres—Non-Equity

FreeStreet
Ron Bieganski - Artistic Director
David Schin - Managing Director
1419 W. Blackhawk
Chicago, IL 60622
773/772-7248
www.freestreet.org
They do not accept unsolicited headshots at present.
Non-Equity – Resident
Founded in 1969. Starting pay is $5.15/hour. They hold season auditions in the fall. The nearest eL stop is Division on the Blue line.

FreeStreet explores who we are and challenges who we become. Since 1969, FreeStreet has been creating model programming within Chicago communities. Current focus is working with Chicago youth and teens.

Their 1999-2000 season included:
 CoTingle
 Cog in the Freak Plan

Frump Tucker Theatre Company
Vincent P. Mahler - Artistic Director
P.O. Box 118315
Chicago, IL 60611-8315
773/883-1090
www.frumptucker.org
Send headshots to the attention of **Vincent P. Mahler**.
Non-Equity – Itinerant
Founded in 1995. Starting pay is nothing.

FrumpTucker is primarily drawn to contemporary, language-rich comedies with serious themes; hence their motto: "We do serious comedy."

Their 1999-2000 season included:
 The Original Last Wish Baby
 Fit To Be Tied - Jeff Nominated: Best Supporting Actress

They accept unsolicited synopses from playwrights and project proposals from directors.

Griffin Theatre
Richard Barletta - Artistic Director
Bill Massolia - Managing Director
5404 N. Clark
Chicago, IL 60640
773/769-2228
www.griffintheatre.com
Send headshots to the attention of **Richard Barletta**.
Non-Equity – Resident
Founded in 1988. Starting pay varies. They hold season auditions in the summer. The nearest eL stop is Berwyn on the Red line.

The Griffin Theatre produces highly original concept pieces for both adults and children that include both original work and adaptations of novels and classic plays.

Their 1999-2000 season included:
 Ella Enchanted
 Loving Little Egypt
 Judas' Mother
 Romeo and Juliet are Alive and Well and Living in Maple Bend
 The Stinky Cheeseman and Other Fairly Stupid Tales
 Catherine Called Birdy

Grounded Theatre
David Lightner - Artistic Director
810 Concord Ln.
Hoffman Estates, IL 60195
847/934-8363
www.pdws-inc.com/grounded
Send headshots to the attention of **David Lightner**.
Non-Equity – Itinerant
Founded in 2000. Starting pay varies.
They accept unsolicited scripts from playwrights.

Theatres—Non-Equity

HealthWorks Theatre
Peter Reynolds - Artistic Director
Steven Raider - Managing Director
3171 N. Halsted
Chicago, IL 60657
773/929-4260
www.healthworkstheatre.com
Send headshots to the attention of **Peter Reynolds**.
Non-Equity – Itinerant
Founded in 1988. Starting pay is $40/per-formance. They hold season auditions in August and December. The nearest eL stop is Belmont on the Red/Brown/Purple lines.
HealthWorks is an educational theatre company committed to working with communities to address critical health and social issues.
Received the 1999 Illinois Theatre Association Children's Theatre Division Award.
They accept unsolicited scripts from playwrights.

Highland Park Players
West Ridge Center
636 Ridge Rd.
Highland Park, IL 60035
847/604-4771
They don't accept unsolicited headshots at this time.
Non-Equity – Itinerant
Founded in 1988. Starting pay is nothing.
Highland Park Players wants to provide a professional quality theatre for the community as well as an outlet for the talents of area residents.
Their 1999-2000 season included:
 The Wizard of Oz
 The Jungle Book
 The Sisters Rosensweig

The Hypocrites
Sean Graney - Artistic Director
Mechelle Moe - Managing Director
P.O. Box 578542
Chicago, IL 60657-8542
312/409-5578
www.the-hypocrites.com
Send headshots to the attention of **Mechelle Moe**.
Non-Equity – Itinerant
Founded in 1997. Starting pay is nothing. They hold season auditions in the summer.
The Hypocrites make theatre live up to its full potential.

ImprovOlympic
3541 N. Clark
Chicago, IL 60657
773/880-0199
773/880-9993 - box office
www.improvolymp.com
Non-Equity – Resident
Founded in 1981. Starting pay was not revealed. The nearest eL stop is Addison on the Red line.
ImprovOlympic is a theatre and a training center. We have one stage for improvisation and a second stage for theatrical endeavors and improv experimental theatre.
They accept unsolicited scripts from playwrights and project proposals from directors.

Inclusive Theatre
847/266-8425
Non-Equity – Itinerant
Founded in 1996. Starting pay was not revealed.

Ch. 7 Theatres 231

Theatres—Non-Equity

Janus Theatre
Terence Domschke - Artistic Director
Sean Patrick Hargadon - Managing Director
P.O. Box 1567
Arlington Heights, IL 60005
847/301-1776
847/931-7247 - box office
Send headshots to the attention of **Terence Domschke and Sean Patrick Hargadon.**
Non-Equity – Itinerant

Founded in 1998. Starting pay is a stipend. Janus Theatre strives to present theatre that is relevant, challenging, and beneficial to the community by revealing the art that life is, and how we poetically dwell within it.

Their 1999-2000 season included:
  The Private Ear & The Public Eye
  The 4-H Club
  The Golden Fleece
  Feydeau's Folly
  Hippolytus

Lifeline Theatre
Dorothy Milne - Artistic Director
Melissa Bareford - Managing Director
6912 N. Glenwood
Chicago, IL 60618
773/761-0667
773/761-4477 - box office
www.lifelinetheatre.com
Send headshots to the attention of **Dorothy Milne.**

Non-Equity – Resident
Founded in 1982. Starting pay is $15/performance. They hold season auditions in spring or summer. The nearest eL stop is Morse on the Red line.
Lifeline creates literary adaptations and original works using an ensemble supported process.
They accept unsolicited synopses from playwrights.

Limelight Theatre Guild of Bensenville
c/o Bensenville Public Library
200 S. Church Rd.
Bensenville, IL 60106
630/415-0894
www.clearnet.org/limelight
Send headshots to the attention of the **Board of Governors.**

Non-Equity – Itinerant
Founded in 1984. Starting pay is nothing. Limelight's motto is "To learn, to experience, and to teach."

Their 1999-2000 season included:
  Whose Life Is It Anyway
  2000 Annual Food Pantry Follies
They accept unsolicited synopses from playwrights.

Low Sodium Entertainment
Aaron Haber - Artistic Director
3741 N. Kenmore #2
Chicago, IL 60613
773/549-3250
www.lowsodiumonline.com
Send headshots to the attention of **Aaron Haber.**
Non-Equity – Itinerant
Founded in 1996. Starting pay is based on the box office. They hold season auditions in August and November. The nearest eL stop is Addison or Belmont on the Red line.
Low Sodium Entertainment is Chicago's underground comedy scene, performing late night, high energy improv for everyone to enjoy.

Their 1999-2000 season included:
  Improvisers Must Be Punished!
  The Evil Show!
  Gameshow!
  Harvey Chucklestein's Hysterical House of Hoo-Haa Stand-Up Comedy!

Theatres—Non-Equity

Mary-Arrchie Theatre Co.
731 W. Sheridan
Chicago, IL 60613
773/871-0442

Murder Mystery Productions
60 Shore Dr.
Burr Ridge, IL 60521
630/887-9988
www.murderme.com
Send headshots to the attention of
Rick Dianovsky - Casting Director.
Non-Equity – Resident

Founded in 1987. Starting pay is $35-60/show. They attend the Unifieds.
Murder Mystery Productions is an interactive murder mystery dinner theatre event, filled with diabolical humor and audience participation.
They accept unsolicited synopses from playwrights and project proposals from directors.

Mystery Shop
Mary Heitert - Artistic Director
551 Sundance Ct.
Carol Stream, IL 60188
630/690-1105
www.themysteryshop.com
Send headshots to the attention of **Mary Heitert.**

Non-Equity – Itinerant
Founded in 1988. Starting pay is $30-45/performance. They hold season auditions in September.
The Mystery Shop is a travelling theatre specializing in adult and children's participatory mysteries and programs.
They accept unsolicited scripts from playwrights.

Neo-Futurists
5153 N. Ashland
Chicago, IL 60640
773/878-4557
773/275-5255 - box office
www.neofuturists.org
They don't accept unsolicited headshots at present.
Non-Equity – Resident
Founded in 1988. Starting pay is nothing. The nearest eL stop is Berwyn on the Red line.
The Neo-Futurists' performances are generally audience-interactive, non-illusory, and head slappingly affordable, including TMLMTBGB, the longest running show in Chicago.
Their 1999-2000 season included:
  Boxing Joseph Cornell
  The Harm in Candor
  Devolution
  The Unfinished Works of
    Sir Linear Scribble
  Lear's Shadow
  Duo Neurotica
  Too Much Light Makes the Baby Go Blind
  Another Lousy Day
  K.

The Noble Fool
P.O. Box 1884
Chicago, IL 60690-1884
773/202-8843
312/988-9000 - box office
www.noblefool.com
Send headshots to the attention of the **Artistic Committee Coordinator.**
Non-Equity – Resident
Founded in 1994. Starting pay was not revealed. The nearest eL stop is North & Clybourn on the Red line.
The Noble Fool is dedicated to elevating the art of comedy. They create and develop ensemble-driven shows utilizing improvsation and music.
Their 1999-2000 season included:
  Flanagan's Wake
  The Baritones
They accept unsolicited scripts from playwrights and project proposals from directors.

Ch. 7 Theatres 233

Theatres—Non-Equity

Northbrook Theatre
Dr. Gregory Dennhardt - Artistic Director
Thom Lange - Managing Director
3323 Walters Ave.
Northbrook, IL 60062
847/291-2367
847/291-2367 - box office
Non-Equity

Open Eye Productions
Noah Simon - Artistic Director
Sara Sevigny - Managing Director
1460 W. Farragut
Chicago, IL 60640
773/293-1557
www.openeyeproductions.com
Send headshots to the attention of **Noah Simon.**
Non-Equity – Itinerant
Founded in 1996. Starting pay is nothing. They hold season auditions in early fall and late winter.

Open Eye is made up of artists for artists; striving to create a well-rounded theatre company.

Their 1999-2000 season included:
Scavenger Hunt
Laughter on the 23rd Floor -
    Jeff Citation: Ensemble
Better Living

They accept unsolicited scripts from playwrights and project proposals from directors.

Pegasus Players
Arlene Crewdson - Artistic Director
John Economos - Managing Director
1145 W. Wilson
Chicago, IL 60640
773/878-9761
www.pegasusplayers.com
Send headshots to the attention of **Casting.**

Non-Equity – Resident
Founded in 1979. Starting pay is a rehearsal stipend plus $25/performance. The nearest eL stop is Wilson on the Red line.

Pegasus does plays with socially relevant and historical content, as well as musicals.

They accept unsolicited scripts from playwrights.

Pendragon Players
Peter Blachford - Managing Director
5020 S. Lakeshore #811
Chicago, IL 60615
773/324-5226
www.pendragonslair.org
They don't accept unsolicited headshots at this time.
Non-Equity – Itinerant
Founded in 1993. Starting pay is $45/performance.

Pendragon Players is a touring readers theatre company. They perform adaptations of classic works of literature in libraries throughout the greater Chicagoland area.

Their 1999-2000 season included:
Three in a Roe by Poe
The Adventures of Sherlock Holmes
The War of the Worlds

They accept unsolicited scripts from playwrights and project proposals from directors.

Pendulum Theatre Company

Bill Redding - Artistic Director
Carolyn Mlakar - Managing Director
2936 N. Southport
Chicago, IL 60657
773/529-2692
www.pendulumtheatre.org
Send headshots to the attention of **Bill Redding**.
Non-Equity – Itinerant

Founded in 1996. Starting pay is a small stipend.

Pendulum Theatre strives for artistic excellence in the production of lesser known scripts of social significance.

Their 1999-2000 season included:
  Abundance - Jeff Recommended
  Kind Lady

They accept unsolicited scripts from playwrights and project proposals from directors.

Pheasant Run Theatre

Diane Martinez - Artistic Director
4051 E. Main St.
St. Charles, IL 60174
630/584-MEGA
www.pheasantrun.com

Plasticene

2122 N. Winchester
Chicago, IL 60614
312/409-0400
www.plasticene.com
Non-Equity – Itinerant

Founded in 1995. Starting pay is nothing. They hold season auditions in July.

Plasticene is a critically acclaimed physical theatre company that builds original non-text-based theatre works and teaches physical and experimental theatre as "The Plasticene Studio."

Porchlight Theatre

L. Walter Stearns - Artistic Director
2936 N. Southport
Chicago, IL 60657
773/325-9884
773/935-6860 - box office
www.porchlighttheatre.com
Send headshots to the attention of **L. Walter Stearns - Artistic Director**
Non-Equity – Itinerant

Founded in 1994. Starting pay was not revealed. They hold season auditions in late August. The nearest eL stop is Southport on the Brown line or Belmont on the Red line.

Porchlight produces intimate and inventive musical theatre.

Their 1999-2000 season included:
  Falsettos - After Dark: Outstanding Performance (Janna Cardin), Jeff Nominated: Musical Direction (Eugene Dizon)
  Collette Collage - Jeff Nominated: Musical Direction (Eugene Dizon), Actress (Suzanne Genz)
  Merrily We Roll Along - Jeff Citations: Choreography (Samantha Fitscher), Musical Direction (Eugene Dizon), Jeff Nominated: Production, Direction (L. Walter Stearns), Actor (Charlie Clark), Actor (Stephen Rader)

They accept unsolicited scripts from playwrights and project proposals from directors.

Theatres—Non-Equity

Profiles Theatre
Joe Jahraus - Artistic Director
Darrell W. Cox - Managing Director
3761 N. Racine
Chicago, IL 60613
773/549-1815
773/549-1815 - box office
Send headshots to the attention of **Darrell W. Cox.**
Non-Equity – Resident

Founded in 1988. Starting pay varies. They hold season auditions in late summer or early fall. The nearest eL stop is Sheridan on the Red line.
Profiles Theatre's primary goal is to bring new works to Chicago that illuminate the determination and resiliency of the human spirit.
They accept unsolicited scripts from playwrights and project proposals from directors.

Prologue Theatre Productions
Anita Grenberg - Executive Director
2936 N. Southport #210
Chicago, IL 60657
847/681-0910
Non-Equity – Itinerant
Founded in 1987. Starting pay is

$25/performance.
Prologue specializes in musicals in a small, intimate setting without the use of amplification.
They accept unsolicited scripts from playwrights and project proposals from directors.

Pyewacket
Kate Harris - Artistic Director
2322 W. Wilson
Chicago, IL 60625
773/275-2201
Send headshots to the attention of **Kate Harris.**
Non-Equity – Itinerant
Founded in 1997. Starting pay is based on box office.

Pyewacket produces high quality, fully staged theatrical productions of "middle tales." As explained by Allan B. Chinen, M.D. "Middle tales offer maps of the mid life passage.
Their 1999-2000 season included:
    The Turn of the Screw - Jeff Citation: Actor (Michael Nowak)
They accept unsolicited synopses from playwrights and project proposals from directors.

Realism Update Theatre
Christina Athanasiades - Artistic Director
2957 N. Pulaski
Chicago, IL 60641
773/685-3077
Send headshots to the attention of **Christina Athanasiades.**
Non-Equity – Resident
Founded in 1987. Starting pay is based on the box office.

Realism Update attempts to produce works that convey moral as well as family and societal values.
Their 1999-2000 season included:
    Titanic
    Much Ado About Nothing
    Twelfth Night
    The Scarlet Letter
They accept unsolicited scripts from playwrights and project proposals from directors.

Theatres—Non-Equity

Red Wolf Theatre Company
David Tatosian - Artistic Director
Susan Block - Managing Director
1609 W. Berteau
Chicago, IL 60613
773/248-9678
312/409-6024 - box office
Send headshots to the
attention of **Susan Block.**
Non-Equity – Resident
Founded in 1997. Starting pay is nothing.

The nearest eL stop is Loyola on the Red line.
Red Wolf produces modern classics geared to the mature actor.
Their 1999-2000 season included:
   Red Address - Jeff Nominated:
      Supporting Actor (Andre W. Whatley)
   Who's Afraid of Virginia Woolf -
      Jeff Nominated: Actress (Susan Block)
   Betrayal
They accept unsolicited synopses from playwrights and project proposals from directors.

Redmoon Theater
Jim Lasko - Artistic Director
Kristen Vurrello - Managing Director
2936 N. Southport - 1st floor
Chicago, IL 60657
773/388-9031
www.redmoon.org
They don't accept unsolicited headshots at present.
Non-Equity – Itinerant
Founded in 1990. Starting pay varies.
Redmoon Theatre produces spectacle theatre, incorporating puppets, masks, objects and physical movement. Much of our work is based in Chicago's Logan Square community.

Runamuck Productions
Heath Corson - Artistic Director
4655 N. Campbell
Chicago, IL 60625
773/784-8100
Send headshots to the
attention of **Heath Corson.**
Non-Equity
Founded in 1995. Starting pay is based on the box office.

Runamuck is a not for profit children's theatre company that adapts literature for the stage. We strive to create children's theatre that engages and entertains the entire family, not just the youngsters.
Their 1999-2000 season included:
   I Left My Sneakers in Dimension X
   Too Many Time Machines
   Food Chain
They accept unsolicited synopses from playwrights and project proposals from directors.

S.T.A.R.
3637 W. 51st
Chicago, IL 60632
773/585-5852
www.chicagostar.org
They don't accept unsolicited headshots at present.

Non-Equity – Itinerant
Founded in 1988. Starting pay is nothing. The nearest eL stop is Midway on the Orange line.
They accept project proposals from directors.

Saint Sebastian Players
773/404-7922
members.aol.com/stsebplyrs
Non-Equity – Resident
Founded in 1982. Starting pay is nothing.
Saint Sebastian Players is a nonprofit, non-Equity company of actors, directors, designers, technicians and administrators. SSP produces three to four mainstage productions annually and several special events, including the annual Monologue Matchup competition and an Annual Banquet including the Sebastian Awards for performance and production.

Theatres—Non-Equity

Schadenfreude
Sandy Marshall - Artistic Director
c/o Heartland Studio Theater
7016 N. Glenwood
Chicago, IL 60626
773/293-0024
www.schadenfreude.net
Send headshots to the
attention of **Sandy Marshall.**
Non-Equity – Resident

Founded in 1997. Starting pay is nothing. The nearest eL stop is Morse on the Red line.

Schadenfreude is committed to developing their individual and group voices through a unique style of writing that yields lively and energetic performances.

They accept project proposals from directors.

Scrap Mettle SOUL
4753 N. Broadway #710
Chicago, IL 60640
773/275-3999
773/275-8949 - box office
They don't accept headshots at present.
Non-Equity – Resident
Founded in 1994. Starting pay is nothing. The nearest eL stop is Argyle on the

Red line.

SMS is an intergenerational community performance ensemble that collects true stories and performs them in an effort to build community understanding in Uptown and Edgewater.

Their 1999-2000 season included:
 Detours Home
 Bigger Then Hope

Sense of Urgency
Edwin A. Wilson - Artistic Director
905 S. Grove - 1st floor
Oak Park, IL 60304
708/386-6669
home.earthlink.net/~thespian13
Send headshots to the
attention of **Edwin A. Wilson.**
Non-Equity – Itinerant
Founded in 1995. Starting pay varies.
Sense of Urgency was founded on the

belief that great theatre can be produced at affordable costs to a diverse audience - selecting neglected classic plays and giving them our full creative energy.

Their 1999-2000 season included:
 A Picture Postcard Fantasy
 The Ruffian on the Stairs
 An Ugly Case

They accept unsolicited scripts from playwrights and project proposals from directors.

Shakespeare's Motley Crew
4926 N. Winchester
Chicago, IL 60640
773/878-3632
Send headshots to the
attention of **Laura Jones Macknin.**
Non-Equity – Itinerant
Founded in 1992. Starting pay is nothing.

SMC produces the works of William Shakespeare and especially his contemporaries.

Their 1999-2000 season included:
 Measure for Measure
 The Roaring Girl - Jeff Recommended

They accept project proposals from directors.

Theatres—Non-Equity

Shattered Globe Theatre
Brian Pudil - Artistic Director
2856 N. Halsted
Chicago, IL 60657
773/404-1237
773/871-3000 - box office
Send headshots to the
attention of **Brian Pudil.**
Non-Equity – Resident
Founded in 1991. Starting pay is $50/week. The nearest eL stop is Fullerton on the Red/Brown/Purple line.

Shattered Globe uses the unique strengths of ensemble acting to re-explore classics and present new plays that examine timeless issues.
Their 1999-2000 season included:
 Real Classy Affair
 Escape From Happiness
 The Lower Depths - Jeff Citation:
  Scenic Design (Kevin Hagan),
  Costume Design (Karen Kawa)
They accept unsolicited scripts from playwrights and project proposals from directors.

Stage Actors Ensemble
656 W. Barry - 3rd floor
Chicago, IL 60657
773/529-8337
theperformanceloft.com
Non-Equity – Resident

Founded in 1978. Starting pay is $150/run. The nearest eL stop is Belmont on the Red/Brown/Purple line.
Stage Actors Ensemble focuses on interracial and multi-cultural productions.
They accept unsolicited scripts from playwrights and project proposals from directors.

Stage Center Theatre
5500 N. St. Louis
Chicago, IL 60625
773/794-2937
773/794-6652 - box office
www.neiu.edu/~stagectr
Send headshots to the attention of **Rodney Higginbotham - Associate Professor.**
Non-Equity – Resident
Founded in 1994. Starting pay is $100/run.

They hold season auditions in May. The nearest eL stop is Kimball on the Brown line.
Stage Center Theatre is a summer stock program that blends working non-union professionals with students in a 2-play summer season.
Their 1999-2000 season included:
 Everybody Loves Opal
 The Miss Firecracker Contest
They accept project proposals from directors.

Stage Left Theatre
Kevin Heckman and Jessi D. Hill - Artistic Directors.
3408 N. Sheffield
Chicago, IL 60657
773/883-8830
members.aol.com/SLTChicago
Send headshots to the
attention of **Jessi D. Hill.**
Non-Equity – Resident

Founded in 1982. Starting pay is one percent of show's gross revenue. The nearest eL stop is Belmont or Addison on the Red line.
Stage Left Theatre is the only theatre in Chicago dedicated to producing plays that raise the level of debate on social and political issues.
They accept unsolicited synopses from playwrights and project proposals from directors.

Stage Right Dinner Theatre
Peter Verdico - Artistic Director
276 E. Irving Park Rd.
Woodale, IL 60191

630/595-2044
630/595-2044 - box office
www.giorgiosbanq.com
Non-Equity

Theatres—Non-Equity

Stockyards Theatre Project
Jill Hughes - Artistic Director
3941 N. Pine Grove #706
Chicago, IL 60613
773/871-6625
www.angelfire.com/il2/stockyards
Send headshots to the
attention of **Jill Hughes.**
Non-Equity – Itinerant

*Founded in 1999. Starting pay is nothing.
Stockyards are the only company in
Chicago dedicated to femaleist theatre
and performance art.
Their 1999-2000 season included:*
   A Chicca Looks at 25:
      A Memoir for the Stage
   Femme Fatalities:
      Four One Act Plays By Women
   Don't Promise

Stone Circle Theatre Ensemble
Jessica McCartney - Artistic Director
915 W. Fletcher
Chicago, IL 60657
773/525-9565
Send headshots to the
attention of **Jessica McCartney.**
Non-Equity

*Founded in 1996. Starting pay is nothing.
Stone Circle focuses less on technical/visual
"spectaculars" and tries to focus on
script/actor-based productions.
Their 1999-2000 season included:*
   The Collector
*They accept unsolicited scripts from
playwrights and project proposals
from directors.*

Summer Place Theatre
P.O. Box 128
Naperville, IL 60566
630/355-7969
www.summerplacetheatre.com
They don't accept headshots
at present.
Non-Equity – Resident
*Founded in 1965. Starting pay is nothing.
The nearest Metra stop is Naperville.
The Summer Place, Inc. is a non-professional, not-for-profit, community theatre*

*group presenting various theatrical presentations in the Naperville area on an
annual basis.
Their 1999-2000 season included:*
   The Fantasticks
   Grease
   Nunsense
   Mame
   Ghost Stories in the Park in the Dark
   Tom Sawyer
   The Legend of Sleeping Beauty
*They accept project proposals
from directors.*

Sweetback Productions
Steve Hickson, Kelly Anchors and David
Cerda - Artistic Directors
1517 W. Rosemont Ave. #3E
Chicago, IL 60660-1322
312/409-3925
Send headshots to the
attention of **Steve Hickson.**
Non-Equity – Itinerant
Founded in 1994. Starting pay is dona-

*tions from the "Pity Pot."
Sweetback produces irreverent,
pop-culture satire.
Their 1999-2000 season included:*
   Valley of the Dolls
   Rudolph the Red Hosed Reindeer
   Queen of the Roundup
*They accept unsolicited synopses from
playwrights and project proposals from
directors.*

Theatres—Non-Equity

Theatre of Western Springs
Tony Vezner - Artistic Director
Jeff Arena - Managing Director
4584 Hampton Ave.
Western Springs, IL 60558
708/246-4043
708/246-3380 - box office
www.TheatreWesternSprings.com
Send headshots to the
attention of **Tony Vezner.**

Non-Equity – Resident
Founded in 1928. Starting pay is nothing. The nearest Metra stop is Western Springs.
TWS is a home for theatre artists from kindergarten through post-retirement, offering training in performing, tech and even the business of running a theatre.
They accept unsolicited scripts from playwrights.

Thirsty Theater
Mitch Newman - Artistic Director
556 W. 18th
Chicago, IL 60616
773/929-6314
312/491-8484 - box office
Send headshots to the
attention of **Mitch Newman.**
Non-Equity – Resident
Founded in 1997. Starting pay is nothing. The nearest eL stop is Roosevelt on the

Red line.
Thirsty Theater's goal is to give actors and directors the opportunity to develop their artistic skills in the Pilsen neighborhood and to expose inner-city children to theatre arts.
Their 1999-2000 season included:
True West
Durang, Durang
Sight Unseen
They accept project proposals from directors.

Timber Lake Playhouse
Brad Lyons - Artistic Director
Pam Sorg - Managing Director
c/o Timber Lake Playhouse - P.O. Box 29
Mt. Carroll, IL 61053
815/244-2035
www.artsaxis.com/tlp
Send headshots to the
attention of **Brad Lyons.**

Non-Equity – Resident
Founded in 1962. Starting pay is $125/week. They hold season auditions in February or March.
Timber Lake is made up of a close-knit family of actors ranging in experience from college to professional, including Equity guest artists.

TimeLine Theatre Company
P.J. Powers - Artistic Director
Pat Tiedemann - Managing Director
615 W. Wellington
Chicago, IL 60657
773/281-8463
312/409-8463 - box office
www.TimeLineTheatre.com
Send headshots to the
attention of **P.J. Powers.**
Non-Equity – Resident

Founded in 1997. Starting pay is nothing. They attend the Unifieds. The nearest eL stop is Wellington on the Brown line.
TimeLine explores humanity through a historical perspective.
Their 1999-2000 season included:
Gaslight
To Live as Variously as Possible
A Cry of Players
They accept unsolicited scripts from playwrights and project proposals from directors.

Ch. 7 Theatres **241**

Theatres—Non-Equity

Timestep Players Educational Children's Theatre Company
Allen McCoy - Artistic Director
P.O. Box 16442
Chicago, IL 60616
773/736-7077
www.timestepplayers.com
Send headshots to the attention of **Allen McCoy.**
Non-Equity – Itinerant

Starting pay is $300/week. They hold season auditions in late February or early March.
Timestep Players is a children's theatre company dedicated to promoting literacy and education throughout the United States by encouraging and motivating children to read through the use of live theatre.
They accept unsolicited scripts from playwrights.

Tinfish Productions
Dejan Avramovich - Artistic Director
Laurie Kladis - Managing Director
4247 N. Lincoln
Chicago, IL 60618
773/549-1888
www.Tinfish.org
Send headshots to the attention of **Dejan Avramovich.**
Non-Equity – Resident

Founded in 1994. Starting pay is $50/run. The nearest eL stop is Western on the Brown line.
Tinfish's goal is to bring to the public productions by or about great European literary figures who are not necessarily associated with the theatre.
They accept unsolicited scripts from playwrights and project proposals from directors.

Tommy Gun's Garage
1239 S. State
Chicago, IL 60605
312/461-0102
www.tommygunsgarage.com
Send headshots to the attention of **Sandy Mangen - General Manager.**
Non-Equity – Resident

Founded in 1989. Starting pay is $3.55/hr plus tips. The nearest eL stop is Roosevelt on the Red line.
Tommy Gun's Garage is an audience-interactive roaring 20's musical comedy revue.

Trap Door Theatre
Beata Pilch - Artistic Director
1655 W. Cortland
Chicago, IL 60622
773/384-0494
www.trapdoortheater.com
Send headshots to the attention of **Beata Pilch.**
Non-Equity – Resident

Founded in 1994. Starting pay is based on tips. The nearest eL stop is Damen on the Blue line or Fullerton on the Red/Brown/Purple line.
Trap Door is committed to seeking out challenging yet obscure works and bringing them to life.
They accept unsolicited scripts from playwrights and project proposals from directors.

Theatres—Non-Equity

TriArts, Inc.
Troy Fujimura - Artistic Director
John Rogers - Managing Director
5315 N. Clark #142
Chicago, IL 60640
773/866-8082 x2
773/866-8082 x1 - box office
www.triarts.org
Send headshots to the attention of
Brian Loevner - Executive Director.
Non-Equity – Itinerant
Founded in 1998. Starting pay is nothing.
TriArts' goal is to provide a fulfilling original artistic experience that unifies all artistic and technical aspects of the production process. TriArts strives to provide the technical aspects - a unified light, sound and set design experience - not only in our own work, but also for other arts organizations in the Chicago area.
Their 1999-2000 season included:
  Desdemona - A Play About
    A Handkerchief
  Hfob-n-Ffos
They accept unsolicited scripts from playwrights and project proposals from directors.

Tripaway Theatre
Karin Shook - Artistic Director
Anita Evans - Managing Director
2714 W. Leland - Garden
Chicago, IL 60625
773/878-7785
www.tripaway.org
Send headshots to the attention of **Karin Shook.**
Non-Equity – Itinerant
Founded in 1994. Starting pay is nothing. They hold season auditions in March or April.
Tripaway is known for its high energy, off-kilter, intensely physical productions of Shakespeare and translations of classics such as Chekhov and Moliere, as well as its own brand of commedia del'arte and puppetry. And puppets doing commedia del'arte. The puppets are taking over...
Their 1999-2000 season included:
  A Midsummer Night's Dream
  Commedia Divino E Profano or
    Scourge of the Doom Pies!
  The Taming of the Shrew
They accept unsolicited synopses from playwrights and project proposals from directors.

Up & Coming Theatre Company
P.O. Box 473
Arlington Heights, IL 60006
847/706-6747
847/718-7700 or
847/437-9494 - box office
pwp.starnetinc.com/starlite/uac/uac.htm
Send headshots to the attention of the **Artistic Director.**
Non-Equity – Resident
Founded in 1993. Starting pay is nothing.
Their 1999-2000 season included:
  Joseph and the Amazing Technicolor
    Dreamcoat
  Grease
  Chess

Ulysses Theatre Company
828 W. Gunnison #3N
Chicago, IL 60640
773/549-0963
www.members.tripod.com/~ulysses_theatre

Theatres—Non-Equity

Village Players
Maura Elizabeth Manning - Artistic Director
1006 Madison St.
Oak Park, IL 60302
708/524-1892
708/222-0369 - box office
www.village-players.org

Non-Equity – Resident
Founded in 1961. Starting pay was not revealed. The nearest eL stop is Harlem on the Green line.
Village Players provides Oak Park's family entertainment.
They accept unsolicited scripts from playwrights.

Village Theatre Guild
P.O. Box 184
Glen Ellyn, IL 60138-0184
630/469-5583
630/469-8230 - box office
www.glen-ellyn.com/vtg
Non-Equity – Resident
Founded in 1963. Starting pay is nothing.

Village Theatre Guild is a community theatre that is not afraid to take risks.
Their 1999-2000 season included:
  Twilight of the Golds
  Ghost in the Machine
  Lost in Yonkers
  The Memory of Water
They accept unsolicited synopses from playwrights.

Vittum Theatre
773/278-7471 x172
773/278-7471 - box office
Non-Equity – Resident
Founded in 1998. The nearest eL stop is Division on the Blue line.

The Vittum Theater rents its versatile state-of-the-art space at a discounted rate to performing artists committed to arts education and outreach.
They accept project proposals from directors.

VORTEX
Gary Charles Metz - Artistic Director
920 Barnsdale Rd.
LaGrange Park, IL 60526
708/352-9120
708/354-4580 - box office
www.northstarnet.org/lpshome/vortex
Send headshots to the attention of **Gary Charles Metz.**
Non-Equity – Resident

Founded in 1996. Starting pay is nothing.
VORTEX prides itself on providing residents near LaGrange Park with original or little-known live theatre at affordable prices.
Their 1999-2000 season included:
  Victim
  Christmas at Farrah's
  Breaking Legs
They accept project proposals from directors.

Walkabout Theater Company
Kristin Schmidt - Artistic Director
Mike Karrys - Managing Director
3241 N. Ravenswood
Chicago, IL 60657
773/248-9278
Send headshots to the attention of **Kristin Schmidt.**
Non-Equity – Itinerant

Founded in 1999. Starting pay varies.
Walkabout Theater Company digs for psychological depth using various disciplines. Almost all their works are from within the group.
They accept unsolicited scripts from playwrights and project proposals from directors.

244 The Book: An Actor's Guide to Chicago

Theatres—Non-Equity

Wheaton Drama, Inc.
111 N. Hale
P.O. Box 4
Wheaton, IL 60189
630/260-1820
Non-Equity – Resident
Starting pay was not revealed.
Wheaton Drama has been in existence since before WWI with a brief suspension in operation around 1918.
Their 1999-2000 season included:
Carousel
Come Blow Your Horn
Wait Until Dark
Our Town
Jerry's Girls

Wing & Groove Theatre Company
Andrew Gall - Artistic Director
1935 1/2 W. North
The Flat Iron Arts Building
Chicago, IL 60622
773/782-9416
www.wingandgroove.com

Winnetka Theatre
620 Lincoln Ave.
Winnetka, IL 60093
847/604-0275 - box office
Non-Equity – Resident
Founded in 1972. Starting pay is nothing. The nearest Metra stop is Winnetka. Winnetka Theatre presents 3-4 shows per season, including musicals and straight plays, sometimes presenting area premieres.
Their 1999-2000 season included:
Cinderella
Lucky Stiff
Big River
They accept project proposals from directors.

WNEP Theater Foundation
Jen Ellison - Artistic Director
Mark Dahl - Managing Director
3210 N. Halsted #3
Chicago, IL 60657
773/755-1693
www.wneptheater.org
Send headshots to the attention of **Jen Ellison.**
Non-Equity – Resident
Founded in 1993. Starting pay is based on the box office. They hold season auditions in July. The nearest eL stop is Belmont on the Red/Brown/Purple lines.
WNEP creates original theater utilizing improvisation, DADA, and collaborative writing and strives to involve the audience in their process. Often confrontational in their approach, WNEP does not believe in the concept of the "passive observer."
Their 1999-2000 season included:
The Mysteries of Harris Burdick
...apocalypse...
My Grandma's a Fat Whore in Jersey
They accept unsolicited scripts from playwrights and project proposals from directors.

Ch. 7 Theatres 245

Theatres—Non-Equity

Women's Theatre Alliance
Janel Winter - Artistic Director
407 S. Dearborn #1775
Chicago, IL 60605-1123
312/408-9910
www.wtac.org
Send headshots to the attention of the **Office Manager**.

Non-Equity – Itinerant
Founded in 1996. Starting pay is nothing. They hold season auditions in September and December.
Women's Theatre Alliance promotes theatre by, for, and/or about women through seminars, showcases, and six-month incubator programs for one-woman shows and for play development.

Workshop Theatre
Michael Colucci - Artistic Director
Thomas Jamroz - Managing Director
1350 N. Wells #F521
Chicago, IL 60610
312/337-6603
Send headshots to the attention of **Michael Colucci**.

Non-Equity – Itinerant
Founded in 1994. Starting pay was not revealed. They attend the Unifieds.
Workshop Theatre explores the entire body of work of one playwright. They accept project proposals from directors.

Your Summer!

Summer Theatre Directory
New Edition December: $19.95
385 Summer Theatres
80 Intensive Training Programs
Combined Audition Times & Places
Apprentice & Internships (Equity & Non-Equity)
And Updated list of overdone monologues

Regional Theatre Directory
New Edition every June: $19.95
435 Regional & Dinner Theatres
Equity & Non-Equity Opportunities
Seasons, Casting, Hiring & Internships
Resources & Reviews of Career Books

Your Future!

Available at **Act I Bookstore**, or direct from Publisher
(802) 867-2223 or www.theatredirectories.com

Improv

The Hypocrites, "Jack, or the Submission"

Improv and the Actor

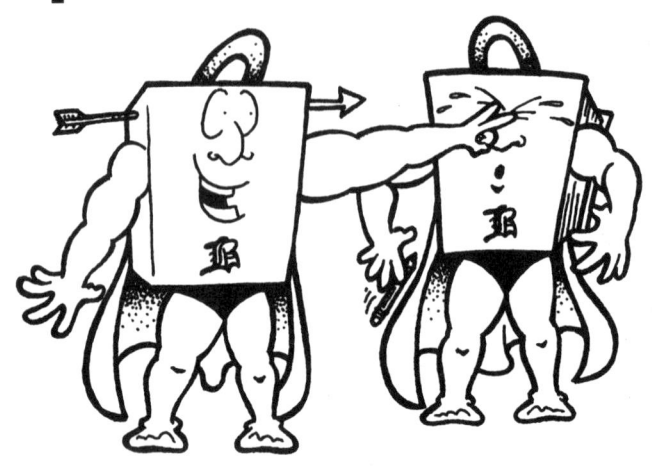

A fool, a fool! I met a fool i' th' forest,
A motley fool;—a miserable world!—
As I do live by food, I met a fool.

By Jason Chin

Welcome to Chicago, without a doubt the greatest city in the world for learning and performing improvisation. Within these city limits you will find more outlets, training centers, teams, and theatres devoted to improvisation than any other city in the world.

An improv show is different from any other kind of theatre; it is a one-of-a-kind experience that will never be experienced. Based on audience suggestions, an improvised show will be funnier or more dramatic depending on the night and cast involved.

Even though improv is first and foremost fun to perform, it also takes months of training and experience to learn how to improvise well. While it is true that just about any "funny" person could take to a stage, get suggestions and do a show, that may not be a show you wish to watch (or be in). Just like any person with a glass of water could be firefighter, that's not necessarily the person you want putting out your blazing house.

A professional (any group that charges money to see their show should be held to these standards) improv troupe will rely on their training to help them make interesting choices and support their fellow players instead of relying on breaking up on stage or flaunting their own rules for a laugh.

Years of training, work and even rehearsal go into the best improv shows. A great improviser is a very good actor because they both rely on the same tools: commitment, relationship, listening and reacting and a dedication to their craft. An improviser uses, not only his/her own instincts and abilities, but his/her teammate's abilities and skills to create a full show.

Improv is a group effort to create a specific set of scenes or games. While most improvisers could be excellent stand-up comedians the reverse usually does not hold true. An improviser's first job is to support the other players on stage by elaborating and heightening what others do and say. It takes time to learn how to do all this.

Yes and....What's the point?

Improvisers are actors, by nature, it's just that their training is different. The skills taught by improv schools are invaluable to an actor: listening and reacting, staying in the moment, making choices that heighten and elaborate the scene and supporting your fellow players. Improv also allows you to become several different people/characters in one show which can be an tremendous asset to an actor. The actor trained in improvisation has an advantage over others not so "blessed." Perhaps the most important ability of an improviser is the ability to adapt. Things are constantly flowing in any improv show and it's the job of an improviser to not only go with that flow but to add to it and make it flow either better or faster. This ability makes script or set changes easier to deal with, a missed cue or line flub becomes part of the show instead of a flaw in a show.

Even though there are no scripts involved, improv can help a writer in many different ways. Many playwrights have said that they become their characters as they write them, or that the characters write themselves. An improviser will play several different characters in one show and sometimes may even do a scene playing several people at the same time. The ability to adapt quickly also comes into play here. When script changes are needed fast, an improv trained writer can handle it. There's a reason why almost all of the writers on Saturday Night Live and the Conan O'Brian Show are improvisers.

The play's the thing

The first thing is to have fun. Improvisers constantly use the word "play" when discussing their performance. "Do you want to play with us?" "Did you play tonight?" "When are you playing next?" This is because improvisation, though set by some general rules, is done in

Improvisation

that magical land of make-believe where we spent a great deal of our childhood. It takes an child's imagination to play with a cardboard box; it takes an improviser's imagination to play with box that isn't there.

Improv, at it's worst, is the worst kind of theater to see. That's why it's improv, there is no sure guarantee that everything will work perfectly. That's why there are classes, to help minimize the chances of sucking. When improv works, it's a wonder to behold. An audience gives more to an improv and gets more as well. There is a spirit of co-operation, of "well, we're all in this together" that bonds an audience with a improv team. That's why improvisers sometimes get applause or laughter from their mistakes as well as their successes.

Once you begin and you discover that love improvisation you may find it addictive. That's why there are so many improvisers in Chicago and beyond. That's why improvisers that have gone on to high-paying TV gigs come back and play. Isn't that something we all wish we could do? Go back to the old neighborhood and play with the kids that live there now?

A level field

Most of the schools of improvisation here in Chicago are based on levels. Each class meets once a week for eight weeks and generally costs about $200 for each eight week session. Since everyone usually begins at level one, even if you have never taken a improv class before you will be with people at the same level. There are several schools of improvisation in Chicago and like all the different martial arts schools (kung fu, karate, tae kwon do) have the goal of making the other guy go down, the improv schools all have the same goal as well: to make the audience laugh. Though there are great differences in the teaching styles of each school they all agree on the fundamental basics of agreement and support. This base knowledge set will help you should you decide to go to several improv schools (as many people do).

Let's take a look at some of the most popular schools and what they aim for.

Second City teaches improv as a means of creating scripted material. This craft of creating scripts from improv has served Second City well for 40 years and is a great ability to have. Students put up shows in the Skybox theater at the end of several levels.

ImprovOlympic teaches improvisation as an artform and performance piece in itself. Created by Del Close and called "long-form improv," or their signature long-form The Harold, their shows are usually 25-40

Improvisation

minutes of uninterrupted, interweaving scenes relating to a single audience suggestion. Students may be chosen to be on one of their performing teams and students put on an improvised show at the end of their course study. The Annoyance Theater teaches fast, fun improv centering on personal growth and development and provides personal attention that may be lacking at the other two major schools. Students put on a show at the end of their course study.

Short-form improv games (a la Whose Line Is It Anyway?), are taught by the Chicago branch of the nation-wide franchise, ComedySportz. Short-form games are sure audience pleasers and rely on the same basic tenets that the other schools teach as well.

The Players Workshop of the Second City has nothing to do with The Second City theater, but also teaches both sketch and improv.

There are several other improv-based theaters like The Free Associates, the Factory Theater, and the Neo-Futurists that offer classes from time-to-time as well. If there is a particular show you enjoy or even a particular performer, ask if there are classes or if he/she are currently teaching somewhere.

The best way to discover what school you should attend is to go to one of their shows. Even on a tight budget most of these theaters offer either 2-for-1s or even free nights. Go see a show and decide whether or not that show is something you would like to perform in. It's really quite that simple.

A quickie before we go

A fast way to experience all of above mentioned theater's shows and teaching styles is the Chicago Improv Fest (www.cif.com), now in its second year. The fest not only hosts groups from around the nation, they provide workshops with some of Chicago's best teachers in one weekend. All of Chicago's improv theaters perform at some point during the fest as well. It's a great way to take a glance at everything Chicago improv has to offer.

Is anyone writing this down?

What if you want to take less risks and guarantee a punchline, or the transcendence of improvisation doesn't appeal to you? Some use improvisation as a basis for scripted material (Second City's famed technique) or they just create scripts from their own fevered imaginations. Chicago, while hosting the largest per capita of improvisers, must

Improv Training

also shoulder the credit (or shame) of the largest proliferation of sketch comedy shows. Similar to their television counterparts, sketch shows are usually comprised of short comedic scenes strung together in a row.

Since TV has bombarded us with sketch shows both good and bad, it might be assumed that sketch is simple to do. This is a tricky proposition; yes, sketch shows are easy to put up, but a good sketch show is very difficult. Having said that improvisation takes training and discovering that there are many schools for such an education, you would think from the preponderance of sketch shows in Chicago, that there would be at least half as many programs dedicated to the creation of sketch comedy. There aren't. There is just one single program dedicated to the teaching of sketch comedy (while several sketch comedy groups have offered workshops in the past, none have lasted long or are expected to continue offering classes) and that is at the Second City.

Since Second City is so successful with their unique brand of show creation (improvised scenes become a scripted show) they are the logical providers of such a class. The Comedy Writing Program teaches students the foundations of scene writing and structure through producing a Second City style show with an ensemble of actors. There are six levels to the Writing Program with each level lasting eight weeks. In an interesting twist, levels 1 through 3 are being offered on the Internet. Students in this program also get the opportunity to view Second City archive tapes for critical dissection and education.

Many of the city's improvisation schools have electives outside of their improv curriculum and may offer a writing class as well. Check with a school of your liking to see what might be coming soon.

Have fun!

Improv Training

ComedySportz
3210 N. Halsted - 3rd Floor
Chicago, IL 60657
773/549-8482
A - First level of training consisting of fundamentals and games.
AA - Advanced scenework techniques and more games.
AAA - Intensive work on Styles, Music, Characters, Dialects and advanced scene work.
Minor League Performance Level- Students workshops and performs an eight week run of their own ComedySportz style show

Improv-Friendly Theatres

ImprovOlympic
(See our ad on page 50)
3541 N. Clark
Chicago, IL 60657
773/880-0199
773/880-9979 - fax
Long Form Improv - Six levels, geared towards performance, classes run eight weeks

The Playground
3341 N. Lincoln Ave.
Chicago, IL 60657
773/871-3793
doug@the-playground.com

Second City
(See our ad on this page)
1616 N. Wells
Chicago, IL 60614
312/664-3959 • 312/664-9837 - fax
www.secondcity.com
Conservatory - The art of improv, Second City revue style
Improv for Actors - For experienced performers with little improv training or as a brush-up course
Writing - Techniques of comedy writing for beginning and advanced writers
Beginning - Foundations of improv for students with limited theatre or improv experience

Improv-Friendly Theatres

These theatres either offer improvised shows or are known for using improv as a major force in creating new works.

ComedySportz
3210 N. Halsted - 3rd Floor
Chicago, IL 60657
773/549-8482

Free Associates
Mark Gagne - Artistic Director
750 W. Wellington
Chicago, IL 60657
773/334-3255
773/975-7171 – box office
773/334-8060 - fax
home.earthlink.net/~free_assoc/

The Second City training center

"The entire recent tradition of American satire can be summed up in three words: THE SECOND CITY."
— Clive Barnes, The New York Times

- Conservatory Program
- Improv for Actors
- Beginning Program
- Acting Program
- High School Program
- Special Workshops
- Comedy Writing Program

CALL: 312.664.3959 or log on to:
www.secondcity.com

Ch. 8 Improv 253

Improv Groups

ImprovOlympic
3541 N. Clark
Chicago, IL 60657
773/880-0199 • 773/880-9979 - fax

Low Sodium Entertainment
3737 N. Kenmore #3F
Chicago, IL 60613
773/549-3250
www.lowsodiumonline.com

Players Workshop's Children's Theatre
Stephen Roath - Artistic Director
2936 N. Southport
Chicago, IL 60657
773/929-6288 • 773/477-8022 - fax
www.playersworkshop.com

WNEP Theater Foundation
Jen Ellison - Artistic Director
Mark Dahl - Managing Director
817 W. Lakeside #807
Chicago, IL 60640-6641
773/334-8661 x1
members.aol.com/WNEP

Improv Groups

Improv groups emerge and vanish in Chicago with startling frequency. Most groups form around a class, last for a while, and then the members go their separate ways. Following are a few groups that have shown above-average permanence.

Baby Wants Candy
773/880-9993

Broken Pilgrims in Gothic Sneakers
1925 W. Newport #F
Chicago, IL 60657-1025
312/974-2110

Detonate Productions
1410 W. Belle Plaine #1
Chicago, IL 60613
773/549-8190

Oui Be Negroes
1432 W. Lunt #208
Chicago, IL 60626
773/274-4563
www.ouibenegroes.com

Sheila Theater Group
4835 N. Kenmore #3
Chicago, IL 60640
773/275-3625

Sirens
Jacqueline Stone
3638 N. Pine Grove #1
Chicago, IL 60613
773/222-7053

Running a Small Theatre Company

An NEA visit gone bad... *This is your spacious, 90 seat theatre?*

Uffish Theatre, "Alcestis"

Theatres for Rent

About Face Theatre
3212 N. Broadway
Chicago, IL 60657
773/549-7943
www.aboutface.base.org
Mainstage:100 - Thrust

American Theater Company
1909 W. Byron
Chicago, IL 60613
773/929-5009
www.atcweb.org
Mainstage:137 - Thrust

Apollo Theater
916 S. Wabash #503
Chicago, IL 60605
312/461-9292
www.apollochicago.com
Mainstage:435 - Thrust

Athenaeum
2936 N. Southport
Chicago, IL 60657
773/935-6860
Mainstage:976 Studio:55 Stage 3:80

Attic Playhouse
410 Sheridan Rd.
Highwood, IL 60040
847/433-2660
www.atticplayhouse.com
Mainstage:94 - Black Box

Bailiwick Repertory
1229 W. Belmont
Chicago, IL 60657
773/883-1090
www.bailiwick.org
Mainstage:150 Second Stage:90 - Thrust

Breadline Theatre Group
1802 W. Berenice
Chicago, IL 60613
773/327-6096
www.breadline.org
Mainstage:40 - Proscenium

Center Theatre
1346 W. Devon
Chicago, IL 60660
773/508-0200
773/508-9584 - fax
Mainstage:60 Studio:25 - Black Box

CenterLight Sign & Voice Theatre
3444 Dundee Rd.
Northbrook, IL 60062
847/559-0110 x237
www.centerlighttheatre.com
Mainstage:100 - Black Box

Chicago Actors Studio
1567 N. Milwaukee
Chicago, IL 60622
773/645-0222
773/645-0040 - fax
www.actors-studio.net
Mainstage:90 - Thrust

Chicago Cultural Center
78 E. Washington
Chicago, IL 60602
312/744-3094
www.ci.chi.il.us/culturalaffairs/

Chicago Dramatists
1105 W. Chicago
Chicago, IL 60622
312/633-0630
Mainstage:77 - Proscenium

Theatres for Rent

ComedySportz
2851 N. Halsted
Chicago, IL 60657
773/549-8080
www.comedysportzchicago.com
Mainstage:200 - Thrust

Corn Productions
4210 N. Lincoln
Chicago, IL 60618
773/278-3274
Mainstage:60 - Thrust

Court Theatre
5535 S. Ellis
Chicago, IL 60637
773/702-7005
www.courttheatre.org
Mainstage:254 - Thrust

Curious Theatre Branch
2827 N. Lincoln
Chicago, IL 60657
773/327-6666
www/enteract.com/~jemlunar

Duncan YMCA Chernin Center for the Arts
1001 W. Roosevelt
Chicago, IL 60608
312/738-7980 • 312/738-1420 - fax
Mainstage:220 Studio: 125 - Proscenium

Excaliber Shakespeare Company
The Harrison Street Galleries Studio Theatre
208 W. Harrison St.
Oak Park, IL 60304
708/366-7832
Mainstage:40 Second Stage:25 - Black Box

Festival Theatre
P.O. Box 4114
Oak Park, IL 60303
www.oprf.com/festival/
Mainstage:300

ImprovOlympic
(See our ad on page 50)
3541 N. Clark
Chicago, IL 60657
773/880-0199
www.improvolymp.com
Mainstage:100 Second Stage:100 - Proscenium

Irish American Heritage Center
4626 N. Knox
Chicago, IL 60630
773/282-7035 x17
773/282-0380 – fax
www.irishamhc.com
Mainstage:600 - Proscenium

Links Hall
3435 N. Sheffield
Chicago, IL 60657
773/281-0824
Mainstage:75 - Black Box

Live Bait Theater
3914 N. Clark
Chicago, IL 60613
773/871-1212
www.livebaittheater.org
Mainstage:70 Second Stage:50 - Black Box

Neo-Futurists
5153 N. Ashland
Chicago, IL 60640
773/878-4557
www.neofuturists.org
Mainstage:149 - Thrust

Theatres for Rent

North Island Center
8 E. Galena Blvd. #230
Aurora, IL 60506
630/264-7202 • 630/892-1084 – fax
www.paramountarts.com
Paramount Arts Centre: 1888 Copley Theatre: 216

Northlight Theatre
9501 Skokie Blvd.
Skokie, IL 60077
847/679-9501 x8
www.northlight.org
Mainstage:850 Second Stage:354 - Proscenium

The Playground
773/871-3793
www.the-playground.com

Profiles Theatre
3761 N. Racine
Chicago, IL 60613
773/549-1815
Mainstage:52 - Proscenium

Realism Update Theatre
2957 N. Pulaski
Chicago, IL 60641
773/685-3077
Mainstage:60 - Proscenium

Red Hen Productions
2944 N. Broadway
Chicago, IL 60657
773/728-0599
www.redhenproductions.com
Mainstage:50 - Black Box

A Red Orchid Theatre
1531 N. Wells
Chicago, IL 60610-7752
312/943-8722
www.a-red-orchid.com
Mainstage:65-70 - Black Box

Schadenfreude
c/o Heartland Studio Theater
7016 N. Glenwood
Chicago, IL 60626
773/293-0024
www.schadenfreude.net
Mainstage:50 - Black Box

Second City
(See our ad on page 59)
1616 N. Wells
Chicago, IL 60614
312/664-3959
312/664-9837 - fax
www.secondcity.com

Stage Actors Ensemble
656 W. Barry - 3rd floor
Chicago, IL 60657
773/529-8337
www.theperformanceloft.com
Mainstage:85

Stage Left Theatre
3408 N. Sheffield
Chicago, IL 60657
773/883-8830
members.aol.com/SLTChicago
Mainstage:50 - Black Box

Strawdog Theatre Company
3829 N. Broadway
Chicago, IL 60622
773/528-9889
www.StrawDog.org
Mainstage:75 - Black Box

The Theatre Building
1225 W. Belmont
Chicago, IL 60657
773/929-7367
773/327-1404 - fax
North: 148 - Black Box
South: 148 - Proscenium
West: 148 - Black Box

Theatres for Rent

Theatre of Western Springs
4584 Hampton Ave.
Western Springs, IL 60558
708/246-4043
www.TheatreWesternSprings.com
Mainstage:414 Second Stage:120 - Black Box

TimeLine Theatre Company
615 W. Wellington
Chicago, IL 60657
773/281-8463
www.TimeLineTheatre.com
Mainstage:75 - Black Box

Tinfish Productions
4247 N. Lincoln
Chicago, IL 60618
773/549-1888
www.Tinfish.org
Mainstage:60 - Black Box

Victory Gardens Theater
2257 N. Lincoln
Chicago, IL 60614
773/549-5788
www.victorygardens.org
Mainstage:199 Second Stage:55 - Thrust

Vittum Theatre
773/278-7471 x172
Mainstage:299 - Proscenium

Wellington Avenue United Church of Christ
615 W. Wellington
Chicago, IL 60657
773/935-0642
773/935-0690 - fax

WNEP Theater Foundation
3210 N. Halsted #3
Chicago, IL 60657
773/755-1693
www.wneptheater.org
Mainstage:45-60 - Black Box

Women in the Director's Chair
941 W. Lawrence #500
Chicago, IL 60640
773/907-0610
773/907-0381 - fax
www.widc.org

Shed some light.
Check out the Lighting Rentals on page 119

Rehearsal Space

Rehearsal Spaces for Rent

About Face Theatre
3212 N. Broadway
Chicago, IL 60657
773/549-7943
www.aboutface.base.org

Act One Studios, Inc.
(See our ad on page 46)
640 N. LaSalle #535
Chicago, IL 60610
312/787-9384
312/787-3234 - fax
www.actone.com

American Theater Company
1909 W. Byron
Chicago, IL 60613
773/929-5009
www.atcweb.org

Apollo Theater
916 S. Wabash #503
Chicago, IL 60605
312/461-9292
www.apollochicago.com

Bailiwick Repertory
1229 W. Belmont
Chicago, IL 60657
773/883-1090
www.bailiwick.org

Belle Plaine Studio
2014 W. Belle Plaine
Chicago, IL 60618
773/935-1890
773/935-1909 - fax

Breadline Theatre Group
1802 W. Berenice
Chicago, IL 60613
773/327-6096
www.breadline.org

CenterLight Sign & Voice Theatre
3444 Dundee Rd.
Northbrook, IL 60062
847/559-0110 x237
www.centerlighttheatre.com

Chase Park
4701 N. Ashland
Chicago, IL 60640
312/742-7518

Chicago Actors Studio
1567 N. Milwaukee
Chicago, IL 60622
773/645-0222
773/645-0040 - fax
www.actors-studio.net

Chicago Dramatists
1105 W. Chicago
Chicago, IL 60622
312/633-0630

Circle Theatre
7300 W. Madison
Forest Park, IL 60130
708/771-0700

ComedySportz
2851 N. Halsted
Chicago, IL 60657
773/549-8080
www.comedysportzchicago.com

Defiant Theatre
3540 N. Southport #162
Chicago, IL 60657-1436
312/409-0585
www.defianttheatre.org

Rehearsal Space

Excaliber Shakespeare Company
The Harrison Street Galleries Studio Theatre
208 W. Harrison St.
Oak Park, IL 60304
708/366-7832

ImprovOlympic
(See our ad on page 50)
3541 N. Clark
Chicago, IL 60657
773/880-0199
www.improvolymp.com

Lifeline Theatre
6912 N. Glenwood
Chicago, IL 60618
773/761-0667
www.lifelinetheatre.com

Live Bait Theater
3914 N. Clark
Chicago, IL 60613
773/871-1212
www.livebaittheater.org

Lookingglass Theatre Company
2936 N. Southport
Chicago, IL 60657
773/477-9257
www.lookingglasstheatre.org

Neo-Futurists
5153 N. Ashland
Chicago, IL 60640
773/878-4557
www.neofuturists.org

Noyes Cultural Arts Center
927 Noyes
Evanston, IL 60201
847/491-0266
847/328-1340 - fax

Porchlight Theatre
2936 N. Southport
Chicago, IL 60657
773/325-9884
www.porchlighttheatre.com

Profiles Theatre
3761 N. Racine
Chicago, IL 60613
773/549-1815

Realism Update Theatre
2957 N. Pulaski
Chicago, IL 60641
773/685-3077

Red Hen Productions
2944 N. Broadway
Chicago, IL 60657
773/728-0599
www.redhenproductions.com

A Red Orchid Theatre
1531 N. Wells
Chicago, IL 60610-7752
312/943-8722
www.a-red-orchid.com

Roadworks
1144 W. Fulton Market #105
Chicago, IL 60607
312/492-7150
www.roadworks.org

Schadenfreude
c/o Heartland Studio Theater
7016 N. Glenwood
Chicago, IL 60626
773/293-0024
www.schadenfreude.net

Ch. 9 Running a Small Theatre Comany 261

Rehearsal Space

Shattered Globe Theatre
2856 N. Halsted
Chicago, IL 60657
773/404-1237

Sheil Park
3505 N. Southport
Chicago, IL 60657
312/742-7826

Stage Actors Ensemble
656 W. Barry - 3rd floor
Chicago, IL 60657
773/529-8337
www.theperformanceloft.com

Stage Left Theatre
3408 N. Sheffield
Chicago, IL 60657
773/883-8830
members.aol.com/SLTChicago

Steppenwolf Theatre Company
758 W. North - 4th floor
Chicago, IL 60610
312/335-1888
www.steppenwolf.org

Strawdog Theatre Company
3829 N. Broadway
Chicago, IL 60622
773/528-9889
www.StrawDog.org

The Theatre Building
1225 W. Belmont
Chicago, IL 60657
773/929-7367 • 773/327-1404 - fax

Theatre of Western Springs
4584 Hampton Ave.
Western Springs, IL 60558
708/246-4043
www.TheatreWesternSprings.com

Timestep Players Educational Children's Theatre Company
P.O. Box 16442
Chicago, IL 60616
773/736-7077
www.timestepplayers.com

Tinfish Productions
4247 N. Lincoln
Chicago, IL 60618
773/549-1888
www.Tinfish.org

Tommy Gun's Garage
1239 S. State
Chicago, IL 60605
312/461-0102
www.tommygunsgarage.com

Victory Gardens Theater
2257 N. Lincoln
Chicago, IL 60614
773/549-5788
www.victorygardens.org

Wellington Avenue United Church of Christ
615 W. Wellington
Chicago, IL 60657
773/935-0642
773/935-0690 - fax

WNEP Theater Foundation
3210 N. Halsted #3
Chicago, IL 60657
773/755-1693
www.wneptheater.org

A brief guide to forming a Not-For-Profit

It shall be to your good: for my father's house, and all the revenue, that was old Sir Rowland's, will I estate upon you, and here live and die a shepherd.

By Robert J. Labate*, of Defrees & Fiske

Creating a not-for-profit corporation is a bit like building your own swimming pool – it's a surprisingly complicated job and you won't know if it works until it's too late. Personal embarrassment aside, the penalty for springing a leak in your not-for-profit (also called a "nonprofit") corporation may be that you are *personally liable* for paying back taxes, so it is worth your while to make sure that all the legal t's are crossed and all the IRS

---

* *This article is provided as a source of information and is not to be construed as legal advice or opinion. You may contact me through my firm's web-site (www.defrees.com), via email at rjlabate@defrees.com or via mail to Robert J. Labate, Defrees & Fiske, 200 South Michigan Ave, Suite 1100, Chicago, Illinois, 60604 (312) 372-4000.*

Ch. 9 Running a Small Theatre Comany 263

Non-for-Protit

i's are dotted before you begin to accept money or sell tickets. The following steps are offered to help you decide whether you want to go the nonprofit route and, if so, how to begin the process.

Step I – Research, plan and think, think, think.

Most successful projects begin with the simple question, "What do I want to accomplish?" Creating and operating a not-for-profit corporation can have many advantages (limiting personal liability and obtaining an exemption from payment of certain taxes being the two most obvious), but these benefits come at a price.

Thus, the first step is to define your purposes and goals. Do you simply want to limit your personal liability should an accident occur at one of your events, or are you primarily interested in obtaining tax exempt status in order to attract funding from the many private foundations which fund only tax-exempt, nonprofit organizations? Are you organizing to produce a single project (such as a documentary film), or do you intend to generate ongoing activities in the community? Do you know who will serve on your Board of Directors (you must have at least three directors), and do you know who will have the right to control and direct the activities of your nonprofit corporation? How will you raise funds in support of your activities, and do you plan to sell goods or services which are related (or unrelated) to the purpose of your nonprofit corporation? The answers to these and similar questions will determine the form and structure of your organization.

One of the best local sources of information on these issues is the Nonprofit Financial Center (www.nonprofitfinancial.org), located at 111 West Washington Street, Suite 1221, Chicago, IL 60602-2706 with the phone number (312) 606-8250. The NFC offers a number of useful handbooks (including one on creating an Illinois nonprofit company) and sponsors training sessions to educate nonprofit companies on topics such as responsible financial management, raising money, legal reporting and public disclosure requirements. If you are seriously considering the creation of a nonprofit corporation, then the NFC, or some similar organization, should be your first stop.

Another excellent source of information is the IRS itself. A significant amount of "plain-English" information on the process of filing for tax-exempt status can be obtained directly from the IRS web-site (www.irs.ustreas.gov) by clicking the section on "Tax Info For Business," or you can go directly to the specific IRS webpage which provides information on tax-exempt organizations (www.irs.ustreas.gov/prod/bus_info/eo). From the IRS site you can download "Publication 557," a 55-page booklet which discusses the rules and procedures for seeking to obtain exemption from federal income tax under §501(a) of the Internal Revenue Code.

Step 2 – Obtain professional advice.

Few things will ruin your day as quickly as having to withdraw a foundation funding proposal, or having to tell a donor that her contribution to your nonprofit corporation is not tax deductible, because the IRS declined your application for tax-exempt status. A one-time reading of all 55 triple-columned, single-spaced pages of IRS Publication 557 together with roughly 150 pages of the Illinois General Not For Profit Corporation Act of 1986 (codified as 805 ILCS 105/101 and available at www.legis.state.il.us) may not be sufficient to enable you to steer clear of potential traps.

My recommendation is that you consult with someone who has done this before, or who is willing to spend a considerable amount of time learning the art of correctly completing and filing the forms required by the state of Illinois and by the IRS. The materials available from the Nonprofit Financial Center will help and Ana Gehant, the NFC's Director of Operations, can provide valuable advice regarding your preparation of not-for-profit materials.

If you don't have a lot of money to spend on hiring an accountant or lawyer, there are several places you can call for assistance. Lawyers For The Creative Arts, 213 West Institute Place, Suite 401, Chicago, 60610 (312/649-4111), itself an Illinois nonprofit corporation, provides low-cost legal assistance in support of the creative arts. If you are truly without funds, either the LCA or one of its volunteer attorneys may be able to assist you.

Another source of low-cost legal assistance is the Small Business Opportunity Clinic of the Northwestern University School of Law (312/503-8576), located at 357 East Chicago Avenue, Chicago, IL 60611. The SBOC Director, Thomas H. Morsch, supervises Northwestern Law School students who perform the majority of the legal services. A list of the services provided by the SBOC is available at its website (www.law.nwu.edu/small-business) or you can send them an email at small-business@nwu.edu.

For approximately $200, plus filing fees, the SBOC will prepare and file your Illinois nonprofit incorporation documents and for an additional $200, plus filing fees, the SBOC will prepare and file your § 501(c)(3) application for tax-exempt status. And if you simply want a consultation, the SBOC will be pleased to arrange it. By any measure this is a terrific deal.

Step 3: Set up your Illinois non-profit corporation.

Now that you have defined your purpose and goals and have reviewed the application process with a professional, you are ready to prepare your incorporation papers and hold your first meeting of directors. Once you've done your homework and enlisted the aid of a professional, the process looks deceptively easy.

The first stop is the Illinois Secretary of State website (www.sos.state.il.us), from which you can download a variety of forms and learn the cost of each filing. Finding the nonprofit forms page is a bit confusing, but it can be located either by using the Not-For-Profit form page URL (http://www.sos.state.il.us/depts/bus_serv/forms.html) or by clicking the following sequence of hot links: Click "Services" on the Secretary of State home page; Click "For Business" on the Services page; click "Download Business Services Forms" on the Business page; and click "Not-For-Profit Forms and Fees" on the Download Business Services Forms page.

Once you download and complete the appropriate forms, you must review them with your advisor to ensure that you provided all appropriate information. For example, one potential trap is how you describe the "Purpose" of your nonprofit company. If your company's stated "Purpose" is too specific, it may not be accepted by the Illinois Secretary of State, but if it is overly broad, it might detract from your application for tax-exempt status with the IRS.

Tom Morsch of the SBOC suggests that careful attention to the wording of the "Purpose" section may make it easier for you to apply for tax-exempt status. "Normally, we add to the purpose clause words like '...within the meaning of section 501(c)(3) of the Internal Revenue Code' and attach, as an additional section 5, a statement about what happens if the corporation is dissolved. The recommended additions are in the NFC handbook."

Remember that the filing of Articles of Incorporation with the Illinois Secretary of State is simply *the first and easiest part* of the process of creating a nonprofit corporation. There are lots of actions which must follow immediately upon the acceptance and certification of your Articles by the state of Illinois, each of which should be reviewed with your advisor.

The list of required post-filing actions is extensive, but here are a few. *Within 15 days* after you receive your certified Articles of Incorporation from the Secretary of State, you must file the certified Articles with (and pay a filing fee to) the recorder of the county in which the registered agent of the nonprofit corporation has its office. Additionally, *you must file* an application to obtain a federal tax identification number for the corporation. The directors of the new nonprofit corporation *must promptly adopt by-laws and elect officers,* upon proper notice. If you have decided to have members, it is recommended that you promptly schedule a first meeting. Be aware that certain charitable organizations are also required to register and to file annual reports with the Office of the Illinois Attorney General.

The structure of your nonprofit company will determine exactly what post-filing actions you must take, so be sure to obtain a complete list of such actions from your advisor. Fortunately, standard forms of by-laws and other documents are available and, in certain circumstances, a number of these actions can be accomplished without conducting a formal face-to-face meeting by the use of waivers and consents. But whether taken formally or informally, a great number of actions must be taken soon after incorporation, so be prepared.

Step 4 - Federal and State tax exemptions.

Unfortunately, creation of an Illinois not-for-profit corporation, by itself, *does not entitle your organization to any form of tax exemption.* Even worse, not all nonprofit entities will qualify for an exemption from federal income taxes (see Publication 557, mentioned above, to determine whether your organization qualifies for tax-exempt status). Even if you qualify, the application process for obtaining tax-exempt status often takes six months or longer! So, if tax-exempt status is essential to the operation of your nonprofit, plan accordingly.

The filing fee alone for applying for tax-exempt status can be as much as $500 (if your organization's gross receipts have been or are likely to be more than $10,000 per year). The Application for Recognition of Exemption requires you to provide detailed information, such as:

• A detailed narrative description of your organization's activities -- past, present and planned;

• The name, address and title of each officer and director;

• The Federal Employer Tax Identification Number of the organization;

• A copy of your organization's Articles of Incorporation and By-laws; and

• Financial Statements (including a detailed breakdown of revenue and expenses) for the current year and for each of the prior three years, or if organized less than one year, proposed budgets for the next two years.

Non-for-Protit

Also keep in mind that once you have filed your application, it is not uncommon for the IRS to contact you to request more specific or additional information.

If you are fortunate enough to obtain a federal income tax exemption, you will also be exempt from Illinois income tax. However, *obtaining tax-exempt status does not mean that you are exempt from all tax payment and reporting requirements.*

Thus, if your nonprofit sells goods or services, it may be required to pay Illinois sales taxes and each year your nonprofit must file annual reports with the IRS and with Illinois Department of Revenue. If your nonprofit company employs people, you will likely be required to withhold "trust fund" taxes from their compensation. If you own property, you may be required to pay real estate taxes. Failure to observe applicable rules and laws, even if innocently done, might result in the revocation of your tax-exempt status or the dissolution of your organization. Each of these issues is complex and any proposed business activity by your organization, as well as the manner in which you solicit contributions, should be discussed at length with a knowledgeable advisor. Nonprofit corporations are wonderful vehicles for accomplishing certain public-spirited goals, but they are not for everyone and creating a nonprofit is certainly not easy. But if you believe that a nonprofit corporation is correct for you, remember that there is plenty of information available on the web and that there are many well-informed organizations available to help you through the process at a reasonable cost.

Looking for a Board?

Look among the Accountants on page 302

Management Training for the Arts

Let us sit and mock the good housewife Fortune from her wheel, that her gifts may henceforth be bestowed equally.

By Mechelle Moe

"The pen is mightier than the sword."

It may not be as appealing as stage combat or dance classes, but business training is a necessity for any and all artistic directors, company managers, or those that have a hand in the administrative muck of running a theatre. And they will need plenty of ink when filling out not-for-profit status forms, designing comprehensive budgets, applying for grants, or writing press releases.

But, as reported in the "Survey of Arts Administration" (new edition: Guide to Arts Administration Training & Research) issued by the American Council for the Arts: "Many arts administrators are not trained as managers and, therefore, lack the requisite skills in strategic planning marketing, personnel and other managerial functions." To put it simply, they don't have the background or knowledge necessary to run a business. (Yes, it is true. Your theatre company is a business.)

Management

And with hundreds of theatre companies inundating the Chicagoland area, the competition for audiences and grant money is pretty steep. A company needs a strong creative management team leading them in order to survive.

But never fear, there is some relief in sight for those of you stuck behind a computer instead of onstage. Thankfully, we're in Chicago, which is a mega resource center loaded with a multitude of organizations geared directly to training the novice in management for the arts.

Probably one of the first resources you should tap into is the **Arts & Business Council of Chicago** (A&BC). There are many facets to the A&BC, all of which operate under the common goal of enhancing management and leadership capabilities of arts organizations by uniting them with the business world. Two programs of particular interest are the Business Volunteers for the Arts (BVA) and the Arts Marketing Center.

According to Deborah Obalil, assistant director of the Arts Marketing Center, the "BVA is designed to provide *pro bono* management assistance to arts organizations." The program recruits experienced business professionals, provides extensive training that teaches them to apply their knowledge and skills to the arts, and then matches the volunteers with small to mid-sized not-for-profit arts organizations as *pro bono* consultants.

There is an application process (including a nominal fee) required to participate in the BVA program. Only organizations that have maintained 501(c)3 status for at least two years will be considered.

As Obalil explains, "Organizations have to have a bearing on what they really need to work on. They are the ones who can get the most out of a volunteer."

Obalil also manages the Arts Marketing Center, which focuses on generating up-to-date information on the ever evolving arts climate, disseminating that information, and developing skills. It is the belief of the program that "armed with the proper information and skills, arts organizations can thrive." The Center provides research and data services, technical assistance/consultation and workshops. The latter are held throughout the year on varying topics including press relations, generational marketing, designing effective marketing plans and community involvement.

"Our workshops are very popular," says Obalil. "We administer evaluation forms at the end, and we are consistently rated above four on a five-point scale."

According to Obalil, the Center uses a variety of experts in the field to

Management

conduct workshops and panel discussions. And although the workshops are primarily geared to mid-sized organizations, Obalil stresses that the information is still pertinent to smaller companies.

For the novice fundraisers, we have the **Donors Forum of Chicago,** which strives "to promote and support effective and responsible philanthropy." The Forum serves as an informational and networking hub for grantmakers, funders, foundations, not-for-profit organizations and market researchers.

If you are researching new grants, the Donor's Forum Library is where you want to go. It houses the largest collection of philanthropic and not-for-profit resources, such as private and corporate foundation directories, grant lists, foundation annual reports and giving guidelines.

Workshops currently offered by the Forum include: The ABCs of Proposal Preparation & Writing, an introductory course for not-for-profits applying for funding from private foundations or corporations; Major Gift and Capital Campaign, which introduces participants to the basic fundraising concepts underlying major gifts and capital campaigns; and Securing Support from Individuals, which teaches basic techniques in soliciting funds from private individuals. Workshops are typically all-day events that range in price from $100 to $140.

There is an overwhelming amount of information available, which may be a little daunting to someone in the early stages of grant writing. That is why they have a capable staff on board to answer any questions. But be warned! The Forum serves all not-for-profit agencies, not just arts organizations. This can be good and bad— bad in the sense that it is not as clear cut or neatly packaged as something you might receive from the Arts & Business Council. You might have to be a bit more savvy in siphoning out the details that pertain to your cause. On the other side, exposure to other not-for-profit organizations can be highly beneficial in eking out new inventive ideas or strategies. First rule of management club—networking is essential.

Barbara Kemmis, director of Library Services at the Donors Forum, hints that more tailored workshops for various sectors—including arts organizations—may be offered in the future. They recently initiated a relationship with Arts Bridge and have collaborated with the League of Chicago Theatres in the past.

Speaking of the nation's first business incubator for the arts, **Arts Bridge** operates three programs—the Incubator Program, Art Works and the Alternative Business Center—that strive to connect "emerging and underserved cultural groups with arts management expertise and a professional business environment."

Management

Founded in 1986, Arts Bridge has assisted over 400 Chicago not-for-profit organizations through their various programs, specifically small to mid-size arts organizations. "We have had people that have had pocket change—meaning a few thousand dollars," says program director Jim Faucett. "And then we have some that are in the Arts Work program that have million dollar budgets. But most [groups] fall between the $100,000-$300,000 range."

According to Faucett, the Incubator Program is the organization's "signature program, it is what Arts Bridge was initially established to do." The program is a residential business training center that provides members technical service (annual business planning, individual management consulting, workshops), administrative support (computer training/assistance, clerical support, bulk purchasing, receptionist services), on site Arts Bridge staff members, facilities (furnished offices, resource library, conference room, kitchen), and equipment (computers, printers, internet access, Xerox, fax, telephone, postage meter). Highly competitive, the program only harbors approximately six to eight groups at a time from various artistic backgrounds ranging from theatre and dance to the visual arts. Depending upon the individual needs and development of the groups, the program length can range from two to six years. The rigorous application/selection/interview process alone takes from six months to a year to complete.

How are groups chosen? Sometimes organizations contact Arts Bridge, oftentimes funders recommend certain troupes, and groups can also be spotted in the Arts Work program (although Faucett stresses that this is not a prerequisite or guarantee for selection). Remember, Chicago is a small community and if you are doing good work, word gets around. Basic criteria includes: 501(c)3 status, 2 years of producing high quality work, and at least one person (paid or unpaid) willing to devote 10-20 hours a week to the administrative process of the company.

Arts Work, a program initiated in 1998, is a non-resident program that offers not-for-profit organizations that are not serviced in the Incubator Program the opportunity to share and participate in the wide range of business development programs and resources that Arts Bridge offers. Two types of membership packages are offered to prospective organizations. An associate membership is offered for $50; benefits include a monthly participation calendar (outlining various workshops and management training events as well as a grant funding calendar), biannual newsletter (features business related articles by business professionals in the field), and discounts including 15 percent at Kinkos. Full membership is $150; it includes all the benefits above as well as technical assistance and management training events (led by management consultants,

Management

business administrators and non-for-profit arts and cultural administrators), access to a comprehensive resource library, and diagnostic consultation. (Membership not for you? Don't fret, Arts Bridge also opens up some of their workshops to the public for a small fee. Admission is limited, and first priority goes to Arts Bridge members. If your not-for-profit organization would like to be notified of their open workshops, give them a call and ask to added to their mailing database.)

But let's get back to the grant calendar—a very handy resource for those of you ready to dip your feet into the funding waters. Arts Bridge does a lot of the painful legwork involved in researching grants that apply to arts organization and compiles a nifty little calendar that includes deadlines, contact information and a brief description of what type of groups they fund. So for those of you that feel the Donor's Forum is a black hole of information, this calendar gives you a headstart on foundations that may be useful to you. But don't think all your homework is done. This is just a sampler list; there is a lot more information out there.

Another benefit of Arts Works is that, through its workshops, it puts your organization in contact with funders. "(Funders) like to do their homework too," says Faucett. "They have a certain type of profile mix they are trying to meet, and this allows them a chance to see new groups. It is also good for groups to put a face to funders, see that they are human."

Finally, the Alternative Business Center offers basic support services to organizations at "better-than-competitive" rates. So if you're looking to put on a more professional air and are tired of having board meetings in your living room, check out the resources at Arts Bridge which include: office space, conference rooms, mailbox rentals, faxing and photocopying.

Another agency that might be of use, especially if you are in the midst of butting heads with the city, is **TAPAS**, a.k.a. Technical Assistance Providers Arts Series. The Department of Cultural Affairs launched this series to teach arts organizations how to work effectively and efficiently with the city and state. Founded in 1998, TAPAS hosts an annual showcase/reception that allows arts organizations an opportunity to meet and greet various service providers to whom they may not be typically exposed.

"The Department of Cultural Affairs is really serving as a catalyst for collaboration by bringing different service providers together through workshops that are affordable," says Keri Butler, cultural programming associate.

Management

And, at $20 a pop, they are affordable. Last year, workshops were offered on a wide array of topics including: Managing a Cultural Facility, a primer for organizations looking to expand, lease or own for the first time; Working with the City that Works (I & II), learn to decipher government lingo, obtain permits, licenses, grants, PPA's, etc; Working with the State, an overview of Illinois state agencies and departments, obtaining not-for-profit status, taxes, tax-exempt status, etc.

"(The) Working with the City workshop has been very successful," says Butler. "We see our role as one of bringing arts organizations and city departments together to break down the barriers and help the arts to understand the difficult issues."

Another way of learning is through example. Available online at www.arts.endow.gov/pub/lessons/index.html is the **National Endowment for the Arts Lessons Learned Toolsite**. This site—"a comprehensive compendium of planning advice"—offers management assistance through case studies and essays collected from a wide range of arts professionals. Local groups are profiled, including Steppenwolf and The Old Town School of Folk Music.

Better yet, if you are looking for something more than an occasional workshop, **Roosevelt University** recently announced a new program offering an MBA in Arts Management headed by Metropolis' executive director Alan Salzenstein. Eight core classes include: Accounting for Executives; Finance for Decision Makers; The Functions of the Executive; Marketing Strategies: Theory and Practice; The Cultural, Managerial and Economic Environment of the Arts; Marketing and Development; Labor-Management Relations; and Legal Environment of the Arts. For more information visit Roosevelt's website at www.roosevelt.edu.

Grants

And for those of you who are weary from processing all this information, The Book is pleased to do a little leg work for you. The following is a list of foundations that might be useful to your organization—remember, this is just a sampler:

Sara Lee Foundation: New Grants
312/558-8604
www.saraleefoundation.org
$5,000-$10,000

Management

Mayer and Morris Kaplan Family Foundation
847/926-8350
$2,500-$25,000

Arts International: The Fund for US Artists, Performing Arts Festivals
212/674-9744
www.artsinternational.org
$500-$10,000

Harris Foundation
312/621-0648
$100-$10,000

United Airlines Foundation
847/700-5714
$5,000-$75,000

Meyer Family Foundation
708/449-7755
$500-$1,000

Frank E. Payne & Selba B. Payne Foundation
312/828-1785
$10,000-$50,000

The Shubert Foundation (Dance & Theatre)
212/944-3777
Varies

R.R. Donnelly & Sons Corporate Giving Program
312/326-8102
www.rrdonnelly.com/public/community
$1,500-$20,000

Richard H. Driehaus Foundation
312/641-5772
Up to $10,000

Recruiting an Active Board of Directors

Who stays Time withal?
With lawyers in the vacation: for they sleep between term and term, and then they perceive not how Time moves.

By Susan Hubbard

Ah, the perfect board. Like the perfect parent really. Someone to watch over you, give you just as much advice as you want to hear, provide you with resources and discreetly look the other way when you screw up colossally.

That's what all theatre companies want. And need. Or is it?

According to companies who can attribute great success to an active board, as well as experts at Chicago's Arts and Business Council Board, theatre companies must already have key elements in place before they can even begin to contemplate recruiting a board. Your company must ask and internally agree upon a number of apparently simple but critical questions.

Who are you? What defines you as a theatre company? In marketing terms, this is known as your "brand" identity. It must be clarified for a potential board member before they can decide whether your company is the right cause for them. Can you say who you are in no more than a couple of well-turned phrases?

What is your mission? Why do you exist? A potential board member must feel that their most passionately held values are embodied and upheld by your organization.

Board of Directors

Who do you serve? This is your audience, otherwise known as your constituency. You must know three key things about them: Who are they; what do they need; and how is your company uniquely positioned to serve them?

What is your vision for the future? Do you know where you want to be as a company in five years? In 10? To a prospective board member, this is as important as who you are today.

What is missing to get you where you want to be? What people, resources, space, equipment, etc. do you need? A potential board member will need to know in order to gain a clear picture of what their role is to be in your success.

What is your articulated battle plan for filling in those gaps. Part of a board member's responsibility is to oversee and scrutinize your plan. Prospective board members are more likely to be impressed with companies that have something from which to work.

Finally, who are the people who can help you fill the gaps and carry out the plan? Every person being recruited wants to know why you have chosen them over all others to invite on your board.

If you can answer these questions, you can begin to think about recruiting for your board.

Why do you need a board?

Chiefly, you need a board to help govern your company and support it financially. According to Producing Director Matt O'Brien of Irish Repertory of Chicago, "When you get to the point where you are looking at your work as a long-term business, to make a living from, you have to ask how can we as a theatre develop our product to become an asset to the Chicago community?" That, according to O'Brien, takes a highly developed and articulated idea of what your company can uniquely contribute to Chicago theatre. And it takes money.

"I don't have the connections," laughs Melissa Vickery-Bareford, managing director of Lifeline Theatre. "I don't know the more affluent theatregoers, or have the influence to get the kinds of sponsorships, or the expertise in physical structures, accounting or marketing that our board members possess." Lifeline's board most recently led a charge that raised over $100,000 to renovate their theatre space in Rogers Park. But the Board's commitment to the company was there from the very beginning in 1983. "One of the first things our early board did," says Melissa, "was take it upon themselves to raise funds to hire key people full time. It has been a big plus to have the board take on the responsibility for specific types of expertise. It frees us to focus on the work, on

Board of Directors

the programming, and where we are going artistically."

"If you want to go the not-for-profit route," says Ken DeWyn, Director of Development for the phenomenally successful Chicago Shakespeare Theatre, "a board is essential."

The board, says DeWyn, is the primary fundraising group in your organization. "Most people don't realize that in a capital campaign 90 percent of your campaign goal comes from 5-10 percent of your giving base. This is one of the reasons why boards are increasingly important. It is your board that drives your major gift work; their contacts provide your company access to the top 10 percent of the wealth population in your region. As an organization, you have to be willing to expend the resources and the personnel to support their efforts."

In recruiting board members, it is important not to assume potential giving capacity too early. Someone who may appear to be able to contribute only very modestly may suddenly surprise you with access to an entirely new network of potential audience and constituents.

The general rule is board members must have a passion for the organization and can either give resources, get resources, or both. "You may have heard of the three W's every organization wants and needs on its board," says DeWyn. "They are wealth, work, or wisdom."

At Chicago Shakespeare Theatre, 70 percent of contributions to their current campaign are coming from the board and board networking, and fully half of that contribution comes directly from the 36-member board itself. "This kind of success entails responsibility," says DeWyn. "As your board grows, you have to be sure you have the staff and the resources to effectively work with these dedicated volunteers."

How to begin

According to Michelle Cohen, program director for Chicago's Arts and Business Council's On Board, when you are considering board recruiting, look first at who currently is part of your organization. This includes your audience, your ensemble members, your volunteers, any "friends" of the organization. "My strategy would be to tell smaller companies to tap into their audiences more," says Cohen. "Sometimes organizations have as their mission serving specific populations yet there is no one inside the organization representing that population. But those are the very people who know about the needs of that population, who can speak to and improve the programs you're doing."

According to Cohen, it's especially important to have groups to whom you want to reach out represented on your board. Again, it depends on your plan. "I can't stress enough that the planning process is key," she says. "Take a hard look at the questions, 'Where are you now? Where do you want to go' – lay out the vision. What are the steps needed to get you there. What kinds of people, background, skills do they need. And then, how are you going to bring them in?"

DeWyn confirms her strategy. "Look within your own ranks for that start-up leadership. Who currently volunteers for you, is involved and interested, who has the passion and the ability to contribute to the organization? Initially, it is friends and family. Some of those earliest board members can become your longest term board members because of their sense of ownership. And as time goes on, those supporters often increase their capacity to contribute many times over."

To begin then, you need a handful of people with the experience, means or interest to contribute to your company and who are willing to identify and cultivate others who can be brought into your company's community.

Says O'Brien, "Ask yourself, 'Who is our audience?' And this defines who your board is. Your audience members will be your board members. And they are the best evangelists for what you are producing."

Recruiting your board comes back to developing your audience. And developing your audience comes back to articulating your identity and your mission statement.

A case in point: Irish Repertory of Chicago

Matt O'Brien formed Irish Repertory of Chicago in 1998 after seven years of critically touted shows by the Splinter Group still proved to be no guarantee for an audience each time they opened a show.

"After awhile, it's no fun to produce on a small scale," he says, "because no one will come to see what you produce on a small scale."

Splinter Group needed to define their audience and, to do that, they needed to bring their own identity as a company into focus, "We were drawn to Irish and Irish-American writers. We were in love with the language, and we were interested in doing work that showcased designers, writers and directors, as well as actors. We believed that our interest would be matched in Chicago by interest in Irish and Irish-American cultural life." The group looked for "a specific project as a benchmark for what we would become," according to O'Brien. They found it in Marina Carr's award-winning play, *The Mai,* which had never been produced here.

The company took two years to plan and develop the project that would define their new identity. Meanwhile, they expanded their audience reach. They exhibited at each Irish-American Heritage Center event and

Board of Directors

created a website with the kind of links that if you type in "Irish" and "Chicago," Irish Repertory Chicago is the first link that comes up. They bought mailing lists specifically composed of Irish-origin names.

"Half the deal is to get yourself and your company name out there in such a way that you have that instant recognition," says O'Neill. "The point is to get people familiar with your product. We want people to know that yes there is a professional Irish theatre company in Chicago and it's called Irish Repertory Chicago, so that when they get the brochure they can say," Oh, we've heard of them and we've heard good things, and they will take a moment to look at the brochure.

The company looked for a moniker that would describe in a nutshell who they were and they came up with "All Irish and Irish-American playwrights."

"The O'Neill we did last year, *Long Day's Journey into Night* is a great play and a showcase for John Mahoney but it's also an important document related to Irish-American culture and what it means to be Irish-American in America." O'Brien said.

Finding the board resources to make the show happen began as a grassroots effort. "Once we knew who we were, it was about finding the connections out there and then laying into it," says O'Brien. "Our people networked. They would go out and find new people and those people would find new people. As potential board members, we looked to approach people who were already involved in charitable work and who had a connection to what we were doing. Then we had the bright idea to call up Lois Weisberg at the Chicago Cultural Center and tell her about what we were doing, and she said, 'I'll call Maggie.'" And Mrs. Maggie Daley became the honorary chair of Irish Rep's Founders Committee, a board devoted strictly to fundraising. "It took us seven years of mucking it up to figure it out," says O'Brien.

Irish Rep's success had to do first with defining themselves as a company and then defining their mission and their audience. O'Brien notes that in smaller, younger theatre companies often the whole mission is really about individual expression rather than long-term community development. "I've been in Chicago theatre for 20 years and seen literally 300 companies come and go. They last three to four years and maybe they've done what they've set out to do, which is to get their people on the stage and further their careers. But if you want to be around for the long term, you need to develop a community."

Irish Rep's inaugural season opened in May 2000 and consistently played to 85 percent capacity, garnering rave reviews and thousands of subscribers. "For seven years before, Splinter Group never got any "marquee" board members who could help take us where we needed to go to make an impact on the community. Like other groups, we were a bunch of artists in our early 30's whose primary identity was as designers and directors. We had to reshape to become Irish Rep."

Due to its success, Irish Rep's board will have to grow to meet the needs of the company's expanding future. By the end of Spring 2002, the company's annual budget will have grown from 80,000-90,000 pre-'98 to 650,000-750,000. One third to one half of this budget will have to be brought in from outside revenue.

"Our Founders Committee is up to the challenge," says O'Brien, "in that they love the association with Irish Rep and what it means. Bringing in friends to see the shows, meet the artists, and develop their interest in supporting the company is a natural extension of this enthusiasm. If you have strong core of people doing this, the artistic and producing staff can concentrate on its work. The center core and importance of any company has to be borne by the community. This is why as a not-for-profit you have to put the community first. We exist to make our interests mesh with theirs. That's why not-for-profits get the tax break, because we are supposedly contributing something good."

O'Brien's advice to smaller theatre companies? "First define your identity as to who you are. If you're not just about being a showcase for your talent, then how do you fit into the Chicago community? What are you doing that is different from the theatre down the street? Figure out who your audience is, where they live, and go after them."

"There's a military saying. 'Hope is not a battle plan.' To get to a certain level, you have to plan. Who is my audience? How do I speak to them? So that by the time the show opens, the audience is there, waiting and eager for what you have to offer."

Identity and Mission: Lifeline Theatre

"Lifeline's KidSeries was founded very early on in 1986, well before other theatres embraced the concept," says Melissa Vickery-Bareford, Managing Director of Lifeline Theatre. "The kids and family focus has helped to define who Lifeline is. Child-friendly programming spills over into the mainstage with one show a year out of three having a strong child element that also appeals to adults. A lot of our board members got involved specifically because of this focus," says Melissa. "And we have kids who started with our kids series, continued through our mainstage Kids and Family program, and who now regularly attend our mainstage productions." Conversely, parents of kids who attended KidSeries have become mainstage regulars. With KidSeries and its

Board of Directors

related programming Lifeline fulfilled an audience need, defined what they were about as a theatre, and established audiences from whom they could draw their board.

Now Lifeline is reaching out to the 70,000 people who live near them in Rogers Park. They've hosted neighborhood organizations and businesses at special events and are planning to launch a specially-priced subscription next year for people living in their zip code area. The 4th of July 2000 weekend saw a packed house of neighborhood kids enjoying a free Lifeline show.

"Our board and our staff really work together," says Melissa. "We have a new business plan that we created last year with the help of the BVA (Business Volunteers for the Arts), a program out of the Chicago Arts and Business Council. It cost us $25 to apply and get a volunteer. I strongly recommend that theatre groups tap into this terrific resource."

With the help of the BVA volunteer, Lifeline has been focusing on where they want to be in five years and planning both financially and artistically. "The simple fact of just planning our season two years in advance has added so much stability," says Melissa. "We are able to plan programs, plan the marketing. As an organization, we're looking forward more than ever before."

Lifeline's current board members came from their audience. Part of their responsibility is to bring new membership into the Lifeline community. "We have Board Nights, where we can all meet each other, three to four times a year. If the new folks show interest, we ask them to join a committee. A benefit committee is really ideal. That way there is a specific event with a specific end that they can help with to see how we all fit. We've gotten away from just asking people right away to join the board. We like to say we're trying to date people before we marry them!"

The right fit

The dating/marriage analogy in relation to board recruiting is echoed by Arts & Business Council's Michelle Cohen. "We like to help organizations understand the special role of the board by saying that the difference between being a volunteer for an organization and being on its board is the like the difference between dating and a marriage. It has to do with the level of commitment. Being on the board entails a bigger time commitment, it entails a financial commitment, and there is a legal side in a board member's role. There's accountability that isn't on a volunteer level. If volunteering is like dating, recruiting a board member is a lot like hiring an employee or preparing for a marriage."

Board of Directors

Cultivating a board member should be a kind of courtship—gradually bringing them in and getting them excited about what your company is doing. But the prospective board member's own values and passions will be the defining factors in their decision to join your board. Also important are size and structure of the organization and its organizational culture. How do the people inside your company relate? Are they businesslike or casual, democratic, or charged by a fiery core of leaders? Does your company thrive on new ideas or does it like to take its time mulling them over? If the latter, and you're recruiting a board member who likes to hit the ground running, that recruit will probably wind up feeling frustrated and undervalued.

You've got your board. Now what?

Even at the most established institutions, the role of the board is constantly under review. The topic was hotly debated at the League of Chicago Theatre's summer 2000 conference. Board members and development staff alike are asking at their meetings—what is enough from a board member, what's not enough, and what's fair. "It's tricky," says Chicago Shakespeare's DeWyn. "We ask them to be on the board, then a peer structure kicks in. One board member is participating at a very high level, and then suddenly that becomes a standard which may not be applicable to everyone."

A Chicago success story, Chicago Shakespeare Company, was just 11 years ago operating out of a one-bedroom apartment on Broadway. Today it has a new seven-story home on Navy Pier with a 525-seat theatre. More than 120,000 people are expected to attend the 2000-2001 season. Their annual budget grew from three million to eight million in two and a half years. The company couldn't have gotten there without their board.

"What you've done with your mission statement and your vision and your plan is created a prospectus for your own success," says DeWyn. "Anybody can put on a play. How have you defined your mission? Is it outreach to the community, educational, supportive of new work or of local artists? A clearly defined mission is necessary to make you distinctive in the Chicago theatre scene."

Chicago Shakespeare is a fine example. Nearly 20 years ago when CST began, no major theatre in Chicago was devoted to a continuing exploration of the Shakespeare canon. Barbara Gaines, CST's founder and long-time artistic director, started a workshop among her friends devoted to the art of performing Shakespeare. They put on their first performance, *Henry V,* upstairs in a bar. But they invited key individuals

Board of Directors

from the community and from that first audience were drawn the first board members, some of whom are still with the company today.

"All of this was possible because Barbara had a big vision," says DeWyn. "She had a mission of Shakespeare for Chicago. Somehow Shakespeare had to get around the misrepresentation people had of him, be released from the ivory tower and plunked back into the public square where he belonged. This was an idea people could rally around. Theatre companies should strive to brand what it is you're going to do and be."

Communicating that to your prospective board members is important. There has to be clarity about what you are and how potential board members fit in, as well as enough flexibility to optimize the different strengths that they bring.

"Identifying your brand comes back to the idea of serving an audience," says DeWyn. "It really gets to the heart of philanthropy to ask what it is you're doing and for whom. When you can define it and communicate it to your potential board members, you help inspire the passion and the loyalty that comes from engaging their highest values. We like to say that Chicago Shakespeare is there above all to make Shakespeare accessible. That's why the new location at Navy Pier fits in with our mission so well. With such a location, we're able to serve a very broad demographic. Shakespeare used to perform among the populace. He would approve of what we're doing."

Susan Hubbard developed and managed the Managing Institutional Advancement program at the University of Chicago's Graham School.

Performink

Chicago's Entertainment Trade Paper, The art, the business, the industry.

www.performink.com

Your source for vital industry news

PerformInk Newspaper is a publication with news and information on the theatre industry in Chicago and the Midwest, including job listings and audition notices. PerformInk's mission is to be a catalyst in the healthy growth of the local theatre industry.

To order call 773/296-4600.

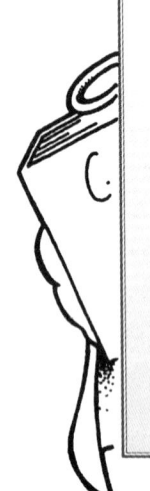

Developing a Pitch

Why 'tis a boisterous
and a cruel style,

A style for challengers;
why, she defies me,

Like Turk to Christian.

By Karin McKie

You see them from afar. They look pleasant, so you sidle up. You introduce yourself. They are cordial, yet distracted, fielding attention from a myriad of other suitors. You scramble to make yourself more attractive, and think of more clever things to say. After a few smart yet fumbled sentences from you, they politely excuse themselves, and you frantically offer a firm handshake while breathlessly asking for their phone number. They reluctantly oblige, and you retreat to the corner of the room, your sweaty hands folding the prized seven digits into your most important pocket.

Are you meeting a potential date at a party? Possibly. Is this perhaps an office mixer schmooze opportunity for you to move to another department? Close. Are you a theatre publicist attempting to wield your powers on an opening night? Indeed. Pitching to the media can be as complex and unnerving as a blind date. But, unlike love, pitching your client and their show can be a calculated success. If you do your homework.

So what are your assignments? Just like you were reminded ad nauseum in school, never underestimate the powers of reading, writing, and 'rithmatic.

The Pitch

Knowing what you are talking about when pitching a show to the media, whether print, electronic (TV and radio), or the newest flavor, ether (i.e. Internet outlets), is crucial. A theatre publicist must be involved in the production of a show from the get-go. This especially includes season selection—the artistic mission and vision questions that are explored during this process always impact a show's eventual coverage. Why is a company doing this play? Is it the 100th anniversary of the playwrights' birth? Does the show cover a topic that's hot in the news? Is this a midwest/American/world premiere? The marketing "cart" shouldn't precede the artistic "horse," yet these two functions are inextricably linked. And the artistic side should continually feed marketing efforts for a production—will the playwright be in town for interviews? Are World War II veterans coming to see this World War II show? Is the lead reprising the same role she did ten years ago? All of this vital information makes your play unique, interesting, and newsworthy enough to get some column inches. Make it a point to engage in continuing dialogue with the director, the playwright, the dramaturg, the designers, the actors and everyone involved to find ways of selling this show.

The theatre is a writing business. The commodity here is language: well-crafted words that convey a time, a place, a relationship, an experience that is human. As a theatre publicist, you are charged with relating the poignancy of a play (a work that is usually years of painstaking process for the author) in simple, concise news releases (and fact sheets, PSA's, etc.).

The hard part is done—the play, that is—and publicists need simply relay the journalistic basics of who, what, where, when and why (see above) in an easily digestible and thought-provoking way. This is not as difficult as it may seem. Always check your facts, and get the basics of what dates and times, what theatre, which address, and the like from the producers. Too many cooks do spoil the soup, but have a few pairs of eyes check the details for accuracy. As mentioned previously, chat with the director and author about their vision and reason for working on the piece and relate that vital information in a few paragraphs. This is your pitch to get features for the production as well as interest for critics to come review the play.

Avoid superlatives like "the greatest story ever told" or "the funniest comedy in the history of the world." That is for critics and the audience to decide. You can state the facts in a creative way, such as "Jefferson or Tony Award winning" or "adapted from the New York Times Bestseller List book." These types of "sound bites" promote the credibility of the show without being too demonstrative. Getting a feature or a review has a lot to do with the "sex appeal" of the show—discerning what is "hot" and "cool"' about your production and communicating that succinctly will get you visibility in this theatre-heavy market.

The written harbingers of the show need to be sent a bare minimum of six weeks in advance (earlier if possible to accommodate long-lead publications, such as monthly magazines). In addition to your excellent written pieces, don't forget other media tools that a publicist often coordinates, such as the ever-important production photos (sent in advance of opening), videos, audio tapes of original show music (if applicable), and the like.

And then there's math. As a publicist, you can only accomplish what your budget (and your wild creativity) will allow. Often with smaller ensembles, monetary constraints can seem insurmountable. True, to a point. But phone calls and e-mails are still relatively free, so research your contact information thoroughly and use it wisely. The Internet is emerging as a fabulous tool for such exploits as finding theatrical associations who offer free or low-cost media lists, libraries that offer funding and grants resources, and even "yellow pages" for good old names and phone numbers.

Remember that theatre artists and their minions (you included) should engage in a symbiotic relationship (not parasitic, as some would posit) with the media. Make their job easier by providing them with clear basic information, sprinkled with some "sex appeal" (see above). Be pleasant and concise when phoning them, including the courteous intro of "Are you on deadline now? Do you have a minute?" The press are indeed people, and I guarantee that if you remember that their dog Sparky had puppies, and you take a moment to ask about their progress, you will be "in like Flynn" when pitching your product. This is like any relationship, so understand their needs (don't pitch a Greek play to someone who historically shuns classics—again, read as much as you can so you know these types of things) and make it pleasant for them to spend a few minutes with you. Never demand media attention—this will assuredly get you nowhere. Instead, be a choreographer that skillfully matches personalities and temperaments with ideas and interests. And, as in love, keep trying. With persistence and an ability to think on the fly, wonderful things can happen.

PR Firms

Carol Fox & Associates
1412 W. Belmont
Chicago, IL 60657
773/327-3830
773/327-3834 - fax

Jay Kelly
2254 W. Grand
Chicago, IL 60612
312/633-1992
312/633-1994 - fax

GSA Advertising
211 E. Ontario #1750
Chicago, IL 60611
312/664-1999
312/664-9017 - fax

Margie Korshak, Inc.
875 N. Michigan #2750
Chicago, IL 60611
312/751-2121
312/751-1422 - fax

K.D.-P.R.
K.D. Kweskin
2732 N. Clark
Chicago, IL 60614
773/248-7680
773/883-1323 - fax

MMPR
Michelle Madden
1636 W. Summerdale #1
Chicago, IL 60640
773/784-8347
773/784-8599 - fax

Performink

Chicago's Entertainment Trade Paper, The art, the business, the industry.

www.performink.com

Your source for vital industry news

Performlnk Newspaper is a publication with news and information on the theatre industry in Chicago and the Midwest, including job listings and audition notices. Performlnk's mission is to be a catalyst in the healthy growth of the local theatre industry.

To order call 773/296-4600.

Five Steps for Audience Development

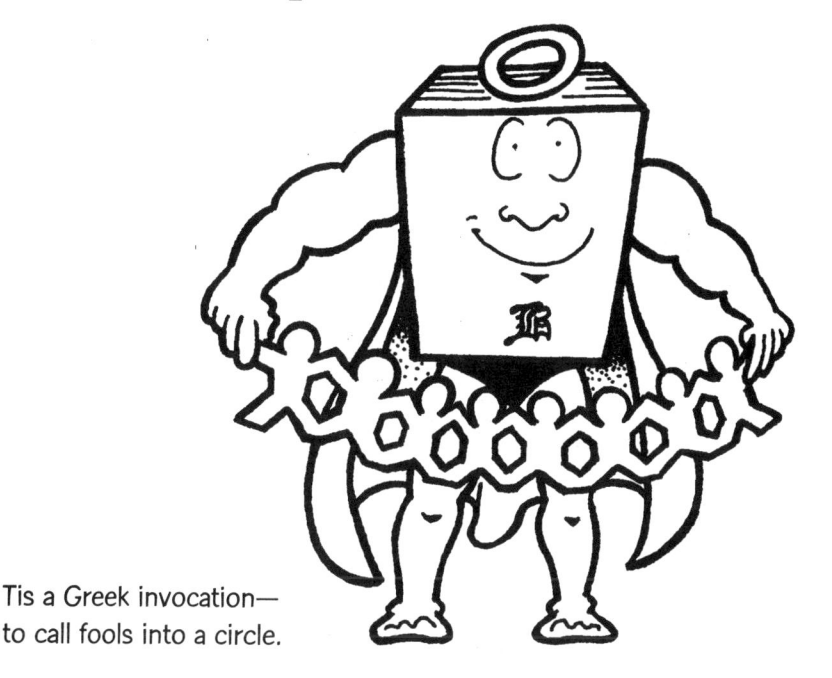

Tis a Greek invocation—
to call fools into a circle.

by Julie L. Franz

There's nothing more exciting than striking out on your own and building your own theatre company. It's tempting to think that if we throw all of our efforts into what goes on the stage, people will magically recognize superiority and show up in droves. But, like any small business, there are thousands of details to tend to outside of artistic excellence that can make or break your business, especially when it comes to attracting, and keeping, audiences.

Much of that has to do with thinking longer term than the next show. It's hard when you're starting, since you're literally financing things from show to show, so this article will focus on things that, hopefully, are easy and inexpensive, but will help set the stage for long-term success.

Audience Development

There are as many wrong definitions of marketing as there are stars in the sky. Marketing is not just promotions, and it's not sales. It's not posters or a good review or a direct mail piece. It's developing a deep understanding of your customer and how they relate to your artistic product. It's customer-focused, and it includes thinking though issues regarding product, price, place and promotion, and understanding the relationship between your artistic product and the customer. Here are five basic audience development issues to think through as you consider starting your own theatre company.

First, make absolutely sure your theatre company really is unique. Chicago is full of actors and theatre companies. To Joe Consumer perusing the CHICAGO TRIBUNE Friday Arts Section in search of something to do, you're just one of hundreds of arts listings. People buy on uniqueness and trust. You can communicate uniqueness in your marketing materials; you build trust with artistic excellence.

In making sure you're really unique, ask yourself why you couldn't have just joined another theatre company. Why, artistically, did you have to strike out on your own? What do you do that no other theatre company does? And answer the question as if you're explaining it to your mom and her friends. (Most ticket buyers and arts decision makers are women.) In other words, use consumer language, or language the common man can understand.

"Ensemble theatre" is one of my favorite phrases, since no one but us theatre professionals has any understanding what it means; it only describes how you're organized, and it's a fact, not a consumer benefit. Tell your mom how and why what she sees on the stage will be different from something out there already. Focus your communications pieces, posters and fliers on benefits, not just facts. It's a fact that you're presenting a certain play on a certain night at a certain time and location. But how will that benefit the customer? Most consumers are unfamiliar with the standard repertory. Tell them what the show is about. Is it a comedy, drama, mystery or musical? Which specific emotions will it stir?

Second, now that you can describe your uniqueness, spend money to have a logo designed by a professional. Having a single, distinct visual image is paramount in the consumer's ability to recognize you in an instant. And it stays with you forever. With a few minor revisions and updates, the Hubbard Street Dance Chicago logo hasn't changed dramatically since their inception. Neither has Steppenwolf's or Victory Gardens'.

Third, budget for marketing and promotions. Again, it's tempting to put all your money and effort into the artistic product, then leave nothing for promotion. It's like throwing the most elaborate birthday party in the world,

Audience Development

but forgetting to budget for invitations. Typically, when first starting out, you'll need about 25 percent of your budget devoted to audience development.

Fourth, take advantage of free promotional opportunities. This means developing a strong press relations program and habitually updating newspaper and website entertainment listings. Deborah Popely of Deborah Popely & Company in Des Plaines touts the following as the "Seven Secrets of Highly Successful Publicists:"

1. Have a smart media strategy that targets publications that reach your audience, includes a unique story angle, looks beyond the usual media, and puts you at the right place at the right time.
2. Pitch a creative story angle, not just the fact that you're mounting a new production.
3. Provide a well-written presentation of that creative story.
4. Provide strong visuals to help make the story come alive.
5. Be fearless and persistent in pitching story ideas.
6. Have a well-researched, up-to-date media list.
7. Have a service orientation toward the media. (You're solving their need for fresh ideas; they're not solving your need for publicity.)

And, don't overlook free listings. The TRIBUNE and SUN-TIMES are great, but focus too on your neighborhood newspaper and newsletters from neighborhood associations and religious organizations. Most of your initial audience will come from a 5-10 minute walk or drive. Make the time to consistently send update listings to the TRIBUNE, state tourism and city tourism websites. They're seen by millions during the year, many of whom are locals.

Fifth, and finally, capture the name, address and phone number of every audience member. It's easier and less expensive to retain a current customer than to get a new one. Why start at ground zero for each show when you can, for less time and effort, invite past audience members, then build a larger audience from there? Use personal letters, newsletters, press releases, etc. to keep your audience informed. Treat them like one of the family, since your most loyal audiences will actually believe they "belong" to your theatre. Hold special receptions or "meet the director" nights to break down the fourth wall and help them become more intimately involved with you and your group.

Time and again, The Arts Marketing Center works with arts groups to help develop new audiences. More times than not, we end up having to go back and "fix" these five areas of marketing and audience development. But if you're contemplating founding your own company, now is

Ch. 9 Running a Small Theatre Comany **291**

Jeff Awards

The Joseph Jefferson Awards

And after, every of this happy number, That have endur'd shrewd days and nights with us, Shall share the good of our returned fortune, According to the measure of their states. Meantime, forget this new-fallen dignity, And fall into our rustic revelry!

By Carrie L. Kaufman

The Jeffs

The **Joseph Jefferson Awards,** or Jeffs as they're commonly called, started in 1967 when four actors got together to honor the best and brightest actors in Chicago. Six awards from seven theatres were given out at the first ceremony in 1968. Thirty-three years later, the Jeffs are split into three different sections, which give out almost 100 awards a year.

Equity Awards

The Equity wing of the Joseph Jefferson Awards judges theatres that have contracts with Actors Equity Association.

Local Equity theatres are judged from August 1 to July 31, with an awards ceremony in late October or November. They are formally called the Joseph Jefferson Awards. What an Equity actor, director, etc. wins that night is a Jeff Award.

And they only win one. For a few years, the Jeff Committee tried giving multiple awards in each category, which is what they do for the Non-Equity Citations. But a consultant the Committee hired told them that the community overwhelmingly preferred to be singled out.

292 The Book: An Actor's Guide to Chicago

Jeff Awards

"At the end of the day, they still really thought the value of the award was more significant if it were for single winners," says current Jeff Committee chair Joan Kaloustian.

Some of those single winners can be for lower tier Equity theatres. Since Equity instituted its new tier system in the mid-90's, a CAT N theatre, which produced a show with only one Equity actor at a very low pay scale, can compete with a major LORT or CAT V theatre that has a budget in the millions and actually come out on top. This has done much to obliterate the distinctions between Equity and non-Equity theatre and also to showcase the remarkable work by people and theatre companies that are non-union—something which is unique to Chicago.

For the 1999/2000 season, for instance, Famous Door Theatre, with its annual production budget of $500,000, won three awards for its production of the Josh Sobel play *Ghetto*. That was the same number of awards Goodman Theatre, with its multi-million dollar production budget, won for *The Odyssey*.

Non-Equity Citations

The **Citations wing** of the Joseph Jefferson Awards, instituted in 1973, is for non-Equity theatres. Citations are judged from April 1 to March 31, with a ceremony in early June. That ceremony is called the Joseph Jefferson Citations. The Jeff Committee is very careful to keep the word "award" away from non-Equity theatre. They structure the non-Equity ceremony to be non-competitive. There are "honorees," who may be called "winners," but there are absolutely no "losers." Of course, with the multiple recipients structure, there have been instances in which four out of the five people nominated have been "honored" with Citations, leaving a very clear "loser."

Non-Resident Productions

About seven years ago, the Jeff Committee began giving awards for touring productions, such as *Show Boat, Ragtime, Aida*. Frankly, these awards have little credibility in the theatre community and are often looked upon—rightly or wrongly—as opportunities for the Jeff Committee to get free tickets to the hot post- or pre-Broadway shows.

That may be a bit unfair, and it may be more of a reflection on the gripers than the Committee. The Jeff Committee argues that they support the theatre community and that the bigger shows—especially when they take up long-term residence—are part of that community. That sentiment sticks in the craw of many small, struggling artists.

There's also the argument that many of these non-resident shows cast

Jeff Awards

out of Chicago and a good deal of the actors may be local. In fact, some of the producers may be too. Shouldn't they be honored? Have they somehow given up their community status by taking or producing a big show?

Eligibility

The Jeff Committee rules for eligibility are Byzantine. Barely anyone in Chicago theatre outside the committee understands them and I dare say there are some people on the committee who would have trouble reciting every single rule. But if you work through the complexities, a remarkably fair, and strangely beautiful, system emerges.

There are two sets of rules. One qualifies theatres and shows to be judged. The other details exactly how a show is recommended—or not.

Qualification

For an **Equity** show to be **Jeff eligible,** it must be produced at a theatre within a 30 mile radius of the corner of State and Madison and in the state of Illinois. Some theatres outside of 30 miles, such as Marriott Theatre in Lincolnshire, were Jeff eligible before this rule was in place and have been grandfathered in. There is no waiting period for a new Equity theatre to begin being judged.

For **non-Equity** theatres, the rules are a bit more stringent. You just can't do the Judy and Mickey thing in a storefront somewhere and expect the Jeff Committee to come. The producing non-Equity theatre must have been in existence for at least two years and have produced at least four productions during those two years, with at least two productions in the preceding year. To keep their eligibility, they have to keep producing at least two Jeff-eligible shows a year (see below). And non-Equity theatres have to be in the city of Chicago, unless grandfathered in. (Circle Theatre in Forest Park was grandfathered in about 10 years ago when the rules changed.) So if you start a new theatre company in your hometown of Naperville (which wouldn't be a bad idea considering there would be little competition and vast audiences), you can't be Jeff eligible. Likewise, if you start a theatre company here and gain a great reputation and maybe even win some Jeffs and you decided to move it to Napervillle, you will lose your Jeff eligibility.

For an individual production to be Jeff eligible, it must have a minimum of 18 performances. In addition, it must have at least two consecutive weekend performances, with at least one weekend night performance per week available to Jeff members.

The Jeff Committee does not judge children's theatre, nor does it judge performance art. Late night shows—which are quite standard in Chicago—are also not eligible. Curtain for an eligible show must be no later than 9:30 p.m. This is not because the Jeff Committee does not like these things (many of them go to ineligible shows just for fun); it's that they have to draw the line somewhere.

For judges to come to a theatre's opening night (or opening weekend) performance, the theatre must put in its request a minimum of three weeks before opening night or the 25th of the preceding month. They would prefer you get them in before the 25th, when the assignments are made. All requests must be in writing.

If the theatre is doing a co-production with another theatre, both theatres must be Jeff eligible. It doesn't matter how long the first theatre has been in existence—or how many Jeff Citations or Awards it has won in the past—if it hooks up with a brand new theatre company, the Jeff Committee won't come.

These rules were instituted as a sort of filter. While there is much good theatre in Chicago, there is a lot of bad theatre here too and, frankly, the Jeff members don't want to waste their time. They figure that if a company has been able to attract audiences and stay afloat for two years, it must be doing some good stuff. Similarly, they feel that if a company is willing to take the risk of putting up an Equity bond and pay its actors, they probably aren't fly-by-night.

Of course, this means that some really good theatre can't be nominated for a Jeff. But it doesn't mean a new theatre isn't on the Jeff's radar screen. Many members show up to good shows by new theatre companies that aren't yet Jeff eligible.

Nominating Process

Over the last few years, some theatres (namely Goodman, Steppenwolf, Marriott's Lincolnshire and Victory Gardens) haven't been happy with the Jeff voting procedures. Too often, they said, good shows or good performances or good design elements would slip through the cracks. So after a couple of years of studies and negotiations, the Jeff Committee and the theatres—represented by the League of Chicago Theatres—came up with a system to include theatre professionals in the judging system. The Advanced Technical (AT) Team adds two theatre professionals to the opening night judges. That's all. It does not add any judges after opening night. Since the AT Team has come on board, more elements that might have slipped through the cracks have been caught, but there are still cracks. And some theatres have still been slighted.

Jeff Awards

As of this writing, the AT Team has only been in existence for Equity shows. The seven judge system will roll out for non-Equity theatres on April 1, 2001.

So here are the old rules, still in existence for non-Equity theatre until April 1, 2001:

Once the theatre has called the Jeff Committee and is deemed eligible, five Committee members are assigned to attend opening night of the non-Equity show. If those Jeff Committee members like the show or categories within the show, then the show is **Recommended.**

Those recommendations come out the day after opening night. Judges must call in their votes by 11 a.m. and theatres are notified by 2 p.m.

The term "recommended," however, does not mean that the Jeff Committee is giving an unqualified endorsement of the show. A show that was particularly awful in all but one area could be recommended because the opening night judges thought that one area was so outstanding—maybe even because it was good despite the rest of the piece—that it deserves to be recognized.

How a show is deemed to be recommended is the most complicated part of the Jeff Committee's rules. There are three ways a show can get recommended under the 5-judge, lame-duck system.

If three judges vote positively in any one category and a fourth judge votes positively in any category, then the show is recommended or nominated. For instance, if three judges loved and voted for the lead actress and a fourth judge loved and voted for the lead actor, even if the fifth judge hated the show entirely, the production is nominated. They don't have to like anything more about the show, though frequently if they like a show, they like it in multiple categories.

That last fact, and a few incidents in which judges have picked lots of categories but no three matched, prompted the Committee to add a second way shows can be recommended or nominated. If at least 10 positive votes—scattered across any of the categories—are cast by all five judges, and each one of the five casts at least one positive vote, then the production is recommended.

If four of the five judges cast a total of 15 or more positive votes, even if the fifth judge didn't cast any positive votes at all, then the show is recommended.

Remember, this is only in effect for non-Equity theatres until April 1, 2001. After that, all the judging switches to the AT Team rules.

Jeff Awards

New AT Team Rules

Under the new rules, seven judges, not five, are sent out for opening night. Five of them are Jeff Committee members, chosen are random just like before. The other two—the AT Team members—are theatre professionals who are not members of the Jeff Committee. They are chosen at random by the League. No one AT Team member can judge more than five Equity and five non-Equity shows a year, which ensures broad participation from theatre professionals. Those seven judges must call in their votes by 9 p.m. the next day, after which the theatre is notified as to whether or not it is recommended.

For an **Equity** show to be recommended under the new rules, five of the seven judges have to vote positively. After that, there must be four or more votes for one single element (like direction) and three or more votes for another single element (like lead actor).

"That's ratcheting up the requirement from what it was," says Kaloustian. "That was part of the goal, to make sure the term 'Jeff Recommended' carried a little more weight."

There are a couple of exceptions to this rule. One is if the show has three or fewer people in the cast. In that case, the criteria is that one single element of the production has to receive four or more votes. They wave the second, three-vote standard.

The other exception is when at least 20 positive votes for anything are cast by five of the seven judges. So if a show got 21 positive votes, but no one element got four positive votes, it still gets recommended—but only if five of the seven judges cast those positive votes. If four judges make those 21 positive assessments, the show is still not recommended.

For **non-Equity** theatres, the criteria are a bit more relaxed. Five out of seven judges have to vote positively, but a show only needs four votes for a single element to be nominated. The three votes for another single element is not necessary for non-Equity shows. A non-Equity show can also be nominated if the production gets a total of 15 votes from at least five judges.

"It's more difficult for folks with teeny, teeny budgets to get technical nominations," says Kaloustian. "When you're spending $3.12 to build a set, your expectations are that it's not going to look like the Goodman."

Once the show is recommended for Equity or non-Equity, the rest of the Jeff Committee is informed and must see the show within 60 days of opening night. They are not told which categories were the ones that garnered the positive votes. They fax, e-mail or mail in their votes in each category after they've seen each show. Those votes are tabulated.

Ch. 9 Running a Small Theatre Comany 297

Jeff Awards

The recipients of the most votes in each category are put onto a final ballot, which is sent out to each of the members at the end of the August 31 (for Equity) or March 31 (for non-Equity) judging season. Those final ballots are the nominations for each category.

After those Award and Citation nominations are made, the committee sends in those final ballots for the winners or recipients. The results of that vote are announced at either the November Awards or the June Citations.

Structure

The Jeff Committee is made up of 45 people dedicated to the theatre industry in Chicago. Quite simply, they love theatre. They see upwards of 125 shows a year and in the busy seasons—around September/October and February/March—they see around six shows a week. Many even see two shows a day on weekends when it's busy.

"This is a labor of love for people. You've got to love it if you're doing it for 125 nights a year with no compensation," says Kaloustian.

As with any awards, there are people who don't like the Jeffs or who discount them. Funny though, Jeff Awards and Citations always seem to show up on people's resumes and in ads for shows or theatres. Over the years, the Committee has been criticized for not being made up of theatre professonals, but truly how many working theatre professionals have time to see other people's work six nights a week?

Currently, over half the Jeff Committee is or has been involved in theatre professionally. Some are teachers, some are actors and playwrights. A couple of critics are on the committee. And there are a good many producers, some still active. Some committee members, says Kaloustian, still have their Equity cards.

Jeff Committee members get a single comp for non-Equity shows and two comps for Equity shows. Frequently, says Kaloustian, members will just use the one comp no matter what the show. Spouses tend to get a bit theatre weary, and the Jeff Committee members tend to go see theatre with each other. But, she adds, they don't talk about the show amongst themselves. I've even tried to engage Jeff Committee members at intermission in conversations about the show and have gotten a nod and a vague answer at best. Wish I could say the same for some groups of critics I've seen at intermission.

The Jeff Committee, no matter what their formal training, is always trying to learn more about theatre and the crafts that come together to make a show. Each meeting they have a speaker or program designed to help them learn more about stage crafts. Designers have taught them about the elements that are not supposed to be noticed. They have talked with directors and dramaturgs. And one cannot discount the point that no matter what one knows about theatre *before* joining the committee, they learn a hell of a lot after seeing 125—often mediocre—shows. I wonder if many theatre artists have that kind of education.

To contact the Jeff Committee, call 773/388-0073.

Helpful Organizations

Arts and Business Council of Chicago
Arts Marketing Center
70 E. Lake #500
Chicago, IL 60601
312/372-1876
312/372-1102 - fax
www.artsbiz-chicago.org

Arts Bridge
Suellen Burns - Executive Director
2936 N. Southport
Chicago, IL 60657
773/296-0948
773/296-0968 - fax
www.artsbridge.org

Association of Consultants to Nonprofits
P.O. Box 4852
Chicago, IL 60680
312/580-1875
www.ACNconsult.org

Center for Communication Resources
Nalani McClendon
1419 W. Blackhawk
Chicago, IL 60622
773/862-6868
773/862-0707 - fax
www.bham.net/soe/ccr

Community Media Workshop at Columbia College
600 S. Michigan
Chicago, IL 60605
312/344-6400
312/344-6404 - fax
www.newstips.org

CPA's for Public Interest
222 S. Riverside Plaza - 16th floor
Chicago, IL 60606
312/993-0393
312/993-9432 - fax
www.icpas.org/cpaspi.htm

Cultural Facilities Fund
78 E. Washington #250
Chicago, IL 60602
312/372-1710
312/372-1765 - fax

Chicago Department of Cultural Affairs
Richard Vaughn - Director of Legal Affairs
312/742-1175
www.ci.chi.il.us/CulturalAffairs

Donors Forum of Chicago
208 S. LaSalle #735
Chicago, IL 60604
312/578-0175
312/578-0158 - fax
www.donorsforum.org

Helpful Organizations

Executive Service Corps of Chicago
30 W. Monroe #600
Chicago, IL 60603
312/580-1840
312/580-0042 - fax
www.esc-chicago.org

Illinois Alliance for Arts Education
200 N. Michigan #404
Chicago, IL 60601
312/750-0589 • 800/808-ARTS
312/750-9113 - fax
www.artsmart.org

Illinois Arts Alliance
200 N. Michigan #404
Chicago, IL 60601
312/855-3105
312/855-1565 - fax
www.artsalliance.org

Illinois Arts Council
100 W. Randolph #10-500
Chicago, IL 60601
312/814-6750
312/814-1471 - fax
www.state.il.us/agency/iac

IT Resource Center
Sarah Oaks - Marketing Director
29 E. Madison #1605
Chicago, IL 60602
312/372-4872 • 312/372-7962 - fax
www.npo.net/itrc

Lawyers for the Creative Arts
213 W. Institute #401
Chicago, IL 60610
312/944-2787
800/525-ARTS
312/944-2195 - fax
www.cityofchicago.org/culturalaffairs/
CulturalProgramming/Lawyers.html

League of Chicago Theatres
228 S. Wabash #300
Chicago, IL 60604
312/554-9800
312/922-7202 - fax
www.chicagoplays.org
The League promotes Chicago's theatre industry through marketing, advocacy, and information services. Programs include Hot Tix, Chicago Theater Guide, Play Money Gift Certificates, Cooperative Advertising and the Annual CommUNITY Conference. The League coordinates the annual non-Equity general auditions in May/June and also hosts the annual theatre industry conference with workshops and seminars open to the public.

Nonprofit Financial Center
111 W. Washington #1221
Chicago, IL 60602
312/606-8250
312/606-0241 - fax
www.nonprofitfinancial.org

Pre-Paid Legal Services, Inc.
(See our ad on page 135)
9242 W. National Ave.
West Ellis, WI 53227
414/329-3047

Season of Concern
203 N. Wabash #2104
Chicago, IL 60601
312/332-0518
312/372-0272 - fax
members.aol.com/sochicago/

The Support Center
3811 N. Lawndale #100
Chicago, IL 60618
312/648-0995
773/539-4751 - fax
www.supportcenter.org/sf/

Living

Around the Coyote, "Double Climax"

Accountants & Tax Preparers

Legal, Tax and Insurance

Accountants and Tax Preparers

American Express Tax and Business Services
Craig Minnick
30 S. Wacker #2600
Chicago, IL 60606
312/499-1649 • 312/207-2954 - fax

Bob Behr
4738 N. LaPorte
Chicago, IL 60630
773/685-7721
773/283-9839 - fax

David P. Cudnowski, Ltd.
70 W. Madison #5330
Chicago, IL 60602
312/759-1040
312/759-1042 - fax
www.lawyers.com/talentlaw

David Turrentine, E.A. Income Tax Service
3907 N. Sacramento
Chicago, IL 60618
773/509-1798
773/509-1806 - fax

Gerald Bauman & Company
75 E. Wacker Drive #2100
Chicago, IL 60601
312/726-6868
312/726-3683 - fax

H&R Block
179 W. Washington
Chicago, IL 60602
312/424-0268 • 312/424-0278 - fax
www.hrblock.com

246 Janata Blvd. #320
Lombard, IL 60148
630/792-1063 • 630/792-1066 - fax
www.hrblock.com

Jay-EMM Acct/Tax/Consulting
735 S. Victoria
Des Plaines, IL 60016
847/679-8270

Joel N. Goldblatt, Ltd.
100 N. LaSalle #1910
Chicago, IL 60602
312/372-9322
312/372-2905 - fax

Katten, Muchin & Zavis
525 W. Monroe #1600
Chicago, IL 60661
312/902-5200
312/902-1061 - fax

Mangum, Smietanka & Johnson, L.L.C.
35 E. Wacker #2130
Chicago, IL 60601
312/368-8500

H. Gregory Mermel
2835 N. Sheffield #311
Chicago, IL 60657
773/525-1778
773/525-3209 - fax

Weiner & Lahn, P.C.
900 Ridge Rd. #F
Munster, IN 46321
708/895-6400
219/836-1515

302 The Book: An Actor's Guide to Chicago

Attorneys

**Chicago Bar Association
Lawyer Referral**
321 S. Plymouth
Chicago, IL 60604
312/554-2001
www.chicagobar.org

**Chicago Volunteer
Legal Services**
100 N. LaSalle #900
Chicago, IL 60602
312/332-1624

David P. Cudnowski, Ltd.
70 W. Madison #5330
Chicago, IL 60602
312/759-1040 • 312/759-1042 - fax
www.lawyers.com/talentlaw

Tom Fezzey
1200 Harder #320
Oak Brook, IL 60523
630/928-0600 • 630/928-0670 - fax
www.lawyers.com/fezzey

Dale M. Golden
25 E. Washington #1400
Chicago, IL 60602
312/201-9730
312/236-6686 - fax
www.dalegoldenlaw.com
The Law Office of Dale M. Golden is a general law practice for the special legal needs of creative artists, entertainment professionals, and companies. It provides a full range of services to the entertainment industry, including negotiation and drafting of contracts, copyright and trademark licensing, business formation, and litigation.

Joel N. Goldblatt, Ltd.
100 N. LaSalle #1910
Chicago, IL 60602
312/372-9322 • 312/372-2905 - fax

JoAnne Guillemette
311 S. Wacker Dr. #4550
Chicago, IL 60606
312/697-4788
800/616-5964 - pgr.
312/697-4799 - fax

Katten, Muchin & Zavis
525 W. Monroe #1600
Chicago, IL 60661
312/902-5200 • 312/902-1061 – fax

Timothy S. Kelley
Attorney at Law
55 E. Washington #1441
Chicago, IL 60602
312/641-3560

Lawyers for the Creative Arts
213 W. Institute #401
Chicago, IL 60610
312/944-2787 • **800/525-ARTS**
312/944-2195 - fax
www.cityofchicago.org/culturalaffairs/
CulturalProgramming/Lawyers.html

**Mangum, Smietanka
& Johnson, L.L.C.**
35 E. Wacker #2130
Chicago, IL 60601
312/368-8500

Pre-Paid Legal Services, Inc.
(See our ad on page 135)
9242 W. National Ave.
West Ellis, WI 53227
414/329-3047

Jay B. Ross & Associates P.C.
838 W. Grand #2W
Chicago, IL 60622-6565
312/633-9000
312/633-9090 - fax
www.jaybross.com

Movie Theatres

Peter J. Strand
McBride, Baker & Coles
500 W. Madison - 40th floor
Chicago, IL 60661-2511
312/715-5756

Fred Wellisch
1021 W. Adams #102
Chicago, IL 60607
312/829-2300 • 312/829-3729 - fax

William Borah and Associates
2024 Hickory Rd. #105
Homewood, IL 60430
708/799-0066 •708/799-0122 - fax

Insurance

Myers-Briggs and Company, Inc.
125 S. Wacker #1800
Chicago, IL 60606
312/263-3215
312/263-0979 - fax

Paczolt Financial Group
913 Hillgrove
La Grange, IL 60525
708/579-3128
708/579-0236 - fax
www.paczolt.com

Ronald Shapero Insurance Associates
Health Insurance Specialists
260 E. Chestnut #3406
Chicago, IL 60611
312/337-7133

Movie Theatres (Cool and Cheap Ones)

Davis Theatre
4614 N. Lincoln
Chicago, IL 60625
773/784-0893

Esquire Theater
58 E. Oak
Chicago, IL 60611
312/280-0101

Facets Multimedia
1517 W. Fullerton
Chicago, IL 60614
773/281-9075
773/929-5437 - fax
www.facets.org

Logan Theatre
2646 N. Milwaukee
Chicago, IL 60647
773/252-0627

Music Box
3733 N. Southport
Chicago, IL 60613
773/871-6604
www.musicboxtheatre.com

Three Penny Theatre
2424 N. Lincoln
Chicago, IL 60614
773/935-5744

The Vic Theatre (Brew & View)
3145 N. Sheffield
Chicago, IL 60657
312/618-VIEW
773/472-0449
www.victheatre.com

Village North
6746 N. Sheridan
Chicago, IL 60626
773/764-9100
www.villagetheatres.com

Village Theatre
1548 N. Clark
Chicago, IL 60622
312/642-2403
www.villagetheatres.com

Health Clubs

Health & Fitness
Health Clubs - Personal Training

Bally Total Fitness
2828 N. Clark
Chicago, IL 60657
773/929-6900
800-FITNESS
www.ballytotalfitness.com

Chicago Fitness Center
3131 N. Lincoln
Chicago, IL 60657
773/549-8181
773/549-4622 - fax
www.chicagofitnesscenter.com

Gorilla Sports
2727 N. Lincoln
Chicago, IL 60614
773/477-8400
773/477-8476 - fax

Gold Coast Multiplex
1030 N. Clark
Chicago, IL 60610
312/944-1030
312/944-6180 - fax
www.gcmultiplex.com

Know No Limits
5121 N. Clark
Chicago, IL 60640
773/334-4728

Know No Limits
3530 N. Lincoln
Chicago, IL 60657
773/404-1950

Lake Shore Athletic Club
441 N. Wabash
Chicago, IL 60611
312/644-4880
312/644-4870 - fax

Lake Shore Athletic Club
1320 W. Fullerton
Chicago, IL 60614
773/477-9888

Lehmann Sports Club
2700 N. Lehmann
Chicago, IL 60614
773/871-8300
773/871-3506 - fax
www.lehmannsportsclub.com

Mint Condition Wellness and Training Center
1111 Pasquinelli Dr. #450
Westmont, IL 60559
630/455-9525
www.InMintCondition.com
A personal trainer is an investment in your health and well-being...choose the best! One-on-One Personal Training in a private, professional setting. Located in the Oak Brook area near the intersection of Rt. 83 & Ogden Ave. Don't you deserve to be in Mint Condition?

Michael Sokol
312/642-4235
312/642-7686 - fax

Webster Fitness Club
957 W. Webster
Chicago, IL 60614
773/248-2006
773/248-3195 - fax
www.websterfitness.com

Women's Workout World
208 S Lasalle
Chicago, IL 60604
312/357-0001

Ch. 10 Living **305**

Nutritionists

World Gym - Hyde Park
1451 E. 53rd St.
Chicago, IL 60615
773/363-1212 • 773/363-2010 - fax
www.worldgymchi.com

World Gym
909 W. Montrose
Chicago, IL 60613
773/348-1212
www.worldgymchi.com

World Gym
150 S. Wacker
Chicago, IL 60606
312/357-9753
312/357-0577 - fax
www.worldgymchi.com

YMCA
800/935-9622

Health Food Stores

Life Spring
3178 N. Clark
Chicago, IL 60657
773/327-1023 • 773/327-1030 - fax

Sherwyn's
645 W. Diversey
Chicago, IL 60614
773/477-1934

Whole Foods Market
1000 W. North
Chicago, IL 60622
312/587-0648
www.wholefoods.com

Whole Foods Market
3300 N. Ashland
Chicago, IL 60657
773/244-4200
www.wholefoods.com

Nutritionists

Lake Shore Naprapathic Center
3166 N. Lincoln #410
Chicago, IL 60657
773/327-0844

Mint Condition Wellness and Training Center
1111 Pasquinelli Dr. #450
Westmont, IL 60559
630/455-9525
www.InMintCondition.com
Let Julie Fulton, RD, LD, and the West Suburban Dietetic Association 1999 Recognized Young Dietitian of the Year, help you modify your eating habits to achieve and maintain your desired weight, control or prevent specific medical conditions, or just eat better.

Rose Quest Nutrition Center
200 N. Michigan #404A
Chicago, IL 60602
312/444-9234

Living Healthy?
Get a Stage Weapon!
on page 119

Weight Control

A Creative Change
Honora Simon, Ph.D.
541 W. Diversey #208
Chicago, IL 60614
312/939-9394
312/939-9594 - fax
www.reducestress.com
Specialties: Stress, Anxiety, Fears, Depression, Relationships
Dr. Honora Simon, board certified psychologist and licensed nutritionist with a 30 year private practice, uses hypnosis for a variety of issues. She states, "I like working with creative, artistic people because they reflect my personality and are open to change and growth." Offering 10 percent discount from this ad.

Professional Weight Clinic
200 E. Ohio #501
Chicago, IL 60611
312/664-2255

Weight Watchers
800/651-6000

Women's Workout World
208 S Lasalle
Chicago, IL 60604
312/357-0001

Counselors

Abraham Lincoln Center Screening & Support
(specialize in children)
1950 W. 87th
Chicago, IL 60620
773/239-7960
773/239-0272 - fax

Associated Psychologists and Therapists
77 W. Washington #1519
Chicago, IL 60602
312/630-1001
312/630-1342 - fax
www.psychologists.org

Community Counseling Center of Chicago
Mental Health Center
4740 N. Clark
Chicago, IL 60640
773/769-0205
773/769-0344 - fax

A Creative Change
Honora Simon, Ph.D.
541 W. Diversey #208
Chicago, IL 60614
312/939-9394
312/939-9594 - fax
www.reducestress.com
Specialties: Stress, Anxiety, Fears, Depression, Relationships
Dr. Honora Simon, board certified psychologist and licensed nutritionist with a 30 year private practice, uses hypnosis for a variety of issues. She states, "I like working with creative, artistic people because they reflect my personality and are open to change and growth." Offering 10 percent discount from this ad.

Hypnotists

Dance Therapy Center
Fine Arts Building
410 S. Michigan
Chicago, IL 60605
312/461-9826 • 312/461-9843 - fax

Kate DeVore, M.A.
4451 N. Hamilton
Chicago, IL 60625
773/334-7203
www.KateDeVore.com
Do you feel ready to make a shift in your life, but in need of guidance? You have the answers, and I can help you clarify them in a safe, loving and supportive environment. I offer a combination of counseling, bodywork and an eclectic set of healing modalities. I am a Reiki Master also certified in Vibrational Healing.

Great Lakes Psychological Providers
111 N. Wabash #1408
Chicago, IL 60602
312/443-1400 • 312/443-1307 - fax

Ann L. Hammon, M.D.
550 W. Surf #101C
Chicago, IL 60657
773/296-2195

Hypnotists

Associated Psychologists and Therapists
77 W. Washington #1519
Chicago, IL 60602
312/630-1001 • 312/630-1342 - fax
www.psychologists.org

Gerald Greene, Ph.D.
500 N. Michigan #542
Chicago, IL 60611
312/266-1456

Harambee Wellness Center
1515 E. 52nd - 2nd floor
Chicago, IL 60615
773/925-6877

Hartgrove Hospital
520 N. Ridgeway
Chicago, IL 60624
773/722-3113 • 773/722-6361 - fax

Howard Brown Health Center
4025 N. Sheridan
Chicago, IL 60613
773/388-1600

Institute for Psychoanalysis
122 S. Michigan #1300
Chicago, IL 60603
312/922-7474 • 312/922-5656 - fax
www.chianalysis.org

Panic Anxiety Recovery Center
680 N. Lake Shore #1325
Chicago, IL 60611
312/642-7954 • 312/642-7951 - fax

Dr. Steigman
4433 W. Touhy #552
Chicago, IL 60646
847/675-7544

Ruth Landis
B.S., M.A., certified body psychotherapist, certified hypnotherapist, Reiki master
773/991-7777
Using a multi-track method rooted in Gestalt therapy, Alexander Technique, Feldenkrais Awareness through Movement, Chakra work, visualization, energy and nature, our work facilitates greater personal awareness, invites physical and emotional healing, freeing the creative spirit and the spontaneous self. $65.00

Meditation

Peace School
3121 N. Lincoln
Chicago, IL 60657
773/248-7959
773/248-7963 - fax

Vajrayana Buddhist Center
827 W. Roscoe #1
Chicago, IL 60657
773/529-1862
www.geocities.com/athens/academy/6362

Zen Buddhist Temple (Chinese Culture Academy)
608 Dempster St.
Evanston, IL 60202
847/869-0554

Religious Groups

Chicago Genesis
A Creative Christian Collective
773/275-3490

Congregation Or Chadash
656 W. Barry
Chicago, IL 60657
773/248-9456

Dignity Chicago (Roman Catholic)
3023 N. Clark - Box 237
Chicago, IL 60657
773/296-0780
www.dignitychicago.org

The Ethical Humanist Society of Greater Chicago
7574 N. Lincoln Ave.
Skokie, IL 60077
847/677-3334
www.ethicalhuman.org

Grace Baptist Church
1307 W. Granville
Chicago, IL 60660
773/262-8700

HAVURA
Jewish Community Group
7316 N. Tripp
Lincolnwood, IL 60712
847/679-8760

Holy Trinity Lutheran Church
1218 W. Addison
Chicago, IL 60613
773/248-1233
www.holytrinitychicago.org

Second Unitarian Church/ Unitarian Universalist
656 W. Barry
Chicago, IL 60657
773/549-0260 - office
773/549-3933 - minister
www.2uchicago.org

Vajrayana Buddhist Center
827 W. Roscoe #1
Chicago, IL 60657
773/529-1862
www.geocities.com/athens/academy/6362

Wellington Avenue United Church of Christ
615 W. Wellington
Chicago, IL 60657
773/935-0642
773/935-0690 - fax

Chiropractors

Advance Center
Dr. Michael Luban
55 E. Washington #1310
Chicago, IL 60602
312/553-2020
312/553-5128 - fax

Belmont Health Care
Lena Granlund
2110 W. Belmont
Chicago, IL 60618
773/404-0909

Chicago Chiropractic Center
30 S. Michigan #400
Chicago, IL 60603
312/726-1353
312/726-5238 - fax

Chicago Neck and Back Institute
5700 W. Fullerton #1
Chicago, IL 60639
773/237-8660
773/237-3159 - fax

Chiropractic Chicago
Dr. Ellisa J. Grossman
407 W. North
Chicago, IL 60610
312/255-9500

Chislof Chiropractic Center
7448 N. Harlem
Chicago, IL 60631
773/763-0400

Graham Chiropractic
Dr. Betty E. Graham
5344 N. Lincoln
Chicago, IL 60625
773/769-6666
773/334-1696 - fax

Greater Chicago Chiropractic
Dr. Dale Zuehlke
561 W. Diversey #221
Chicago, IL 60614
773/871-7766
773/871-0781 - fax

Franklin D. Ing
2451 N. Lincoln
Chicago, IL 60614
773/525-2444
773/525-9989 - fax

Progressive Chiropractic Rehabilitation & Wellness Center
2816 N. Sheffield
Chicago, IL 60657
773/525-WELL
773/525-9397 - fax
www.progressivechiro.net

Dr. Kevin Regan
Holistic Practitioner
55 E. Washington #1630
Chicago, IL 60602
312/578-1624
312/578-8717 - fax
www.doctorkev.com

Seaman Chiropractic Center
4941 W. Foster
Chicago, IL 60630
773/545-2233
773/545-8383 - fax

Dr. Briana S. Skarbek
513 Waukegan Rd.
Northbrook, IL 60062
847/509-0005

Stiles Chiropractic Offices
48 E. Chicago
Chicago, IL 60611
312/642-1138

Naprapaths

Belmont Health Care
Lena Granlund
2110 W. Belmont
Chicago, IL 60618
773/404-0909

Karen L. Bruneel
4770 N. Lincoln #6
Chicago, IL 60625
773/769-1133
773/769-1134 - fax

Chicago National College of Naprapathy
3330 N. Milwaukee
Chicago, IL 60641
773/282-2686
773/282-2688 - fax
www.naprapathy.edu

Lake Shore Naprapathic Center
3166 N. Lincoln #410
Chicago, IL 60657
773/327-0844

Acupuncture

Advance Center
Dr. Michael Luban
55 E. Washington #1310
Chicago, IL 60602
312/553-2020
312/553-5128 - fax

American Acupuncture Association
65 E. Wacker
Chicago, IL 60601
312/853-3732

Beth Braun Ph.D.,C.M.T.
Miro Center for Integrated Medicine
1639 Orrington Ave.
Evanston, IL 60201
847/733-9900
847/733-0105 - fax
www.mirocenter.org

Chicago Acupuncture Clinic
Dan Plovanich, Dipl. Ac.
3723 N. Southport
Chicago, IL 60613
773/871-0342
773/871-0348 - fax

Chiropractic Chicago
Dr. Ellisa J. Grossman
407 W. North
Chicago, IL 60610
312/255-9500

East Point Associates, Ltd.
Mary Rogel & Unsoo Kim
1525 E. 53rd #705
Chicago, IL 60615
773/955-9643
773/955-9953 - fax

Graham Chiropractic
Dr. Betty E. Graham
5344 N. Lincoln
Chicago, IL 60625
773/769-6666
773/334-1696 - fax

Franklin D. Ing
2451 N. Lincoln
Chicago, IL 60614
773/525-2444
773/525-9989 - fax

Massage

Know No Limits
3530 N. Lincoln
Chicago, IL 60657
773/404-1950

Progressive Chiropractic
Rehabilitation & Wellness Center
2816 N. Sheffield
Chicago, IL 60657
773/525-WELL
773/525-9397 - fax
www.progressivechiro.net

Dr. Kevin Regan
Holistic Practitioner
55 E. Washington #1630
Chicago, IL 60602
312/578-1624 • 312/578-8717 - fax
www.doctorkev.com

Seaman Chiropractic Center
4941 W. Foster
Chicago, IL 60630
773/545-2233
773/545-8383 - fax

Dr. Briana S. Skarbek
513 Waukegan Rd.
Northbrook, IL 60062
847/509-0005

Massage

**American Massage
Therapy Association**
Illinois Chapter
708/484-9282
708/484-8601 - fax

Back to One
5342 N. Winthrop
Chicago, IL 60640
773/561-5893

Bodyscapes, Inc.
Massage Therapy Clinic
820 Davis #216
Evanston, IL 60201
847/864-6464

Beth Braun Ph.D.,C.M.T.
Miro Center for Integrated Medicine
1639 Orrington Ave.
Evanston, IL 60201
847/733-9900
847/733-0105 - fax
www.mirocenter.org

Karen L. Bruneel
4770 N. Lincoln #6
Chicago, IL 60625
773/769-1133
773/769-1134 - fax

Chiropractic Chicago
Dr. Ellisa J. Grossman
407 W. North
Chicago, IL 60610
312/255-9500

Chislof Chiropractic Center
7448 N. Harlem
Chicago, IL 60631
773/763-0400

Diamond Beauty Clinic
151 N. Michigan #1018
Chicago, IL 60601
312/240-1042

Alexander Technique

Greater Chicago Chiropractic
Dr. Dale Zuehlke
561 W. Diversey #221
Chicago, IL 60614
773/871-7766
773/871-0781 - fax

Hair Loft
14 E. Pearson
Chicago, IL 60611
312/943-5435

Heidi's Salon
110 E. Delaware
Chicago, IL 60611
312/337-6411
312/337-7174 – fax

Leslie Kahn
Licensed Massage Therapist
1243 N. Damen
Chicago, IL 60622
773/276-4665

Know No Limits
3530 N. Lincoln
Chicago, IL 60657
773/404-1950

5121 N. Clark
Chicago, IL 60640
773/334-4728

Mario Tricoci
Hair Salon & Day Spa
900 N. Michigan
Chicago, IL 60611
312/915-0960 • 312/943-3138 - fax

Massage Therapy Professionals
3047 N. Lincoln #400
Chicago, IL 60657
773/472-9484 • 773/472-8590 - fax

Progressive Chiropractic
Rehabilitation & Wellness Center
2816 N. Sheffield
Chicago, IL 60657
773/525-WELL
773/525-9397 - fax
www.progressivechiro.net

Rodica European Skin & Body
Care Center
Water Tower Place - Professional Side
845 N. Michigan #944E
Chicago, IL 60611
312/527-1459
www.facialandbodybyrodica.com

Seaman Chiropractic Center
4941 W. Foster
Chicago, IL 60630
773/545-2233 • 773/545-8383 - fax

Sun Center
1816 N. Wells - 3rd floor
Chicago, IL 60614
312/280-1070
www.home.earthlink.net/~suncenter

Alexander Technique

Chicago Center for the Alexander Technique
Ed Bouchard
5415 N. Sheridan #1005
Chicago, IL 60640
773/728-3235

Ch. 10 Living 313

Yoga

The Academy of Dance Arts
1524 Centre Cr,
Downers Grove, IL 60515
630/495-4940

Belle Plaine Studio
2014 W. Belle Plaine
Chicago, IL 60618
773/935-1890
773/935-1909 - fax

Bodyscapes, Inc.
Massage Therapy Clinic
820 Davis #216
Evanston, IL 60201
847/864-6464

Dance Center of Columbia College
1306 S. Michigan
Chicago, IL 60605
312/344-8300
312/344-8036 - fax
www.colum.edu

Global Yoga and Wellness Center
1823 W. North
Chicago, IL 60622
773/489-1510

Hedwig Dances
Administrative Offices
2936 N. Southport #210
Chicago, IL 60657
773/871-0872
773/296-0968 - fax
www.enteract.com\~hedwig

North Shore School of Dance
107 Highwood
Highwood, IL 60040
847/432-2060
847/432-4037 - fax
www.northshoredance.com

NU Yoga Center
3047 N. Lincoln - 3rd floor
Chicago, IL 60657
773/327-3650
www.yogamind.com

Peace School
3121 N. Lincoln
Chicago, IL 60657
773/248-7959
773/248-7963 - fax

Sivananda Yoga Center
1246 W. Bryn Mawr
Chicago, IL 60660
773/878-7771
www.sivananda.org/chicago

Temple of Kriya Yoga
2414 N. Kedzie
Chicago, IL 60647
773/342-4600
773/342-4608 - fax

Tracy Vonkaenel
4057 N. Damen
Chicago, IL 60613
773/279-8879

Yoga Circle
Gabriel Halpern - Director
401 W. Ontario - 2nd floor
Chicago, IL 60610
312/915-0750
www.yogacircle.com

Tai Chi

Dance Center of Columbia College
1306 S. Michigan
Chicago, IL 60605
312/344-8300 • 312/344-8036 - fax
www.colum.edu

Physicians

ARR/Alternative Reproductive
2000 N. Racine
Chicago, IL 60614
773/327-7315
773/477-0287 - fax

Beth Braun Ph.D.,C.M.T.
Miro Center for Integrated Medicine
1639 Orrington Ave.
Evanston, IL 60201
847/733-9900
847/733-0105 - fax
www.mirocenter.org

Center for Human Reproduction
750 N. Orleans
Chicago, IL 60610
312/397-8200
312/397-8338
312/397-8394 - fax

Harambee Wellness Center
1515 E. 52nd - 2nd floor
Chicago, IL 60615
773/925-6877

Howard Brown Health Center
4025 N. Sheridan
Chicago, IL 60613
773/388-1600

University Family Physicians
1953C N. Clybourn
Chicago, IL 60614
773/348-1414
773/348-1477 - fax

University of Chicago Physicians Group
4640 N. Marine
Chicago, IL 60640
773/564-5333
773/564-5334 - fax

Women's Health Resources
3000 N. Halsted #309
Chicago, IL 60657
773/296-3500

Clean bill of health?
Check out the Dance Classes on page 54

AIDS Resources

Harambee Wellness Center
1515 E. 52nd - 2nd floor
Chicago, IL 60615
773/925-6877

Horizons Anti-Violence Hotline
773/871-2273

Horizons Community Service
Gay and Lesbian Hotline (6-10pm)
773/929-4357

Howard Brown Health Center
4025 N. Sheridan
Chicago, IL 60613
773/388-1600

Stop AIDS
3651 N. Halsted
Chicago, IL 60613
773/871-3300
773/871-2528 - fax
www.howardbrown.org

Test Positive Aware Network
1258 W. Belmont
Chicago, IL 60657
773/404-8726
773/404-1040 - fax
www.tpan.com

Grooming & Appearance

Salons

Alfaro Hair Design
3454 N. Southport
Chicago, IL 60657
773/935-0202

Nancy Angelair Salon
1003 N. Rush
Chicago, IL 60611
312/943-3011

Curl Up and Dye
2837 N. Clark
Chicago, IL 60657
773/348-1000 • 773/348-2802 - fax

Diamond Beauty Clinic
151 N. Michigan #1018
Chicago, IL 60601
312/240-1042

Hair Loft
14 E. Pearson
Chicago, IL 60611
312/943-5435

Heidi's Salon
110 E. Delaware
Chicago, IL 60611
312/337-6411
312/337-7174 - fax

J. Gordon Designs, Ltd.
2326 N. Clark
Chicago, IL 60614
773/871-0770
773/871-2514 - fax

Cosmetic Surgery

Philip James
710 W. Diversey
Chicago, IL 60614
773/248-9880

Marianne Strokirk Salon
361 W. Chestnut
Chicago, IL 60610
312/944-4428 • 312/944-4429 - fax
www.mariannestrokirk.com

Mario Tricoci
Hair Salon & Day Spa
900 N. Michigan
Chicago, IL 60611
312/915-0960
312/943-3138 - fax

Media Hair & Makeup Group
Maureen Kalagian
708/848-8400

Molina Molina
54 W. Maple
Chicago, IL 60610
312/664-2386

Niko's Day Spa
2504 Clark
Chicago, IL 60657
773/472-0883

Paul Rehder Salon
939 N. Rush
Chicago, IL 60611
312/943-7404

Salon Absolu
1216 W. Belmont
Chicago, IL 60657
773/525-2396

Timothy Paul Salon
200 E. Delaware
Chicago, IL 60611
312/944-5454 • 312/944-5460 - fax

Trio Salon Ltd.
11 E. Walton
Chicago, IL 60611-1412
312/944-6999 • **877/944-6999**
312/944-9572 - fax
www.triosalon.com

1913 Central St.
Evanston, IL 60201-2227
847/491-6999
www.triosalon.com
"Chicago models turn to TRIO...for many of the shortest, coolest looks seen on the hottest new faces in town...(TRIO) has been recognized nationally for its creative and technical works...(the) name (being) synonymous with flattering, precision cuts and picture perfect stylings." MODERN SALON. Open Seven Days A Week.

Cosmetic Surgery

Associated Plastic Surgeons
Dr. Otto J. Placik
680 N. Lake Shore #930
Chicago, IL 60611
312/787-5313
800/232-0767
847/398-1784 - fax

Chicago Hair Institute
Ron Corniels
20 E. Ogden
Hinsdale, IL 60521
630/655-9331 • 630/655-9381 - fax

Dr. Diane L. Gerber
680 N. Lake Shore #930
Chicago, IL 60611
312/654-8700

Ch. 10 Living **317**

Skin Care

Wafik A. Hanna, M.D.
12 Salt Creek Ln. #225
Hinsdale, IL 60521
630/887-8180 • 630/887-8188 - fax

Raymond Konior, M.D.
1 S. 224 Summit #310
Oakbrook Terrace, IL 60181
630/932-9690 • 630/932-8125 - fax
www.thenewyoudoc.com

Liposuction Institute of America
Dr. Leon Tcheupdjian
1700 W. Central Rd.
Arlington Heights, IL 60005
847/259-0100 • 847/398-3855 - fax
www.lipodoc.com

New Dimensions Centre for Cosmetic Surgery
60 E. Delaware - 15th floor
Chicago, IL 60611
312/440-5050
312/440-5064 - fax
www.nd-plasticsurgery.com

New Image Specialists
James M. Platts, Jr., M.D.
34 E. Oak #400
Chicago, IL 60611
312/951-2694
312/951-6492 - fax

Skin Care

Cheryl Channings
54 E. Oak - 2nd floor
Chicago, IL 60611
312/280-1994
312/280-1929 - fax
www.channings.com

Hair Loft
14 E. Pearson
Chicago, IL 60611
312/943-5435

Heidi's Salon
110 E. Delaware
Chicago, IL 60611
312/337-6411
312/337-7174 - fax

Marilyn Miglin Institute
112 E. Oak
Chicago, IL 60611
800/662-1120
312/943-1184 - fax
www.marilyn-miglin.com

Mario Tricoci Hair Salon & Day Spa
900 N. Michigan
Chicago, IL 60611
312/915-0960
312/943-3138 - fax

Nouvelle Femme
1157 Wilmette Ave.
Wilmette, IL 60091
847/251-6698

Rodica European Skin & Body Care Center
Water Tower Place - Professional Side
845 N. Michigan #944E
Chicago, IL 60611
312/527-1459
www.facialandbodybyrodica.com

Salon Absolu
1216 W. Belmont
Chicago, IL 60657
773/525-2396

Dentists

Electrolysis

Amber Electrolysis
3734 N. Southport
Chicago, IL 60613
773/549-3800

Carol Block Ltd.
Permanent Hair Removal
70 E. Walton - 2nd Floor
Chicago, IL 60611
312/932-0345
www.cyberconnect.com/carolblock/home.htm

Water Tower Hair Removal
845 N. Michigan #972W
Chicago, IL 60611
312/787-4028
312/787-4092 - fax
www.purelazer.com

Dentists

Belmont Dental Care
3344 N. Lincoln
Chicago, IL 60657
773/549-7971
773/348-7544 - fax

Dr. David B. Drake
739 W. Belmont
Chicago, IL 60657
773/248-8813 • 773/248-8898 - fax

Dr. Jeffrey Gaule
3120 N. Ashland
Chicago, IL 60657
773/281-7550
773/281-0808 - fax

Gold Coast Dental Associates
Dr. Jeffrey Weller
1050 N. State - Mezzanine
Chicago, IL 60610
312/654-0606
312/654-1606 - fax

**Dr. Martin Lieberman & Dr.
William T. Tetford**
5419 N. Sheridan #105
Chicago, IL 60640
773/728-9200

**Lincoln Park Columbus
Dental Associates**
2551 N. Clark #700
Chicago, IL 60614
773/348-7008
773/348-5810 - fax

**Lincoln Park Cosmetic
and General Dentistry**
424 W. Fullerton
Chicago, IL 60614
773/404-0101

Dr. Craig Millard, D.D.S., P.C.
30 N. Michigan #920
Chicago, IL 60602
312/726-5830
312/726-7290 - fax

Michelle Rappeport, D.D.S.
3056 N. Southport
Chicago, IL 60657
773/935-4960

Ravenswood Dental Group
1945 W. Wilson
Chicago, IL 60640
773/334-3555
773/334-5771 - fax

Ch. 10 Living **319**

Public Service

Dr. Marianne W. Schaefer
4801 W. Peterson
Chicago, IL 60646
773/777-8300
www.the-toothfairy.com

Dr. Joseph S. Toups
25 E. Washington #1325
Chicago, IL 60602
312/263-6894

Dr. Glenn Ulffers, D.D.S.
1001 N. Clark
Chicago, IL 60610
312/337-1318 • 312/642-5166 - fax
All phases of general dentistry emphasizing cosmetics including bleaching, porcelain veneers, and crowns. All done in a friendly environment in order to make the apprehensive patient comfortable. Nitrous oxide analgesia is available for those who are most fearful.

Dr. Gray Vogelmann
155 N. Michigan #325
Chicago, IL 60601
312/819-1104

Dr. Roger M. Wills
30 N. Michigan #1414
Chicago, IL 60602
312/332-7010
312/332-1812 - fax

Dr. Ieva Wright
333 N. Michigan #2900
Chicago, IL 60601
312/236-3226
312/236-9629 - fax

Public Service Phone Numbers

ArtLaw Hotline
312/944-ARTS

Attorney General
312/814-3000

CTA/PACE Information
312/836-7000

Equal Employment Opportunity Commission
Chicago, IL
312/353-2713

IRS Taxpayer Information
Chicago, IL
800/829-1040

Movie Phone
312/444-FILM

Chicago Park District
Chicago, IL
312/747-2200

Police (Non-Emergency)
Chicago, IL
312/746-6000

Post Office Information
312/654-3895

Ticket Master
312/559-1950

Women's Bureau
U.S. Department of Labor
233 S. Dearborn #1022
Chicago, IL 60604
312/353-6985
312/353-6986 - fax

February 2001

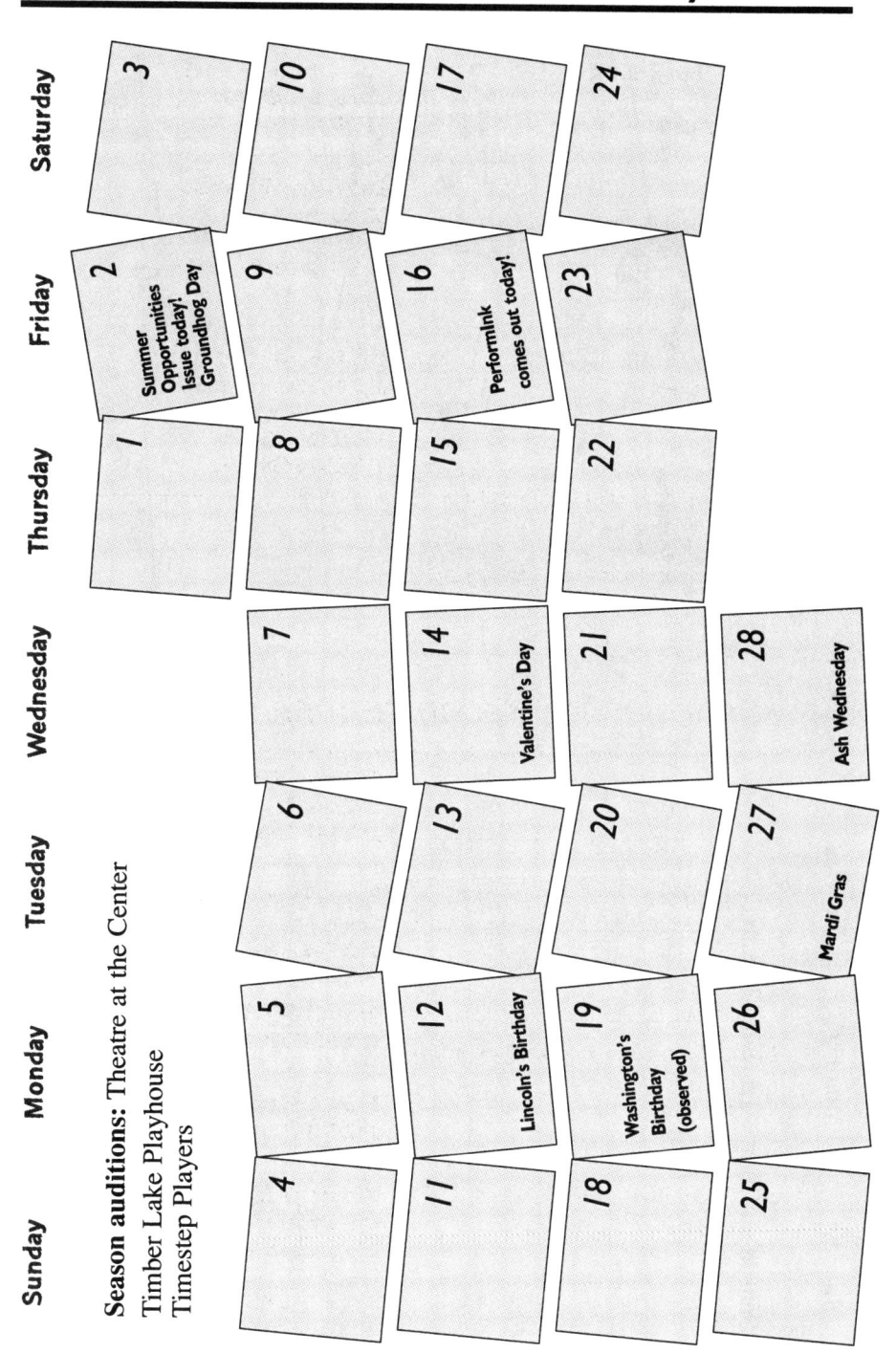

Sunday	Monday	Tuesday	Wednesday	Thursday	Friday	Saturday
				1	2 Summer Opportunities Issue today! Groundhog Day	3
4	5	6	7	8	9	10
11	12 Lincoln's Birthday	13	14 Valentine's Day	15	16 PerformInk comes out today!	17
18 Washington's Birthday (observed)	19	20	21	22	23	24
25	26	27 Mardi Gras	28 Ash Wednesday			

Season auditions: Theatre at the Center
Timber Lake Playhouse
Timestep Players

Calendar 321

March 2001

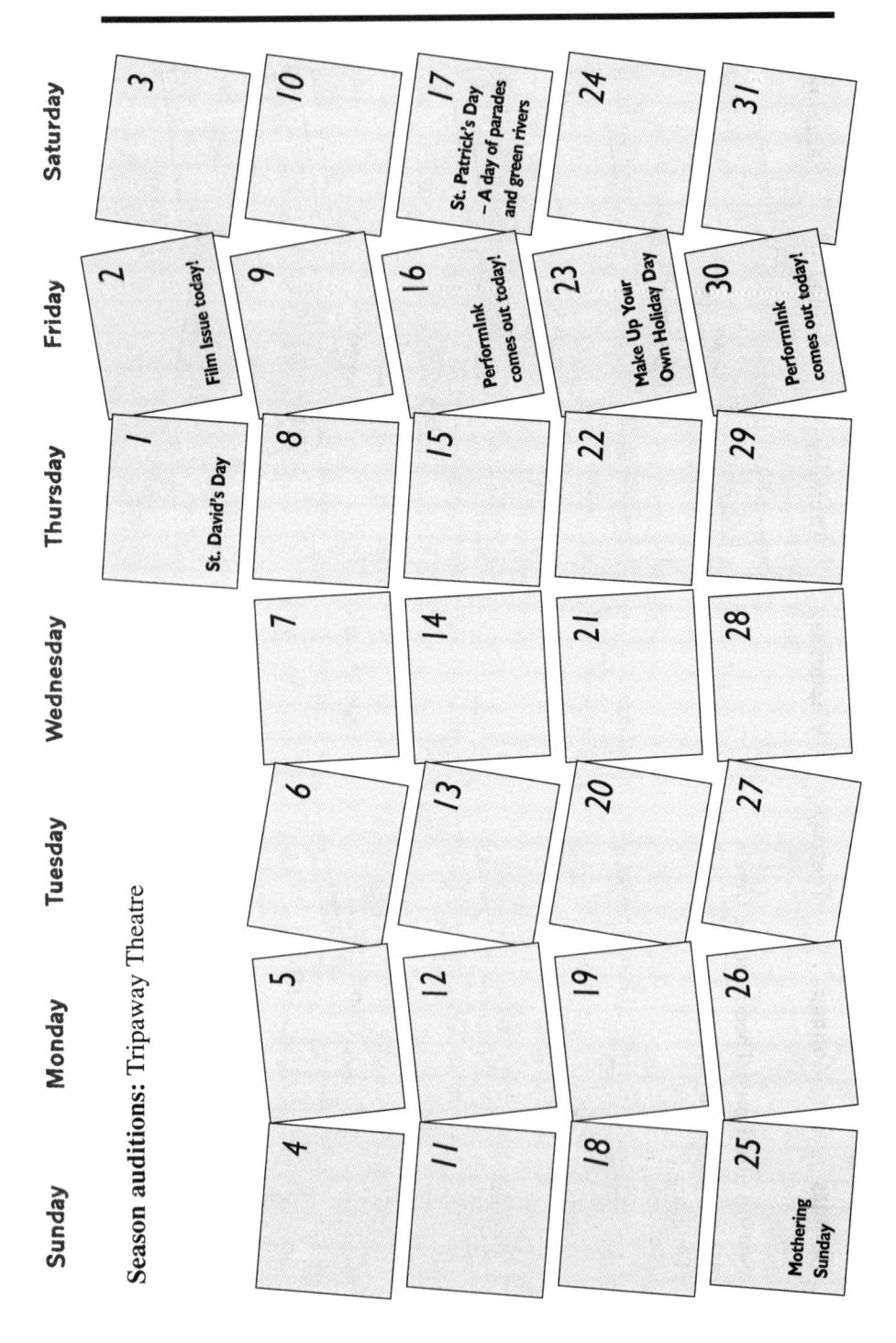

	Sunday	Monday	Tuesday	Wednesday	Thursday	Friday	Saturday
		Season auditions: Tripaway Theatre			1 St. David's Day	2 Film Issue today!	3
	4	5	6	7	8	9	10
	11	12	13	14	15	16 PerformInk comes out today!	17 St. Patrick's Day – A day of parades and green rivers
	18	19	20	21	22	23 Make Up Your Own Holiday Day	24
	25 Mothering Sunday	26	27	28	29	30 PerformInk comes out today!	31

322   The Book: An Actor's Guide to Chicago

April 2001

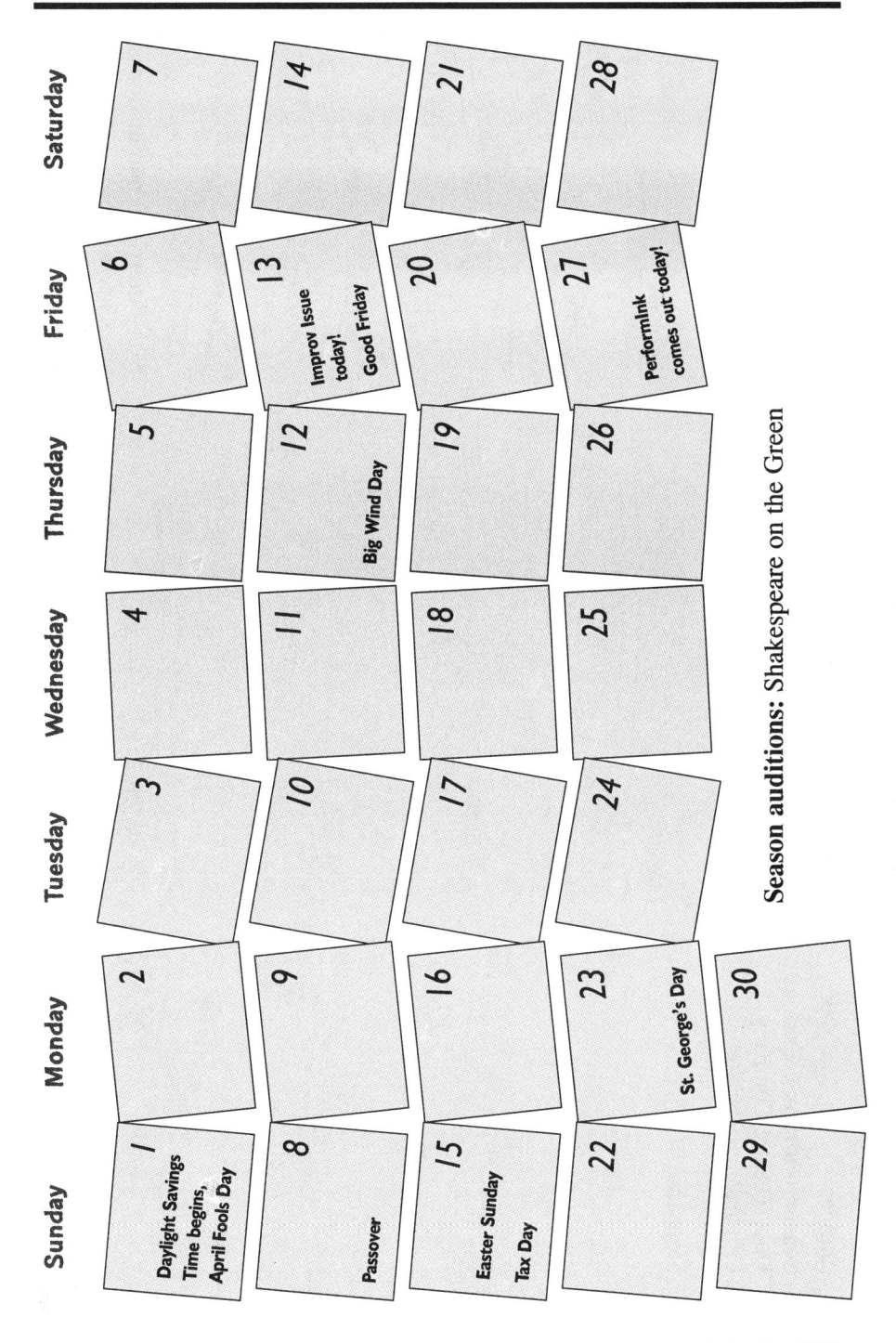

Sunday	Monday	Tuesday	Wednesday	Thursday	Friday	Saturday
1 Daylight Savings Time begins, April Fools Day	2	3	4	5	6	7
8 Passover	9	10	11	12 Big Wind Day	13 Improv Issue today! Good Friday	14
15 Easter Sunday Tax Day	16	17	18	19	20	21
22	23 St. George's Day	24	25	26	27 PerformInk comes out today!	28
29	30					

Season auditions: Shakespeare on the Green

Calendar 323

May 2001

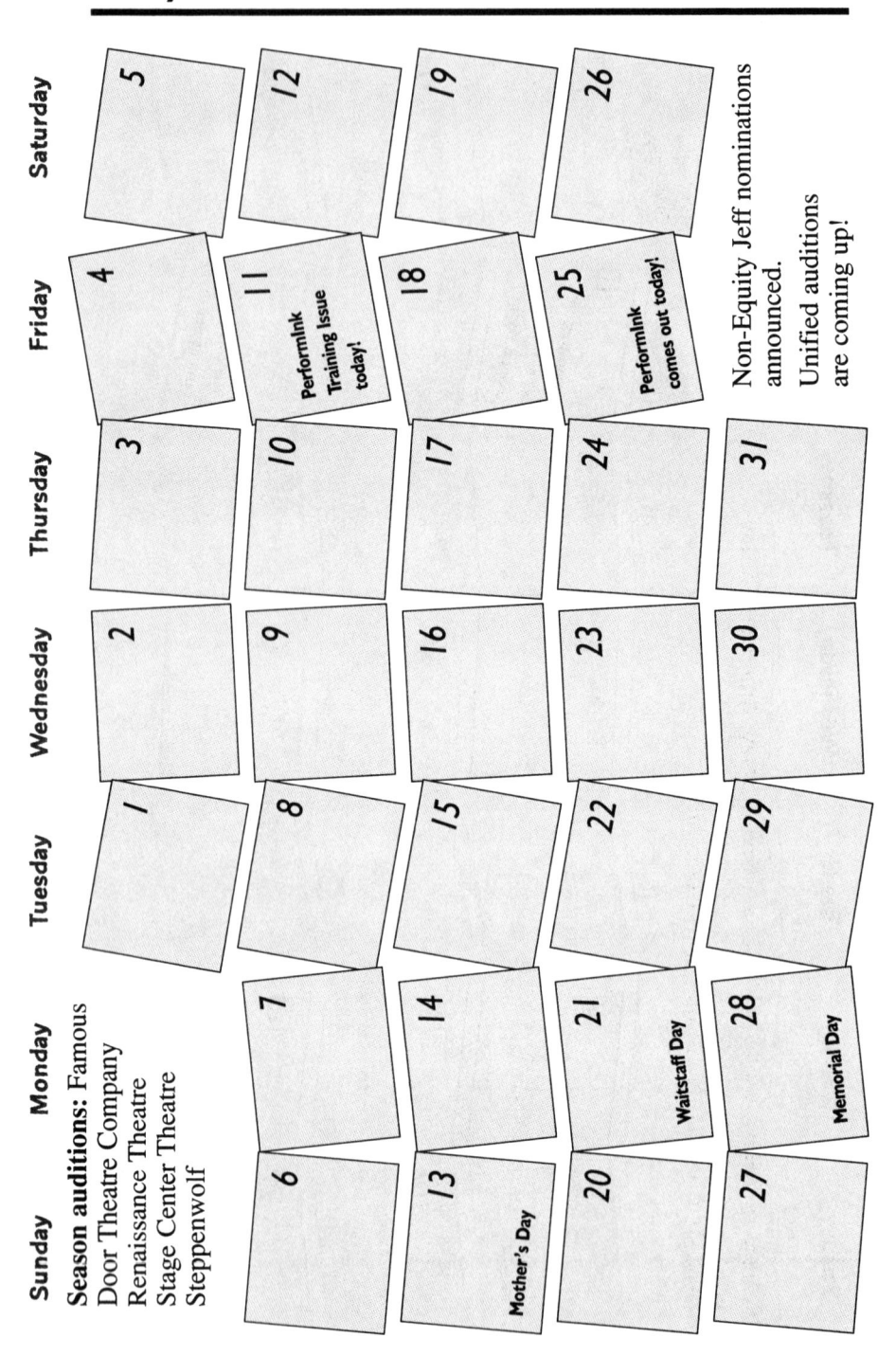

Sunday	Monday	Tuesday	Wednesday	Thursday	Friday	Saturday
		1	2	3	4	5
6	7	8	9	10	11 PerformInk Training Issue today!	12
13 Mother's Day	14	15	16	17	18	19
20	21 Waitstaff Day	22	23	24	25 PerformInk comes out today!	26
27	28 Memorial Day	29	30	31		

Season auditions: Famous Door Theatre Company, Renaissance Theatre, Stage Center Theatre, Steppenwolf

Non-Equity Jeff nominations announced. Unified auditions are coming up!

324 The Book: An Actor's Guide to Chicago

June 2001

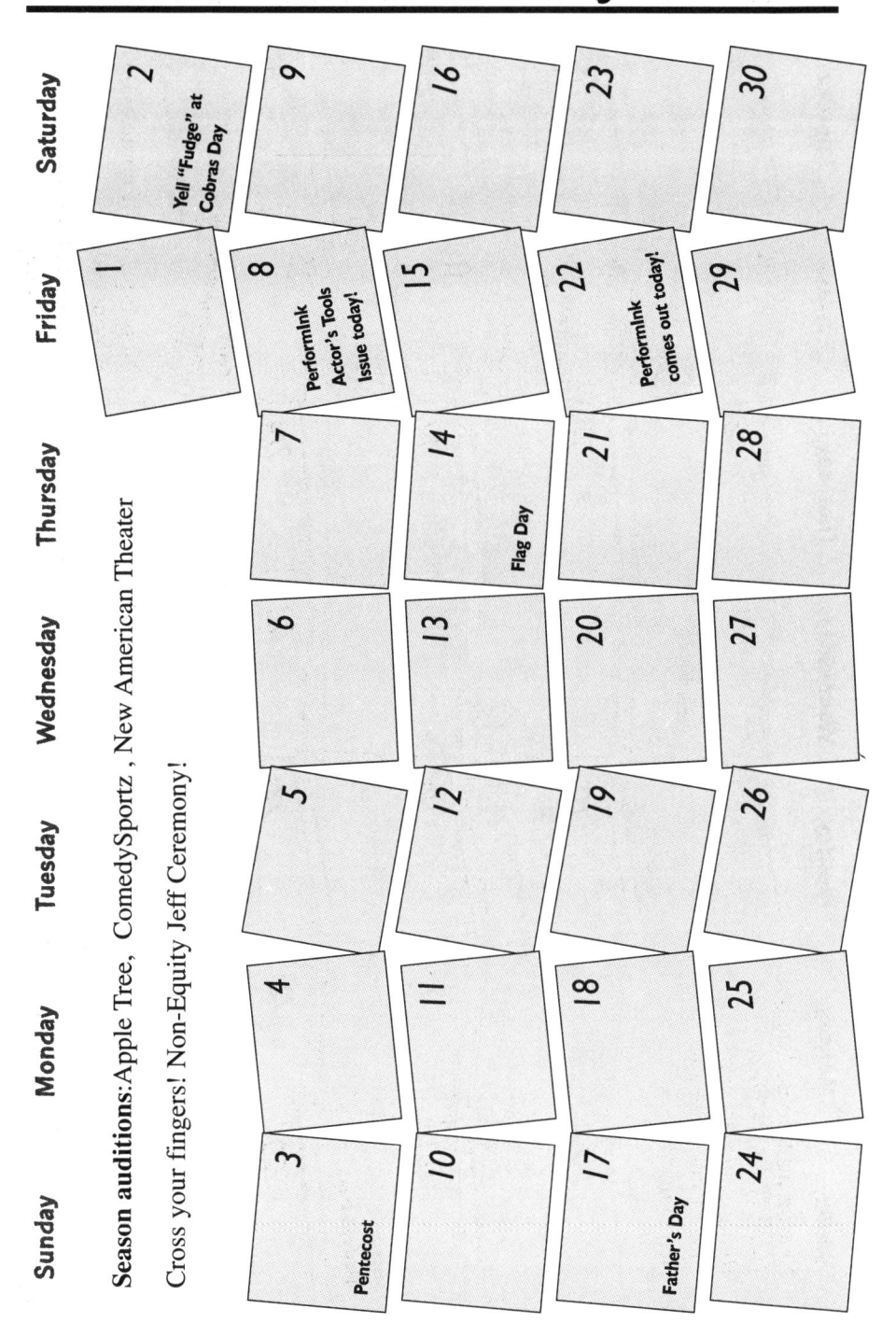

Sunday	Monday	Tuesday	Wednesday	Thursday	Friday	Saturday
					1	2 Yell "Fudge" at Cobras Day
3 Pentecost	4	5	6	7	8 PerformInk Actor's Tools Issue today!	9
10	11	12	13	14	15	16
17 Father's Day	18	19	20	21 Flag Day	22	23
24	25	26	27	28	29 PerformInk comes out today!	30

Season auditions: Apple Tree, ComedySportz, New American Theater

Cross your fingers! Non-Equity Jeff Ceremony!

Calendar **325**

July 2001

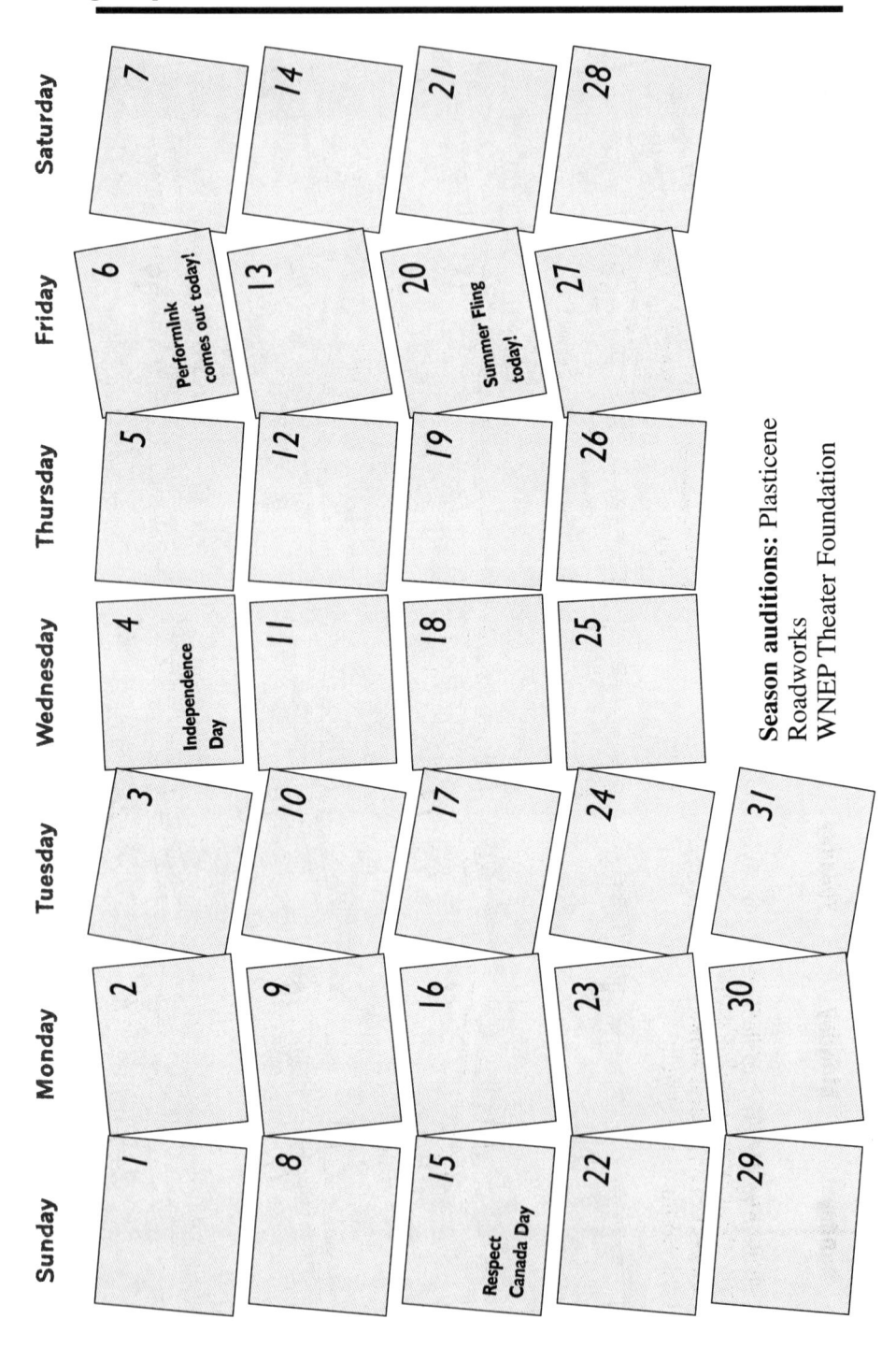

Sunday	Monday	Tuesday	Wednesday	Thursday	Friday	Saturday
1	2	3	4 Independence Day	5	6 PerformInk comes out today!	7
8	9	10	11	12	13	14
15 Respect Canada Day	16	17	18	19	20 Summer Fling today!	21
22	23	24	25	26	27	28
29	30	31				

Season auditions: Plasticene
Roadworks
WNEP Theater Foundation

326 The Book: An Actor's Guide to Chicago

August 2001

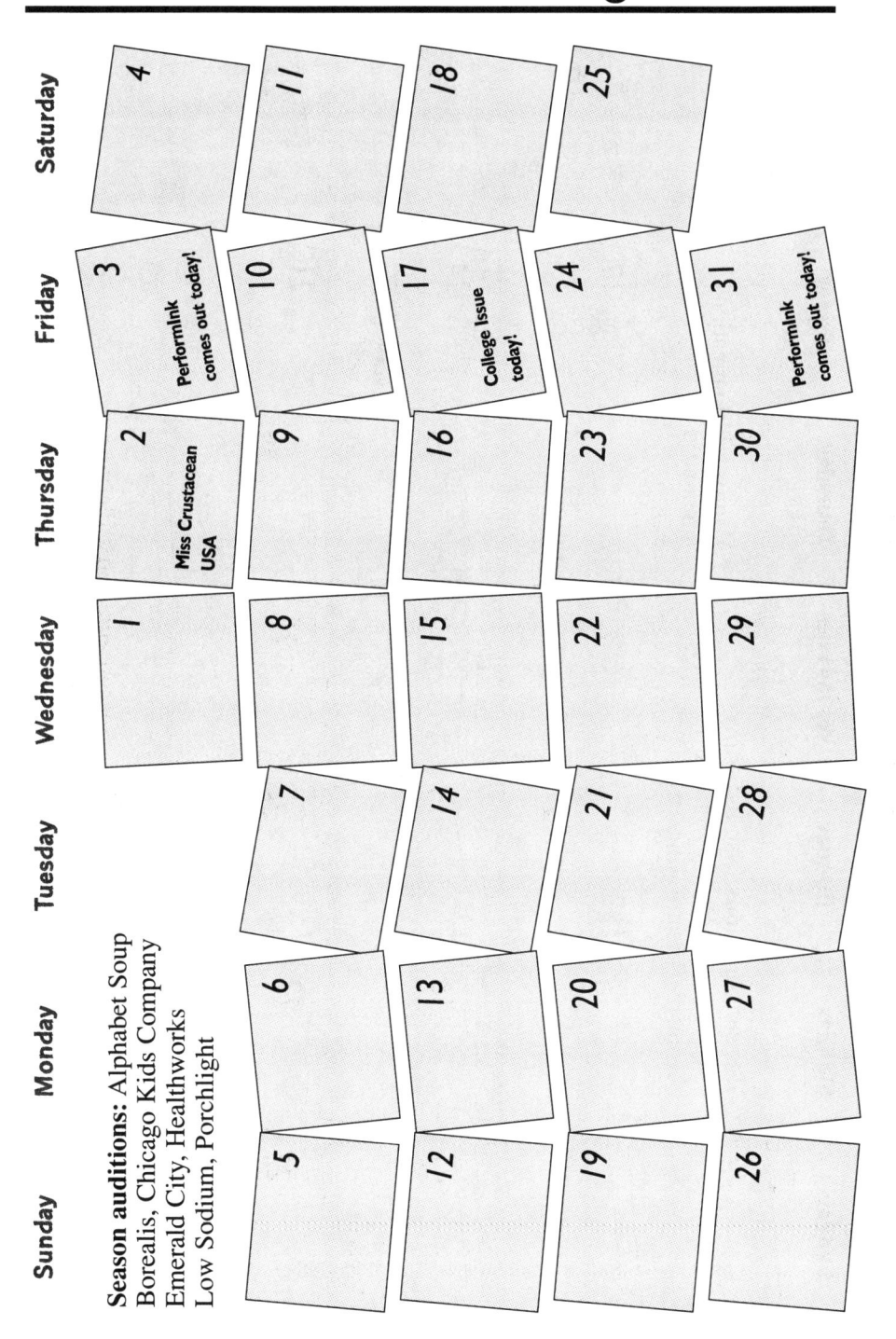

Sunday	Monday	Tuesday	Wednesday	Thursday	Friday	Saturday
			1	2 *Miss Crustacean USA*	3 *PerformInk comes out today!*	4
5	6	7	8	9	10	11
12	13	14	15	16	17 *College Issue today!*	18
19	20	21	22	23	24	25
26	27	28	29	30	31 *PerformInk comes out today!*	

Season auditions: Alphabet Soup Borealis, Chicago Kids Company Emerald City, Healthworks Low Sodium, Porchlight

Calendar 327

September 2001

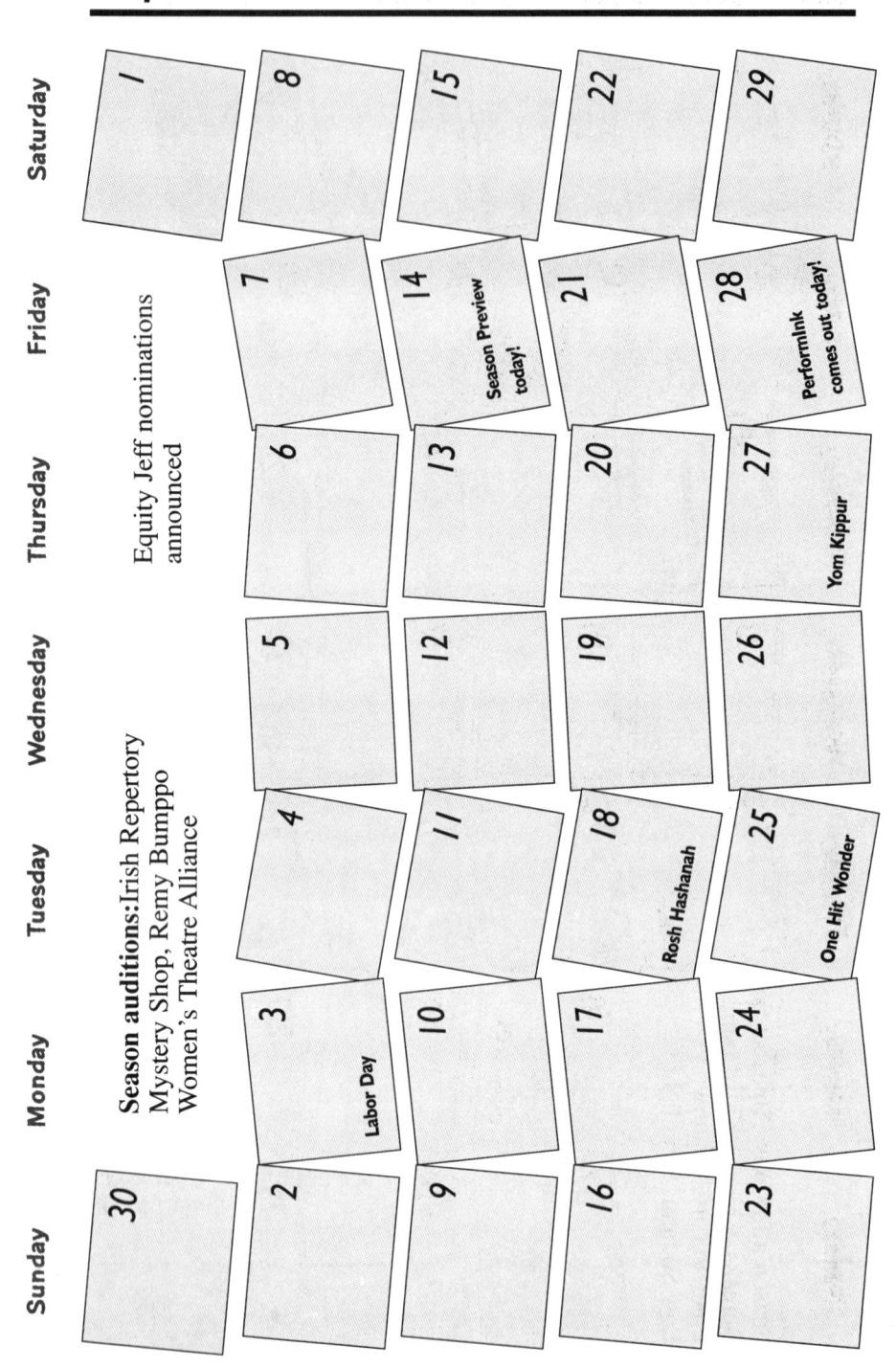

Saturday: 1, 8, 15, 22, 29

Friday: 7, 14 (Season Preview today!), 21, 28 (PerformInk comes out today!)

Thursday: Equity Jeff nominations announced, 6, 13, 20, 27 (Yom Kippur)

Wednesday: 5, 12, 19, 26

Tuesday: 4, 11, 18 (Rosh Hashanah), 25 (One Hit Wonder)

Monday: Season auditions: Irish Repertory, Mystery Shop, Remy Bumppo, Women's Theatre Alliance; 3 (Labor Day), 10, 17, 24

Sunday: 30, 2, 9, 16, 23

328   The Book: An Actor's Guide to Chicago

October 2001

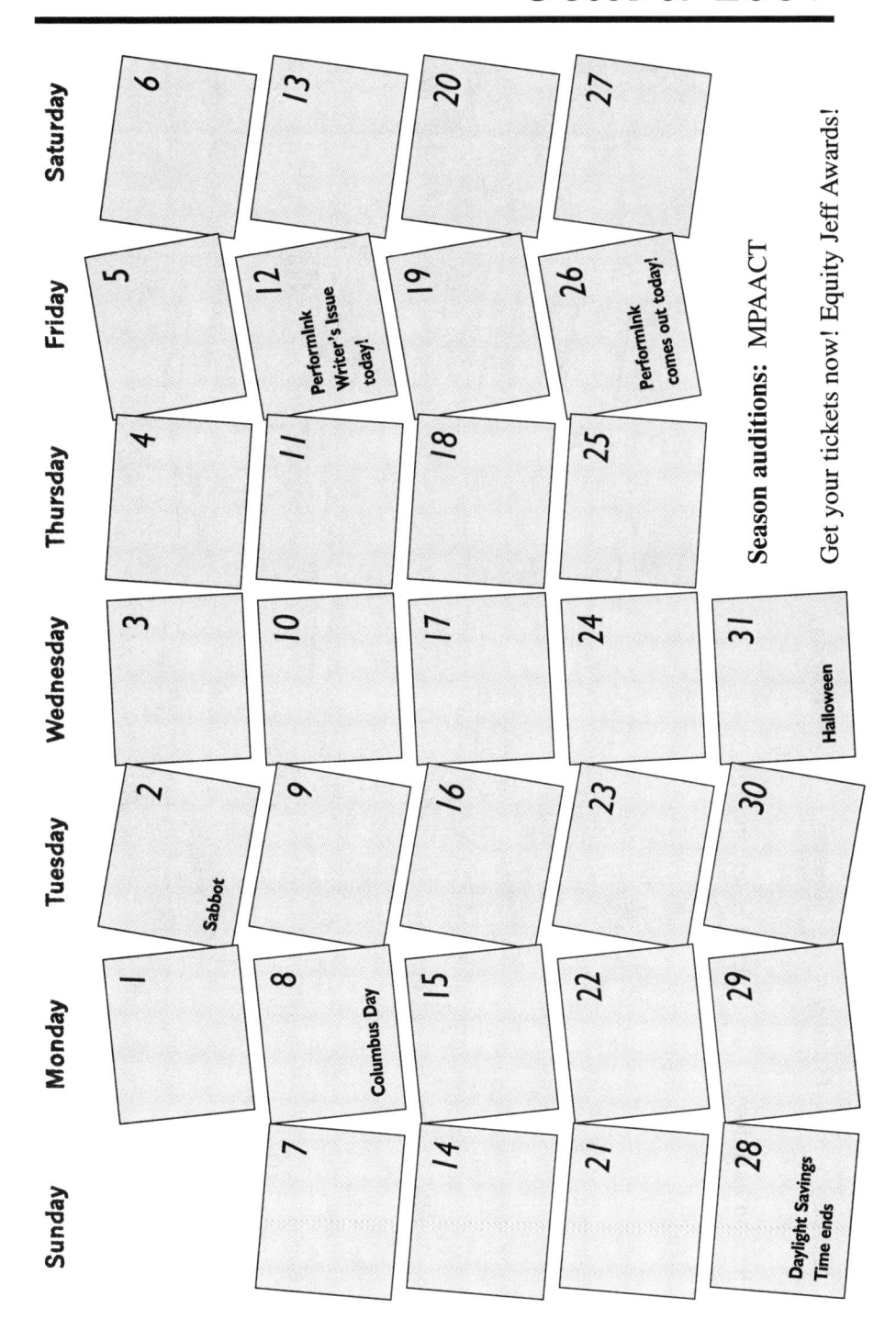

Sunday	Monday	Tuesday	Wednesday	Thursday	Friday	Saturday
	1	2 Sabbot	3	4	5	6
7	8 Columbus Day	9	10	11	12 PerformInk Writer's Issue today!	13
14	15	16	17	18	19	20
21	22	23	24	25	26 PerformInk comes out today!	27
28 Daylight Savings Time ends	29	30	31 Halloween			

Season auditions: MPAACT

Get your tickets now! Equity Jeff Awards!

Calendar 329

November 2001

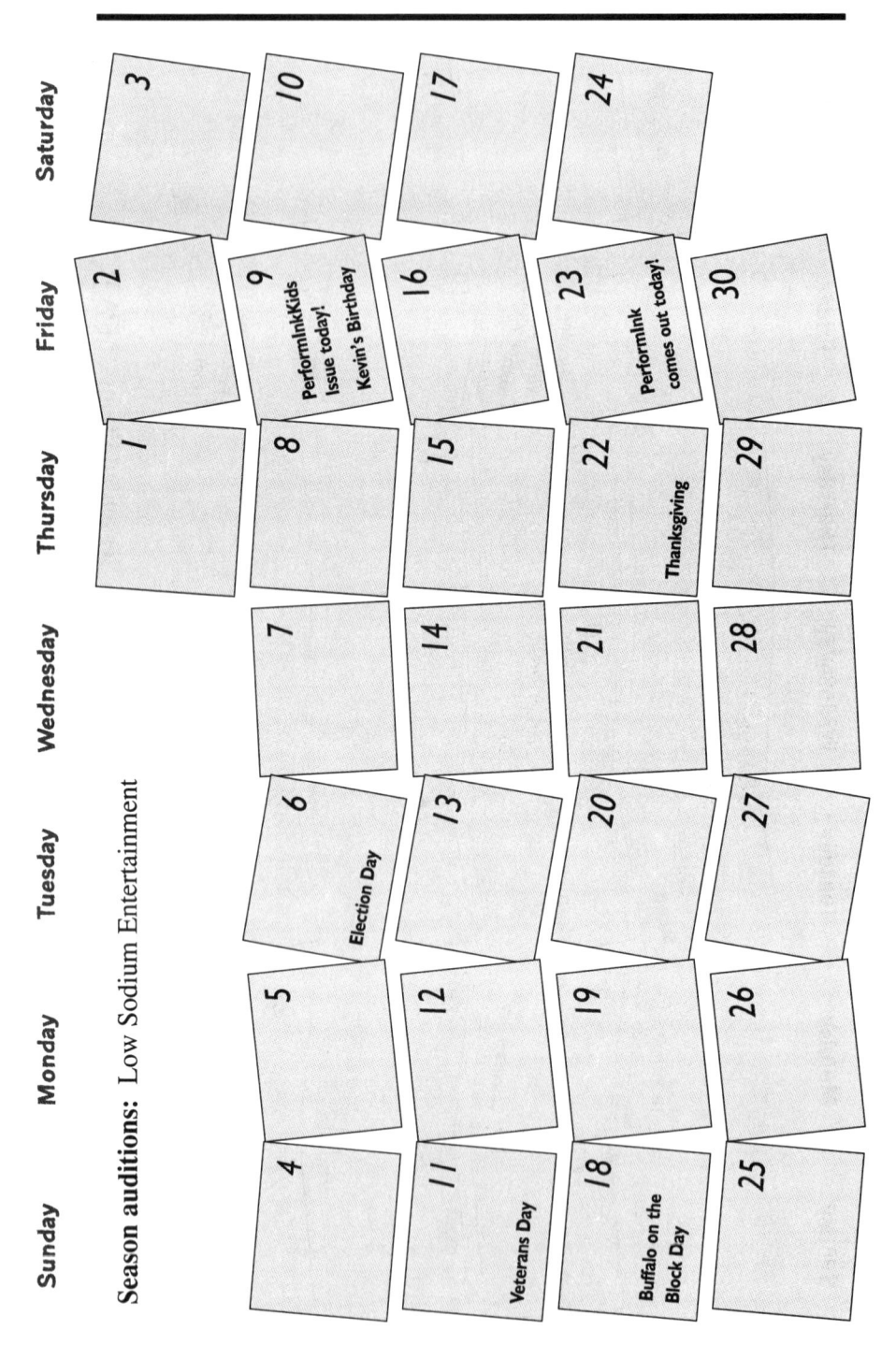

Saturday: 3, 10, 17, 24

Friday: 2, 9 (PerformInkKids Issue today! Kevin's Birthday), 16, 23 (PerformInk comes out today!), 30

Thursday: 1, 8, 15, 22, 29 (Thanksgiving)

Wednesday: 7, 14, 21, 28

Tuesday: 6 (Election Day), 13, 20, 27

Monday: 5, 12, 19, 26

Sunday: 4, 11 (Veterans Day), 18 (Buffalo on the Block Day), 25

Season auditions: Low Sodium Entertainment

330 The Book: An Actor's Guide to Chicago

December 2001

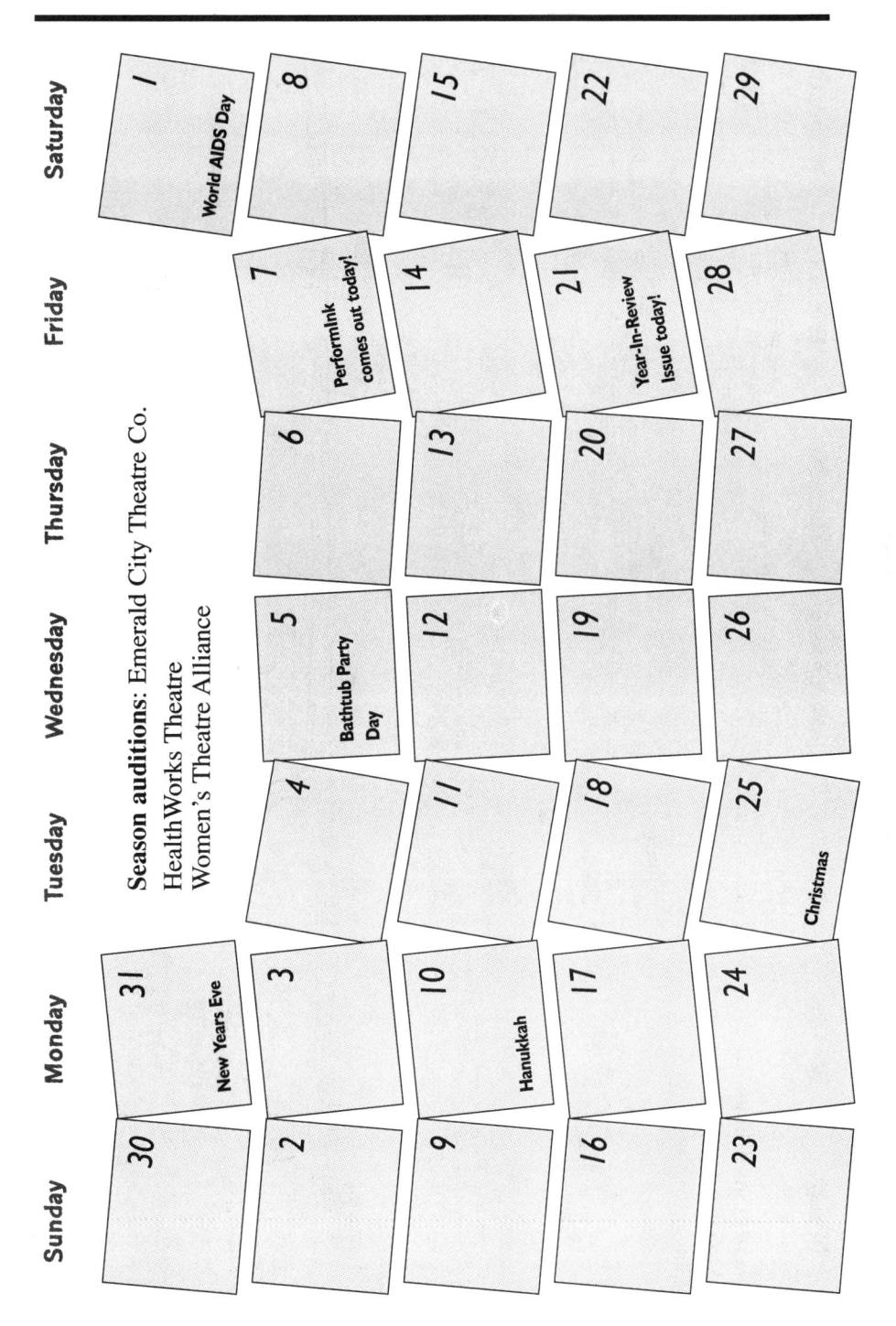

Sunday	Monday	Tuesday	Wednesday	Thursday	Friday	Saturday
			Season auditions: Emerald City Theatre Co. HealthWorks Theatre Women's Theatre Alliance			1 World AIDS Day
2	3	4	5 Bathtub Party Day	6	7 PerformInk comes out today!	8
9	10 Hanukkah	11	12	13	14	15
16	17	18	19	20	21 Year-In-Review Issue today!	22
23	24	25 Christmas	26	27	28	29
30	31 New Years Eve					

Calendar 331

January 2002

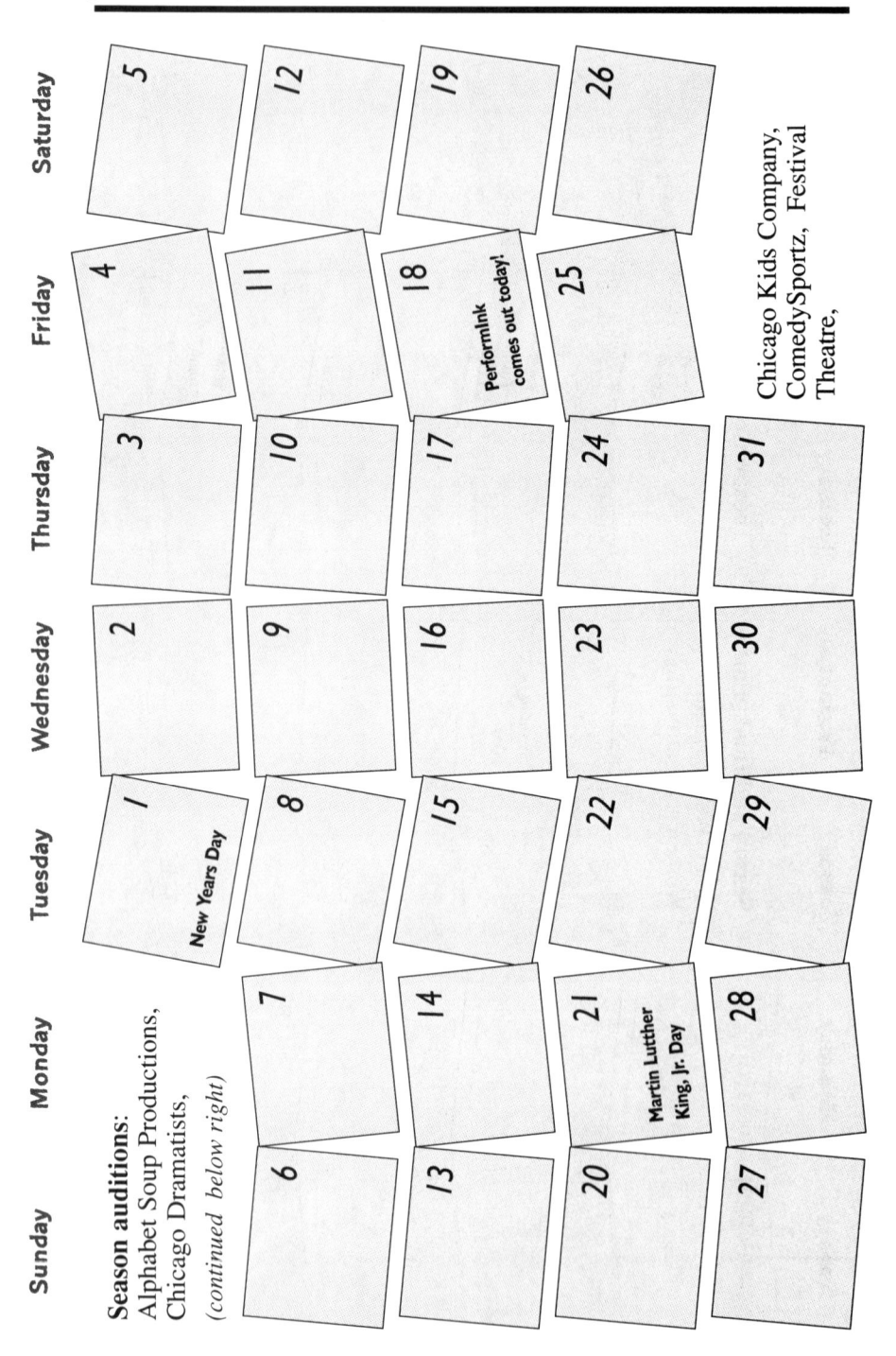

Sunday	Monday	Tuesday	Wednesday	Thursday	Friday	Saturday
		1 New Years Day	2	3	4	5
6	7	8	9	10	11	12
13	14	15	16	17	18 PerformInk comes out today!	19
20	21 Martin Luther King, Jr. Day	22	23	24	25	26
27	28	29	30	31		

Season auditions:
Alphabet Soup Productions,
Chicago Dramatists,
(continued below right)

Chicago Kids Company,
ComedySportz, Festival
Theatre,

332   The Book: An Actor's Guide to Chicago

February 2002

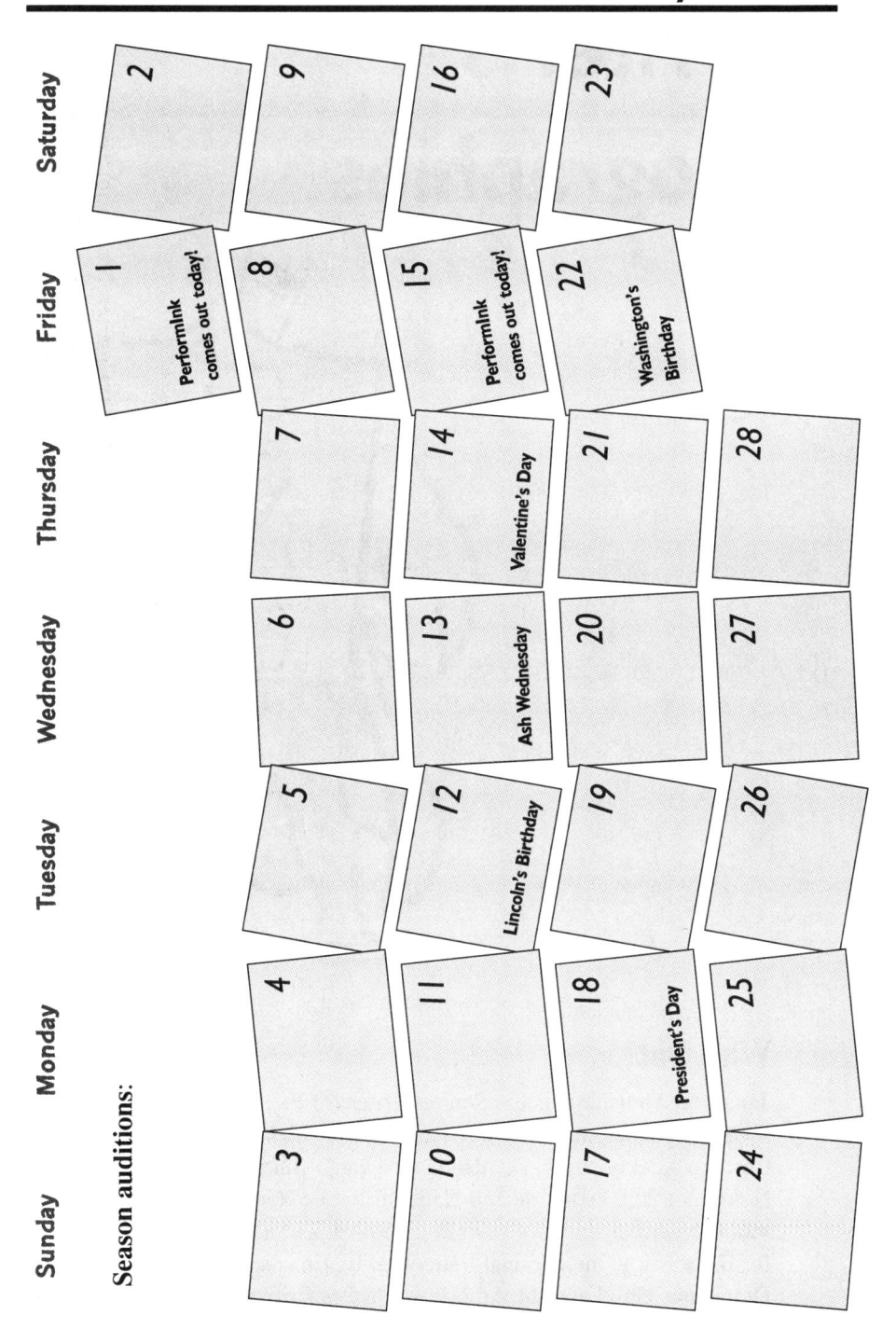

Sunday	Monday	Tuesday	Wednesday	Thursday	Friday	Saturday
	Season auditions:				1 PerformInk comes out today!	2
3	4	5	6	7	8	9
10	11	12 Lincoln's Birthday	13 Ash Wednesday	14 Valentine's Day	15 PerformInk comes out today!	16
17	18 President's Day	19	20	21	22 Washington's Birthday	23
24	25	26	27	28		

Calendar 333

Writer's Biographies

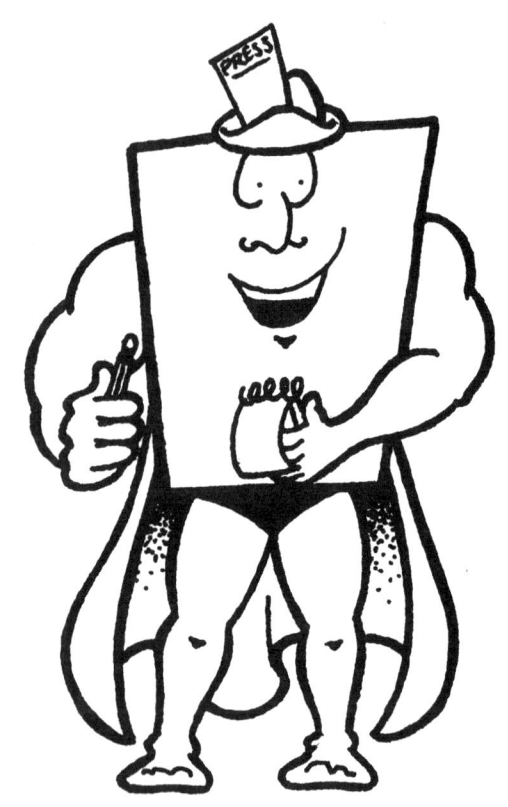

Who Dat?

Jonathan Abarbanel is the Senior Writer for PERFORMINK, Chicago's trade newspaper, and the Theater Editor for the WINDY CITY TIMES, a Chicago weekly paper. He also is an award-winning theatre critic for NORTH SHORE MAGAZINE and National Public Radio affiliate WBEZ; a senior contributor to CHICAGO FOOTLIGHTS; and a featured columnist for BACKSTAGE, the national trade weekly. He is a member of the Dramatists Guild and the American Theatre Critics Association.

Biographies

Dexter Bullard is an award-winning director, teacher, and acting coach with ten years experience in Chicago theater. Dexter has directed for The Second City, Next Theatre, A Red Orchid Theatre, and American Theater Company as well as with Plasticene, an experimental physical theater company which he founded in 1995. Dexter teaches physical acting at The Plasticene Studio and improvisation at The Second City Training Center. Dexter has taught acting and performance at Roosevelt University, UIC, Columbia College, The School of The Art Institute, The Audition Studio, and The Actors' Center.

Jason R. Chin has performed, directed and hung up coats at most of Chicago's improv theaters. He is currently the Associate Artistic Director for the ImprovOlympic.

Julie Daly has been an actor in Chicago for the last eight years. She has been seen on many Chicago stages and in a handful of commercials, industrials and independent films. She is also a part-time staff member at PERFORMINK.

Adrianne Duncan is a newly relocated Los Angeles actress and singer and former vice president of The Actor's Connection. Her film and television credits include the independent feature The Chameleon with Seymour Cassel, CBS' Early Edition, Home Alone III, and numerous commercials, including Payless ShoeSource, AT&T and Head & Shoulders. She has worked with such Chicago theatres as Chicago Shakespeare Theatre, National Jewish Theatre, Organic Theatre, Stage Left and Bailiwick Repertory. A graduate of the theatre program at Northwestern University, she collaborated extensively on the acting guide "Chicago Connection" and has also contributed to "The Book" and PERFORMINK newspaper.

Julie Franz Peeler, Director, National Arts Marketing Project Julie is an accomplished market researcher and marketing strategist in both the for profit and non-profit arena. She worked actively with the arts and funding communities to develop the four programs of the Arts Marketing Center. Success in Chicago led to a grant from American Express to expand AMC into seven additional cities as the National Arts Marketing Project. That grant was renewed in 2000 and the program will expand into an additional four US cities this year, while international alliances also are being explored. While working at major international advertising agencies, she developed growth plans for Fortune 500 clients, as well as for the U.S. Olympic Committee. At

335

Biographies

the same time, Julie actively volunteered her business skills in the Chicago arts community. She examined mid-size business giving habits for The Goodman Theatre, developed a member retention plan for The Museum of Contemporary Art, and researched parent's attitudes towards arts education for ArtSmart, an awareness program of the Illinois Alliance for Arts Education. She holds a BA in Journalism from Loyola University of Chicago and a Masters in Management in Marketing and Non Profit Management from the Kellogg Graduate School of Business at Northwestern University.

Kevin Heckman has edited "The Book" for the last four years, as well as serving as listings editor and critic for PERFORMINK. Additionally, he works as a director, actor, lighting designer and teacher. He's worked with a number of companies including Shakespeare Repertory, Apple Tree, Illinois Theatre Center and Bailiwick. He's co-Artistic Director of Stage Left and a member of The Aardvark's artistic collective. Kevin attended Wesleyan University in Connecticut where he received degrees in theatre and mathematics.

Kyle Hillman is a director/actor working in or around the Chicago land area. Since receiving his Master's Degree from Roosevelt University, Kyle has worked as the Theater Manager for Village Players Theater, casting assistant for ReginaCast and currently works at the central office of the Actors Equity Association. To help pay his bills, Kyle often works as a computer consultant and independent web designer. He has designed an Internet presence for several Chicago land theatres and related industry businesses.

Susan Hubbard is a writer and filmmaker living in Chicago. She has been a professional grantwriter, a not-for-profit training manager, and a volunteer fundraiser for the arts. She developed and managed a certificate program for fundraisers, Managing Institutional Advancement, for the University of Chicago's Graham School. Working with instructors and students from diverse organizations in the Managing Boards and Constituency Development module provided her with countless affirmations of the approaches presented by the companies in this article.

Carrie L. Kaufman is the publisher of PerformInk, PerformInk Books and PI Online.

Robert J. Labate, a partner at the law firm of Defrees & Fiske, concentrates his practice in the area of entertainment law, representing independent production companies (both film and music), actors, screenwriters, musicians, authors and talent agencies in a broad spectrum of

Biographies

contract, copyright and related litigation issues. He also has significant experience in general corporate law and financial restructuring matters. Bob writes a monthly "Law and Entertainment" column for Performink (www.performink.com) and speaks at film production seminars jointly sponsored by The Independent Feature Project and the Chicago Academy of Visual Arts.

Karin McKie has been working in public relations and marketing for over 13 years. She is principal of her own firm, Tree Falls Productions, which provides comprehensive public relations, marketing, writing, and editing primarily for Chicago-based theaters and arts organizations. She is a published author, actor, director, and lecturer in the US and abroad. She was honored as one of TODAY'S CHICAGO WOMAN MAGAZINE's "100 Women Making a Difference" for her HIV/AIDS education promotional work. Industry recognition includes a Capital Region Emmy Award and a PBS Promotions Award. No se vende lo que no se enseña.

Mechelle Moe is the editor of PERFORMINK and an associate editor of The Book. She serves as Producer for The Hypocrites theatre company and as an actor has collaborated with Lifeline, A Red Orchid, Prop and The Hypocrites.

Ben Winters After two years as a writer and theater critic in Chicago, where he worked for everyone from PERFORMINK to NEWCITY to the CHICAGO TRIBUNE, Ben Winters recently relocated to Los Angeles.

THE END

Notes:

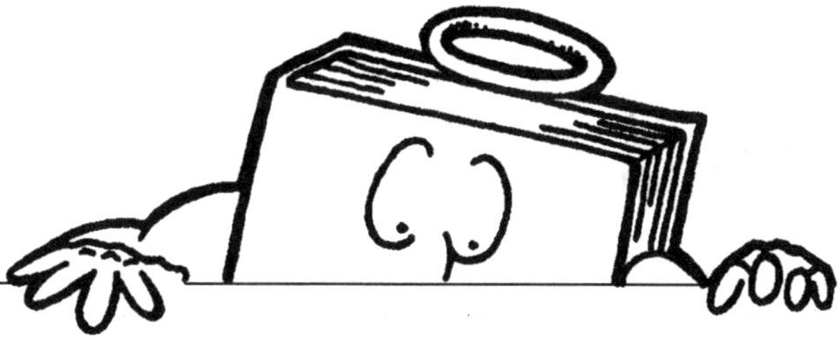

Notes:

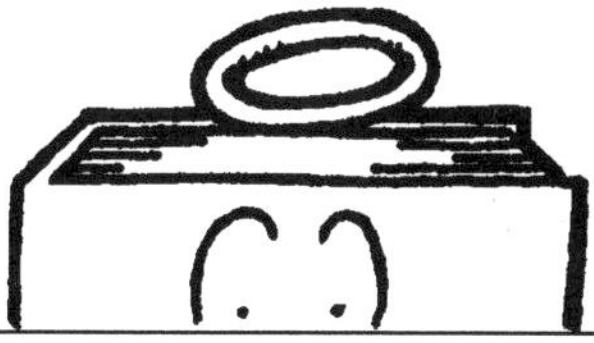

CTA eL Train System

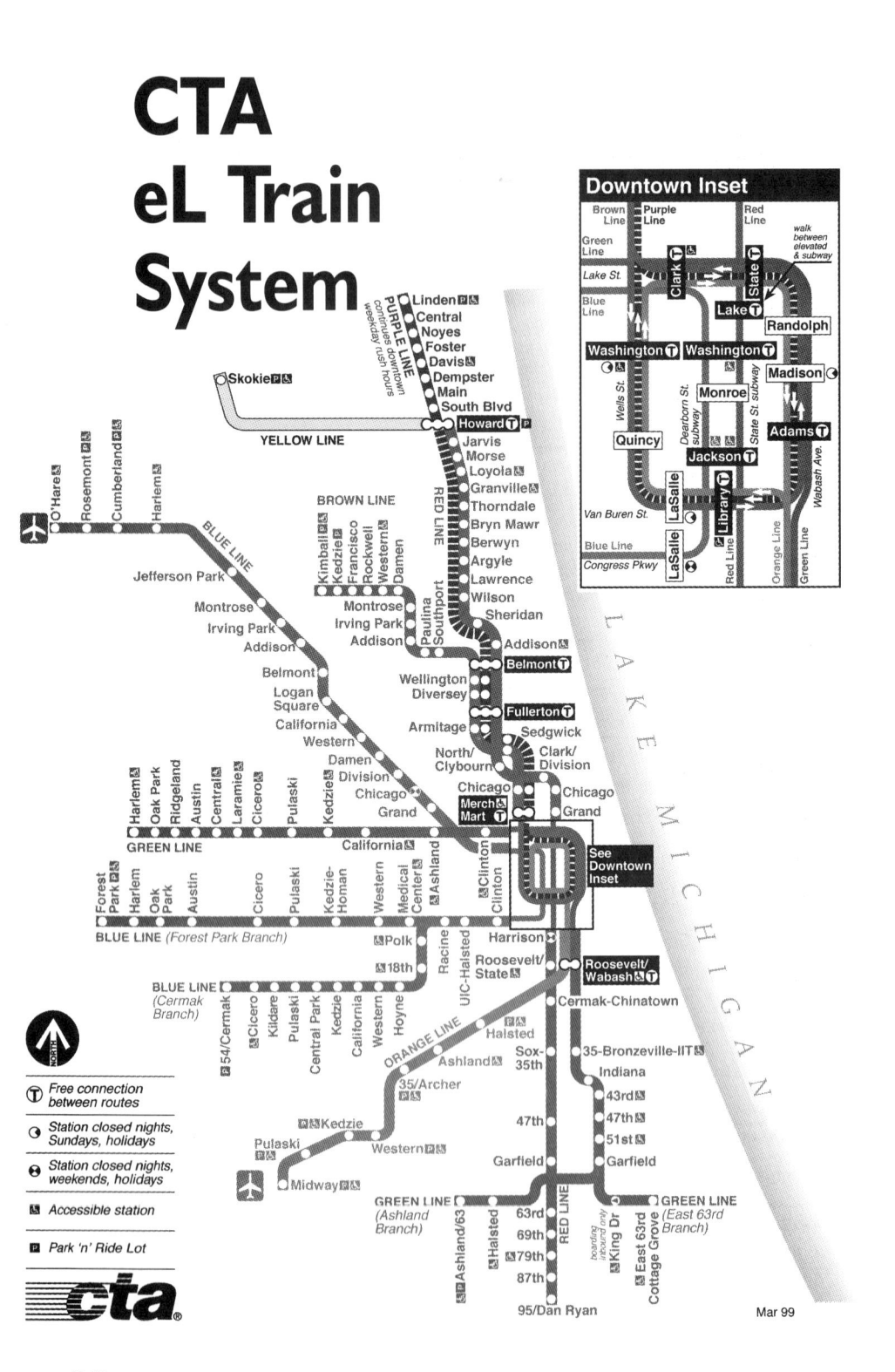

Advertisers Index

A Personnel Commitment 346
A&B Photography 98
ABC Pictures 98
Active Temporary Services 31
Act One Studios 46
Actors Workshop 52
Advanced Personnel 29
Andrew Collings Photography 88
A-PAKS 99
Appropriate Temporary . . .Back Cover
Audio One 64, 148
The Audition Studio 49
Bosco Productions 149
Brosilow Photography 91
Chicagoactors.com 105
Chicago Casting Center 142
The Choice for Staffing 33
City Staffing 30
Classic Photography, Inc. 87
Credible Communications 158
DePaul University -
    Community Music Division 67
Fantasy Headquarters 116

ImprovOlympic 50
Ruth Landis 61, 308
The Larko Group . . .Inside Front Cover
McBlaine & Associates 139
Brian McConkey 90
National Photo Service 96
New Actors Workshop 48
New Tuners/Theatre Building 218
Pete Stenberg Photography 94
Pre-Paid Legal Services, Inc. 135
Proven Performers 32
Quantity Photo 99
Robert Erving Potter Photography . .92
Rick Mitchell Photography 93
Season of Concern 176
Second City 59
Jeremy Sklar 60
Smart Staffing 131
Peggy Smith-Skarry 68
Sound Advice 63
Temporary Opportunities
    . . . . .Inside Back Cover
Theatre Directories 118, 246

Order a subscription to

Perform*ink*

Chicago's Entertainment Trade Paper. The art, the business, the industry.

Your source for vital industry news

PerformInk Newspaper is a publication with news and information on the theatre industry in Chicago and the Midwest, including job listings and audition notices. PerformInk's mission is to be a catalyst in the healthy growth of the local theatre industry.

Name _____
Business Name _____
Address _____
City _____ St _____ Zip _____
Phone _____
Fax _____
e-mail _____
website _____

___Send me a 1-year subscriptions to PerformInk. I have enclosed my check or money order for $32.95. Please bill the credit card number below for $32.95.

___ Send me a copy of the 2001 edition of "The Book: An Actor's Guide to Chicago" for $15 plus a $5 shipping and handling fee. I have enclosed my check or money order for $20, which includes the $5 shipping and handling fee. Please bill the credit card number below for $20.

___ Send me both a subscription to PerformInk and "The Book: An Actor's Guide to Chicago" for a total of $47.95 ($32.95 for a subscription and a discounted subscriber price of $10 for "The Book," and a $5 shipping and handling fee.

___ I have enclosed my check or money order for $_____.

___ Please bill the credit card number below for $_____.

Visa/MasterCard/Discover # _____, Exp. _____

**Send to:
PerformInk, 3223 N. Sheffield - 3rd floor
Chicago, IL 60657**

Order more copies of

The Book: An Actor's Guide to Chicago!

Every religion has its text, Chicago theatre has The Book!

Name _____
Business Name _____
Address _____
City _____ St ____ Zip _____
Phone _____
Fax _____
e-mail _____
website _____

___ Send me a copy of the 2001 edition of "The Book: An Actor's Guide to Chicago" for $15 plus a $5 shipping and handling fee. I have enclosed my check or money order for $20, which includes the $5 shipping and handling fee. Please bill the credit card number below for $20.

___ Send me both a subscription to PerformInk and "The Book: An Actor's Guide to Chicago" for a total of $47.95 ($32.95 for a subscription and a discounted subscriber price of $10 for "The Book," and a $5 shipping and handling fee.

___ I have enclosed my check or money order for $_____.

___ Please bill the credit card number below for $_____.

Visa/MasterCard/Discover #_____, Exp. _____

**Send to:
PerformInk, 3223 N. Sheffield - 3rd floor
Chicago, IL 60657**

1-800-GET-A-JOB

Audition Blues got you down? Visit the friendliest agency in town.

Since 1947, we have been helping Chicago's aspiring performers in their short and long term employment needs. If you have the personality, skills and the desire to work, give us a call or stop by to see us.

We are here to help you!

- *Temporary*
- *Permanent*
- *Computer training*
- *Resume assistance*
- *Flexible Schedules*
- *No fees to applicants*
- *Weekly pay periods*

**Temporary Staffing ◆ Permanent Placement
Executive Recruiting**

A Personnel *Commitment*®

208 South LaSalle St.◆ Suite 189 Chicago, IL 60604
312/251-5151   Fax 312/251-5154